VYING FOR ALLAH'S VOTE

South Asia in World Affairs Series
T. V. Paul, *Series Editor*

OTHER TITLE IN THE SERIES
Afghan Endgames: Strategy and Policy Choices for America's Longest War,
Hy Rothstein and John Arquilla, editors

VYING FOR ALLAH'S VOTE

Understanding Islamic Parties, Political Violence, and Extremism in Pakistan

HAROON K. ULLAH

Georgetown University Press
Washington, DC

FOUNDATION BOOKS

FOUNDATION
BOOKS

Foundation Books is an imprint of Cambridge University Press India Pvt. Ltd.

Cambridge House, 4381/4 Ansari Road, Daryaganj, New Delhi 110 002

www.cambridgeindia.org

This edition is published by Cambridge University Press India Pvt. Ltd.
by arrangement with Georgetown University Press, Washington DC, USA

First South Asia edition 2014
Reprinted 2014

Printed in India at Sanat Printers, Kundli

ISBN 978-93-82993-84-1 Hardback

To Amber, Ami-ji, Abu-ji, and family,
and to He who bestows all blessings

CONTENTS

ILLUSTRATIONS

Tables

Figures

ACKNOWLEDGMENTS

I am indebted to many individuals and institutions for their support of this project. The American Institute of Pakistan Studies (AIPS) and the William J. Fulbright Fellowship Program both awarded grants that funded part of my extensive research and fieldwork. Special thanks to the AIPS committee: Mark Kenoyer, Anita Weiss, Kamran Asdar Ali, and Will Glover for their support of my book from its early stages.

I also owe a deep debt of gratitude to Harvard's Kennedy School of Government and the University of Michigan. In particular, my heartfelt thanks go to Robert Mickey, Ronald Inglehart, Mary Corcoran, Anna Gryzmala-Busse, Ashutosh Varshney, Mark Tessler, Tarek Masoud, Asim Khawaja, and Barbara Metcalf. Each of them helped shape my academic training and has provided lively intellectual discussions that enriched and extended my work. Many thanks to Vali Nasr, whose mentorship and groundbreaking research on Muslim democratic parties and Jamaat Islami inspired me to carry on with my research. I am also grateful to Harvard's Belfer Center for Science and International Affairs for their generous support with a fellowship during 2007–9. The fellowship allowed me to expand the scope of the project, and I learned a great deal from the world-class scholars at the Center.

I am also grateful to several leading policymakers and diplomats at the US State Department for their mentorship and support of the project. Particular thanks to former US Ambassador to Pakistan Cameron Munter for the opportunity to be part of his staff in Pakistan, and for his enthusiastic interest in the project. I extend my gratitude to Jeremy Rosner for his guidance and careful attention to methodology. My hearty thanks to Tim Lenderking, Rick Olson, Dick Hoagland, Kathryn Schalow, Peter Brennan, Dan Feldman, Irfan Saeed, Tom Miller, Robin Raphel, Walter Douglas, Mark Davidson, Jonathan Pratt, Adnan Mirza, Vinay Chawla, Nicole Chulick, Rick Waters, Brent Hartley, and Jonathan Henick. From them I learned valuable concepts regarding policymaking and public diplomacy. My deepest thanks and admiration go to the late Ambassador Richard C. Holbrooke, on whose team I served; his passion for diplomacy and the region was remarkable and left a lasting impression on all who knew him.

I must also acknowledge my debt to the political and civil society activists, scholars, media persons, and journalists in Pakistan, Afghanistan, Bangladesh, Egypt, and Morocco, who shared with me their experiences and insights into the dynamics of political parties and democratization. For sharing information and providing access, my thanks to the leaders in the Pakistan Muslim League, Jamaat Islami, Jamiat Ulema Islam, Tehreek-i-Insaf, Pakistan Peoples Party, Muttahida Quami Movement, and Awani National Party. It is at these political rallies that I first heard the campaign slogan "*A vote for us is a vote for Allah!*" which inspired the title of this book. In Pakistan, Mumtaz Ahmad's mentorship and legendary scholarship served as a model. In addition, I am indebted to Mosharraf Zaidi, Adil Najam, Moeed Pirzada, Amineh Hoti, Mohammed Mallick, Mohammed Waseem, Daniyal Aziz, Maleeha Lodhi, Najam Sethi, Taimur Rehman, Shahid Khan, Rasul Baksh Rais, Imtiaz Gul, Zahid Hussain, and Ahmad Rashid for sharing their profound understanding of politics in Muslim-majority countries.

The research and writing of this book has spanned the course of several years. Throughout this period I have benefited greatly from an ongoing intellectual exchange with many scholars and colleagues who engaged with the ideas in my book and suggested valuable refinements to the manuscript. These people include Akbar Ahmad, Peter Lavoy, Shuja Nawaz, Hassan Abbas, Christine Fair, Joshua White, Marvin Weinbaum, Quinn Mecham, Imtiaz Gul, Andrew Wilder, Lisa Curtis, Qamar ul-Huda, Moeed Yusuf, Peter Mandaville, Peter Bergen, Bruce Reidel, Matt Nelson, Steve Coll, Anatol Lieven, Pippa Norris, Joseph Nye, Sanjeev Khagram, Parag Khanna, Alexander Evans, Imam Mohammed Magid, Jonathon Brown, Intisar Rabb, Barney Rubin, Steve Cohen, Dan Markey, Mirza Baig, David Coolidge, Rashad Hussain, Huma Yousef, Hamada Hamid, Maya Tudor, Shahzad Bhatti, Zareena Grewal, Mehmood Kazmi, Shaarik Zafar, Al-Husein N. Madhany, and Hussain Haqqani. I developed my own ideas through my association with these scholars and topical experts. Of course, the responsibility for any omissions or errors in this manuscript are entirely my own. Further, the views expressed are my own and do not represent the US State Department.

I must also extend thanks to several of my colleagues for their outstanding and meticulous support during the preparation of this book, most importantly to Sarah Jordon Watson for her incredible work, as well as Nadia Shoeb and Liz Golberg. The team at Georgetown University Press has shown great care and editorial expertise throughout the publication process. My sincere thanks especially go to editors Don Jacobs and T. V. Paul, as well as the entire staff. I am indebted to my agent Don Fehr at Trident Media Group for his hard work and continued belief in the importance of the project.

Lastly, during the long period it took me to design, research, and write this book, my family has been wonderfully supportive. As the great poet Muhammed Iqbal (1877–1938) wrote: "You are an eagle, and your station is much higher than the royal palaces—beyond the mountains and higher." I am grateful to my wife Ambereen for her unwavering faith and care in my academic endeavors, as well as for her generosity and forbearance. I am especially thankful for her editing of various drafts of the manuscript; her improvements were significant. To my loving parents I dedicate this manuscript, Dr. Kaleem and Zarfshan Ullah, for instilling us with an appreciation of poetry and Allama Iqbal—and who have set a high bar for civic activism and scholarship while providing the best role models one could ever ask for. To my siblings, Sarah, Noor, Imran, and Muneer, for their help on the project, inspiration, and support throughout the process, I extend my deep gratitude.

CHAPTER 1

INTRODUCTION

In early 2011, the prominent Pakistani politician Salman Taseer was assassinated by a gunman who believed he had insulted Islam by expressing politically moderate views and defending the rights of women and religious minorities. At the time of his death Taseer was the governor of Punjab, Pakistan's most populous province, and had been a well-known figure in Pakistan for decades. He was a founding member of the Pakistan People's Party (PPP), a supporter of President Zulfiqar Ali Bhutto's democratization campaign in the 1960s, and a trusted adviser to the president's daughter, Benazir Bhutto, during her terms as prime minister. Taseer was also a successful businessman, having founded a full-service brokerage house and a telecom company. Throughout his career, Taseer was outspoken in his belief that democracy and pluralism are inseparable and that all religious minorities (including members of the Ahmadiyya sect, whom many Pakistanis consider to be non-Muslims) should be allowed to vote in general elections.

Such opinions are antithetical to the positions of hard-line clerics who believe that Taseer's version of democracy is tantamount to Westernization and the destruction of true Islam in Pakistan. Shortly before his death, Taseer had particularly outraged clerics by criticizing Pakistan's strict blasphemy laws as unjust and indefensible. (In Pakistan, making a statement that is construed as offensive to Islam can result in penalties ranging from a fine to capital punishment.) Taseer had spoken out in defense of a Christian woman, Aasiya Bibi, who was convicted under the blasphemy laws, saying she had not committed a crime and should be released from prison. He argued that the extremists were abusing the blasphemy laws and that Islamic law should not supplant the laws of the state.

While Taseer was certainly aware that his political beliefs put him in danger (he had received numerous death threats over the years and even served time in prison), to the end he refused to be silenced. On January 4, 2011, as Taseer was leaving Islamabad's Kohsar Market, where he had met a friend for lunch, a member of his own security team stepped forward with a machine gun and fired a volley at the governor from ten feet away. Taseer was struck twenty-six times and died instantly.

I was living in Islamabad a few blocks from Kohsar Market when Taseer was assassinated. I knew the area in Islamabad well. The Kohsar Market is a popular meeting place for expatriates and Islamabad's upper classes, while a park across the street is often full of middle-class Pakistani families enjoying a day out. The area is considered one of the safest in Islamabad, and the assassination there of a well-known (and well-guarded) member of the establishment sent a clear message: Opponents of Pakistan's religious right could be targeted anywhere, at any time.

As shocking as Taseer's assassination was, the response to his death was even more so. When the assassin, Malik Mumtaz Hussain Qadri, a member of the "moderate" Sufi organization Ahl-Sunnah Wa Jamaat, entered a courtroom several days after the murder, he was met by cheering crowds that showered him with flowers. In the following weeks, Pakistan's Islamic confessional parties led marches of up to forty thousand people honoring Qadri's "heroic" action and celebrating Taseer's death. Even more disconcerting, Pakistan's moderate political leaders remained silent. They issued bland statements acknowledging his passing but did not speak out against the mass rallies in support of vigilante Islamism. The provincial court judge who found Qadri guilty of murder was forced to flee Pakistan, and extremist groups successfully pressured the government to suspend the case against Qadri indefinitely.

The assassination of Taseer was by no means the first time religious extremists have used violence to silence moderate Pakistani voices. Benazir Bhutto, the long-exiled former prime minister and champion of the middle class and women's rights, was fatally attacked with gunfire and explosive devices as she left a campaign event in December 2007. There is still some dispute over who masterminded Bhutto's assassination, but strong evidence indicates that members of al-Qaeda–affiliated organizations were involved in its planning and execution.

But Pakistan's political history also includes many instances of surprising moderation on the part of even the most conservative religious parties. In Karachi in 2005, for instance, a broad coalition of parties—including the secular, leftist PPP and the deeply religious, conservative Jamaat-e-Islami (JI)—formed to oppose the government-supported parties in elections for municipal governing councils (called Local Bodies).[1] The wary détente between the PPP and the JI was all the more remarkable given the two parties' long history of electoral competition and extra-electoral conflict. In 1979, for instance, the military regime of General Mohammad Zia ul-Haq, a well-known JI supporter, executed PPP founder Zulfiqar Ali Bhutto, Pakistan's first democratically elected head of government and the father of PPP leader Benazir Bhutto. As the elder Bhutto himself supposedly remarked at his trial, "I appointed a Chief of [Army] Staff belonging to the Jamaat-i-Islami and the result is before all of us."[2]

Twenty-five years later, however, the two parties were able to mend fences long enough to confront their common enemy, the Pakistan Muslim League–Quaid-i-Azam, a "king's party" formed and supported by military leader Pervez Musharraf and Pakistan's army and intelligence services. The JI, at least, had a second motivation as it was losing support among its base (the urban middle and lower-middle class) to Jamaat-ud-Dawa (JuD) the front organization for the banned militant group Lashkar-e-Taiba. The alliance with the PPP, therefore, presented the JI with its best chance of being able to form a government and in the process hopefully win back some of the support it had lost to JuD.[3]

Of course, it could be argued that the parties' moderation in municipal elections is not the best predictor of their behavior on the provincial or national level. Furthermore, Pakistan's religious parties had at best an uneasy relationship with Musharraf, who supported the international campaign in Afghanistan and promoted a policy of "enlightened moderation" when it came to religion. But the JI's and PPP's willingness to work together in the face of the threat from an antidemocratic force shows that Pakistan's political parties, no matter their religious orientation, are fierce defenders of democracy when they are being kept out of power through undemocratic means.

Given Western fears of a "radical Islamist takeover" in Pakistan, perhaps better proof of the essential pragmatism of Pakistan's political parties—religious and otherwise—is the performance of the Muttahida Majlis-e-Amal (United Council of Action [MMA]), a broad coalition of religious parties that united to contest elections in 2002. The MMA is a fascinating example of the complexity of Pakistan's religious politics, as it brought together a diverse group of actors with markedly different religious traditions, from the austere modernism of the JI to the more traditionalist Barelvi practices of the Jamiat Ulema-e-Pakistan and even the Shiism of the Islami Tehrik Pakistan. (I discuss the MMA at greater length in chapter 5.) That some members of the coalition have been closely linked to sectarian violence makes its formation even more remarkable.

The MMA (likely aided by the military and intelligence services) was very successful in the 2002 elections and won, most importantly, sufficient seats to form a government in the North-West Frontier Province (NWFP). Now known as Khyber Pakhtunkhwa (KPK), the province is a strategically crucial area for Islamic militancy in Pakistan and Afghanistan; not only does it border the tribal areas, where most Pakistani militants find refuge, it has a significant militancy problem in its own territory. Given certain MMA politicians' public sympathy for the militants and the coalition's declared goal of instituting sharia law in Pakistan, many foreign (and Pakistani) observers feared that an MMA government in Pakistan would provide a safe haven for militancy and allow the "Talibanization" of Pakistan.

Yet while the MMA did pass controversial sharia legislation, its implementation of Islamic law was slow and cautious. More remarkably, however, was the near-complete about-face its members performed on the issue of terrorism and internal security. Although MMA members continued to oppose Pakistan's continued cooperation with the international war in Afghanistan, they stopped insisting that the United States immediately close its bases in Pakistan.[4] Prominent MMA leader

Maulana Fazlur Rehman declared that the Taliban had erred by trying to institute an Islamic system by force; the MMA, by contrast, would try "to bring about an Islamic revolution in accordance with the wishes of the people who voted for us."[5] Less than two years into its administration, the MMA became embroiled in a battle with Musharraf over his attempt to legalize his position as Pakistan's chief executive. This fight sapped much of the coalition's energy, and disagreement among the parties over whether to strike a bargain with Musharraf eventually led to its disintegration. In the next general election, in 2008, the people of the KPK voted in a resolutely secular party, and the MMA has never been able to regain the political success it experienced in 2002.

The religious parties that made up the MMA were deeply conservative, but their experience in government casts doubt on any easy assumptions about how religious parties will behave both in and out of power. Pakistani history shows that religious parties can be as pragmatic and flexible as secular parties are. Moreover, there is a wide variety of such parties, and the differences among them are too often hidden by such blanket terms as "Islamist." Pakistan's religious parties compete not only with secular parties but also with militant groups (for support, if not votes) and—perhaps most frenetically—with each other.[6] This competition at times leads to extremism, but it is as likely to lead to moderation. Above all, participation in the electoral process leads to pragmatism. Parties may prefer radical policies, but first and foremost they seek to remain in power.

What is driving political extremism in Pakistan? What does it mean that political moderates are either silenced or targeted? And how should the United States and other Western nations engage with extreme confessional parties in such nations as Pakistan, Afghanistan, Egypt, Tunisia, and Indonesia, where Islamists hold both political and moral authority? The murder of Salman Taseer underscores the fact that religion, politics, and policy are inextricably linked in Muslim-majority democracies, and the implications of these links are not well understood in the West. Furthermore, the recent strong showing of Islamic confessional parties in the Arab Spring—particularly in Egypt, Tunisia, and Morocco—shows they are a force to be reckoned with. Despite an increasing amount of scholarly interest in the issue, the phenomenon of Muslim democracy is still only poorly understood.[7]

One way to navigate the politics of Muslim-majority democracies is to examine their parties. And among the least understood components of these democracies are the politico-religious (confessional) parties themselves. The lens of party politics is particularly appropriate for the study of Pakistan, which had political parties well before there were elections to contest; indeed, some of its parties trace their roots back to a time before the country even existed. The deep roots of party politics in Pakistan mean that any discussion of Pakistani politics that ignores the role of these parties will be impoverished.

In this book I analyze the origins, ideologies, bases of support, and electoral successes of the largest and most influential confessional parties in Pakistan. I develop a new typology for understanding and comparing the discourses put forth by these parties in the hopes of addressing one fundamental question: What drives Islamic confessional parties to become extreme, encourage violence, and inhibit democratic reform? In order to explain these groups' often surprising flexibility, I introduce a theoretical model, the sharia-secular model, that illustrates their movement (in both directions) along a highly fluid continuum, from support for the creation of an Islamic theocracy in Pakistan to a more secular approach.

The Pakistani case, as I shall show, provides preliminary answers to many of the most important questions that Westerners have about the role of Islamic parties in democratic political life. To a certain extent, pursuing these answers requires us to abandon some of our preconceptions about such parties. We often ask, for instance, whether participation in elections will lead Islamic parties to moderate their views, but Pakistan's history shows us that participation in elections is equally likely to lead to moderation *and* extremism. Where a party falls on the continuum depends on how it reads the political tea leaves. Just as American candidates play to their base during the primaries and then move to the center for the general election, Pakistani candidates may say one thing while campaigning and act rather differently once they are elected.

Do Islamic parties secretly hope to win power through the ballot box and then cancel any further elections and institute a theocracy? Of course, it's impossible to know what grandiose fantasies political leaders (of any persuasion) might nurture, but Pakistan's history provides a clue. The JI, Pakistan's best-organized and most-cohesive religious party, was offered the chance to work with military dictator Zia ul-Haq on his "Islamization" program, the closest Pakistan has ever come to instituting an Iranian-style theocracy. Despite the golden opportunity this overture presented to institute its preferred form of Islamic governance in Pakistan, the JI eventually broke with Zia over the issue of elections, with JI leaders insisting that they take place and eventually joining the opposition when they did not. While the JI's stubbornness may simply show that Pakistan's religious parties are intent on holding power in their own right, rather than being the military's pet politicians, the fact remains that every one of Pakistan's military rulers has eventually met with massive resistance in which the religious parties have played an important role. Pakistanis, at least, are unlikely to submit to theocracy any time soon, and Pakistan's religious parties, whatever their true views on democracy, are even less likely to present the sort of unified front that would make such a theocracy possible.

Perhaps more than any other state today, Pakistan provides a vision of the future of Muslim democracy. Pakistanis have on three occasions voted a center-right, Islamic but not Islamist party into office and did so most recently with the resounding victory in the 2013 elections of the Pakistan Muslim League–Nawaz (PML-N). The party has already ruled Pakistan for five years, and its two previous administrations provide ample material for a study of Islamic democracy, at least in its South Asian form. The PML-N presents itself as a party of and for Muslims, and at times (including in the 2013 elections) it has made alliances with extremist groups and courted the religious vote by passing sharia-inspired legislation. But the bulk of the party's efforts while in power have been devoted to two ends—first, ensuring its own future success by distributing patronage to key supporters and constituencies and, second, putting Pakistan on a sound economic footing by encouraging trade and industry and developing the country's infrastructure. PML-N leader (and namesake) Nawaz Sharif has shown himself a master at playing to the overwhelmingly religious Pakistani electorate while running the country as the pragmatic businessman that he is.

The viability of the center-right approach in present-day Pakistan was also proved by the 2013 campaign's most surprising success story, the explosive rise to political power of Imran Khan's Pakistan Tehrik-e-Insaf (Pakistan Movement for Justice). While Khan and his party had languished in the political wilderness for years, in Pakistan's current climate his particular mix of anti-Americanism, vague piety, and promises of an end to corruption proved extraordinarily effective. The Pakistan Tehrik-e-Insaf's success in 2013—it controls the government in one Pakistani province and looks set to play a major role at the center—makes clear that Islamic democracy has an enormous constituency in Pakistan.

The long-term effects of this balancing act are unclear. It is certainly true, as many liberal Pakistanis lament, that the country is undergoing a rightward shift. The tendency of Pakistani politicians to pander to religious extremism—a trend whose roots go back to the 1970s—plays a role in this phenomenon; in fact, it may end by nurturing religious political forces too powerful to be easily managed. (It could be argued that Pakistan's current acute internal security crisis is a sign that the government is already reaping what it has sown.) But Pakistan's politicians have proven themselves to be remarkably adaptable and deeply committed to democracy, while its political parties—whether secular, Muslim democratic, or Islamist—are far too diverse, competitive, and fractious to submit easily to even religiously unimpeachable single-party rule.

CHAPTER 2

ISLAM AND DEMOCRACY IN PAKISTAN

There are few nations where the rise of extremist political groups is of greater international significance than Pakistan. Poised with a fully loaded nuclear arsenal at the crossroads of religious extremists, nationalist fervor, and the war on terrorism, Pakistan's importance to global geopolitical stability and international peace is inescapable. While Pakistan's Islamic parties still depend on military patronage, its current democratic transition will depend on how Islamic parties contribute to civilian rule and mobilize support for political reform.

Islamic Confessional Parties

Political scientist Stathis Kalyvas has defined "confessional" political parties as organizations that leverage aspects of religious ideology and culture to mobilize, recruit, and campaign in electoral contests.[1] Confessional movements have developed out of many religious traditions in many countries. Jews in Israel, Christians in Brazil, and Hindus in India have all formed political parties whose platforms draw from and focus on religious tradition. Islamic confessional movements, however, are of particular interest in the post-9/11 world. The recent ascendancy of Islamic parties in Turkey, the Gaza Strip, Indonesia, and Egypt poses opportunities and challenges for international relations in an era of international terrorism and division between the Islamic and Western worlds.

A common perception among Western populations, and even policymakers, is that Islamic parties affiliate with, support, or fund militant Islamist terrorist groups. Although little empirical evidence supports this claim, the perception remains. This notion creates a generalized fear of Islamic party electoral successes on the grounds that terrorist groups will be afforded safe haven, patronage, and encouragement. It is widely believed that Islamic governments will be reluctant to support, and might even undermine, Western antiterrorism efforts that target organizations within their borders.

Policymakers and activists in the West are also concerned that democratic rule itself will be irrevocably compromised as strongly religious Islamic parties gain power. Even if these groups rise to power through democratic means, so the argument goes, they may be driven to impose theocratic rule to block future elections and revoke democratic rights. This concern is greater regarding Muslim nations than for other nations with a similarly dominant and politically active religious majority, because Hindu, Jewish, and Christian states have a much longer history with, and demonstrated commitment to, democratic rule and greater experience with explicitly confessional parties that are also entirely committed to the democratic process. For the populations of most Muslim-majority nations, democracy is a relative novelty, and they do not necessarily regard it as the only option. Moreover, while democracy itself is not widely perceived as contrary to the precepts of Hinduism, Judaism, or Christianity, and while the majority of Muslims support democracy, a prominent strain of Islamic thought still argues that true religious piety and democracy are incompatible.[2]

The idea that democracy and Islam are in conflict is based partly on the belief that democracy must necessarily be both liberal and secular.[3] The conflation of democratic process, liberalism, and secularism is problematic. Secularism is, of course, a deeply contested concept, and its definition varies widely. Western secular liberal thinking emphasizes the importance of the separation of church and state; proponents of "Indian secularism," such as Rajeev Bhargava, speak of a "principled distance" between religion and state rather than an impenetrable wall; and some theorists, such as Talal Asad, question the very possibility of division, arguing that the secular state is not walled off from religion but instead seeks to control it.[4] Yet each of these conceptions of the secular approach is often described as incompatible with orthodox Islam, which advances the principle of *tawhid*, or the "oneness of God," and recognizes the presence of the spiritual in all things, including affairs of state. The removal of divinity from the affairs of state (as opposed to the removal of the state from the affairs of divinity) is thus seen as an invitation to amoral rule.[5] This perceived "slippery slope" is expressed in Humeira Iqtidar's interviews with members of Jamaat-e-Islami and Jamaat-ud-Dawa, the Islamist militant group, who used the terms *ladiniyat* ("a state of being without religion") and *dahriyat* (a "refusal of religion") when discussing what English speakers would call secularism.[6]

The perceived conflict between Islam and democracy is also based on the fact that some historical Islamic constructs are at odds with democratic governance. The most notable of these is a belief in the caliphate, or the rule by an Islamic leader ordained by God rather than by political leaders elected by fallible citizens. While this model would be hard to reconcile with democracy, a more modern interpretation of the caliph depicts each person as called by God to stewardship, responsibility, and service, which does not preclude elections.[7]

The concern among some non-Muslim observers and Western officials that Islam is incompatible with democracy and that Islamic political parties will permit their nations to become bastions of theocratic rule and training grounds for terrorists informs current international relations. In actuality, these fears demonstrate how poorly understood confessional Islamic parties in Pakistan and other Muslim-majority nations are.

Islamic confessional groups vary hugely in their ideologies, constituencies, political strategies, platforms, and electoral successes. In some countries, Islamic parties play key roles in national governments, while in others they attract less than 2 percent of the vote. In some countries, Islamic parties build powerful coalitions, while in others they fail to get a foothold. In Turkey, the Islamic Adalet ve Kalkinma (Justice and Development) Party (AKP) has won two national elections in a row; in nearby Azerbaijan, the Islamic party has been banned from electoral competition. In Pakistan, which is 97 percent Muslim, Islamic (although not Islamist) parties have won a majority share in national governments, but Senegal (94 percent Muslim) has never had an Islamic party.[8] The existence and persistence of such a range of Islamic confessional party success suggests that Islam, as a basis for political organization, is neither an irresistible narcotic nor a destructive force that will drive a nation to abandon all semblance of democracy. A sober look at the history, organization, and conduct of Islamic parties in Pakistan will show that these groups face the same practical challenges—and are sensitive to the same practical constraints—that all political actors do.

In this book I lay out a new typology for understanding Islamic confessional parties based on a close examination of politics in Pakistan. Contrary to the prevailing monolithic approach, which sees all Islamic parties as "Islamists," I argue that Islamic parties exist on a spectrum—what I call the sharia–secularism continuum—from those who believe that Pakistan should be governed by Islamic law, with little or no lay person's input, to those who believe that religious authority has no place in governance.[9] Furthermore, the parties frequently move back and forth along this spectrum in order to gain political advantage. Despite this ideological diversity, however, Islamic parties can be organized into three distinct types, each with their own ideological underpinnings, organizational structures, and political strategies. And while Islamic parties incorporate aspects of their religious traditions and theology into their platforms, party leaders are not singularly (or even primarily) committed to pursuing a purely ideological agenda. Like all political parties, Islamic confessional parties want to compete and win elections.

This reality has been overlooked in the literature on Islamic parties because most current scholarship makes the false assumption that such parties are primarily or solely interested in winning *national* elections. The nature and frequency of party instrumentalism, however, become clear only when we take seriously these parties' interests in winning *local* elections as well. The literature also mischaracterizes voters' motivations, assuming that economic deprivation or generalized Islamic militancy drives the electorate into the arms of far-right Islamist political parties. My research shows that voters make much more sophisticated calculations about their self-interests and that these calculations vary considerably at the national and local level.

The case of Pakistan reveals that electoral participation does not necessarily yield moderation; however, it does lead to instrumentalism, or, in other words, pragmatism. In fact, Islamic political organizations frequently engage in political strategies that require them to condone actions, including using extra-electoral means (violence) and forming coalitions with militant and secular organizations, that run contrary to their own platforms. Recognizing that Pakistani Islamic parties are as tethered to practical political considerations as is any other party has huge implications for our understanding of what drives political extremism and how to create incentives for moderation.

Party Types and Extremism: The Sharia–Secularism Continuum

While all Islamic confessional parties agree that Islamic tenets should inform governance, they vary tremendously in how strictly they interpret religious laws and how significant they believe the government's role in enforcing those laws should be. I refer to this range of belief as the sharia–secularism continuum.

For the sake of convenience, I will group Pakistan's Islamic parties into two main types—the Islamists and the Muslim democrats.[10] This categorization is certainly not meant to suggest that there are strict, permanent, or even obvious demarcations between the parties in these two groups; in fact, the opposite is the case. As I emphasize throughout this book, when the political context demands it, Pakistan's Islamic parties move toward and away from each pole of the continuum with remarkable ease.

On the far end of the continuum are those parties, which I call Islamist parties, that are committed to imposing sharia law and building a theocratic state. These groups seek to empower religious leaders, institutionalize Islamic governance, command adherence to Islamic law and traditional religious texts, base citizenship on religious affiliation, and remodel the economic system according to passages in the Quran that govern interest payment. In this book I treat all religiously fundamentalist parties as Islamist parties. Their strictly literal reading of religious texts leads them to adopt exclusionary policies with regard to community members who do not share their religious beliefs. I argue that the Islamist category is itself overly broad and conflates two distinct types of organizations. In this book I recognize two main types of Islamist parties—network Islamists and hierarchical Islamists. As discussed at greater length in chapter 3, these party types differ in terms of their location on the sharia–secularism continuum, bases of support, leadership structures, mobilization and messaging strategies, and substantive policies.

Muslim democrats, in contrast to Islamists, exist much closer to the middle of the sharia–secularism continuum. These parties are Muslim in that they believe that Islamic teachings should inform public policy and support calls for civil enforcement of some religious laws. But they do not look to the Quran for specific policy prescriptions, promote a literal interpretation of religious texts, or support major political or economic reforms derived from a narrow view of the Quran.

Any use of the term "sharia" must come with some caveats. The fact that Islamist parties share roughly similar conceptions of the role that sharia should play in governance should not obscure the significant differences in their political programs, their different interpretations of what sharia entails, or the contested nature of the term "sharia" itself. J. M. Otto, for instance, identifies four different senses of sharia, of which the first and most universal is the abstract law of Allah as revealed in the Quran. But since the Quranic law must be applied (and, according to some, interpreted), sharia in the modern sense also includes the works of the classical jurisprudents, the historically and geographically contextual bodies of interpretation produced by Muslims courts over the past thousand years, and finally the contemporary "spectrum of principles, rules, cases, and interpretations that are developed and applied at present." In most Muslim societies, therefore, "the variety of meanings of sharia has given rise to a flexible . . . discourse about sharia and law which moves smoothly from one definition of sharia to another."[11] The PTI made a stunning debut in the 2013 elections garnering almost 20 percent of the popular vote, key seats in the National Assembly, and provincial coalition control in KPK. The result of sharia's long historical development has been a multiplicity of interpretive schools, or *fiqh*, each with its own understanding of the particulars of the law. In Pakistan in particular, this diversity is increased by the different ideological and theological groundings of the Islamist parties.

Furthermore, in Pakistan the twin poles of the sharia–secularism continuum can be defined by referring not only to a group's attitudes about the role of religion in government but also to the group's beliefs regarding jurisdiction, or the authority to say what the law is. The grounds for this debate were laid almost at Pakistan's birth. The text of the 1949 Objectives Resolution, which was meant to establish the principles of the future constitution, guarantees both "fundamental rights including equality of status, of opportunity and before law, social, economic and political justice, and freedom of thought, expression, belief, faith, worship and association"; and that "Muslims shall be enabled to order their lives in the individual and collective spheres in accordance with the teachings and requirements of Islam as set out in the Holy Quran and the Sunna."[12] But Islamists and Muslim democrats (not to mention the secular parties) strongly disagree as to who should be able to mediate any conflicts that may arise between these foundational principles—that is, the secular courts or the *ulema* (and if the latter, which *ulema*).

Pakistani prime minister Liaquat Ali Khan, who introduced the resolution, specifically rejected the idea that a state governed in accordance with Islamic principles must (or even could) be a state governed by "ordained priests, who wield authority as being specially appointed by those who claim to derive their rights from their sacerdotal position."[13] In 1952, however, Prime Minister Khwaja Nazimuddin proposed to the Constituent Assembly that a board of *ulema* (Muslim clerics and scholars) should be established to rule on the compatibility of proposed legislation with the Quran. Although the proposal was voted down, Pakistan's Islamist parties have not conceded defeat.[14]

Differences regarding what sharia entails exactly, and who has the right to define and enforce it, help explain the surprising fact that Islamic parties that occupy much the same space on the continuum are as likely to disagree with one another as they are with groups to their right or left. Parties closely spaced on the continuum will often compete more fiercely with each other than with their supposed ideological opponents. A roughly shared structural vision for Islam's role in Pakistan does not ensure that parties will agree on the details of a future Islamic state or on the best way to achieve it. Furthermore, as this book shows, parties locked in a close electoral race will often make surprising ideological shifts as they angle for votes. A party's original position on the continuum constrains its options for ideological maneuvering, but it does not dictate them.

Throughout the book I use the phrase "Islamic parties" to refer to all Islamic-based political groups, "Islamist parties" to refer to more extreme confessional groups, and "Muslim democratic parties" to refer to more liberal confessional groups. (The nomenclature "Muslim democrat," drawn from Pakistan's political environment, should not be misconstrued as synonymous with classical Western liberalism.) I use the term "extremism" to indicate engagement in a very specific set of behaviors that arguably pose a threat to democracy. In this context, extremism does not refer to political thought that is far from the center of the sharia–secularism continuum. For my purposes, a political party is defined as "extreme" if it meets two of the following three criteria: (1) adopts exclusionary policies based on rigid classifications of morally valid behavior, (2) uses inflammatory rhetoric about the divide between the morally upright and the morally corrupt as a mobilization tool and incitement to action, and (3) engages in extra-electoral tactics, including militant action and violent enforcement of religious practice.[15]

In addition to challenging the misperception that Islamic confessional parties are homogeneous and universally extreme, my research also upends the assumption that the policies and positions of Islamic parties, particularly Islamist parties, are fixed and immutable. Quite the contrary. Confessional parties in Pakistan move along the sharia–secularism continuum over time, depending on the political environment and organizational incentives. A central finding of this book is that confessional parties become more extreme or more moderate in order to maintain political viability.

Muslim Democracy in Pakistan

Scholars of Pakistan traditionally assign its political parties to one of three main groups: *socialists*, represented by the Pakistan People's Party (PPP); *nationalists*, represented by the Pakistan Muslim League–Nawaz (PML-N); and *Islamists*, such as the Jamaat-e-Islami, as well as a number of smaller parties. I argue, however, that this typology obscures the fluid boundaries between the PML-N and the Islamist parties, and that while the PML-N has inherited the name of Muhammad Ali Jinnah's original Muslim League, it has morphed into a new party.

While Islamism, nationalism, and socialism are fairly well defined, the concept of Muslim democracy requires further elucidation. I borrow the term from the work of Vali Nasr, who first coined it in his 2005 article "The Rise of 'Muslim Democracy.'" Although Nasr includes the PML-N as a prime example of a Muslim Democratic party, as he puts it,

> Muslim Democrats view political life with a pragmatic eye. They reject or at least discount the classic Islamist claim that Islam commands the pursuit of a *shari'a* state, and their main goal tends to be the more mundane one of crafting viable electoral platforms and stable governing coalitions to serve individual and collective interests—Islamic as well as secular—within a democratic arena whose bounds they respect, win or lose. . . . The rise of the Muslim Democrats has begun the integration of Muslim religious values—drawn from Islam's teachings on ethics, morality, the family, rights, social relations, and commerce, for example—into political platforms designed to win regular democratic elections.[16]

Nasr believes that Islamists "view democracy not as something deeply legitimate, but at best as a tool or tactic that may be useful in gaining the power to build an Islamic state."[17] He thus distinguishes Muslim democratic parties from Islamist parties by their commitment to democratic values and from ordinary secular parties by their explicit desire to integrate their Muslim faith and their political agendas. While I argue that the pragmatism that Nasr believes characterizes Muslim democratic electoral politics can in fact be found in parties all along the sharia–secularism continuum, it is this ultimate belief in democracy that distinguishes the Muslim democrats from their counterparts further along the continuum toward Islamism.

The concept of confessional democracy, as Nasr makes clear, is not a new one. As can be seen in the development of Christian democratic parties in nineteenth-century Europe, a number of political organizations have sought to forge political identities based on religious identity and often without the full support of the religious hierarchy. Kalyvas shows how the transformation of mass Catholic political organizations into modern political parties often involved a process of declericalization, and even secularization, as lay activists refused to submit to the commands of Catholic authorities. Furthermore, he argues that the appearance of confessional parties strengthened rather than weakened secular democracy, politicizing the religious populations of Europe and giving them a reason to engage in the democratic process. The process resulted in parties that, owing to their mix of religious values and emphasis on social welfare, were difficult to classify on the usual conservative–liberal axis.[18]

While Muslim democracy is equally concerned with making mass appeals to voters while bypassing the religious hierarchies, it differs from its Christian counterpart in a number of ways. Perhaps most important, as Nasr writes, "Muslim Democracy, unlike Christian Democracy, cannot measure itself against an authoritatively expressed core of political and religious ideas that transcend national boundaries. . . . Muslim Democrats . . . lack a clear, unified message. They seem instead like the inchoate offspring of various ad hoc alliances and pragmatic decisions made in particular political circumstances."[19] Thus there is no "Muslim democratic" position on any particular political question; instead, each party is left to construct its own platform and to triangulate its political strategy in its own national context. What unites the Muslim democratic parties, from Turkey's AKP to Pakistan's PML-N, is their use of the language of Islamic values to sell an essentially moderate agenda to a deeply religious electorate. The viability of this strategy can be seen in the PML-N's success at sidelining the more explicitly Islamist parties such as the JI, which at one point seemed poised to play a major role in Pakistani politics on the national level.

In the context of Pakistan, however, given the PML-N's pragmatism and primarily economic focus, as well as the oft-noted fact that the PPP and the PML-N "share virtually the same manifestos, many of the same members of the National Assembly, and the same sole objective of winning and holding onto power at all costs," does it make sense to describe the PML-N as an Islamic party at all?[20] This problem of classification is one that impacts the discussion of many moderate Islamic parties. Charles Kurzman, for instance, notes that Turkey's AKP, which is nearly universally accepted as an Islamic party, "has removed almost every reference to Islam from its electoral platforms, and instead describes itself simply as a 'conservative' party."[21]

The study of Pakistani political parties faces the opposite problem when it comes to classification. In overwhelmingly devout Muslim Pakistan, few parties or politicians are likely to entirely jettison Islamic rhetoric or to pass up the chance to gain a few extra votes by appealing to Muslim values. Hence the left-wing PPP begins a list of its four founding principles with the slogan "Islam is our faith," and both parties made copious references to Islam and Islamic values in their published platforms (known as manifestos) in the 2013 national elections. Yet from its inception the PPP has been challenged by parties closer to the sharia end of the continuum on Islamic grounds, and it is widely viewed as a secular party because of its leaders' secular leanings and its socialist economic program ("Socialism is our economy" is the third of the PPP's four founding principles).[22] Although its first platform, composed for the 1970 elections, promised to mix socialism and "Islamic idealism," party insiders recognized that the PPP's stated program was an illusion, and in truth the party was solely guided by the political instincts of its largely secular leader Zulfiqar Ali Bhutto.[23] Although Bhutto at times attempted to appeal to Islamic leaders, promulgating bans on drinking and gambling shortly before his overthrow by the military, these moves were widely seen as desperate attempts to head off the public protest that followed his manipulation of the 1977 elections.[24]

The PML-N, by contrast, has made a point of appealing to the Islamist constituency and has at times entered into (admittedly politically convenient) electoral alliances with the Islamist parties.[25] The most significant of them, the Islami Jamhoori Ittehad (Islamic Democratic Alliance [IJI]), was formed with the military's guidance for the purpose of opposing the PPP in the national elections of 1988 (the first to take place after Gen. Mohammad Zia ul-Haq's death). The alliance, which included the PML-N and the Islamist parties of the Jamaat-e-Islami and the Jamiat Ulema-e-Islam (Party of Islamic Scholars [JUI]), was seen as the defender of the policies promulgated during the Zia period, most particularly his Islamization campaign.[26] (The alliance collapsed in the run-up to the 1993 national elections as both the PML-N and the JI sought to win a parliamentary majority in their own right, providing an example of the far-from-united front presented by Pakistan's confessional parties.) The PML-N has been led from its founding by Nawaz Sharif, who personifies the party and its policies as much as the Bhuttos have been identified with the PPP. In his many electoral contests against Benazir Bhutto, Sharif was careful to emphasize his Pakistani education (in contrast with Benazir's secular Western upbringing) and his closeness with religious leaders.[27]

Nasr identifies a number of structural factors that he believes are conducive to the rise of moderate parties with pragmatic approaches to democracy and that, in turn, suggest the conditions under which Muslim democracy is likely to flourish in the future. Unsurprisingly, given that Nasr views the PML-N's rule during the 1990s as a prime example of Muslim democracy in the making, all of the structural factors apply to Pakistan: a military that plays a dominant (and moderating) role in national politics, a vocal and influential private sector, and hotly contested elections in which no party manages to hold power for long.[28] The result is a particularly nonideological political system in which the major parties eschew grand gestures in an attempt to win the favor of the "median voter."

Clearly not all of the structural factors associated with the rise of Muslim democracy are desirable from the standpoint of Pakistan's development as a democracy. The bitter cut and thrust of Pakistani electoral politics, combined with Muslim democracy's nonideological stance, can result in petty political contests, with politicians seemingly more concerned with acquiring power than with what they will do once they have it. And the Pakistan Army—whose cooperation with

Islamists in the post-Zia era has led the PML-N to seek the ideological middle—has had a particularly pernicious effect on Pakistan's democratic consolidation, weakening Pakistan's civilian political parties in order to maintain its image as Pakistan's sole competent power center. But in a Muslim democracy, Nasr argues, the Pakistan Army may have created a phenomenon that it is not able to control without resorting to a full-blown coup.

The Rise of Muslim Pakistan

Pakistan presents an ideal focus for a study of Islamic confessional parties, not only on account of its current strategic importance, but also because the concept of an Islamic political identity first arose on the Indian subcontinent nearly four hundred years ago. From the eighth to the nineteenth centuries, a series of empires, many of them Islamic, ruled the territory that is now Pakistan. The Mughal Empire, the last of these Muslim dynasties, was the dominant power in northern India from the mid-1500s to the mid-1700s. As the Mughals weakened, however, they lost their grip on their various vassal states and faced increasing challenges from independent Hindu and Sikh kingdoms. As the British encroached farther into India during the eighteenth century, they took advantage of this division to play feuding neighbors off one another.

Against this backdrop of decline, a distinct Muslim political identity began to develop, as seen in the writings of eighteenth-century religious thinkers such as Shah Wali Ullah. Wali Ullah sought to harmonize revelation and reason in order to allow Muslims to exercise individual judgment in matters of Islamic law and to unite in the face of the growing threat from the (Hindu) Maratha Kingdom.[29]

As Muslim intellectuals lamented the loss of an Islamic state and sought to restore the "lost glory of Islam," religion became more central to the political identities of Muslims on the Indian subcontinent. According to the 1772 plan of Governor Warren Hastings, Muslim and Hindu populations under East India Company rule were governed by different sets of religiously based personal laws.[30] The East India Company's twin prerogatives of maximizing revenue and maintaining control without resorting to the military guided this approach, which had the unintended effect of vindicating Muslim intellectuals' claims of Muslim exceptionalism. Nineteenth-century scholars, such as Syed Ahmed Khan (1817–98), Altaf Hussain Hali (1837–1914), and Muhammed Iqbal (1878–1938), engaged in a passionate quest to understand and halt the political decline of the Muslim community.

In 1858, the British crown issued a noninterference proclamation, which gave India's regions autonomy in the organization and regulation of local commerce. The proclamation created a favorable environment for Muslims to mobilize around their distinctive religious identity. While the Muslim movement was far from monolithic, its disparate parts did share an underlying acceptance of Muslims' fundamental religious difference from Hindus.

Subsequent British reforms, originally intended to avoid communal antagonism in India, had equally powerful unintended consequences and eventually led to the formation of the first explicitly Muslim political parties. The Indian Councils Act of 1892 initiated a policy of separate Hindu and Muslim representation on government councils, and the 1905 partition of Bengal (into majority Hindu West Bengal and majority Muslim East Bengal, now Bangladesh) further fueled Muslim calls for separate political representation. The Morley-Minto reforms of 1909 further institutionalized religious divisions by forcing Muslims and Hindus to vote in separate electoral blocs: Muslims could vote only for Muslim representatives and Hindus only for Hindu representatives. The reforms marked a watershed moment in Indian communal politics, codifying the belief that religious identity was the basis of political identity.

The new political order was separate and unequal, relegating Muslims to the status of a permanent minority. The ascendant Hindu political class thus had little incentive to negotiate any power-sharing agreements with their Muslim counterparts. This combination of increasingly rigid political-religious identity and numerical disadvantage spurred the rise of parties founded to represent the Muslims of the subcontinent, with the most prominent among them being the Muslim League (founded in 1906). The rise of an explicitly Muslim political movement in opposition to the secular nationalist Indian National Congress caused the political landscape to become immediately polarized along communal lines. This condition persisted even as it became clear that Indian independence was on the horizon.

After World War II, the British lost their will to hold on to India. The colonial administrator proposed establishing a loose federation of Indian states with a weak national government. While the leadership of the Muslim League found this proposal attractive, Congress objected because it wanted to maintain majority control over a strong centralized state. Congress proposed keeping separate electoral systems, which would allow the Muslim League to participate as a minority party, but it was unable to adequately reassure the league that Muslims' rights would be protected in an independent India. Over the next few years, political squabbling, gridlock, and personal hubris finally led the British to formally partition the Raj into the two states of India and Pakistan in 1947. The mass of India divided Pakistan into two halves, West and East Pakistan. The Dominion of Pakistan became the Islamic Republic of Pakistan in 1956.

Democracy in Pakistan

As was true of many of Britain's former colonies in South Asia, independent Pakistan was not established as a true democratic republic. Its system of government was cobbled together from a host of competing traditions, including feudalism, Islamism, tribalism, and Western-style representational government. As a result, Pakistan has veered wildly and sometimes violently between democratically elected governments and military dictatorships. Until 2013, no elected civilian Pakistani government had ever completed a full term and made a constitutional transfer of power; indeed, civilian chief executives have been imprisoned, assassinated, executed, or removed from power in a coup carried out by the military alone or with the cooperation of Pakistan's military.[31] Governments occasionally have been voted into office, but until now none had been voted out.

In 1958, only eleven years after the nation's founding, General Mohammad Ayub Khan staged the first coup d'état. Pakistan's founding fathers had mobilized the Muslims of British India (particularly those of the Hindu-majority areas) by appealing to their fear of Hindu domination. But when the time came to govern an independent state, the Muslims did not have the requisite resources or unity of purpose to legislate effectively. With the support of the military and of feudal elites, Ayub Khan abrogated the constitution and outlawed political parties.[32] Since then, while the military has intermittently returned to the barracks, it has never allowed civilians to rule completely. Succeeding Ayub Khan was another military ruler, General Agha Mohammad Yahya Khan, who temporarily reinstated party democracy and allowed elections to be held in December 1970.[33] Although Yahya Khan proved unwilling to actually surrender the reins of power, the 1971 war between India and Pakistan, and the catastrophic loss of East Pakistan after Pakistan's defeat, spelled the end of his military regime.

Each one of Pakistan's four military leaders has claimed that he was a reluctant coup maker. Yet each of the military coups has involved elaborate troop movements and legal maneuvers that could not have occurred as part of a spontaneous military action. Pakistani coup makers have either abrogated or suspended the constitution and then legitimized their actions via the rulings of a complicit judiciary. In Musharraf's case, for instance, he installed new Supreme Court judges after the coup to ensure a favorable verdict on his rule and amended the original constitution to better accommodate military intervention.

While generals have ruled Pakistan for more than half of the state's existence, Pakistanis have steadfastly maintained a nominal commitment to democracy. Acknowledging this reality, every one of Pakistan's military rulers—Generals Ayub Khan, Yahya Khan, Zia ul-Haq, and Musharraf—has tried to claim that he was building the conditions for democracy instead of destroying it. Current Chief of Army Staff General Kayani stands as a remarkable exception to this trend. Almost every military leader has expressed the hope of imposing martial law for only the bare minimum time necessary to restore stability and then turning the government over to its elected representatives. And each military leader has attempted to legitimize his rule by holding elections, a sign that "the supreme source of legitimacy continued to lie with the constitution."[34] But Ayub remained in power for a decade, Zia ruled for eleven years, and Musharraf had to be forced out of office and out of the country. (Following his return to Pakistan in the spring of 2013, he was put under house arrest outside Islamabad to await trial on multiple counts of treason and murder.) Had Yahya Khan not lost East Pakistan, he too might have remained in charge for several more years.

Pakistan's military rulers have all announced elaborate reform programs to clean up national politics that were essentially campaigns to eliminate political opponents. Ayub Khan introduced the Elective Bodies Disqualification Ordinance, which enabled him to remove those politicians who had been elected before martial law was imposed on the grounds of corruption. Yahya Khan demanded that politicians participating in the 1970 election demonstrate a commitment to Islamic ideology and national integrity. After the election, a number of parliamentarians elected from East Pakistan were discharged because they did not satisfy this criterion. Zia expelled an entire generation of public officials and then introduced new qualifications for future politicians. Musharraf used corruption charges and the lack of academic qualifications as bases for disqualifying experienced politicians from holding office. Whenever a civilian leader has questioned the military's authority or vision, he or she has been removed from power. Meanwhile, the military elite leveraged the country's strategic value to secure aid from allies abroad and allocated a huge portion of the nation's budget for defense. In 1994–95, defense accounted for more than a quarter of Pakistan's expenditures.[35] Its unofficial expenditure is even larger, as even under civilian rule, Pakistan's generals continue to make military policy and drive a huge portion of the state's budget into their own coffers.[36]

Today, Pakistan operates as a kind of patronage democracy, as defined by political scientist Kanchan Chandra. In a patronage democracy, elections are held and the results are sometimes adhered to, but the elections are not always completely free and fair. Furthermore, the polity lacks a commitment to individual rights and liberties and to a system of checks and balances. In patronage democracies, elections are important because they determine not who will hold political power but who will control patronage networks and thus have the power to distribute jobs and discretionary spending.[37] Policy is dictated less by elected legislators than by a group of powerful economic, military, and religious leaders who primarily serve the elites. The national government does not necessarily follow the rule of law and will step outside the bounds of its constitutionally mandated powers when expedient.

Party politics in Pakistan are overlaid on and subtly interactive with far older systems of political organization, systems that predate Pakistan's founding as a modern democracy. Factions, or blocs, bound together by patron-client relationships, characterize politics at the local level. Stephen Lyon's summary of the ethnographic literature on these political groupings notes five common observations: the groups "cut across socioeconomic boundaries," they are "led by individuals who must conform to the shared cultural values of the followers," they "are organised around personal loyalties rather than common ideology or even common interest," individuals may belong to more than one faction and thus will choose which alliance to invoke in a particular situation, and the Pakistani political scene features contractual alliances (alliances formed for economic and political benefit) that, while they can be dissolved, are often long-term arrangements.[38]

The majority of rural Pakistanis come into contact with the state—and, by extension, formal politics—via the mediation of their landlord, who heads their contractual alliance. Landlords may or may not be politicians themselves, but they do participate in politics on the provincial or national level, usually by promising the votes of their local faction to a politician who in turn provides the village with services. On the village level, therefore, landlords fulfill many of the roles that are normally associated with the state, including securing and spending public development funds and assisting villagers in navigating the bureaucracy.[39] Landlords' connections to provincial-level politicians, who are in turn connected to national-level power brokers, allow them to obtain and distribute such important favors as jobs.

Matthew Nelson's work on politician-constituent relations in Punjab Province provides specific examples of how the patron-client relationships function in Pakistani politics.[40] Nelson shows that most rural Punjabis assess their representatives, whether on the local or national level, not on the politicians' ability to craft and promote new legislation that will advance the people's interests but on their ability to help them avoid the impact of Pakistan's laws on the inheritance of land. Since the 1970s and Zia's Islamization campaign, these laws have been gradually changed to better reflect Islam's insistence that female heirs receive a share of the land, but the changes have brought them into direct conflict with tribal custom, which dictates that only males inherit land. Thus Nelson's survey of local landowners and district court cases found that constituents believe the politicians' most important job is to craft out-of-court settlements and keep lawsuits out of the courts. As far as land law is concerned, the most important politician in a village may not be the district's member of the National Assembly but the *patwari* (local record keeper), who, for a fee, can alter the records of land ownership in a particular citizen's favor. As Lyon put it, by arranging for their clients to avoid the mandates of Pakistani law (whether in questions of land distribution or merely passing through customs at the airport), politicians show that they are "stronger than rules."[41] Their influence attracts more clients, who in turn increase their political power.

That said, Pakistan's period of democratic rule from 1988 to 1999 did allow some of the features of a functioning democracy, such as horizontal class-based voting, to develop. Andrew Wilder's excellent and groundbreaking study of national politics in Punjab tracks the PPP's decline over that period and the coincident rise of Nawaz Sharif's PML-N.[42] Wilder shows that the PPP had a firm grip on Punjabi rural constituencies and continued to win a majority of Punjab's seats in the National Assembly well into the 1990s, but it steadily lost ground in the cities and towns, where an anti-PPP movement, primarily comprising middle-class businessmen, coalesced around Sharif's promise of economic growth. The culmination of this trend was the 1997 election, in which the PML-N won 107 of the 113 National Assembly seats from the Punjab and was well on its way to commanding a two-thirds majority in the assembly.

Contrary to the popular assumption that *biraderi* (tribal) associations dictate voting behavior, Wilder argues that not only party identification, especially in northern and central Punjab, but also the party's effectiveness in distributing patronage and development funds are becoming an increasingly common factor in decision making. Punjabi voters are thus unlikely to vote for a candidate whose party they deem unlikely to capture a majority or at least a plurality in the National Assembly and thus would not possess the clout necessary to direct significant resources back to its members' constituencies. This patronage-focused voting behavior has proved a high hurdle for those Islamist parties that attempt to compete on the national level. The belief that such parties will never become major players in the National Assembly is thus far a self-fulfilling prophecy.

In such a political system, where elections, if they occur, are not the route to real political power, it is fair to ask why parties form at all. I address this matter in depth in chapter 3, but what is worth establishing here is that given Pakistan's weak commitment to democratic processes, confessional parties may operate in the system one day and outside it the next.[43]

The Role of Religion and Islamic Parties

Islam has figured centrally in the political system and national identity of the Islamic Republic of Pakistan since the nation's founding, but its prominence has been matched by the vigorous disagreement over the degree to which Islamic laws and principles should be made manifest in Pakistan's legal, political, and economic structures. For nine years after independence, Pakistan's first leaders—primarily secularists, traditional economic elites, or religious authorities—were unable to ratify a constitution because of differences over the role of Islam in the system of laws.[44] In 1952, the Jamiat Ulema-e-Islam proposed that the constitution should stipulate that a board of *ulema* would serve as the final arbiter of any proposed legislation's compatibility with Islamic law. After a hard-fought public campaign, the proposal was rejected in the National Assembly by a vote of 276 to 91.[45] The two sides eventually reached a compromise that satisfied no one. Pakistan would henceforth be an Islamic Republic with a Muslim head of state, and a constitutional provision would stipulate that Muslims be allowed to live in accordance with the principles of Islam. Pakistan's first constitution mandated that the Quran be taught in schools, but it did not impose sharia law and was deliberately vague about Islam's role when setting public policy.[46] Yet the rights of religious minorities, most notably the Ahmadiyya Muslim sect, were given only minimal protection.

Politicians and ordinary Pakistanis continued to debate the proper role for Islam in the state, but this constitutional dispensation remained essentially in place until the ascent of General Zia in 1977. Zia overthrew Zulfiqar Bhutto's second democratically elected administration and assumed power at a time of extraordinary upheaval. The 1977 elections that saw Bhutto returned to power had been a hard-fought contest between the PPP and the Pakistan National Alliance (PNA), an opposition coalition. When the PPP won in a landslide, the PNA accused it of having rigged the election and launched a Pakistan-wide campaign of civil disobedience. As unrest spread, the army seized the pretext to impose martial law and then created a military government led by Zia, the army's commander in chief.[47] Although Zia's first speech in his new role promised elections within ninety days, he rapidly convinced himself that his vision for Pakistan required his own personal guidance, and he looked for ways to legitimize military rule.[48] The decision to rule as a military dictator meant that Zia needed to make new friends and quickly; moreover, he also needed to find a solution to the puzzle of national consolidation that had confounded his predecessors. Islam, and Pakistan's Islamists, was the obvious choice.

Pakistan in the 1970s had increasingly moved toward the Islamization of public life. In 1974, for instance, the Islamist parties won their decades-long campaign to have the Ahmadiyya sect declared non-Muslim. Not only did the PPP-controlled parliament pass a law declaring the Ahmadiyya non-Muslim, but it also amended the 1973 constitution to ensure that an Ahmadi could not hold the posts of president or prime minister (although the probability of such an event was already close to zero).[49] William Richter argues that this trend had its roots in the trauma of losing East Pakistan in 1971, but he agrees that it came to a head during the 1977 electoral campaigns when the PNA, which was dominated by religious parties, used Islam to attack Bhutto and brought religious issues into the national political debate as never before.[50] Lacking a real platform or political agenda, the PNA relied almost entirely on appeals to religion, as seen in its slogan, which promised a *Nizam-i-Mustafa* (system of the Prophet).[51] Bhutto and the PPP responded by making a significant shift to the left on the sharia–secularism continuum, removing the word "socialism" from party literature, promising to make Friday the weekly holiday, and billing its platform as one of "Islamic egalitarianism."[52]

Zia himself was a personally pious man, who during his time as chief of the army staff had distributed religious literature to the officer corps. He recognized "Islamism could endow the state with the . . . legitimacy" that a predominantly Punjabi military dictatorship inherently lacked and that it held the promise of unifying a country riven by ethnic divisions.[53] Since there was only one Islam and Pakistan was an Islamic state, he could thus portray any expression of ethnic, regional, or political difference as "antithetical" to Islam. As Zia himself once succinctly put it, "One God, One Prophet, One Book, one country, one system—no dissension!"[54]

Unlike Bhutto, however, who trimmed his sails to fit the prevailing winds, Zia's strategic and sincere Islamization program was "an ideologically inspired programme aimed at establishing a 'true Islamic society' in Pakistan."[55] As such, it was designed to touch every aspect of Pakistani life. Ian Talbot divides the legislative and formal aspects of Zia's program into four main areas: "judicial reform, implementation of the Islamic Penal Code, economic activity and a new educational policy."[56]

Judicial and legal reforms were some of the first parts of the Islamization program to be implemented. In 1979, Zia promulgated the notorious Hudood Ordinances, which set Islamic punishments—whipping, stoning, and other fatal methods—for crimes ranging from adultery and drinking to gang robbery.[57] As with much of the Islamization program, the Hudood Ordinances had a dual purpose—to bring Pakistani criminal law into line with sharia and, in their focus on the sanctity of private property, to remind the lower classes that the Bhutto era was over.[58] Although Zia also established Shariat Benches on the high courts and the Supreme Court in 1979, the following year the High Court Shariat Benches were eliminated and a Federal Shariat Court was created. "These benches, comprised of Muslim judges of the respective courts, were empowered to examine any law or provision of law and to decide whether or not it was 'repugnant to the injunction of Islam as laid down in the Holy Quran and Sunnah of the Holy Prophet.'"[59] In 1981, Zia appointed three *alims* (religious leaders and scholars) to the Federal Shariat Court, marking the first time members of the *ulema* had ever served on a Pakistani court.[60] But Zia, to the great disappointment of his Islamist supporters, limited the jurisdiction of the Shariat courts, which were not empowered to review the constitution or any laws relating to the financial or economic system.[61] The Shariat courts simply became further implements of state control, "used less as a means of creating an ideological system of justice and more as a powerful tool of social control in the hands of state leaders."[62]

The reforms with perhaps the longest-lasting impact on Pakistani society came in the area of education. The Zia regime rewrote the standard textbooks used in Pakistani schools to create a semi-mythic narrative of Islamic Pakistan under siege by Hindu India.[63] Quranic and Islamic study was made a mandatory part of both public and private education, Zia founded a sharia faculty at the Quaid-i-Azam University, and the government made efforts to modernize and mainstream the religious school, or *madrasah*, system by both increasing public funds available to such institutions and encouraging the *ulema* to adopt modern educational standards.[64] With this last step, the government officially recognized degrees issued by *madaris* (plural of *madrasah*), and their students were eligible to receive public scholarship funds. Government recognition thus led to explosive growth of the religious school system, as the number of primary schools attached to mosques increased by twelve thousand in 1983 and 1984 alone.[65] As the *madaris*' role in educating religious leaders expanded to include the production of government bureaucrats, their basic ethos changed as well and was seen most signally in new curricula, which included secular subjects meant to prepare students for public service. This change, and the government's increased involvement, was anathema to many members of the *ulema*. As with many aspects of the Islamization campaign, the educational reforms eventually drove a wedge between the military and religious leaders.

As his stubbornness on the question of constitutional review and his quest to control the religious education system make clear, Zia—as were leaders of Pakistan both before and after his reign—was not interested in outsourcing state functions to religious institutions; instead, he saw Islamization as a process of bringing religious institutions under the control of the state.[66] (According to some definitions of secularism, Zia's program was thus an essentially secular one.) Furthermore, he was sufficiently pragmatic to bend when circumstances required. After Pakistan's Shia population led massive protests, he exempted the Shia from the new Islamic taxes on wealth and land (which are not condoned in Shia Islam).[67]

Zia's pragmatism and his state-centric approach eventually caused friction with Pakistan's religious organizations. The JI, for instance, was an integral part of the first wave of the Islamization program. A long-time admirer of JI leader Syed Abul A'ala Maududi, Zia placed JI members in important cabinet posts and brought them into his inner circle of advisers.[68] The JI used its link to the Muhajir population to pacify that group's demands for democracy; the JUI did the same with the Baluch and the Pashtuns.[69] But a rift developed between the military and the JI after 1979, as the JI began to realize that Zia had no intention of ever relinquishing power to civilian parties and Zia decided that the military, not a political party, was the organization best suited to lead the creation of an Islamic state.[70] The split, however, was never total. Religious parties were torn between the devil that they knew—Zia's statist and occasionally half-hearted Islamization efforts—and the devil that they feared, namely, a possible PPP government should democracy be restored. Thus, in the early 1980s, the Islamist parties abstained from participating in the pro-democracy movement in Sindh Province, contributing to its collapse.[71]

Islamization was primarily an urban phenomenon. Zia did attempt to co-opt rural religious leaders, who had historically been PPP supporters. As the JI and other Islamist parties helped to build support for the regime in the cities, the *pirs* (Islamic religious figures whose authority is hereditary and not based on education) extended Zia's power networks in the countryside.[72] Richard Kurin's anthropological work in a Punjabi village, however, suggests that the Islamization campaign had little if any noticeable effect on the lives or opinions of Pakistan's rural poor.[73] Zia's focus and his primary constituency was the lower middle class, often urban, of the provinces of Punjab, Sindh, and North-West Frontier (now the Khyber Pakhtunkhwa). He wooed them with a "promise to protect the sanctity of *chador* (the veil) and *chardivari* (the four walls of a house)," symbolizing women's honor and private property.[74]

As might be expected, Zia's Islamization campaign was far from a panacea for Pakistan's ills, and Pakistan is still struggling with its consequences. Zia's push to Islamize Pakistan gave new valence to the question of what "Islam" means and who defines it. The campaign deepened the Sunni-Shia divide (a rift that has current lethal consequences for Pakistan's Shia population), and caused significant discontent in traditionally Sufi areas such as Sindh, leading to a near rebellion in that province.[75] The elections without parties strengthened ethnic and biraderi ties but to the detriment of national cohesion and future attempts at democracy.[76] Although Zia did not originate the policy of supporting militant groups in Kashmir and Afghanistan, funds flowing to such groups, particularly the mujahideen in Afghanistan, increased drastically under his tenure.[77] Furthermore, the explosion in the *madrasah* system under Zia ensured that such groups would have a steady supply of willing recruits.[78] Thus the Zia regime contributed significantly to the growth of Pakistan's "Kalashnikov culture."

While many formal aspects of Zia's Islamization program were rolled back under Benazir Bhutto's PPP government in the 1980s, it continues to influence modern Pakistani politics. One area in which Zia's policies still have enormous effect is the politicization of Pakistan's Islamic institutions. While certain members of the *ulema* had been involved in politics even before Pakistan's creation, Islamization, with its emphasis on the role of the *ulema* in defining and leading Islam, created irresistible new incentives for *alims* to become involved in politics and improve the status of the *ulema* in Pakistani Islam.[79] As Nasr writes, "The centrality of madrasahs to state-led Islamization meant that the ulama would remain in control of Islamic learning at a time when Islam was poised to define public policy and lay claim to modern sectors of the economy and society. It also meant that they would develop a more prominent role, laying claim to Islamism and its central role in state and society after 1980. The state thus helped create an ulama wing of Islamism, which would increasingly assert itself at the cost of the lay Islamist thinkers and organizations."[80] Indeed, the role of *madaris* and their graduates in Zia's Islamization program was so great that even non-*ulema* Islamist parties such as the JI (whose founder, Maududi, had vociferously criticized the *ulema* and the Islamic educational system) began to found *madaris* of their own.[81]

Zia's reforms, and the resulting contest to win a share of government largesse, also sharpened a preexisting trend in which religious cleavages—not only between members of different faiths but also between different sects and subsects of Islam—assume highly political dimensions. Thus Alix Philippon describes the struggle for supremacy among Pakistan's varied religious traditions as a fight for secular as well as divine authority.[82] Leaders of the Sufi-inspired Barelvi sect, for instance, who claim to represent a majority of Pakistan's Sunni Muslims, "deem that their being 'representative' of the religiosity of the population should translate into a hegemonic situation in the political field."[83] Their relative lack of political clout is a continual frustration to the Barelvis. In a fascinating observation, Joshua White suggests that the Barelvi leaders' silence following Salman Taseer's assassination by a member of the sect was an attempt "to buttress their own standing within the Barelvi community, and to raise the profile of the Barelvis vis-à-vis their Sunni competition by exploiting an issue that played well with both their own constituency and with the Sunni public at large."[84] (The Barelvis deeply venerate the Prophet Muhammad and thus highly support the blasphemy laws that Taseer opposed.)

Pakistan had been an Islamic nation before Zia came to power. Twenty-five years after his death it still retains some features of what William Ziring called the "Islamic State," or a rigidly authoritarian entity that "seeks to [reinforce Pakistani unity] by demonstrating the effectiveness of the ruling authority's coercive power."[85] The Zia era created political alignments—with the military, Islamists, and businessmen on one side and the PPP, ethnic parties, and the landed class on the other—that long outlasted his reign, which ended in an unexpected, still mysterious, and deadly plane crash in 1988. And at least for the foreseeable future, Zia's efforts solidified the formation of a powerful "Islamic vote" in Pakistani politics.

While debate over the proper role of Islam still rages in Pakistan, its people generally accept the overlap between affairs of state and of the soul. The separation between religion and politics considered so desirable in Western democracies simply does not exist in Pakistan. The "hand of Allah" and references to God's will are seen and felt everywhere. The Pakistani constitution begins, "In the name of God, the Beneficent and the Merciful." Confessional parties use slogans such as "Islam is the solution." Banners on election booths remind voters, "Islam is our destiny, in this life and the hereafter." And the Pakistani legal system does incorporate aspects of sharia with its sharia courts, religious laws governing marriage and inheritance, and the infamous blasphemy laws, which ban defamatory speech against Islam or its prophet. Children in public schools all over Pakistan are required to memorize "Bilad-e-Islamia," a poem by Muhammed Iqbal that deplores political leaders who tout themselves as Muslims but are devoid of a genuine spiritual attachment to the blessed prophet.

Post-Zia Pakistan has also seen an increasing shift toward an embrace of political, as opposed to simply personal, visions of Islam. The most recent data on Pakistani public opinion shows that Pakistanis are more likely than citizens of most Muslim countries to believe that there is only one interpretation of sharia (61 percent, putting Pakistan fourth on a list of twenty-two countries); 84 percent of Pakistanis think sharia should be made the law of the land (the sixth-highest percentage in thirty-eight countries surveyed and up from 79 percent in 2007); and 86 percent maintain that the punishment for apostasy should be death.[86] But while Pakistan's Muslims express a strong adherence to the principle of Islamic governance, they differ widely as to what it involves. For example, they are roughly equally split on whether Pakistan's current laws follow sharia, with 41 percent reporting that they do and 45 percent that they do not. (Of the latter group, however, 91 percent believe that not following sharia is a bad state of affairs.)[87]

This discrepancy illustrates the point made by C. Christine Fair, Neil Malhotra, and Jacob Shapiro, who argue that for many Pakistanis the term "sharia" connotes general good governance rather than the enforcement of specific laws.[88] Their groundbreaking research shows that more than 95 percent of respondents to their survey believe that a government that rules according to sharia law "provides services, justice, personal security, and is free of corruption," while only 55 percent believe that sharia also or primarily means meting out the use of physical punishments, such as stoning, amputation, and so on.[89] The people's vague understanding of what sharia law entails therefore allows politicians to attempt to share in its popularity without committing themselves to any particular policy. And the strong support for sharia law among Pakistanis makes moving to the left on the sharia–secularism continuum a perpetually viable electoral strategy.

Pakistani opinion is not likely to swing back toward moderation any time soon, as shown in two recent polls (from 2009 and 2013) of young Pakistanis ages eighteen to twenty-nine. Members of this cohort, who were born during Zia's tenure or slightly afterward, are five times as likely to identify themselves as Muslims first rather than as Pakistanis first.[90] While in 2009 their opinions were essentially evenly split (33 percent to 32 percent) between democracy and sharia law as the best system of governance for Pakistan, by 2013 sharia law had surged ahead, with 38 percent of respondents listing it as the best option versus 32 percent for military rule and 29 percent for democracy.[91] Young Pakistanis are also deeply pessimistic, with 94 percent of them reporting that Pakistan is headed in the wrong direction.[92] This statistic has gone up from 80 percent in 2009.[93]

In light of these findings, I closely examine the origins, organization, and behavior of Pakistan's three largest Islamic parties, each of which represent one of the three party typologies: Muslim democrats, hierarchical Islamists, and network Islamists. The Pakistan Muslim League (PML), a Muslim democratic party, was originally founded in 1906 to counter the power of the Hindu elite of British India. It remained the most prominent Islamic party in the subcontinent throughout the first half of the twentieth century and led the movement for an independent Muslim state of Pakistan.

Almost from its birth, however, challengers found the league insufficiently far-right and did not believe it would safeguard the interests of devout Muslims. The modernizing, hierarchical Islamist party, Jamaat-e-Islami, was founded in 1941 to push for broader adoption of sharia law. The JI is now the largest and most influential Islamist party in Pakistan and South Asia. The network Islamist party,

Jamiat Ulema-e-Islam, was formed in 1945. Originally focused on establishing religious institutions and *madaris* and issuing *fatwas* (religious edicts) about religious practice in modern society, the JUI slowly became more interested in formal electoral politics. It is now a dominant political player in Pakistan's rural provinces.

Other Islamic confessional parties in Pakistan include the Pakistan Muslim League–Quaid (PML-Q), Jamiat Ulema-e-Pakistan–Fazlur (JUI-F), Jamiat Ulema-e-Islam–Sami (JUI-S), Jamiat Ulema-e-Pakistan (JUP), Tehreek-e-Insaf (PTI), Tehrik-e-Jafaria Pakistan, and Markazi Jamiat Ahle Hadith (JUAH). As noted Islamic studies scholars Jonathan Brown and Intisar Rabb emphasize, sharia's long historical development has been a multiplicity of interpretive schools, or *fiqh*, each with its own understanding of the particulars of the law. Islamic parties are important participants in Pakistani politics and have achieved electoral success on the national, provincial, and district levels. Combined, they have won at least 10 percent of the seats in the National Assembly in each election in the last twenty years. Since 1990, Islamic party candidates have held more than twenty federal ministerial positions and served as assembly speakers in four provincial legislatures. Islamic parties have held majority control in provincial legislatures six times, including in the strategically important Khyber Pakhtunkwha. They have eked out important victories on the district level as well, for example, winning the mayorship in Bahawalpur, Punjab, in 2005.

That said, Pakistani confessional parties have had less electoral success than Pakistan's overwhelmingly Muslim population might suggest. Secular parties have often dominated politics, particularly on the national level. The most prominent among them, the socialist Pakistan People's Party, was founded in 1971 by Zulfiqar Bhutto. Bhutto led a populist revolt against the military bureaucracy and built the first grassroots political movement in Pakistan. The Muttahida Quami Movement (United National Movement, MQM), based in Sindh, is supported primarily by Muslim immigrants from India, while the Awami National Party (ANP) is a Pashtun party based in Pakistan's northern region. Each of these secular parties has fared well at various points—the PPP has governed Pakistan on four occasions—and has joined governing coalitions.

A close look at the data reveals that the inability of Islamic parties to consolidate electoral gains or make meaningful inroads in new electoral arenas is more often the result of competition from other Islamic parties rather than from secularists. Such in-group bias is explored in depth in chapter 6. Essentially, my research reveals that the closer two parties are to each other on the sharia–secularism continuum, the more vicious and intractable their political battles are likely to be. These disputes are not merely academic or political disagreements. The frontier areas of Pakistan and Afghanistan are experiencing a decades-long civil war, with each side promoting a different version of Islamic politics.

Plan of the Volume

In chapter 3 I analyze in detail the political theory behind the development of confessional Islamic parties and the structural and organizational models they adopt. I argue that it is vital for social scientists to begin using theoretical constructs that are specific to the developing world rather than simply importing theories that have been used to explain party formation and organization in Western developed democracies. I then describe a three-part typology of Islamic parties in Pakistan.

Chapters 4 and 5 look closely at the development, motivations, and behavior of Muslim democratic and Islamist confessional parties in Pakistan, respectively. I focus on the ideological forces that guide party formation and the resulting organizational features. Drawing on historical and ethnographic data and firsthand interviews with 160 party leaders and supporters conducted as part of my field research in Pakistan, I examine the formative and electoral experiences of Pakistan's three largest Islamic political parties.

In chapter 6 I address the issue of voter motivation as it relates to party behavior. I examine why conventional theories to explain voter support for confessional parties are not adequate in the Pakistani context, and I introduce original survey data to suggest the basis for a new theory of Islamic voter decision making. I provide evidence drawn from a unique thought experiment conducted with 455 Pakistani voters to gain a fuller understanding of the in-group bias phenomenon. Based on this reconceived notion of party formation and voter motivation, in chapter 7 I address the matter of Islamic party behavior. I argue that Islamic parties become less ideological and more instrumental (in some cases using extra-electoral means, street power, and even violence) over time, shifting their positions and platforms to achieve maximum electoral success in their target regions and races. In chapters 8 and 9 I examine the implications of this research for our understanding of what drives political Islamic extremism, applying its conclusions to the cases of Egypt, Turkey, and Afghanistan.

I have used several methods to investigate the core research questions presented in this book. Qualitative data includes interviews with political elites, focus groups, and careful examination of primary and secondary archival materials at Punjab University and Quaid-i-Azam University. Quantitative data includes close analysis of local and national election results, survey results, and voter behavior experiments. This book is one of the first to apply both qualitative and quantitative methods to a scholarly study of political parties and party systems in Pakistan.

Finally, I discuss the policy implications of building a new understanding of Islamic confessional parties. Oversimplified and uninformed depictions of party politics in Pakistan have negatively affected international policy, resulting in the mismanagement or total neglect of potentially vital relationships. Awareness of the broader context, history, and motivations underlying the behavior of Islamic confessional parties could vastly improve the ability of diplomats to navigate Pakistan's ever-changing and often bewildering political terrain. More specifically, understanding that Islamic political parties are motivated as much by voter turnout as by righteousness should impact relations with Islamic allies and antagonists and should potentially open new opportunities for diplomacy. Given the events in 2011 in Tunisia, in Egypt, and across the Middle East, the likelihood is that Islamic confessional parties such as the Muslim Brotherhood will accrue greater political power moving forward. To engage these organizations in a productive dialogue, it is essential that Western policymakers understand what drives such parties toward moderation or extremism.

CHAPTER 3

ISLAMIC PARTIES IN PAKISTAN

It may seem natural, even obvious, that an overwhelmingly Muslim country such as Pakistan should be home to confessional Muslim political parties. But the existence and persistence of Islamic political parties in Pakistan were not givens. Although the Islamic parties of what is now Pakistan predate the existence of the republic itself, Pakistan's political system is not a particularly hospitable place. Cheating and manipulation routinely taint elections, and the parliamentary assemblies and executive offices to which political candidates aspire are often merely rubber stamps or puppets of powerful private interests. The puzzle of party persistence is compounded by the fact that the costs and risks associated with participating in electoral politics are significant. Campaigns are time consuming, exhausting, and financially expensive, and successful parties may be the target of pushback by the military sector if its leadership feels sufficiently threatened, rendering victories at the ballot box merely symbolic.

Why, given this environment, do Islamic parties form at all? What are the motivations, conditions, and processes of party formation in developing Muslim democracies? Why have confessional parties persisted for Pakistan's entire history? In this chapter I examine the existing literature on the founding of confessional parties, much of which is based on studies of party emergence in Western European democracies, and the growing body of literature devoted to specifically Islamic party formation. I discuss the ways in which the present theoretical tools fail to explain the emergence of religious parties in developing nations in the Islamic world, and I provide a new theoretical framework for explaining the rise of confessional parties in countries like Pakistan. Based on this broad theory of Islamic party formation and organization, I am able to identify and describe three main types of confessional Islamic parties in Pakistan and provide a firm basis for better understanding their methods and conduct.

For the purposes of this discussion, I define an organization as a "political party" as soon as it nominates a candidate for electoral office. Indeed, whether the organization resembles a traditional political party or even describes itself as such, entry into an electoral contest is both necessary and sufficient for it to be defined as a party. This definition of party formation, while admittedly rather basic, is consonant with most existing definitions. Political scientists Anthony Downs and

Joseph Schumpeter use similarly minimalist definitions of parties: "a team of men seeking to control the governing apparatus by gaining office in a duly constituted election" and "a party is a group whose members propose to act in concert in the competitive struggle for political power," respectively. Other students of party formation, such as Giovanni Sartori, also require that the party have some hope of success: "a party is any political group that presents at elections, and is capable of placing through elections, candidates for public office."[1]

Party Formation in Developed Democracies

With so many directions a movement can go, the question remains, why select the electoral route? The political science literature includes a number of studies of party emergence and the incentives that lead actors to create confessional political parties.[2] Most theoreticians have based their conclusions on studies of secular or Catholic confessional party formation in developed Western democracies.[3] Many authors have focused on parties as a solution to the problems of collective action; adopting a microeconomic perspective, they argue that parties are the result of rational, self-interested decision making.[4] These authors assert that when political actors grow weary of intractable political dilemmas and ineffectual legislative rule by cycling majorities and unstable coalitions, they attempt to intervene by creating a new party organization. According to Gary Cox and Matthew McCubbins, winning over legislators is crucial to party formation; to build membership and clout, the new party leadership offers legislators public goods, such as appropriations and campaign funds. In addition, the party must build its reputation among the electorate so that candidates and voters can easily use their party affiliation as shorthand for their shared interests and ideals. The establishment of a party also serves as a bulwark against the "free rider" problem, because a party's reputation and platform serve as long-term commitment devices, binding party members to the party organization.

Posing a significant problem in parliamentary systems, a free rider benefits from the collective action of others without contributing personally to creating the goods or product. The principle may apply in a wide variety of circumstances, but in this case it refers to those who gain benefits from a policy or practice without expressing support for the system or organization that produces or promotes the policy. Members of Parliament, for example, may be able to satisfy their agenda simply by forming temporary associations with other members on a case-by-case basis. Without more permanent formal allegiances, members may be free to pursue policies to the detriment of one-time associates or may avoid publicly taking unpopular stands. Political parties formalize such associations and coalitions, making reciprocity and accountability explicit through party membership.

In exploring the origins of the party system in the United States, John Aldrich basically agrees with Cox and McCubbins, although he emphasizes the natural advantages of the party organization in the context of legislative bodies.[5] He argues that coalitions and parties—basically, durable and binding coalitions—are created in response to legislative bargaining problems. Aldrich's work focuses on the period between 1790 to 1860, when members of the US Congress were grappling with important decisions about debt repayment and the government's structure. The formation of parties in this context was a natural reaction to the range and complexity of the issues put forth and the instability created by frequently cycling majorities. In this context, "it is reasonable to conclude that parties arose out of the step-by-step strengthening of factions into political parties as a means of avoiding consequences of voting disequilibrium."[6] Once a party formed on the legislative level, it had an interest in building a general membership and mobilizing votes in order to enhance its strength, thus leading to the transformation of legislative parties into mass parties. In both Cox and McCubbins's and Aldrich's analyses, political entrepreneurs already engaged in parliamentary politics have an incentive to initiate party formation in order to effect legislative outcomes and shape public policy.

Other scholars argue that party formation is a way for previously inactive or disenfranchised contestants to influence policy and the political system. This explanation is especially relevant in the case of the early socialist and Catholic confessional parties of nineteenth-century Europe. Przeworski and Sprague, for instance, note that the first socialists primarily sought not to change labor conditions but to build self-contained and self-sustaining communities. Their focus only changed when they decided that any changes in workers' lives in the near future required electoral participation. Kalyvas observes that Catholic political activists traveled a similar route, first embracing self-quarantine from the larger society and then coming to terms with the realization that true political power required engagement.

In addition to motive, party formation requires opportunity.[7] Most theorists, working in the context of developed democracies, see changes in the existing political institutions or in the underlying social cleavages as prime opportunities for party formation. Seymour Lipset and Stein Rokkan argue that modern European party systems were shaped by a series of conflicts over state building, religion, and class that took place between the Protestant Reformation and the Industrial Revolution.[8] The sequential interaction of these conflicts resulted in distinct and highly durable social identities or cleavages that still form the basis of the different national parties. The Industrial Revolution, for example, exacerbated long-standing urban versus rural conflicts and produced distinct urban coalitions and rural coalitions in the national legislatures of most European countries. Urban-rural tensions were most intense during the earliest phases of industrialization, and this period saw working-class parties emerge across Europe. Lipset and Rokkan argue that social cleavages were translated into embryonic party systems even though barriers to political participation were relatively high and large groups of people were still disenfranchised. According to this view, barriers to participation can create an opportunity for parties to form and give a voice to those who are unable to vote. In fact, this subtlety is often missed or glossed over. One cannot and should not assume that fringe elements can neither participate in nor become a democratic force, now or eventually.

In the case of Catholic confessional parties, an ideological cleavage developed between anti-ecclesiastical and anti-Catholic governments and the Church. Facing attempts to legislate against the Church, Catholics recognized a need to engage in the political sphere.[9] Kalyvas identifies a three-stage process of Catholic confessional party formation as it occurred in Belgium, the Netherlands, Austria, Germany, and Italy.[10] In the *organizational strategy* stage, Catholic organizations began mobilizing outside the electoral arena, rallying Catholic believers to help counter anti-ecclesiastical sentiment and anti-Church legislation. In the *participatory strategy* stage, confessional organizations entered the political arena and formed powerful coalitions with conservative parties, leading to impressive electoral results. The success of this strategy empowered Catholic activists and encouraged them to use their political capital to engage in the third stage of the process, the *formation* of confessional parties. Ultimately, the leadership of these parties freed themselves from the Church's control, developed more centrist platforms, and broadened their voter bases. The strategic choices of both Church leaders and their conservative allies led to the empowerment of new political actors.[11] In a sense, the Church became a victim of its own success; it could neither prevent the formation of confessional parties nor control their strategy and platform.

Each of these theories of party formation relies heavily on an assumption of parliamentary efficacy. Cox, McCubbins, Kalyvas, and Aldrich assume that party formation is based on a desire to achieve specific political, economic, or social ends by obtaining greater power in the Parliament. But this move is only rational if the parties (as units of power) can have a substantial influence in Parliament and if that Parliament plays a meaningful role in creating policy. Similarly, Kalyvas argues that the Church's political activities and eventual Catholic party formation were a strategic response to its opponents and were attempted only after non-electoral activities had failed.[12] The implication is that electoral success would afford the Church enough power to force policy changes when other strategies could not, but it would only have been true if Parliament indeed had been efficacious.

Party Formation in Developing Democracies

These theories about the motivation, conditions, and processes associated with the emergence of political parties have questionable relevance for developing democracies and particularly for those that have Muslim majorities, such as Pakistan.

Political parties in Pakistan have developed in a very different environment from those in Western Europe. Pakistan's parties emerged in the context of European colonial rule. Furthermore, the Indian subcontinent is home to a complex and often conflicted patchwork of religious, ethnic, and linguistic groups without parallel in modern Europe. Finally, the previously discussed theories, which are based on a presumption of parliamentary efficacy, are limited in explaining party formation in a country where elections are infrequent and fraught with irregularities and where parliaments are bereft of any real authority.

Other authors have noted this poor fit between political typologies based on Europe's experience and the realities of developing democracies. "There is hardly any political system of the South Asian countries . . . that fits satisfactorily into the classical schemes of either the political sociologist's or institutionalist's view on the formation and structuring of party systems," writes Clemens Spiess.[13] He argues that the pervasive presence of "clientelist linkages and charismatic leadership" throughout South Asia makes a good deal of political theory irrelevant, and he contends that the true underpinnings of party formation in Southeast Asia are regionalization, intensive factionalism, and widespread dynastic and family rule. These patterns, Spiess asserts, are indigenous expressions of the culturally and historically grounded political patterns that presage party formation.[14]

Spiess correctly assesses the poor fit between models of political party formation developed from Western secular governmental systems and those common to South Asia. His identification of regional, dynastic, familial, and factional power divisions is also an accurate description of central patterns of South Asian politics. However, as this book makes apparent, political realities in Pakistan (and likely throughout South Asia) involve an even more complex set of variables and considerations than Spiess indicates, with the result that party formation there bears almost no resemblance to that in the Western world. Political parties in Pakistan are formed in the contexts that Spiess decribes, but factors such as religious identity, class, language, and ethnic identity (which often cross national boundaries) also play a significant role.

Clearly, the traditional account falls short of adequately describing party formation in Pakistan, particularly regarding Islamic party formation. A few scholars have attempted to answer the call for a more regionally specific model. As Kalyvas writes, in emerging democracies, the political process has not yet become routinized: "Elections are not yet the only game in town."[15] In this context, South Asian political parties (Islamic confessional parties included) are formed not solely to push policy through the legislature but also to achieve other, nonlegislative, objectives. While those parties do have aspirations to shift policy, potentially through political channels, these observations suggest that their initial motivation in holding public offices is not strictly to affect changes in policy.

A primary motivation for party development in emerging democracies, particularly those with a history of colonial rule, is that winning electoral contests opens access to state resources, such as earmarks for pet projects, jobs, or control over specific markets.[16] Kanchan Chandra has termed it "patronage democracy." Although the comparison is not exact, there are similarities between political party formation in modern emerging democracies and those in nineteenth-century Europe. As the shift from feudalism to democracy began, elites tried to retain power through electoral politics, trading votes for patronage.[17] In the early days of European democracies, electoral success did not translate neatly into political power, just as it does not in modern developing democracies in many Muslim nations. Political parties in Europe were initially vehicles for elites to maintain long-standing socioeconomic and ethnic inequities in the face of growing suffrage.

The conditions required for party formation are not necessarily the same in developed European democracies as they are in developing democracies. Numerous authors have argued that in developed democracies, some kind of institutional change needs to occur that heightens tensions over long-standing ethnic, cultural, linguistic, religious, or class cleavages. Such institutional shifts occurred in Europe when the authority of the Catholic Church declined during the Protestant Reformation and when feudalism was overthrown during the Industrial Revolution. Modern developing democracies, however, have not witnessed this sort of profound, internal institutional shift. The biggest change has instead been gaining independence from colonial rule. As the foreign powers that had constrained political organization for decades or centuries left, domestic groups for the first time were able to access the goods available to political contenders. That these changes were externally rather than internally driven has had a lasting impact on the region, though, stunting modernization and the development of stable constitutional systems.[18] The earliest political parties in Pakistan emerged essentially in reaction to Western imperialism and have had a very difficult time transitioning away from opposition and taking up the work of state building. (This outward focus is still evident in the case of modern hard-line Islamist organizations and is discussed in greater depth later.)

Parliamentary systems in developing countries tend to wield little real power, but they are ideal vehicles for patronage and graft. The ability to gain access to patronage benefits for supporters is a necessary precondition for party formation in an emerging democracy.[19] Electoral winners are able to establish client-patron relationships that are the modern analogues of the feudal relationships that predominated in the nineteenth and early twentieth centuries.[20] In many cases, long-standing elites are able to retain their preeminence through electoral contests by becoming the brokers of public goods.

Party formation in developing democracies also seems to follow a distinctive process, which obtains regardless of the type of party—secular or confessional—being formed. The first stage of the process is *elite organization*, or the mobilization of groups that held power prior to or during colonial rule. Elite power may be based on regional, socioeconomic, ethnic, cultural, linguistic, and religious identity. In the context of the dissolution of the colonial power structure, these identities become more salient and elite status in a subgroup becomes preeminent. Those who hold elite status in a subgroup, and are motivated by a desire to retain their status and privilege and to increase them through governance restructuring, organize around their shared identity to pursue some portion of the newly available power and state goods. Thus, even though a party may have a confessional cast, the underlying reason for elite mobilization need not be religious.

The second stage of the process is *legitimization* and *state recognition*. Legitimization means the party agrees to play by the rules of the electoral game and to work within the state's institutional constraints. Pakistani parties achieved legitimacy only after they came to terms with the creation of an independent state and set out to influence the state apparatus by participating in electoral politics. (Some confessional parties, for instance, had been against partition.) A secondary aspect of legitimization is gaining formal recognition by the state. Only political parties that are registered with the appropriate ministry (currently the Election Commission) can have their names or *intikhabi nishaan* (party symbol) on the ballot boxes. The state also can ban parties or restrict their publicity at ballot boxes. This point is important given the country's high illiteracy rates.

In Pakistan, as in most parliamentary systems where coalitions reign supreme and majority parties rely heavily on smaller parties to form controlling blocs, the state has an incentive to recognize newly formed parties as vehicles for delivering the support of additional subgroups of voters, thus consolidating state power.[21] Big parties will often try to co-opt smaller parties, offering them ministerial positions in return for their support of their patrons' agenda. Secular parties may even form alliances with smaller confessional parties, depending on the specific constituencies involved. In Muslim-majority nations, secular parties know that if they shun confessional parties they may offend a public highly attuned to religious symbolism. Rather than risk drawing public ire, secular parties allow confessional parties into the game.

Parties that achieve legitimacy and state recognition then enter the third formative stage, *mass mobilization*. At this point, parties must engage in a variety of mobilization strategies in order to build their base beyond the core group of initial supporters. To a large extent, mobilization strategy is dictated by party elites and the source of their authority. Chapters 4 and 5 address how mobilization strategies vary widely among confessional Islamic parties depending on party type. It is important to note that once confessional parties receive initial recognition from the state, they begin to oppose the state on ideological grounds in order to establish their political legitimacy with voters.

Islamist Party Formation

The contingent nature of Islamic party formation in Pakistan can be seen in the number of Islamic political organizations that have intentionally avoided becoming parties in the true sense of the word. Tablighi Jamaat (TJ), for example, is a religious revivalist group that, while a contemporary of the two main Islamist parties, has refrained from party formation. TJ arose in response to Hindu revivalism and out of a desire to increase religiosity among nonpracticing Muslims. It seeks to unite Muslims from all social and economic classes around the common goal of adherence to the practices of the Prophet Muhammad. TJ uses a grassroots approach, has an informal organizational structure, and keeps an introverted institutional profile—all to great effect. TJ has no permanent membership, and members can easily join or leave the group; but since its inception in 1926 it has still grown explosively from a small local sect to a multinational movement with adherents in more than 150 countries. TJ is arguably more effective at mass mobilization than any of the Islamic political parties are because the organization focuses only on communicating one simple message of religious devotion through direct, personal interactions.

The key difference between revivalist movements such as TJ and Islamist political parties is that the former are concerned solely with the spiritual reformation of individual Muslims, not the imposition of spiritual law by the state. Their allegiance is not to Pakistan but to Islam. This universal focus forestalls party formation and has historically placed groups such as TJ at odds with the state, which in turn remains the suspicious international nature of TJ.

Establishing political parties is not the only form of Islamic political behavior. Robert Quinn Mecham catalogs six types of Islamist political mobilization, of which party formation is only one. According to Mecham, Islamist movements may be either individualist, communal, or statist, meaning that they focus on the promotion of sharia at one of these levels of aggregation.[22] Mecham also categorizes Islamist political movements as either *accommodative*—such movements work within the existing system—or *militant*, meaning they work outside it. While he does not give an example of a militant individualist movement, he does provide examples of the other five types of organizations predicted by his matrix.

More important, Mecham acknowledges that groups can quickly move from one category to another. Political parties may become revolutionaries and vice versa. He also notes that movements may shift their focus from the state to the community to the individual and back to the state. Mecham's conclusion supports one of the underlying arguments of this book: Categories designed to describe the range of Islamist political behavior cannot be rigid. They are driven by pragmatic issues other than ideological commitments. Beyond the most introverted or quietist groups, Islamist organizations are highly susceptible to the electoral context and highly adaptive. Unlike most political parties in Western democracies, Islamist political parties may simultaneously engage in the electoral process (accommodation) and violent protest (militancy), and they may target both national (state) and local (communal or individual) audiences at the same time.[23] This analysis better explains Islamist parties in Muslim-majority states, which at times have supported extreme actions and rhetoric for political benefit rather than because their ideological commitments required taking such positions. In other words, they look at what position will get them the most votes and influence.

Many scholars believe that the origins of political Islam lie in the reaction to Western influence. By the nineteenth century, Pakdil Kesgin writes, "the West had infiltrated Islamic lands politically, economically, and militarily. . . . The intrusion of culture into Muslim societies, and the neo-liberal economic policies and their consequences on Muslim countries were the reasons for the rise of political Islam in the 20th century."[24] In order to preserve the cultural heritage of traditionally Islamic lands and to combat Western influence, Islam was "reconstructed as a revivalist ideology against the domination of the Western World."[25] It is understandable that indigenous people would focus on upholding their cultural values in the face of a dominating foreign presence, but given the wide variety of formations available to Islamist groups, why do they choose to mobilize as quasi-traditional parties as opposed to any of the other options available? This question has gained increasing salience since 9/11 and the Arab Spring. Scholars have also asked which conditions might convince militant Islamist groups to accept a peaceful political process (at least to the extent of contesting elections).

Much of the academic discourse surrounding Islamist political parties is thus focused on the moderation-extremism debate and the associated "moderation-inclusion hypothesis." As defined by Jillian Schwedler, this theory posits that inclusion in the political process will lead radical groups to moderate their views.[26] Scholars such as Carrie Rosefsky Wickham, in her study of the formation of Egypt's Al-Wasat Party, have indeed found that the very action of inclusion in the political process can prompt Islamists to soften their views on such important issues as the role of non-Muslims in an Islamic state and the position of women in society.[27] But, as Schwedler notes in a crucial insight, mere participation in elections or democratic processes—behavior that might appear to indicate the embrace of liberal and democratic norms of governance—is alone insufficient as an indicator of moderation; participation is a form of political behavior that a group might adopt for purely strategic purposes while continuing to harbor a more radical political agenda.[28]

Furthermore, as Janine Clark notes in her study of the behavior of Jordan's Islamic Action Front, even those Islamist groups that do participate in politics may maintain "red lines," or policy positions that they are not willing to negotiate.[29] Scholars have thus focused on establishing mechanisms for determining when and in what manner moderation has indeed taken place. Schwedler identifies three "distinct analytical lenses" for addressing this question. The first examines moderation primarily as a function of the group's behavior, the second lens examines moderation of a group's ideology, and the third focuses on ideological moderation on the individual level.[30]

The universe of Pakistani Islamic organizations, where groups choosing to operate outside the organized political realm range ideologically from TJ to the Pakistani Taliban and legitimate political parties espouse views all along the sharia–secularism continuum, provides strong evidence for abandoning any facile distinction between moderates and radicals based solely on their decision to participate in the political process. Recognizing the poverty of such a distinction, in recent years a number of scholars have begun to question this dichotomy. Janine Clark and Jillian Schwedler, for instance, in their study of female participation in Islamist movements, replace the two-dimensional moderate-radical axis with a four-dimensional grid that charts groups according to their stance on the necessity of strict interpretation of sharia law and the degree to which they are willing to accommodate themselves to the pluralist, democratic political process.[31] This model preserves the possibility (important for any study of Pakistani politics) that a group can behave in an increasingly accomodationist manner while not moderating its ideological stance. It also demonstrates that a group that has long been committed to the political process can move back and forth along the ideological spectrum without abandoning its attitudes toward electoral participation.

The Pakistani experience, which is outlined in later chapters, provides significant empirical support for those theorists of Islamic party behavior who argue that the very act of participation tends to change a group's views (or at least create more flexible ideologies), or what Schwedler describes as "the strategic moderation of behavior model."[32] Mona El-Ghobashy, for instance, argues that the participation of Egypt's Muslim Brotherhood in politics (even the limited participation allowed under the Hosni Mubarak regime) had the unintended consequence of leading it to moderate its political views. She maintains, "One of the most visible byproducts of the Ikhwan's political engagement has been a decisive move away from the uncompromising notions of Sayyid Qutb . . . and toward a cautious reinterpretation of the ideas of founder [Hassan] al-Banna."[33]

Yet this process is far from inevitable; indeed, inclusion does not inevitably lead to moderation. Schwedler's work on Islamist parties in Jordan and Yemen, for instance, shows that participation in a (somewhat limited) political space has led Jordan's main Islamist party to moderate some (although not all) of its views while Yemen's Islah Party, a similar group, has not moderated.[34] In Pakistan as well, the behavior of Islamist political parties, which regularly move back and forth along the sharia–secularism continuum on certain issues when political advantage requires it, shows that political inclusion is unlikely to moderate the behavior of Islamist groups across the board. This relative unpredictability—and the fact that the ideological movement of Pakistan's Islamist parties is far from unidirectional, suggests that studies of Islamist parties must go "beyond moderation" (as Joshua White puts it) and focus instead on how parties actually behave in and out of office.[35]

But while studies go some way toward answering the question of what conditions are necessary for Islamist groups to enter politics, their applicability to Pakistan is limited. Most studies have focused on the decisions of violent groups to lay down their weapons and endorse peaceful political contestation; in short, they have focused on their passage from violence to politics. Not one of Pakistan's Islamist parties, however, started out as a violent group. Quinn Mecham studied Hamas and Hezbollah, two groups that at one point vehemently rejected the political process but now are active participants. He makes perhaps the clearest statement of why Islamist groups decide to form as political parties, given the many other options available to them. He also identifies three conditions that must be fulfilled in order for an Islamist group to enter politics. Decision makers "in the movement" must be (1) "in polities where parties can legitimately compete for some power, (2) believe that their electoral returns will be strong and increase the reputation or visibility of the movement, and (3) expect that electoral outcomes will lead to a significant increase in their resources or policy influence."[36] As he notes, these conditions apply equally well to secular, confessional, and Islamist parties; but he argues that leaders of Islamist movements, which face a greater risk of losing prestige by participating in an electoral contest, will be particularly careful to ensure the conditions are met before taking the plunge. Mecham's focus on party leaders places his theory among the entrepreneurial models of party behavior that visualize parties as formed by "individuals [who] get into the business of party leadership out of self-interest rather than altruism. That is to say, they become party leaders because they expect to benefit from this activity."[37]

Mecham's theory has the advantage of parsimony, and its universal applicability demonstrates that Islamist leaders make the same sorts of calculations about entering the electoral market that their secular counterparts do. Furthermore, he avoids the red herring of the moderation-extremism debate; rather, he focuses on the question of why Islamist groups chose to enter the political market and not on why they chose to eschew violence. His instrumentalist approach offers perhaps the best lens through which to understand Pakistani Islamists' decision to participate in electoral politics. Similarly, Vickie Langohr argues that Islamist groups whose popularity primarily derives from their reputation as social service providers will enter politics as relative moderates in order to protect their social service networks from political encroachment. Once a group has entered politics, its social service network becomes an important source of votes and thus even more worthy of protection.[38]

Participation in electoral competition confers an aura of legitimacy and is a potentially powerful means for a group to attract new members to its cause. Electoral contestation, even when unsuccessful, can lend legitimacy to groups that might otherwise have remained invisible. This case is especially true for ideologically driven groups that enter politics with little hope of electoral success on the national level. In Pakistan, many Islamist political entrepreneurs are religious figures first and foremost, either local members of the *ulema* or clerics who preside as imams at local *masjids* (mosques). *Masjids* in rural areas are isolated and largely autonomous, which means these institutions must sustain themselves with *zakat* (offerings) from the faithful who attend prayers. The imam's personal income is also directly related to the size of his following and the donations.

Stephen Lyon's discussion of *pirs* makes clear that they are fundamentally similar to politicians in that their status may be the result of their religious authority, but their power comes from their ability to do favors.[39] Some of their actions, such as finding jobs for their devotees, are remarkably similar to the functions performed by secular leaders.[40] The same is true for religious leaders of all stripes. Islamist parties and religious leaders have learned that participating in and winning local elections increases the visibility, prestige, and authority of the religious enterprise. Elections act as a catalyst for a virtuous cycle: more influence means more members, larger congregations. The religious power of a local imam can be converted into political power, and the political power of a local *nazim* (mayor) also can be used to enhance the power of a religious order. Indeed, these offices mutually uphold and enhance each other on a local level.

The Sharia-Secular Model of Confessional Party Behavior

Academic studies of political Islam are rich and varied but contain a few shortcomings. First, scholars in the field, as noted earlier, tend to focus on the choice between violence and political participation while excluding subtler distinctions among the various forms of political participation. Second, they also treat the "Islamist political party" as a unitary entity with contours that remain largely unvaried across national boundaries and historical contexts. As shown in the next section of this book, however, confessional political parties vary widely—even in a single country—in terms of their organization, their ideological commitments and strategic objectives, and the methods they use to pursue their goals.

Third, many studies of religious parties or extremist organizations are closely focused on a single group's behavior, despite the growing recognition among political scientists and area specialists that such groups cannot be fully understood when studied in isolation; rather, as with other types of political parties, they must be studied in a context of party competition. As Humeira Iqtidar points out, "Most of the literature on Islamism either assumes relative homogeneity particularly with regard to shared goals, or does not provide any extensive comment on the existence and impact of competition among the various groups."[41] This approach, however, has inherent limitations. As Schwedler writes, "Just as Islamist parties practice and contest politics within a context of multiple and overlapping public spaces, so do they encounter, overlap, and come into conflict with other dimensions of Islamist activism."[42] Thus, Iqtidar's study of the Jamaat-e-Islami places that political party in context by comparing it to Jamaat-ud-Dawa (JuD), a hard-line Islamist organization with strong ties to militant groups. Iqtidar makes clear that the JI and JuD certainly compete—not for votes, since JuD does not contest elections, but for "access to and control of funds, constituencies, legitimacy, and a role in shaping the future" of Pakistan.[43]

These flawed studies can be attributed, at least in part, to the general lack of engagement between scholars of political Islam and political scientists who study secular parties (or religious parties based in other faiths). Sultan Tepe observes that "although religious parties are critical parts of their respective political systems, there is a tendency in the literature to treat them as sui generis or in isolation."[44] Thus, the inclusion-moderation debate regarding Islamist parties goes on in seeming ignorance of the forty-year debate on the determinants of political extremism in the American context. Many of the currently available theories of Islamic party behavior assume not only that moderation takes place along a single axis but also that parties, once included in democratic electoral competition, will moderate their views on policy.

The latter assumption seems to be implicitly based on the orthodox moderation thesis of American political party behavior. The theory posits that parties pursuing a rational vote-maximizing strategy will move to the center in order to conform as closely as possible to the views of the median voter.[45] Yet even the empirical data from American elections does not seem to fit this theory.[46] In fact, politicians from states where opposing parties are well-balanced (and thus elections are hard-fought and close) are less responsive to the center than those from states where their party has a comfortable margin. This finding directly contradicts the orthodox position.[47] For many scholars the orthodox view has been further called into question both by a shift toward increased polarization in American politics and by the attitudes of politicians and campaign strategists, who frequently play to the base rather than seek the center.[48]

While many areas of this debate are not applicable to the Pakistani context, some scholars have sought to discover situations in which selecting "extreme" positions (with "extreme" being defined simply as taking positions that are to the left or the right of the median voter) can be shown to be a winning strategy using rational choice theory. Perhaps most influentially, in a 2005 study Edward Glaeser, Giacomo Ponzetto, and Jesse Shapiro show that the two main American political parties practice what the authors call "strategic extremism" when it comes to issues (such as abortion) associated with religion.[49] Strategic extremism is when parties take positions that do not reflect the actual views of the party's politicians; instead, they diverge in either direction from that of the median voter only for vote-maximizing purposes. While not unique to Pakistan or Muslim nations, scholars who study politics of Muslim nations have not yet understood how this practice plays out in such nations.

Assuming that a politician can win by an "intensive" margin rather than an "extensive" one (i.e., assuming that a sufficiently mobilized base can make up for an alienated center), Glaeser, Ponzetto, and Shapiro find that in a single-issue model, "extremism increases with the variance of voter preferences, the informational asymmetry between a politician's supporters and his opponent's, and the ability of politicians to target political messages to their supporters."[50] When more than one issue is at play in an election, extremism more likely will be seen with those issues that are characterized by a greater heterogeneity of public opinion and that tend to define informational groups rather than cut across them. In the researchers' example, if voters are united in an informational group according to their views on religion, then strategic extremism is more likely on religious issues than on economic ones.

Similar to Glaeser, Ponzetto, and Shapiro's study, I develop a rational choice model that explains when Islamic (or secular) parties will adopt or abandon extreme positions. The model envisions two political parties (party 1 and party 2) competing to win votes from a constituency made up of two unequal groups—constituency A, which forms the majority, and constituency B. Assume that party 1 will always express support for (and, if elected, pursue) parties favorable to constituency A, while party 2 naturally favors constituency B but will not necessarily make that view public. Party 2 is thus faced with a choice in the electioneering period: It can reveal its true preferences, losing constituency A's support and thus the election, or it can claim that it will pursue policies that are favorable to constituency A in an attempt to win enough votes to capture a majority. Making the latter choice will usually involve backing legislation during the run-up to the elections that is favorable to constituency A (and may in fact be costly to constituency B). (The model is mathematically solved in appendix 1.)

Should party 2 win support for constituency A but use the bulk of its time in office to enact its preferred policies (those favorable to constituency B), it will face a further dilemma in the next elections: How can it convince the once-burned and now presumably twice-shy constituency A to back it again? One strategy, according to the model, is to increase its appeal to constituency A by promising to pursue policies even more favorable to constituency A than those proposed by party 1. As party 2 is in power immediately before the election, it will be required to signal credible commitment by actually enacting policies that are highly preferred by constituency A, even if they are highly costly to constituency B.

In the Pakistani context, it is easy to see how this dynamic can lead to moderate parties embracing extremism and to extreme parties embracing moderation. The outcome all depends on the composition of the electorate in a particular district. For example, if constituency A—the larger group, whose preferences will ultimately determine the election—supports Islamist policies, then both party 1 and party 2 will outdo themselves in an attempt to prove their conservative bona fides.

If constituency A is more moderate in its views on the role of religion in governance, however, the parties will present themselves as moderates. Should party 2 triumph in the elections, however, it is likely to express its true preferences by passing pro-sharia legislation and will have to swing back to the center during the next election.

The system does have an internal check in that the parties are not likely to pass legislation that would cost them more than they would gain by winning the election. Suppose party 2 is a moderate party supported by business interests and others with an international outlook but it is campaigning for office in a deeply religious district whose inhabitants favor sharia law. Party 2 likely will promote itself as sharia friendly during the election period but once in office will pursue policies favorable to its true constituency. Therefore, to regain the voters' good graces as the election draws near, party 2 will need a showpiece legislative agenda to convince at least some part of the pro-sharia faction to support the party once again. The costlier such an agenda to party 2's real interests, the more likely it is to convince the voters that party 2 is a good bet. But party 2 will not choose an agenda that will destroy all the benefits of its winning the election in the first place. For instance, if the capitalists who depend on their ability to borrow money or loan it out at interest are its true constituency, party 2 is very unlikely to pass legislation banning *riba* (interest).

Islamic Confessional Party Organization

Variations in confessional Islamic parties in terms of their elites, ideological underpinnings, degree of opposition to the existing regime, and initial access to patronage networks all have a profound impact on the parties' organization and conduct. To compare and discuss the full range of existing parties, first it is necessary to create an adequate system of categorization that takes into account the specific circumstances and histories facing political parties in developing democracies. In doing so, I rely on Richard Gunther and Larry Diamond's party typology, which represents a complete departure from previous methods of party modeling. Their model categorizes parties in developing nations according to three criteria: formal organization, programmatic commitments, and strategic objectives and behavioral style. Using these three criteria, the authors have described fifteen general types of parties, offering a much wider variety than is possible under conventional models.[51] Gunther and Diamond's framework is particularly relevant to examining Pakistan's party system given that it is a developing democracy characterized by low rates of literacy, immature mass communications, and a large and impoverished rural population. Under such circumstances, Gunther and Diamond predict that the role of regional and local elites will be significant and that clientelist and charismatic politics will dominate. Indeed, both hold true for Pakistan.

Organizational structure, Gunther and Diamond's first level of classification, refers to the size of party leadership; the relationships among these leaders; the relationships between the leader, the voters, and the intermediaries; and the relationships with ancillary organizations. A party's formal organizational structure is a product of the party's origins and becomes so enmeshed in collective memory that it tends to reproduce itself over time; thus ordained by the party's past, organization is predictive of the party's future. As Gunther and Diamond write, a "party comes into existence within a specific social and technological context . . . that may . . . leave a lasting imprint on the nature of the party's organization for decades to come."[52] While parties can be formed around a variety of cleavages, in the Pakistani context the most significant are religion, regional issues, and economics. Parties tend to be formed by people with similar religious, regional, and economic backgrounds, and in turn they heavily impact their parties' formal organizational structure.

Parties that arise as a means for feudal elites to maintain power in the face of expanding suffrage are led by small cadres of said elites and rely on organizational bonds forged by close personal relationships and shared interests.[53] The leadership of such parties is reflective of the sharp class cleavage in Pakistani society, with its huge divide between the landed families and the impoverished masses. With only a few lateral relationships at the apex of their hierarchical structures and virtually no direct connection to the majority of voters, national elites depend on strong vertical linkages to local elites who can sway blocs of voters via fiduciary obligations and direct material patronage.[54] The emphasis on these vertical relationships also means there is little use for ancillary organizations, resulting in an organizational structure that is aptly defined as thin.[55] Parties that arise as the result of grassroots mobilization, meanwhile, often rely on a highly organized mass membership and guerrilla networks.

Gunther and Diamond's second criterion for differentiating political parties is their programmatic commitment—that is, whether a party is instrumentally driven by the desire to win votes, ideologically driven by its philosophical and/or religious belief systems, or both. My research of Islamic parties in Pakistan shows, over time, that parties may shift their focus from ideological to instrumental concerns. Still, basic programmatic commitments derive directly from a party's origins. As noted previously, European denominational parties, for instance, began when the Catholic Church sought to maintain power in an increasingly secular and anti-ecclesiastical political landscape. But as large segments of the population were against the Church, none of the Christian parties adopted a program of turning their countries into theocratic states. Rather than seeking a return to Church or even explicitly Christian rule, they instead sought to expand Catholics' political role in societies that had undergone significant secularization. Pakistan, by contrast, was specifically founded as an Islamic republic, and the vast majority of the electorate is still devoutly Muslim. Pakistan's confessional parties thus have leeway to make more explicitly religious programmatic commitments. That is not to suggest, however, that all Islamic parties have similar ideological origins. As described in depth in chapter 4, Muslim democrats can be safely characterized as having primarily instrumental roots and thus similar programmatic commitments.

Gunther and Diamond's third level of analysis concerns a party's strategic objectives and behavioral style and refers to whether a party is "tolerant and pluralistic" or "protohegemonic" in its agenda and in its strategies for implementing that agenda. A party may either support the existing political system or seek to overturn that system. Gunther and Diamond argue that there are two subtypes of religious parties—pluralist denominational mass parties and religious fundamentalist parties—and the latter seeks to organize the state and society around a strict reading of religious doctrinal principles. Consistent with this division, Pakistan's Islamic parties can be broken into two religious subgroups—Muslim democrats, who tolerate religious diversity in public and political life, and protohegemonic Islamists, who demand that sharia be the law of the land.

In the next section, in addition to categorizing Pakistan's Islamic parties according to Gunther and Diamond's criteria, I analyze the connections between their *form*, or their organization, and their *function*, or the policies they espouse. Further, I examine the social affiliations and the particular social, historical, and political contexts that gave rise to each party type. A party's social affiliations dictate which institutions it has access to, from which social groups it draws its leadership cadre, and how it conducts its recruitment efforts. I also look at the degree to which each party type is integrated with or has access to state networks, such as national and regional assemblies, the bureaucracy, and the military. Finally, I discuss the internal structural dynamics that determine whether parties are able to police their own members and stay "on message."

Typology of Islamic Confessional Parties in Pakistan

Building on previous scholarship and applying it to the Pakistani context, I have developed a new party typology that recognizes three distinct types of Islamic confessional parties: Muslim democrats, hierarchical Islamists, and network Islamists. As discussed previously, other analyses and theories of Islamic party formation have often failed to distinguish among these groups; instead, they treat all Islamic confessional parties as Islamists and assume the preeminence of religious ideology in their agendas. More recent work has distinguished between Muslim democrats and Islamists in a broad sense, but it has identified ideology as the sole distinction between them and has treated the latter as a homogeneous group. The typology presented in table 3.1, however, distinguishes important subgroups under the Muslim confessional umbrella and identifies significant differences in ideology, structure, constituency, and strategy among the three party types. Each of these

Table 3.1. Typology of Islamic parties

	Muslim democrat	Hierarchical Islamist	Network Islamist
Structure	Thin, hierarchical organization with high walls to entry	The most narrow Islamic party structures	Broad-based structure of loosely affiliated actors
Elites/entrepreneurs	Highly educated technocrats from the economic elite and middle classes	Highly educated religious and intellectual elites from universities	Less educated religious elites from madrasah system
Commitments	Pragmatic economic and political interests	Religious ideological commitments to state adoption of sharia	Religious ideological commitments to state adoption of sharia
Social affiliation	Economic/social elites	Intellectual and religious elites	Underclass and religious leaders
State incorporation	High, virtually indistinguishable	Moderate incorporation through technocrats	Low, virtually no access to state goods
Social penetration	Low, economic elites a small numerical minority	Low, mostly urban intellectuals	High, deeply embedded in rural underclass
In-group policing	Moderate, strong personalistic affiliations limit policing	High, rigidly controlled hierarchy ensures compliance	Low, autonomous highly independent actors

fundamental characteristics informs and is informed by a party's origin, relationship to the electorate, degrees of incorporation into state or religious networks, distinctive patterns of regional penetration, and unique challenges to party discipline. After the following brief summary of the differences between these parties based on Gunther and Diamond's criteria, chapters 4 and 5 discuss in depth the characteristics, histories, and electoral successes of the Muslim democratic and Islamist parties, respectively.[56]

Muslim democratic parties, such as the PML-N, are organizationally thin and clientelistic.[57] Leadership is limited to a small number of elites who exercise significant power over the strategic and ideological direction of the organization. Relationships in the party are predominantly personalistic and are formed either between elites who are members of the same social, ethnic, or economic class or between voters and patrons who are linked through fiduciary connections.[58] The relationships between voters and party elites tend to be sharply vertical, linking elites to local political entrepreneurs, who are in turn linked to small blocs of voters.

Chandra refers to such parties as "centralized," meaning that the party leadership—prominent intellectuals, civil servants, and professionals—holds power tightly and does not allow members or different social or economic groups to rise in the party.[59] Given that the founders and leaders of these groups are closely aligned, economically and culturally, with the ruling class, Muslim democrats tend to be programmatically committed to maintaining the status quo. They rely on the symbolic and cultural power of religious messaging but do not promote a religious agenda. Their domestic agenda calls for respect for religious values while their foreign policy focuses on so-called Muslim causes, such as the independence of Kashmir. Party platforms, however, are kept deliberately vague in order to allow for maximum political flexibility. Of the three party types, Muslim democrats are the most committed to using democratic means to secure their programmatic agenda. Muslim democrats tend to take an incremental approach to creating change and argue that improvements are best achieved by working in the existing political system.

Islamist groups, by contrast, are defined by their programmatic commitment to imposing sharia law. They adopt such mottoes as *Aik Klauda, aik Jamaat, aik Zindagi* ("One God, one party, one life") and claim that unification under Islamic principles would rid the nation of all social ills. Islamist political leaders are typically religious figures who are able to turn religious authority into political authority.

Hierarchical Islamists, such as the Jamaat-e-Islami, are organizationally similar to Muslim democrats in that their founding elites are also prominent intellectuals from prestigious institutions, and their party structure is composed predominantly of vertical relationships. The difference is that hierarchical Islamist elites are religious intellectuals from prestigious Islamic institutions rather than wealthy landowners or technocrats. (In a nation with a literacy rate of 57 percent and where less than 50 percent of the citizens have a primary education, being university educated is synonymous with being elite.[60]) Hierarchical Islamist parties maintain a narrow structure through careful policing of rigid rules governing their membership and awarding of posts. Well-trained leaders organize local groups and serve as gatekeepers of the party.

Network Islamists are organizationally much flatter, broader, and more accessible than other Islamist groups and draw their leadership from a diverse group of *ulema* with local or regional constituencies. Individual political entrepreneurs in network Islamist parties, having been trained in *madaris* rather than universities, tend to have less formal education than those of either Muslim democratic or hierarchical Islamist parties. They are more socially connected to the rural and poor voters of their constituencies and have greater autonomy than do their Muslim democratic and hierarchical Islamist peers. While these patterns give network Islamist parties greater social connectivity for mass mobilization, they tend to have low incorporation into state networks, making them less attractive to voters in national elections. They are able, however, to deliver essential goods at the local level and thus fare well in local elections.

Both hierarchical and network Islamists tend to be less strategically committed to working through the democratic process than Muslim democrats are. The Islamists are also more inclined to argue not only that change must be wholesale, rapid, and radical, but also that it may be achieved both by votes and by acts of violence.

As demonstrated in subsequent chapters, the structures and other characteristics of the different party types have considerable impact on their mobilization strategies. Because of their position as local religious leaders, network Islamists are able to make direct appeals to their constituents via religious venues, and they are more likely to enjoy close social proximity to and frequent social interactions with voters. Muslim democrats and hierarchical Islamists, by contrast, must work to overcome the distance from the voting population created by narrow hierarchical structures. Each group bridges the distance in distinctly different ways. Muslim democrats draw on their social connections to elites who control vote banks, while hierarchical Islamists predominantly draw on connections to urban mosques and universities. The Muslim democratic parties' strategy is markedly more effective, and as a result, hierarchical Islamists have historically been the least effective of the party types in their mobilization efforts.[61]

CHAPTER 4

MUSLIM DEMOCRATIC PARTIES

Origins and Characteristics

Conventional wisdom holds that political parties in democracies will grow more moderate over time by participating in the electoral and governing processes. As noted previously, this assumption is largely based on observations of socialist parties in nineteenth-century Europe, but it does not apply to Islamic parties in developing Muslim states. Today's Muslim democratic parties are not simply yesterday's Islamist parties that have moderated over time, and in Pakistan's current political climate, some modern Islamist parties have an incentive to become more, rather than less, extreme. In Pakistan, the moderate confessional parties were actually the first to appear on the scene and have a distinctly different history than that of their religiously extreme counterparts. In this chapter I examine the historical roots of the Muslim democratic movement in Pakistan, typify the basic party organization and ideology, and look closely at the historical and modern experience of the country's oldest and most influential Muslim democratic party, the Pakistani Muslim League.

Prior to 1600, Muslims and Hindus on the Indian subcontinent lived alongside one another in relatively peaceful, if cool, accord. The height of Islamic influence in South Asia came during the rule of the Muslim Mughal Empire, which, beginning in 1526 with its overthrow of the Delhi Sultanate, eventually extended its rule over much of the subcontinent. Although by the early 1700s the Mughals had begun their decline and their territories were gradually eaten away by various Hindu rivals, they retained titular power for another 150 years. Simultaneously, between 1600 and 1858, Britain's East India Company conducted a piecemeal conquest of the region. Initially operating as a business venture that shared its profits with the Mughal emperors and Hindu maharajahs, the company gradually reshaped the system of agricultural production in India. As they became increasingly dependent on the company's access to a global marketplace, Indian rulers conceded more and more economic power to the British. The East India Company began to exploit its economic dominance and purchased land, allowing India's feudal lords to retain their aristocratic titles and direct control of the peasants while bringing them decisively under British control. The British Crown formally took control of the Indian states in 1858 and continued to operate the British East India Company.[1]

Even before Britain formally assumed sovereignty over the subcontinent, it had perfected a divide-and-conquer approach to governance in India, imposing different laws and provisions on the various Hindu and Muslim princely states. Although the British Raj was heavy handed in its dealings with all the peoples of the subcontinent, Muslims and Muslim culture were subjected to discriminatory practices from the start. It is unclear where the roots of this pattern lie, though it most likely reflected the East India Company's assessment of power relations in the region. In 1793, the British imposed a land tax system (the permanent settlement system) that allowed tax collectors to take over ownership of lands and then rent them back to the peasants.[2] It was not practiced uniformly, however. Some peasants paid taxes through the Madras system, which allowed peasants to pay taxes directly to the state and circumvent landlords. The effect of this divided tax regime was to bankrupt many landowners in the Bengal region (now divided between Bangladesh and Pakistan), most of whom were Muslim. The disparities worsened when the British made the position of *zamindar* (tax collector) hereditary; since 90 percent of the *zamindars* of Bengal were Hindu, the path to *zamindar* status and its associated wealth was effectively closed to most Muslims.[3]

In addition to taxation inequities, the British engaged in an aggressive land acquisition process, most importantly through the adoption of the Doctrine of Lapse, a policy under which the crown could annex princely states when their sovereign died without a direct biological heir or when the British deemed him incompetent.[4] This policy certainly did not exclusively target Muslims, but given the already decimated power of the Mughal Empire, its effects were more devastating on the Muslim power minority. The Doctrine of Lapse ensured that resentment toward the British was felt at every level of society, including by the nobility, because it "revealed a consistent determination to substitute an English for an Indian civilisation."[5]

This discontent at times erupted in several minor uprisings against British authorities.[6] It was not until 1857, however, that Indian military personnel and civilians of both major faiths rose up in opposition to Britain's stranglehold on the subcontinent. The uprising, which became known as the Sepoy Rebellion, was violently put down, but it led the British to end the East India Company's Raj and bring India under direct rule of the crown. The British saw the Bengal Army (one of three Anglo-Indian regiments at the time) and the Bengali people in general as the prime movers in the rebellion. As Bengal was predominantly Muslim, this belief fed the British view that the rebellion itself was mostly led by Muslims.[7] With the onset of crown rule, Muslim elites who had dominated the region for centuries under the Mughal Empire suddenly found themselves the subjects of a distant Christian monarch and members of the religious, economic, and social underclass. Hindu moneylenders, who had been quick to learn the

English language, study English law, and seek employment with the colonial authorities, replaced Muslims in leadership positions and became further privileged over Muslims.

Crown officials ingeniously exploited the complex interplay of identities and social status in the region—correlated with but distinct from the issue of religious identity—to exacerbate local divisions and prevent collective action against colonial rule. Some manipulations of these preexisting divisions had such dramatic effects on the political landscape that they are still felt today. In 1900, Britain outraged Muslims by making Hindi the official language of what was then known as the United Provinces (now called Uttar Pradesh), the largest state in the subcontinent. At the time, Muslims made up no more than 30 percent of India's overall population and were not evenly dispersed throughout the subcontinent. They were the majority in several small states but were the minority in key regions, such as the United Provinces. The designation of Hindi as the official language intensified growing Muslim fears of repression by Hindus. Language has remained a contentious issue throughout the region and was a catalyst for the civil war that resulted in the creation of modern-day Bangladesh.

In 1911, the British decided to move the colonial capital from Calcutta to Delhi, which also provoked significant opposition among Muslims.[8] Calcutta was home to a high concentration of Muslims who feared further erosion of their status by losing their proximity to the capital. Regionalism remained salient after partition and, with the language issue, eventually contributed to the war between West Pakistan and East Pakistan (the latter became Bangladesh in 1971). Regional differences remain important in modern Pakistan, and sharp divisions exist between the rural frontier regions and the urban areas.

By the early twentieth century, the intense focus on religious and regional divisions, the prospect of increasing opportunity for Indian self-government, and the persistent uncertainty over the distribution of resources had created ideal conditions for confessional party development. Growing increasingly fearful of religious, economic, and geographic isolation, Muslim elites came to recognize their need to organize and mobilize. Muslim agitation did have an effect: In 1905 the viceroy split Bengal into two provinces, creating a new Muslim-majority province of East Bengal. Muslim leaders welcomed the move and hoped that it would reduce the power of Hindu landlords over the rural Muslims of East Bengal.[9] (The partition of Bengal was equally unpopular among the leaders of the Indian National Congress, who six years later succeeded in having it annulled.[10]) In September 1906, Muslim elites gathered in Lucknow, the capital of Uttar Pradesh, and strategized new ways to protect their interests. Their original goal was to pressure the British government to restore some semblance of equity between themselves and the ascendant Hindu elites. That December, at a meeting in Dhaka (now the capital of Bangladesh), this group founded the All India Muslim League, a distant precursor of the first Muslim democratic political party. Its aims were given as "promoting feelings of loyalty to the British" and "protecting and advancing the political rights of Indian Muslims."[11]

At the start, the league was dominated by adherents of Sir Syed Ahmed Khan's Aligarh Movement, which sought to increase Muslim political power by preparing young Muslims to operate in the British system.[12] (The league was officially formed on the last day of the All India Muhammadan Educational Conference, a gathering of Muslim educators and elites from across India that was organized by the Mohammedan Anglo-Oriental College [later Aligarh Muslim University].) Khan's approach—strategic assimilation as the way to Muslim empowerment—was reflected in the principles of the league, which was strongly pro-British. The move to initiate the party's formation was also supported in a letter to the conference delegates from Sir Sultan Mohammad Shah, also known as the Aga Khan, leader of one of the largest sects of Shiite Muslims.

The Muslims' emergence as a political force was the result of both motivation and opportunity. British acceptance of the All India Muslim League in 1906, the first of several legitimizing actions, helped facilitate the party's organizational development. And with the Morley-Minto reforms of 1909 and the Montague-Chelmsford Act of 1919, the British government enacted laws that allowed for greater Indian self-governance.[13] Violence and terrorism had been escalating as a result of the partition of Bengal, and senior British officials believed that increasing Indians' authority would defuse the growing crisis. As a result of these reforms, for the first time seats on legislative councils were allotted to elected representatives. While British appointees would still be in the majority on the councils, even this slight opening of the electoral process marked a watershed moment for proponents of Indian self-government. Furthermore, in response to Muslims' concerns that a first-past-the-post electoral system would consign the Muslim minority to living under Hindu rule, the British stipulated that 25 percent of the legislative council seats would be reserved for Muslims. The Government of India Act of 1919 further increased Indians' political rights and opened more government posts to Indians.

Ideology and Structure

The historical origins of the Muslim nationalist movement critically shaped the Muslim League's organization and structure. Founded by social elites, labor union leaders, wealthy industrialists, and landowners who united in order to safeguard their interests in a chaotic and inhospitable political arena, from its inception the Muslim League was a tool of the elite and reflected elite aspirations. Many of the founders were landowners under the *sirdar* system, a feudal economic system that predated, and was permitted to coexist with, British colonial rule. Under the *sirdar* system (which resembled the practice of sharecropping in the United States), elite landowners were able to maintain significant social and economic power by renting arable land to peasants. Rents were sufficiently high that peasants barely earned a subsistence income, ensuring their continued dependence on the landowners and the economic value of the system.

Since the Muslim nationalist movement had been formed to serve the interests of the elites and maintain well-established social and economic hierarchies, the Muslim League's internal party organization was narrow and highly centralized. Using Gunther and Diamond's terms, the formal organization of the Muslim League was thin and clientelistic.[14] Membership in the league was not open to the public and was dictated by contemporary social structures and hierarchies. The Aga Khan, the head of the Ismaili Shiite sect and a leading proponent of creating a political force to secure Muslim interests, was appointed the Muslim League's first honorary president. Other officers, including six vice presidents, a secretary, and two joint secretaries, were drawn from elite social networks in various geographic regions across pre-partition India. This pattern has been perpetuated in the Muslim democratic parties that are the league's heirs. Their high-level leaders and strategists (also known as political entrepreneurs) are typically well-educated secularists who have ties to Western institutions and the ruling elite in Pakistan. They are deeply incorporated into incumbent political networks and have access to the levers of power and patronage.[15]

The ideological roots of the Muslim nationalist movement were essentially secular. The primary goal of the elites who founded the Muslim League was to preserve the economic, educational, and social system that kept them in positions of relative power. While references to religious affiliation and Muslim identity held deep cultural significance (particularly to the extent that profound divisions existed between Muslims and Hindus), actual religiosity and adherence to strict religious codes were not part of the Muslim nationalist platform. Indeed, the very economic system the league was founded to defend would have been upended by conversion to sharia law, which is widely understood to prohibit *riba* (interest payments) and thus the practice of money lending. Put plainly, state imposition of religious law was antithetical to the interests of the league's most important constituents. (As Matthew Nelson's work shows, important constituencies in modern-day Pakistan continue to oppose the imposition of Islamic law as contrary to their economic interests.[16])

For the first four decades of the movement's existence, the Muslim League viewed itself and conducted itself as a representative of urban socioeconomic elites, predominantly the landowners and captains of industry. It was almost wholly disconnected from the concerns of the illiterate laboring classes that made up the majority of Muslims (and Hindus) in pre-partition India. Rooted in the goal of protecting Muslim elite interests (and gaining advantages over Hindu elites), the Muslim League was primarily concerned with securing a return to the balance of power that had existed during the heyday of the Mughal Empire. Since the attempted rebellion against the British had resulted in the loss of Muslim power, the Muslim League was intent on repairing the relationship between Muslim elites and the British.

The league did not develop aspirations to mobilize the uneducated masses until at least the 1930s. Until then, the Muslim League's posture and language toward the Muslim masses verged on the offensive. In northwest India, for example, where the indigenous population had launched repeated armed rebellions against British rule, the Muslim League's founding determination to promote "feelings of loyalty to the British" won it few friends. The party's structure inhibited mass mobilization, since it operated as an alliance of convenience among elites who were economically, religiously, and socially distinct from the larger population. The league was mainly a phenomenon of the urban areas of Uttar Pradesh, where a substantial minority of Muslims felt oppressed by the Hindu majority.[17] In the area that would become Pakistan, the Muslim League's sphere of influence was essentially confined to the cities of Lahore and Karachi. The party did not even seek to address the interests of the rural landowning elites in the North-West Frontier Province or East Pakistan because its leadership was so concentrated in urban areas. The league claimed a very narrow linguistic following as well. Dominated as it was by Urdu speakers, the party paid little attention to Muslims' cultural and linguistic diversity.

The Muslim League was not merely indifferent to or disconnected from the Muslim masses but was even actively antipathetic toward their traditional religiosity. Prior to partition, the league publicly criticized the pillars of popular Islam, including the *ulema*, *madaris*, and *alims*, all of which Muslim League leaders regarded as backward.[18] Mohammedan Anglo Oriental College, in many ways the alma mater of the Muslim League, was itself founded in response to concerns (later shared by the league) that Islam as practiced was holding Muslims back from progress. Sir Syed Khan had established the college in an effort to close the growing educational gap between Muslims and Hindus, believing that the training provided in *madaris* ill-prepared their students for positions of power in India. *Madrasah* education, Sir Syed felt, was inadequate because it focused exclusively on religion and gave too little attention to modern Western educational principles and material. He saw the failure of such schools to teach English, which was rapidly becoming the language of power, as particularly harmful. Khan was a practicing Muslim who had published commentaries on the Quran, but he was convinced that the path to Muslim regeneration lay in the integration of Islam with the best of Western thought.[19]

It was in this context that the Muslim League was born, driven by a philosophy that viewed a too conservative religiosity as a barrier to the educational, economic, and political advancement of Muslims. The Muslim League's disdain for the religious proclivities of India's Muslims was so profound that the Muslim political activist Syed Abul A'ala Maududi (who went on to found Jamaat-e-Islami) actually hid his ordination as an *ulema* to protect his political credentials.[20]

The league's early antagonism to state-sponsored Islam is reflected in key political decisions of the period, particularly the decision to refuse to support the highly popular Khilafat Movement.[21] The Khilafat Movement was a religious and political effort to support the Ottoman caliphate, which, in the wake of its defeat in World War I, was at risk of being partitioned by the Western powers, especially the British. Although the Ottoman caliphate had no direct power over Indian Muslims, it was an important symbol of Islam, and its fall would signify Islam's global decline. Numerous clerics and *alims* rallied to the cause of the caliphate, preaching a pan-Islamic resurgence. Their message was popular among a large segment of the Indian Muslim population, but because the Khilafat Movement promoted nonviolent political action against the British, the Muslim League refused to endorse it. The ironic result was that the caliphate's supporters ultimately formed an alliance with the Indian National Congress.

As the popularity of the Khilafat Movement shows, the league's ambivalence was far from the only attitude toward religion that Indian Muslims expressed. By the mid-1920s, the league was simply one, and not even the most popular, of a diverse group of parties that had organized to contest the province-level elections created under the 1919 Montague-Chelmsford reforms.[22] Outside the traditional party system, furthermore, Ian Talbot recognizes four broad categories of response to the loss of Muslim power in the subcontinent: modernism, reformism, traditionalism, and Islamism or fundamentalism.[23] While the Aligarh Movement and, later, the Muslim League acted as the representative of the first strain, the others found expression as a political party or mass movement.

The league's eventual quest for partition and the establishment of a Muslim state, therefore, must be seen in the context of a diverse array of solutions to the problem of Muslim weakness in the subcontinent. Deeply religious Muslims, such as Syed Abul A'ala Maududi, had very different views of Muslim nationalism. Maududi, a committed Indian nationalist, was at the same time "fervently and consistently" opposed to the idea of a separate Muslim state in South Asia.[24] He believed that a formal or superficial commitment to Islam did not in itself distinguish Indian Muslims from their Hindu neighbors and that Muslims needed to become more perfectly Islamic before they could found a truly Islamic state.[25] Maududi's ideas are discussed at length in chapter 5, but at this point it is enough to acknowledge both his stance and the fact that long before Pakistan's birth the meaning of a "Muslim state" was already hotly contested.

Pakistani Independence

In the first decade of the twentieth century, the predominantly Hindu Indian National Congress began pressing the British to allow India greater self-governance and to enlarge Indians' representation and suffrage. Consistent with its goal of improving relations between the British colonialists and India's Muslims, the Muslim League took a more conciliatory approach, instead pushing for increased Muslim representation within the current system. The result of Britain's negotiations with the league was the Morley-Minto reforms of 1909. Under this legislation, seats on legislative councils for the first time would be filled by election rather than appointment. The Muslim League, concerned about competing against the numerically superior Hindus, sought and obtained guarantees that 25 percent of assembly seats would be reserved for Muslims (a disproportionate number, given Muslims' representation in the population as a whole) and that Hindus would be barred from voting for Muslim seats.

As with many parties in colonial and postcolonial nations, the history of the Muslim League is as much about its charismatic leaders as it is about formal institutions.[26] The league's early leaders were drawn exclusively from the ranks of the social and economic elite, and it has always displayed a strong tendency toward dynastic rule. The most important leader of the Muslim League was arguably Muhammad Ali Jinnah, a British-trained lawyer and member of the Congress. Jinnah, who shared that party's view that Indians needed more direct control over their destiny, had become a member of Congress in 1906. He supported its calls for reform and enhanced governmental powers but did not at first support its push for independence. He joined the Muslim League in 1913. By virtue of his membership in both organizations, Jinnah was able to bring the league into closer political alignment with the Congress. In 1916 he engineered the Lucknow Pact between Congress and the league; the agreement sought to cooperatively seek self-government for all Indian people. To win the league's support, the Congress promised that an even greater share (30 percent) of seats in a future national assembly would be reserved for Muslims.

Jinnah understood that the British had long successfully employed divide-and-conquer tactics to weaken the indigenous population of the subcontinent. He pursued unity not only with the Muslim elite but also between Hindus and Muslims, arguing that intercommunal cooperation was essential to Indian self-governance. Even after he withdrew from the Congress in 1920, concerned that the party had become too stridently opposed to the British, Jinnah remained hopeful that Muslims and Hindus could work together for greater Indian self-government. But the Lucknow Pact proved to be the high-water mark of Muslim-Indian cooperation. The late 1920s and early 1930s saw a number of failed attempts at negotiation between the two groups, souring some Muslims on the idea of a united India.[27] In 1933 the political theorist and Muslim activist Choudhary Rahmat Ali published a pamphlet titled "Now or Never," in which he proposed creating a separate nation, to be called Pakistan, composed of the northern (Muslim-majority) territories of India.[28] Although the league would not officially adopt the "Pakistan demand" for another seven years, Rahmat Ali's proposal gradually gained steam among Muslim elites and, to a growing extent, the Muslim masses.[29]

By 1935 all of India's political parties were struggling to adjust to quickly changing circumstances.[30] The British had devolved more meaningful democratic powers to Indians (in part through the Government of India Act of 1935) through expanded suffrage and direct voting, thus forcing Indian parties to undertake a type of mass mobilization that had been previously unnecessary. Even as India, including the Congress, moved toward more overt resistance to British rule, Jinnah continued to seek agreement with congressional leaders and continued to call for a unified independent India.[31] Congress's response to his outreach was lukewarm at best, as seen in the disappointing results of a 1928 committee to outline the principles of a future Indian constitution. Known as the Nehru Report, it rejected Jinnah's proposals for separate constituencies or weighting of the Muslim vote.[32]

Congress had little incentive to heed Jinnah's demands for minority protections in an independent India, particularly after the debacle (for the league) of the 1937 provincial elections. The first fruits of the 1935 Government of India Act and the league's first electoral test on the national scene were an unmitigated disaster. League-sanctioned candidates did not win an outright majority of seats in a single province; only one league member was elected in Punjab (where votes backed an anti-partition government) and none were returned either in the Sind or the North-West Frontier Province (an almost entirely Muslim province whose voters chose a Congress government). "In each of the [Muslim] majority provinces, Jinnah's strategy had been repudiated by the voters' choice," while Congress did better than expected in the Muslim minority areas, the league's heartland.[33] The election thus weakened the Muslim League's position as it strengthened that of Congress, which not only won control in six provinces but, by receiving a significant share of the Muslim vote, vindicated its claim to represent all of India's citizens.[34] Jinnah recognized that the political tides had turned; moreover, the party needed to develop its mass appeal and reach out to the traditional power brokers, the landlords and *pirs* (Sufi religious authorities) whom it had long ignored.

It was not until 1940 that Jinnah and the Muslim League took up the cause of independence. In that year the league promulgated the Lahore Resolution, a statement of its intent to seek a separate sovereign Muslim state. The demand for Pakistan was not universal among the league's leadership, but Jinnah had successfully made the case that a separate homeland was the only way to protect Muslim interests.[35]

Furthermore, in a move that would have major repercussions for Pakistan's future, Jinnah and the league began to use religion as an explicit and effective rallying point for their demand for a separate Pakistan. Although many of the league's long-term members remained primarily concerned with preserving the economic system rather than rallying for freedom of worship, the league's appeal to religion and religious identity was particularly effective with the mass of Muslim voters. This move was a particular departure for Jinnah, who in 1920 had "denounced the participation of the ulema in politics . . . [and] appealed to 'the intellectual and reasonable section of Muslim opinion'" to take control of the debate over the role of Muslims in the subcontinent.[36] Indeed, in 1937 he had flatly rejected Muhammed Iqbal's contention that "'the only way to solve the problem of bread for Muslims' was to enforce the 'Law of Islam,'" and the idea was particularly anathema to Jinnah given the likelihood that the *ulema* would have to be involved in interpreting and enforcing Islamic law.[37] But given the league's lack of popularity among the rural masses, Jinnah finally agreed to a compromise whereby the league exploited already-existing fears of Hindu chauvinism and developed propaganda focusing on Congress's "totalitarian" tendencies and the threat it posed to Muslim culture.[38] The cry of "Islam in danger" had already been raised in the 1937 elections; now Muslim League assemblies across India denounced Congress as harboring secret plans of instituting "Hindu Raj" and reducing Muslims to a "state of serfdom."[39]

But Jinnah did not control every league propagandist, and there proved to be a thin line between the claim that Islam was in danger and an appeal to voters that was more directly based on a narrow understanding of religious faith. In the Punjab, where the multifaith Unionist Party had triumphed in the 1937 elections, the campaigns of the 1940s were particularly steeped in religion. Local league organizers told Muslim voters that if they voted against the league they were no longer Muslims, that their marriages would become null and void, and that they could not be buried in Muslim cemeteries.[40] The campaign achieved results. One Unionist campaign worker recounted voters all over the province telling him that if they did not vote for the league they would "become kafir."[41] What's more, as momentum shifted in the league's favor during the period 1937–46, the party began to attract the support of the *pirs*, who often commanded their followers to vote for the league wholesale and whose religious authority "sanctified the Muslim League cause."[42]

By 1945, the league was seen as the authoritative voice of India's Muslims and won electoral contests in both urban centers and far-flung provinces.[43] Although the Indian National Congress still maintained that it attracted the majority of voters, regardless of religious distinctions, the league was in fact very successful in the 1945–46 general elections, taking all the Muslim seats in the Central Assembly, the majority of Muslim seats in Sindh and Bengal, and seventy-five of the eighty-five possible in Punjab.[44] Jinnah shrewdly entered into a pact with the weakened Unionist Party that allowed the Muslim League to retain its title as the sole representative of Indian Muslims and the Unionists to retain their grip on Punjabi patronage networks. With such provincial deals in place, the league's political activities during 1946 were completely focused on the question of partition. Despite Jinnah's continued efforts, the league and Congress failed to reach a compromise on a plan that would keep India united.

The combination of the Indian people's widespread resistance led by Mahatma Gandhi, the economic strain from fighting World War II, and the mutiny in the Royal Indian Armed Forces led the British to hurriedly relinquish all political control to local political leaders by the mid-1940s. On August 15, 1947, the last British viceroy, Lord Louis Mountbatten, signed the law granting independence to the two separate nations of India and Pakistan.[45] Immediately after Pakistan's creation, Jinnah gave two speeches in which he expressed his vision of Pakistan as an Islamic state but not a theocratic one. Addressing the citizens of the new state, he said, "You are free; you are free to go to your temples, you are free to go to your mosques or any other place of worship in this state of Pakistan. . . . You may belong to any religion or caste or creed—that has nothing to do with the business of the State."[46] But he also made clear that his model would not be that of the Mughal Empire under Akbar, as Lord Mountbatten suggested, but an Islamic state founded by the Prophet Muhammad himself.[47]

The details of Jinnah's vision for Pakistan were destined to remain unclear. The Muslim League's electoral strength began to dissipate almost immediately after independence. Jinnah's death from tuberculosis in 1948 and the assassination of his immediate successor, Liaquat Ali Khan, only three years later devastated the party's leadership. Jinnah had suffered from tuberculosis for years but kept his illness private until he suddenly succumbed to a massive hemorrhage. A number of explanations for Khan's assassination have been put forward, but many scholars believe it was orchestrated by rural landlords hoping to block passage of legislation that would have redistributed land to long-term renters. Because the Muslim League was so dominated by urban elites, provincial rural elites had long felt that their interests were as threatened by the league's ascendance as by Hindu or British rule. These regional landlords had not supported partition, and when the league clearly indicated it would indeed attempt to consolidate economic and political power in the urban centers of a newly independent Pakistan, it is likely they tried to topple the government through extralegal means.

The deaths of Jinnah and Khan left the party leaderless and the Parliament deeply divided over the proper role of Islamic law in governmental policy, as well as over the proper division of power between the eastern and western wings of Pakistan. The debate was so intense that it took nine years for the legislature (acting as a Constituent Assembly) to complete a constitution.[48] When the "ulema faction" in the assembly moved to make implementation of sharia part of the Constitution, the Muslim League's representatives in the assembly, who generally shared Jinnah's feelings regarding the involvement of the *ulema* in politics, resisted on the grounds that the imposition of such laws would lead to radical economic reforms and the redistribution of wealth. Iskander Mirza, Pakistan's first president (and a Muslim League member until 1955) warned that "we can't run wild on Islam; it is Pakistan first and last."[49] Amid these disputes, the Muslim League elected new leadership and appointed a committee to determine how to alter the economic structure in Sindh and Punjab, provinces dominated by enormous landed estates. The committee's recommendation that land reform should reduce the legal size of landholdings and permit the direct purchase of land was ignored. Widespread infighting ensued, resulting in the creation of two factions in the Muslim League and endless defections of political players from one to the other.

The scramble for material advantage among members of the new Parliament diminished their allegiance to the principle of democracy. The Parliament was evenly divided between factions represented by the league and, after 1955, the Republican Party, which were distinguished less by their positions on the issues than by personal animosity. Their heads attempted to win over unaffiliated legislators by offering them such perks as trading licenses.[50] Some elites even began quietly to push for the dissolution of the deadlocked Parliament and the imposition of military rule, hoping that it would preserve the pseudo-feudal system that favored their private interests. Lacking the foundation provided by shared ideological commitments, the alliances between Muslim League leadership and local power brokers that had brought the league to power before partition now ensured complete parliamentary stagnation. Regionalism, factionalism, and personal feuds meant that real power in Pakistan remained in the hands that had held it for generations.[51] One contemporary observer described it as similar to "Hobbes' state of nature where every political or provincial group fought against every other group . . . a ceaseless and ruthless struggle for power."[52]

Craig Baxter et al. argue that from the beginning, "constitutional government in Pakistan has been more sham than substance," and it is true that independent Pakistan has spent more time under military leaders than democratically elected governments.[53] Even the nominally democratic post–partition government had thin democratic credentials. The Muslim League had little grassroots support in Pakistan at the time of partition, Jinnah (like other league leaders) "failed to see it as his responsibility to cultivate popular support," and elections were decided by local power brokers, not the people.[54] Given the realities of the legislative process, the major product of Pakistan's Parliament was not policy but patronage. According to Gunther and Diamond, clientelist parties are most likely to develop in "rural, premodern societies, under conditions of geographical isolation from a dominant centre of government, coupled with low levels of functional literacy and poorly developed transportation and communications media."[55] Those conditions aptly describe Pakistan circa 1950; indeed, political power became synonymous with the ability to control the distribution of jobs and other resources. The *biraderi* (kinship networks) in the Muslim League (and other parties) dictated the chain of distribution of goods, or what Gunther and Diamond describe as "durable patterns of loyalty . . . linked with the exchange of services and obligations."[56] Although the Muslim League ran a divided and ineffectual government, until 1955 the party did hold the overwhelming majority of seats in the National

Assembly, which gave its political leaders control of government appointments, jobs, and funds.

Once the immediate threat of Hindu domination had been eliminated, the Muslim League again became primarily associated with elitist secularism in the minds of poor, rural voters, and the party began to lose influence. The party suffered major losses in the 1954 provincial elections and in 1957 lost control of the national government to General Ayub Khan, who placed Pakistan under martial law.[57] Despite these setbacks and a persistent inability to mobilize mass support, the Muslim League and its derivative Muslim democratic parties have managed to retain some power in Pakistani politics. At the founding of the nation, regardless of the ideological considerations of the electorate, allegiance to the Muslim League was the only means of gaining access to state goods. More than any other party examined in this book, the Muslim League, because of its affiliation with economic elites, has been able to remain highly incorporated in state networks. During recurrent periods in Pakistan's history, factions of the Muslim League were absorbed in a ruling military regime (as during Ayub Khan's tenure), and the party then literally became synonymous with the state, giving it ample financial support to advance its agenda and buy clout.[58]

Modern Muslim Democrats: The Muslim League and Its Competitors

Today, several political parties portray themselves as heirs to the original Muslim League. The two largest are the All Pakistan Muslim League (a coalition of the PML-Q [Quaid], PML-J [Junejo], and PML-F [Functional]) and the Pakistan Muslim League-N (Nawaz). While the All Pakistan Muslim League and the PML-N joined forces at one point, they have since split over regional and ethnic disputes.

The Pakistan Muslim League-Nawaz

The Pakistan Muslim League-Nawaz is the largest and most successful of the current Muslim democratic parties, with its status as Pakistan's most important party cemented by its overwhelming victory in the 2013 elections. The party takes its name from its founder, Nawaz Sharif, a wealthy businessman and a conservative politician who has served as prime minister twice. Sharif's first term as prime minister ended when President Ghulam Ishaq Khan dismissed him in 1993 on charges of corruption and incompetence; his second ended when General Pervez Musharraf ousted him in a military coup. He began his historic third term in June 2013, with his party commanding a formidable majority in the National Assembly.

Nawaz Sharif's political career began during General Zia's presidency. He was one of a group of young up-and-coming leaders of the Pakistan Muslim League, which had been reconstituted as a king's party when Zia ended martial law in 1985. Under the leadership of Muhammad Khan Junejo, the PML held (nominal) power at the center and in all four provinces, and Sharif became chief minister of Punjab.[59] Zia hoped that a power-sharing agreement with an elected civilian government would forestall criticism from pro-democracy forces.[60] But in 1988, with the PML and Junejo proving more independent than he had planned, Zia dismissed Junejo, placed himself at the head of the government, and announced party-less national and provincial elections.[61] As it turned out, Zia died before the elections could take place, but his actions split the PML in two, with one group supporting Junejo and the other, headed by Nawaz Sharif, backing Zia.[62]

Sharif's loyalty to the military made him a natural candidate for a leadership position in the Islami Jamhoori Ittehad (IJI), the new coalition being assembled by the army's intelligence service to counter the Pakistan People's Party.[63] The IJI, a hodgepodge of conservative and Islamist parties, quickly realized that the PPP's weakest flank was its "avowedly secular" platform, and the IJI worked effectively to mobilize the Pakistanis' religious sentiments and even ginned up posthumous adulation of Zia, who had been widely disliked while alive.[64] The situation was compounded by Benazir Bhutto's strategic (mis)calculation that "at the dawn of democracy there was no need to appeal to Islam," and she abandoned efforts to court the Islamist parties.[65] "The result," Nasr writes, "was that between 1988 and 1990 the IJI effectively adopted a democratic style and rhetoric to strengthen its Islamic platform, and the PPP was unable to reciprocate."[66] This approach brought the IJI and Nawaz Sharif to power in the 1990 elections. Continuing dissension among factions of the PML, however, eventually resulted in a final breakup of the party, which split into the Nawaz and Junejo parties.[67]

Although the PML-N has taken the Muslim League's name, it can hardly claim to be a direct descendant of the earlier party. Perhaps the two groups' closest similarity is the fact that the leaders of both parties had roots outside what is now Pakistan. The majority of the Muslim League's leaders had their political power bases in the cities of north-central India while the PML-N's leadership ranks are disproportionately populated by the descendants of immigrants from Kashmir (including Nawaz Sharif and his brother Shahbaz) and East Punjab.[68]

But the common face of the two parties hides important differences. They became clear only months into Sharif's first term as prime minister, when he introduced a Shariat bill, or a constitutional amendment to make the Quran and the Sunnah "the supreme law of the land."[69] Sharif, in stark contrast to Jinnah's coolness toward religion and distrust of the *ulema*, was known to be both "ideologically and emotionally committed" to the bill.[70] That said, Sharif's credentials as a pragmatist shone through in his handling of the legislation; despite his early promises and pressure from his Islamist coalition partners, the bill that was eventually passed was not a constitutional amendment and actually had little effect on the status of Islamic law in Pakistan's legal system. Most important, it did not resolve the debate about who had the ultimate right to declare legislation repugnant to sharia, nor did it change the secular courts' long-standing and fairly lenient interpretation of the constitution's repugnancy clause.[71] The next year, with his coalition falling apart, Sharif declared that he would attempt to amend the constitution to make sharia the law of the land.[72] This amendment failed, but during his second administration, he renewed the quest for an amendment in 1998.[73] Since the main Islamist parties had performed execrably in the 1997 national elections while the PML-N experienced unprecedented success, Sharif's second attempt to pass a sharia amendment cannot be chalked up to a desire to keep them in the coalition. Instead, he used religion as a wedge issue and to highlight the differences between the PML-N and the PPP.

The deep ideological differences between the PML-N and the original league can be attributed, at least in part, to the former's roots in the military regime and particularly to Zia's Islamization campaign. During the Zia years the league simply added a facade of democratic legitimacy to military rule by rubber-stamping Zia's policies. As discussed in chapter 2, they were primarily designed to appeal to the conservative, religious lower-middle classes of Punjab and urban Sindh. Although the PML and Zia did not always see eye-to-eye, the PML was anxious to win the support of the pro-Zia constituency and quickly assume his mantle.[74] Zia, at least in part through his instrumental use of Islam, had built a stable coalition of supporters (businessmen, the military, and the lower-middle classes), and the PML recognized that the best way to tap into this voting bank was to invoke religion. Thus, the 1990 party manifesto of the IJI coalition, of which the PML was the dominant member, promised "to establish the supremacy of the Qur'an and Sunnah 'in every sphere of life.'"[75]

With these voters, the PML did not limit its appeal to religious issues, however; Sharif's first speech as prime minister promised not a religious government but an efficient, honest, and economical one.[76] His first administration governed accordingly, and while the Shariat bill was its only major legislative success on the religious front, Sharif passed truly groundbreaking economic legislation that significantly liberalized Pakistan's economy.[77] Sharif, who comes from a family of successful industrialists, has successfully presented himself as the friend of Pakistan's businessmen (and those who hope one day to achieve that status).

This focus on development and economic reform was particularly evident in the 2013 election season, when Sharif campaigned on the two greatest achievements of his previous administrations—the controlled nuclear explosions of 1999 and the construction of Pakistan's first national highway.[78] The PML-N's election manifesto put economic recovery at the top of its agenda, followed by development-related issues such as energy and agriculture. Pakistan's internal security problems were far down the list of priorities, and Sharif did not mention them in the personal letter that accompanied the manifesto.[79]

This silence may have resulted from the PML-N's having received an unexpected campaign donation from the Tehrik-e-Taliban Pakistan (TTP). The group had announced in early April 2013 that it considered Pakistan's three main secular parties—the PPP, the Awami National Party, and the Muttahida Quami Movement—to be "legitimate" targets.[80] Further, it warned Pakistanis to stay away from rallies organized by the three parties. The announcement only formalized the already clear fact that the TTP had long been engaged in a war of attrition against the ANP, having killed more than seven hundred ANP members and supporters since 2008.[81] The threat still had major consequences for the 2013 campaign. While Nawaz Sharif and Imran Khan of Pakistan Tehrik-e-Insaf were able to hold large campaign rallies that attracted thousands of supporters, the PPP, ANP, and MQM were forced to cancel mass gatherings, and their candidates rarely appeared in public, especially in the northwest.[82] PPP chairman Bilawal Bhutto, the son of Benazir Bhutto and the party's hope for the future, did not stay in Pakistan during the campaign. Security fears kept him in Dubai.[83]

As the Taliban's declaration shows, the PML-N, despite its largely secular, development-heavy agenda, is still somewhat acceptable to the country's militant right. Following its usual practice of shoring up its Islamic bona fides by partnering with more right-wing organizations, the PML-N ensured the TTP's continued quiescence by handing out party tickets to former members of the banned anti-Shia group Sipah-e-Sahaba Pakistan. One such candidate, Chaudhry Abid Raza Gujjar, had been convicted on murder charges relating to a 1998 terrorist attack that killed six people. Despite Pakistani electoral laws that exclude candidates who have been convicted of major crimes, the Lahore High Court approved his candidacy.[84] Sardar Ebad Dogar, another such PML-N candidate, had offered a 20-million-rupee bounty on Salman Taseer's head.[85] Both candidates' constituencies are known for high levels of sectarian violence.

Sharif's popularity, his reputation as an economic wizard and an excellent manager, his relatively free hand in campaigning, and his party's deep support in Punjab, where his brother, Shahbaz Sharif, has served as chief minister since 2008—all of these factors made for a powerful electoral combination. The PML-N captured 126 National Assembly seats, 117 of them from Punjab. With the addition of 19 independents who announced their intention to caucus with the PML-N and 31 minority and female representatives (apportioned based on the PML-N's share of the directly elected seats), the party controlled 176 representatives, or more than half of the 342-member house.[86] It won an astonishing majority in the Punjab Provincial Assembly, with 305 of the 358 total seats; was the largest party in Balochistan, with 17 of the 62 seats in its provincial assembly; and remained a player in Khyber Pakhtunkhwa, with 14 seats. The PML-N was thus the only party to make a respectable showing in more than one province.[87]

Pakistan Tehrik-e-Insaf

While the PML-N is not the only party to stake out positions that can be described as "Muslim democratic," for many years it was by far the most successful. The PML-N's position, however, was challenged in the 2013 elections by Pakistan Tehrik-i-Insaf (PTI), a party that the famous Pakistani cricket player Imran Khan founded in 1996. Despite Khan's star power, for the first fifteen years of its existence the PTI experienced little electoral success.

Its situation began to change in 2011, one of the worst years for Pakistani-US relations in recent memory, over the Raymond Davis incident and the killing of Osama bin Laden in Abbottabad, Pakistan.[88] Khan took advantage of his countrymen's popular anger to raise his own profile. In contrast to the reactions of the PPP, which welcomed bin Laden's death, and the PML-N, which issued pro forma protests against the US incursion into Pakistani airspace and mainly aimed its criticism at the PPP government, Khan and the PTI made anti-Americanism the focus of their public message.[89] Khan announced that the PTI would hold a sit-in to block the North Atlantic Treaty Organization's supply routes into Afghanistan and castigated the army for having failed to counter or even notice the raid.[90] Khan's visibility and his popular stance on the issue had their effect, and a poll of urban Pakistanis performed in mid-2011 found that 68 percent wanted him to lead Pakistan (as opposed to 11 percent for then-President Asif Ali Zardari).[91] Khan capped off the year with a massive rally of 160,000 people in Lahore, historically the heartland of the PML-N. He promised the mostly young crowd of supporters that he would halt American activity, pull the Pakistani military out of the tribal areas, and end the Indian "occupation" of Indian Kashmir.[92]

Khan's boldly anti-American stance and his image as an outsider and a "Mr. Clean" who would end corruption and bring real change to Pakistani politics rapidly catapulted him to stardom over the course of 2011 and 2012.[93] Similar to President Obama, Khan had galvanized disillusioned, young voters by using social media and a promise of reforms. In 2012, he was the most popular politician in Pakistan, with a 70 percent favorability rating.[94] But most political analysts agreed that given the reality of Pakistani politics, maintaining Khan's outsider status while also winning elections would be difficult, if not impossible. Through 2011, his party lacked the political power brokers (often called "electables") who determine local elections in Pakistan, with one Pakistani paper remarking, "There is not a single leader in PTI who is known among the masses, except for Imran Khan."[95] Perhaps even more important than name recognition is local-level patronage power, and the PTI was notably short in that regard. As one Pakistani author wrote, "Charisma alone does not take care of the traditional *thana/katcheri* [police station/district court] issues. Parties like the PPP and PML-N have deep roots down to the *mohalla* and *galli* [neighborhood] level, their tentacles entrenched inside the social structure knitted around kinship and patronage."[96]

In late 2011 through early 2012, Khan worked to remedy this deficiency, bringing two well-known political operators (former PPP and PML-N members) on board.[97] But in doing so he risked making PTI look like all the other parties. The strains that this course produced were made clear in the PTI intraparty elections, when the members chose the party's union councils, or local-level organizations. The union councils then voted on the party leadership. (PTI is the only Pakistani party to hold intraparty elections on such a wide scale. JI candidates are elected, but only *rukn* [full members] are able to vote, leaving JI's hundreds of thousands of activists without have voting rights.) Although the competition between various factions of the PTI broke out violently at some polling stations, PTI officials insisted that the intraparty elections were valuable publicity and had succeeded in elevating many members of the lower classes to leadership roles in the party.[98]

Khan's political positions were somewhat unique in Pakistani politics. His economic policies, to the extent that they existed, were liberal, with Khan describing himself as seeking to create a Scandinavian-style welfare state in Pakistan.[99] His views on religion and foreign policy, however, were far more conservative. With Pakistanis aware of his jet-setter past (and former marriage to a woman of Jewish descent), Khan took pains to "cast himself as the archetypal confused sinner who has discovered the restorative certainties of religion and is outraged over the decadence of his own class."[100] Unsurprisingly this self-portrayal involved many references to Khan's own piety and the rebirth of his Muslim faith. A week before the elections, the party combated rumors that it was courting the Ahmadi vote with a press release in which it promised that once in power it would neither seek to repeal nor alter the provisions of the Constitution that declare the Ahmadis to be non-Muslims and prohibit them from calling themselves Muslims nor do anything to offend Muslim sensibilities.[101] Although taking a pro-Ahmadi stance would have been political suicide, many of Khan's more liberal supporters were disappointed that he so thoroughly and publicly rejected the community. Khan's views on the drone war, Pakistan's relationship with the United States, and particularly the necessity of negotiating with, rather than fighting, the Taliban placed him closer to the JI than the PML-N on the sharia–secularism spectrum.[102]

Khan's "rightward tilt" in the lead-up to the 2013 elections, one Pakistani magazine argued, was "a well thought-out and planned strategy" to win the religious conservative vote.[103] An important example of this approach was PTI leader Javed Hashmi's public expressions of support for Hafiz Saeed, the leader of the terrorist group Jamaat-ud-Dawa. After the United States offered a ten-million-dollar reward for information leading to Saeed's capture, Hashmi called Saeed a "preacher of peace" and, while addressing a large rally in Multan, declared that "a social worker . . . can never be a terrorist but all those declaring him a terrorist are the real threat to the peace of the world."[104] Khan himself indicated his conservative bona fides by speaking at a conference held in honor of former Jamaat-e-Islami amir Qazi Hussain Ahmed.[105] Other participants at the conference included leaders of the Difa-e-Pakistan Council, a loose coalition of extremist groups, many of which operate as fronts for terrorism.[106]

The 2013 elections were both an unprecedented success and something of a letdown for the PTI and its supporters. Far from sweeping the PTI into a majority in the National Assembly and Khan into the post of prime minister, the elections saw the PTI win only 28 of the 272 open National Assembly seats, a figure that was dwarfed by the PML-N's 126.[107] (The PTI also received 7 of the seats reserved for minority and female parliamentarians, bringing its total up to 35.) But this result was a massive improvement over its showing in the 2008 elections, in which even Khan himself had failed to win a seat. The PTI was particularly strong in KPK, where it won 17 of the 35 National Assembly seats from that province. But it was far from proving itself a national party, having won no seats in Balochistan, only one in Sindh, and only 8 compared to the PML-N's 117 in Punjab.

Although the PTI won almost as many seats as the long-established PPP, its failure to do well nationally is indicative both of the PML-N's deep roots in Punjab and of the PTI's lack of support among the working classes and rural poor (or, to put it another way, its lack of support among those who can dictate the votes of the working classes and rural poor). As Mohammed Hanif reported in *The Guardian*, Khan "was relying on votes from Pakistan's posh locales. He probably forgot that there was a slight problem there: not enough posh locales in Pakistan. . . . He appealed to the educated middle classes but Pakistan's main problem is that there aren't enough educated urban middle-class citizens in the country. And the masses, it appears, were not really clamouring for a revolution but for electricity."[108]

Perhaps more important, as far as actual governance is concerned, the PTI won 35 of 99 seats in the KPK Provincial Assembly, or nearly three times as many as the second-highest vote-getter, the PML-N. This strong showing enabled the PTI to form a coalition government with the support of the Jamaat-e-Islami (7 seats) and some of the smaller parties. Upon his election as chief minister, PTI member Pervez Khattak promised to enact a number of anticorruption measures while largely avoiding the subject of religion. His coalition partner, JI leader Sirajul Haq, urged the assembly, however, to emulate great Muslim leaders of the past and "take guidance from Madina and Makkah [Mecca]."[109] The men's two speeches (both delivered at the opening of the assembly) indicate that the PTI's strategy in the province would focus on secular governance issues while relying on its coalition partners to provide the administration with a veneer of Islamic credibility.

Meanwhile, in trying to consolidate and maintain support, Muslim democratic parties face an enduring electoral predicament because their core constituency of wealthy landowners and well-educated urban technocrats alone cannot provide enough votes to ensure electoral success. Muslim democrats have to win votes from a large percentage of illiterate, poor rural voters with whom they have little credibility and to whom they have limited access. These main political operatives are cosmopolitan professionals who are not well integrated into local communities or religious networks and lack opportunities to make personal connections with voters.

One time-tested strategy Muslim democrats use to counter these deficiencies is to enlist support from social, political, and business leaders who can coerce or influence blocs of voters. For example, a Muslim democratic technocrat may have the power to appoint administrators to the local Water and Power Development Authority. These administrators control the flow of electricity to key areas and can keep power flowing to or from targeted districts during load-shedding hours, when electricity has to be shut off to parts of the grid due to heavy demand. (Load shedding can last ten to fourteen hours, bringing households and small businesses to a halt.) Provincial Muslim democratic stakeholders also control access to extremely valuable public housing in some areas. Private housing is prohibitively expensive for average citizens in some areas, so housing allotments are one way for party officials to reward loyalists and mobilize grassroots support. Because Muslim democrats in general have maintained a high degree of incorporation in state agencies, their parties are able to offer benefits to supporters in the form of money, jobs, goods, and bureaucratic favoritism.

The source of Muslim democrats' patronage power derives mainly from their members' long-standing connections to the federal civil service and the forty-five federal ministries in Islamabad. Down at the provincial and local levels, the civil service weakens, and so too does the Muslim democrats' ability to direct patronage and wield leverage. At the assistant secretary or director level, however, Muslim democrats are able to distribute patronage through their budgetary powers, their ability to allocate jobs, or their influence over the regulation and implementation of laws, licenses, records, and contracts.

Their ample funding allows Muslim democrats to use sophisticated marketing tactics and media technology to produce memorable political messages. Muslim democratic parties conduct large-scale, anonymous marketing campaigns that make use of big billboards sporting claims that "Pakistan loves China" or "Pakistan's future is bright" and colorful pamphlets spouting Pakistan industrial potential. Muslim democrats are quick to look for savvy ways to reinforce populist messages, whether promoting tax reform or the elimination of corruption. Pakistan's media market has grown enormously, going from three TV channels to more than sixty-two TV channels in less than ten years. Muslim democrats use regional TV channels to test their messages and put party leaders on nightly news shows that are starved for political content. (These channels operate 24/7 but do not have access to nearly enough fresh content. So they often loop the same twenty minutes of footage for hours to a viewership of thirty to forty million people.)

Muslim democrats also engage in negative political campaigning, a tactic that Islamist party members are supposedly precluded from using. They often cite their opponents' lack of education, lambasting them for their "lack of educational degrees" and in some cases accusing them of having purchased fake degrees. Muslim democrats will often discuss economic corruption in detail on the campaign trail. Ads or campaign stump speeches will recite addresses of stolen property, lavish trips taken abroad, and the types of schools attended by the children of political opponents. And because Muslim democratic parties do not have to follow rigid standards of religiosity, they have a great deal more linguistic latitude in crafting political messages. For example, Muslim democrats will routinely talk about "violations" of Islamic ethos and values without specifying legalistic definitions. While Islamists are quick to specify inner and outer boundaries of behavior, Muslim democrats are able to use religious symbolism to criticize without having the religious credentials to cite textual scripture or fatwas.

Modern Muslim democrats do not share their predecessors' criticisms of sharia and open disdain for devout followers. Islam is the common identity around which a concept of Pakistani nationalism has grown, and Muslim democratic parties have come to align themselves, substantively and rhetorically, with a form of "Islam lite." Muslim democrats simultaneously allude to the benefits of liberal secularism and make vague references to a shared Islamic identity. This use of nonspecific religious allusions is a mainstay of Muslim democratic campaigning. Even though these groups are far less committed to religion than Islamists are, the Muslim democrats' religious messaging is easy to transmit and can be interpreted to mean what the listener wants to hear.

While the Muslim democrats' interest in religious enforcement is low, they are willing to make concessions to religion when it is strategically expedient, as seen in Sharif's handling of the Shariat bill and the sharia amendments. Muslim democrats make visible policy concessions to demonstrate a commitment to the welfare or interests of the poor, rural electorate in a phenomenon known as signaling. One recent example of signaling is the Muslim democrats' muted response to the recent assassination of Governor Salman Taseer, the liberal secularist killed for opposing the enforcement of harsh religious laws. The Muslim democrats' silence was in deference to the popular outrage over Taseer's perceived support for "blasphemists." Such signaling is a delicate balancing act, of course, since the adoption of sharia law is not in the interests of the party's core constituency. But signaling is an important mobilization tool because these actions resonate with the electorate.

Regional factionalism continues to be an issue for Muslim democratic parties, as economic interests vary considerably between urban and rural parts of the country. These differences are what led the original Muslim League to split into so many competing subgroups. Interestingly, each faction has been fairly effective at in-group policing. Political operatives are able to command the group's members to conform to a core political message and thus project a coherent image on the national level. Because the personal power and individual political fortunes of the intellectuals and professionals who lead Muslim democratic parties are dependent on their positions in the party apparatus, they are committed to toeing the party line and building partnerships, even across great distances. The various factions of the Muslim League have also proved exceptionally effective at keeping their members away from any involvement in violent extra-electoral strategies. This success has allowed the Muslim League to present itself as the party of free democratic government and the most legitimate participant in the electoral process.

Muslim democrats have historically done far better than hard-line Islamists in national elections. In each of the last seven elections since 1988, Muslim democrats have either won the largest number of seats in the National Assembly or at least a number sufficient to form a significant opposition to the government in power. The split between the PML-Q and PML-N in 2002 (over how best to deal with Musharraf) meant that Muslim democratic power was sharply divided. With the support of the Musharraf government, the PML-Q handily won the majority of seats in the 2002 election (the legitimacy of which has been seriously questioned). In 2008, the PML-N rebounded, winning seventy-one seats and coming in second only to the Pakistan People's Party. The electoral failure of the pro-Musharraf PML-Q was seen as a rejection of Musharraf himself. These patterns are clearly demonstrated in table 4.1.

Muslim democrats have also performed well in some provincial elections, although their strength is clearly nationally based. These parties' provincial strength is regionally specific. Muslim democrats have won in urban Punjab but have failed to gain traction in rural provincial areas such as northern Sindh and parts of southern Punjab.[110]

Despite the general rule that Muslim democrats are more moderate in their policy and language positions than their Islamist counterparts, they are not without variation along this dimension. The political climate of Pakistan is such that at times, more extreme positions are politically expedient. In keeping with Anthony Downs's theory of political economy and with the sharia-secular model, Muslim democrats shift their platforms to suit the occasion.[111] As demonstrated in subsequent chapters, Islamists also modify their positions for political reasons, but in the current environment Muslim democrats are more motivated to vary from their traditional policy and ideological bases.

Perhaps the most common way in which Muslim democratic parties have moved in the direction of extremism at one time or another is by forming coalitions with more extremist groups. The Pakistan Muslim League and its descendants have done so on more than one occasion. In 1977, the PML joined Jamiat Ulema-e-Islam, Jamaat-e-Islami, Jamiat Ulema-e-Pakistan, and others in a nine-party alliance called the Pakistan National Alliance to oppose Zulfiqar Ali Bhutto's PPP.[112] In addition to the ideological shift implied by this marriage of convenience, the party became a participant in proclamations and actions that also belied its moderate roots. The PNA ran on a platform that explicitly made implementation of sharia its main objective, and when the PPP won in a hotly disputed election, the PNA supporters

Table 4.1. Number of National Assembly seats won by major political parties, 1988–2013

Party	1988	1990	1993	1997	2002	2008	2013
Pakistan People's Party (PPP)	93	44	89	18	72	97	32
Pakistan Muslim League (Nawaz)[a]	43	85	73	137	15	71	126
Pakistan Tehreek e-Insaf (PTI)[a]	n/a	n/a	n/a	n/a	n/a	n/a	28
Pakistan Muslim League (Quaid)[a]	n/a	n/a	n/a	n/a	100	42	2
Jamaat Islami (JI)[a]	11	16	3	5	—	—	3
Jamiat-Ulema-e-Islam (JUI)[a]	7		—	2	—	—	10
Muttahida Majils-e-Amal (MMA) Pakistan[a, b]	n/a	n/a	n/a	n/a	50	6	n/a
Awami National Party	2	6	3	10	1	10	1
Muttahida Qaumi Movement (MQM)	13	15	—	12	13	19	18
Other parties/Independents	38	35	42	28	21	27	52
Total turnout (%)	43.07	45.46	40.28	35.42	39.21	42.40	
Total seats	207	207	210	212	272	272	

a. Denotes an Islamic party, as defined in chapters 1-2.

b. Formed in 2002, the MMA is a coalition of religious parties that includes the JI and JUI, along with four others.

became embroiled in violent conflicts that eventually provided the pretext for General Zia and the military to impose martial law. In 1988, the PML joined Islami Jamhoori Ittehad, a nine-party alliance with the Islamist parties, to contest the strength of Benazir Bhutto, who was then leading the PPP. The IJI was also seen as more extreme and religiously conservative than would be expected from the PML's involvement.[113] Although the IJI failed to capture a majority in the 1988 elections, in 1990 it successfully ran on a platform calling for ethical and moral reform of government in response to widespread allegations of corruption in the Bhutto government.

Since 2000, in the face of US and Western military action in Afghanistan, anti-Western sentiment has risen noticeably in Pakistan, making it politically advantageous to express more extreme positions or at least to be silent in the face of extremism. The movement across the Afghan border of Islamist personnel (and anti-Western ideology) into Pakistan not only has boosted the Islamists' strength in the frontier regions but also has increased the popular appeal of extremist action, even to the extent that the assassinations of moderates have been met with approval from a disturbingly large segment of the population.[114] As alarming as these extreme actions are, the historical patterns of the Muslim democrats suggest that any rightward movements will be motivated by political strategy rather than by any real shift in ideology. Thus, after failing to win an outright majority in the National Assembly in the tarnished 2002 elections held under Musharraf, the PML-Q eventually reached a political bargain with the Islamist Muttahida Majlis-e-Amal, despite the latter group's desire to institute sharia law and its vociferous opposition to the United States. The MMA agreed, after more than a year of debate, to abstain from voting against a constitutional amendment that would legitimize Musharraf's role as president of Pakistan.[115]

Some of this trend toward extremism can be attributed to the Muslim democrats' attempts to engage with new types of voters. Muslim democrats are acutely aware of the possibility that newer parties, such as the MQM, will cut into their support. To counter these developments, Muslim democrats have tried to mend fences with various extremist groups, such as Jamaat-ud-Dawa and Sipah-e-Sahaba Pakistan, which have loyal constituencies in central and southern Punjab. Sometimes these alliances take the form of seat adjustments, in which the two groups seek to minimize anti-PPP vote splitting by mutually agreeing which elections each party will contest and promising to support their rivals in districts where they do not field a candidate.[116]

As this book stresses throughout, this change in strategy is not ideological but rather pragmatic. Muslim democrats began to compromise elements of their worldview to make space for pragmatic considerations that allow for their survival and growth. Chapters 5 and 6 explore when electoral strategies lead to instrumentalism and how political calculations about when, where, and from whom to elicit votes can drive parties to adopt more extreme positions.

CHAPTER 5

ISLAMIST PARTIES

Origins and Characteristics

As a definitional matter, all Islamist parties support state enforcement of religious law and practice.[1] Beyond that fundamental point of agreement, however, there is significant ideological diversity among Pakistan's Islamist parties, which vary in their interpretations of Islamic texts and views of how sharia should functionally operate in Pakistan. Yet differences over more practical matters, such as organizational structure, are actually more predictive of political behavior and electoral success. The organizational model an Islamist political party adopts has much less to do with religious ideology than with the socioeconomic background and class affiliation of party leaders. In this chapter I describe the historical rise of Islamist political parties in Pakistan, examine the two main organizational models of Islamist parties (hierarchical and network), and look closely at the political experiences of the two oldest and most influential Islamist parties of each type—Jamaat-e-Islami and Jamiat Ulema-e-Islam—demonstrating that their degree of extremism (as evidenced by political behavior) is more linked to political expediency than it is to ideology.

As explained in chapter 4, the Muslim democratic movement—the Muslim League in particular—was launched by primarily urban-based Muslim elites. Jinnah and the other leaders of the Pakistan movement eventually came to a political compromise with the feudal elites who for centuries had controlled the territory of modern-day Pakistan. These landowners wanted to protect their financial interests in any future state, no matter its ideological bent. The original Muslim League was thus founded on a nationalistic and economic ideology, not a religious one; indeed, some leaders of the movement could fairly be regarded as antireligious.

The origins of Islamist parties in Pakistan could not be more different. They were born out of fervently religious movements, adopted explicitly religious programmatic commitments, and drew their leadership from the ranks of the country's most revered religious authorities. Notwithstanding the explicitly religious historical base of Islamist parties, their entry into the political arena is marked by policy decisions and practices that frequently contradict their ideological groundings but that are consistent with the organizational and individual self-interest that economic theorists view as driving parliamentary politics.[2] Thus although the ideological premises of Islamist parties remain relatively stable across time, their policies and statements shift with the variation of political and social conditions.

Prior to the official establishment of the British Raj in 1857, the various Islamic leaders of the subcontinent had very different connections to politics and political power, varying across region, sect, and class. These variations ultimately shaped the kinds of religious political parties that developed in Pakistan. In general, however, there is evidence that Islamic religious leaders had frequently combative relationships with the British. Muslim clerics have long defined themselves as protectors of the Islamic faith in India, and the British Raj was a clear adversary during the period of colonization. Clerics constituted an estimated quarter of the approximately 200,000 of Muslims killed during the Sepoy Rebellion of 1857.[3] The perception that the British targeted Muslim leaders reinforced notions of Islam's being under siege from Western powers.

In 1866, a group of Muslim clerics built a *madrasah* at Deoband (now in Uttar Pradesh, India) called the Dar ul-Ulum (House of Knowledge). Dar ul-Ulum became the center of a religious revival movement devoted to the purification of Islam and continues to be one of the most influential Islamic learning centers in the world. The Deobandi movement, as it became known, swept across South Asia as graduates of the seminary founded new *madrasahs* throughout India and Afghanistan. The movement was popular because it suggested a more authentic response to Western rule and provided an outlet for Muslim grievances. Deoband was a reformist and revivalist movement, but it also rejected the modern rationalistic Islam championed by reformers such as Sir Syed Ahmed Khan. Instead, its leaders believed that "a strong disavowal of modernity could hasten their way back to the re-creation of a lost Islamic glory."[4]

The new *madrasahs* trained scholars, priests, and lawyers who prioritized the preservation of Islamic religion, culture, and heritage. Deobandi scholars argued that the decline of Islam was rooted in a lack of religious education and Muslims' consequent susceptibility to straying from the true course of Islam; thus the movement's clerics, first in India and then globally, issued hundreds of thousands of new legal rulings to provide guidance to the faithful on daily matters. Their *fatwas* ranged from the mundane to the fundamental. If one was touched by a dog, one had to redo the ablution for ritual prayers; women should pray in their houses instead of at mosques; and *madrasah* education was far superior to that offered in Western-style schools. This effort increased regulation of the private sphere and gave Deobandi scholars great influence over the daily activities of their followers.

Their rejection of politics initially kept the Deobandi from clashing with the British. Deobandi adherents believed that it was Muslims who needed to be reformed, not the state. While their strict religious order and separate way of life did not win them many friends in the colonial government, their avowed stance against partition (and hence the Muslim League) gave them some protective cover.

The British allowed Deobandi scholars to organize conferences, travel around South Asia to give sermons, and establish a press to disseminate their teachings. Deobandi founders skillfully built the religious seminary as an autonomous institution, divorced from British politics and financially supported by individual Muslims.

Indeed, the source of Deoband's strength was its role in religious education in South Asia. For many Muslims, Deobandi *ulema* became the final arbiters of what was and was not "true Islam," a powerful and empowering role. By the time of partition, more than four thousand students had graduated from Dar ul-Ulum; many of them went on to found new *madrasahs* across South Asia. Deobandi scholars also held national conferences on religious rulings, giving them a visible platform from which to address a mass following and build consensus.[5] Urdu-language print media published the speeches and commentaries and disseminated them internationally.

The Deobandi were not overtly political at first, presenting themselves as "inward looking and primarily concerned with the Islamic quality of individual lives."[6] This original stance has not entirely disappeared. The Deobandi movement gave rise to the Tablighi Jamaat, an apolitical religious revival organization that has members throughout much of the Muslim world. But in the wake of the dismantling of the Mughal Empire, the brutal suppression following the Sepoy Rebellion, and the imposition of direct British rule, some Deobandi leaders decided they had suffered enough political and cultural losses.

Deobandi opposition to British rule took a variety of forms, including armed resistance. In the World War I era, a group of *ulema* engaged in the Silk Letter Conspiracy, a failed attempt at armed insurrection. The conspirators planned to overthrow British rule in India with the help of the Germans and Turks and establish a pan-Islamic government stretching from Turkey to India. The British discovered the plot and arrested the ringleaders.[7]

This setback was not the end of Deobandi political involvement. In 1919, a group of Deobandi *ulema* formed the Jamiat Ulema-i-Hind (Organization of Indian Scholars [JUH]).[8] Using nonviolent tactics, the JUH set out to put political pressure on Britain to retain the Ottoman caliphate and grant India independence. The organization did not favor partition, instead promoting an Indian nationalist platform. The group's mission and tactics fit well with those of Mahatma Gandhi and the Indian National Congress, leading the JUH to join the congress in a Hindu-Muslim alliance. (Many JUH members, including some of its most important leadership, in fact remained in India after partition and continued to be involved in political life.)

The onset of partition also occasioned a split in the Deobandi movement. The JUH was representative of an activist (and actively anti-Pakistan) trend in the movement, but other Deobandis had historically eschewed politics of any kind.[9] With the creation of Pakistan and the dissolution of the imperial British power structure in the mid-twentieth century, however, some members of this latter group recognized that they could no longer afford to remain on the political sidelines. Their continued opposition to political involvement meant that they risked ceding power in the new state to the Muslim League, which Deobandi scholars regarded as deeply irreligious and harmful to the cause of Muslim purification. Once they had committed to entering politics, their previous failure to take a vocal stance against Pakistan made it far easier for them to participate in Pakistani politics than it would prove to be for members of the JUH. This historically antipolitical faction in 1945 would found the JUI, which became the foremost Deobandi political party in Pakistan. But the lure of politics also proved too strong to resist for those members of the JUH who ended up in Pakistan, for they were already a naturally political group. Despite their initial opposition to the state, they were anxious to play a role in shaping its future. As one JUH leader put it, "We are fortunate that we had no role in the sin of creation of Pakistan, but being here we have every claim to its politics and future."[10]

Jamaat-e-Islami: A Hierarchical Islamist Party

Syed Abul A'ala Maududi founded Jamaat-e-Islami in August 1941. Maududi was born to a wealthy family in what is now Maharashtra, India. His personal history is one of an elite upbringing, social isolation, and high expectations for academic excellence.[11] Maududi was initially homeschooled by his father (an attorney who had attended Aligarh College) and private instructors. Ultimately, he was sent to a *madrasah* and then to the premier Deobandi institution of higher learning, Dar ul-Ulum. His father's sudden death cut short Maududi's formal training, but his life continued to revolve around intellectual and academic pursuits as a journalist and author. He had shown a gift for writing in Urdu early on, and after his father's death he became a journalist, editing a small Urdu paper by the time he was seventeen and winning increasingly prestigious journalism jobs during his mid-twenties. He eventually edited the two leading Deobandi journals—*Muslim* and *al-Jamiyat* (the latter was the house organ of the JUH).[12] (Although Maududi certainly came from a Deobandi background, the JI has never officially promoted Deobandi thought at the expense of the various competing Sunni traditions of Ahle Hadith, Barelvi, and so on. Today its ranks include Sunnis of diverse religious backgrounds and even a few Shiites.[13])

During his years as a journalist, Maududi wrote several essays defending Islam and explaining his vision of Islam as a nonviolent faith.[14] He was a strong supporter of the Khilafat Movement, but unlike the participants in the Silk Letter Conspiracy, he argued for the preservation and protection of Islam by nonviolent means. He eventually became editor and chief writer for *Tarjuman al-Qur'an*, a Muslim revivalist journal. *Tarjuman al-Qur'an* served as the main channel for disseminating Maududi's vision of Islam, in which the faith was increasingly figured as both a personal and political identity.

By the early 1940s Maududi had grown deeply suspicious of the Shuddhi and Sangathan Hindu revivalist movements and the increasingly Hindu orientation of the Indian National Congress. The congress had refused to honor its agreement with the Muslim League that Muslims would constitute 30 percent of the National Assembly and was unwilling to maintain the separate Hindu and Muslim electoral systems instituted in 1909. Maududi did not support the Muslim League's move toward creating a separate state of Pakistan or the Indian National Congress's pursuit of a single Indian nation, believing that neither option would lead to the establishment of Islam as the unique and sole identification of Indian Muslims. In his writings, Maududi argued for the importance of a separate Muslim identity and a Muslim state that facilitated and increased piety in its people. In the face of assaults to Muslim existence, including harassment, interference with Islamic religious practice, and discrimination, Maududi proposed forming a Muslim theo-democracy in which Islamic law would guide public policy in all areas of life. (Maududi specifically rejected the term "theocracy" to describe his ideal state, arguing that the truly Islamic state would be ruled not by the *ulema* but by the entire Muslim community.[15]) In 1941, seventy-five clergy and lay people who had been influenced by Maududi's writings attended a meeting in Lahore, where Maududi founded the Jamaat-e-Islami as a vehicle for developing and establishing such a state.[16] He was the party's first *amir*.

Jamaat-e-Islami was initially made up of Urdu-speaking elites who felt that Dar ul-Ulum was not sophisticated enough in its public outreach.[17] During the first years of its existence, JI membership was highly exclusive; being a card-carrying member was akin to membership in a fraternity or union. Thus, at the time of partition, six years after its founding, it had only 625 members, less than 400 of whom lived in Pakistan.[18] But these small numbers belie its potential impact. In 1945, for instance, roughly 10 percent of the members were *ulema* with their own *madrasahs*, allowing them to inculcate their students with the group's message.[19] Maududi believed that Indian Muslims should see themselves not as a nation but as an ideological movement, as the socialists or communists did.[20] Thus, the JI was consciously designed as a vanguard party, and its leadership looked to recruit highly committed Muslims who were willing to devote significant time and energy to the mission.[21] The JI focused on building political structure, not mass support, and tried to wield influence in targeted areas, such as the design of Pakistan's first constitution. Maududi did not want Islam to be confined to the private sphere or limited to individual religious practice. He felt that Islam should inform governance, political communities, and public institutions. He wanted the JI to influence the debate across the Muslim world.[22]

Although JI was established as a political party, in its early form it functioned initially more as a revivalist movement focused on reforming the minds and behavior of individual Muslims and on converting Indian Hindus to Islam. As Vali Nasr observes, the JI was more of a holy community than a political party, expecting its members to observe the sovereign rule of Allah and demonstrate their devotion in their behavior.[23] But Maududi's vision differed from that of contemporary Muslim revivalists who held that individual devotion could drive broad social and religious change. Instead, Maududi argued that only in a fully Islamic state, shielded from the corrupting influences of Hinduism and the West, could individual Muslims achieve true reformation. Muslims had to live under both social and political rules of Islamic law in order to engage in meaningful personal spiritual development.[24] Such a position necessarily demanded political engagement to pursue the institution of sharia as state law.[25]

Maududi opposed partition, because the Muslim League proposed founding a secular state for Muslims rather than an Islamic state ruled according to Islamic law. At the JI's first meeting, the group identified eight issues of focus, one of which was the conversion of non-Muslims. Maududi's grand vision likely involved converting India's Hindus and creating an ideal Islamic state in a unified India. But as Britain moved hastily toward granting independence, and as support for the Muslim League grew, Maududi recognized that partition would occur and that the JI had to change its strategy in order to participate effectively in the fight to shape Pakistan's future. After partition Maududi chose to move to Pakistan and began to work toward establishing the JI as an opposition party. (The JI continued its work in India through its fellow organization Jamaat-e-Islami Hind.) At this point, the party adopted the Quranic verse "Ud-Khulu Fis-Silmi Kaffa" (Enter in Islam full fledged) as its slogan.

The Jamaat-e-Islami rapidly positioned itself as a thorn in the side of the Muslim League, even to the extent of denying the legitimacy of the state. In 1948, for instance, Pakistan covertly sent paramilitary groups into Kashmir in an attempt to wrest it from India's control, describing the action as a jihad. Maududi rejected this religious rationalization for the covert war, writing that true jihad could not be carried out secretly. Opposing the Pakistani government's Kashmir agenda was an extraordinary step, especially at a time of high tension with India. The government accused Maududi of being pro-Indian and jailed him for his statements.[26] But Maududi and the JI were not content to work entirely outside the organs of state power; despite Maududi's dislike of the conservative *ulema*, he allied himself with them in the debate over the Islamic content of the new Pakistani constitution.[27]

The JI offers the most well-articulated programmatic objectives of any of Pakistan's Islamist parties, largely because they were honed and disseminated through Maududi's writings rather than through a committee of clerics and scholars.[28] Although Maududi's voluminous work defies easy summarization, the JI's ambitions can be summarized in three goals: on the personal level, seek individual obedience to God; on the social level, eliminate inconsistencies between Muslims' professions of faith and their actual lives; and on the political level, assert Islamic leadership in all areas of life. The scope of this proposed Islamic leadership certainly includes Pakistan, but theoretically it describes a universal ideal. As one JI leader told me, "We will not cease until sharia law is throughout the Muslim nations. As it is written, Islam will someday be the faith of all on this earth."[29] According to the JI, the third goal drives the group to build a Muslim vanguard, a group of pious Muslims of exceptional ability who can lead an Islamic state. The party contends that Islamic leadership cannot be established without such a vanguard.

Organizationally, the JI is Pakistan's oldest and most prominent example of a hierarchical Islamist party. According to party doctrine, 90 percent of Pakistan's Muslims are pious but deeply ignorant about the fundamentals of their faith, and 5 percent are educated but have been corrupted by Western values. Thus, the remaining 5 percent, the well-educated faithful, are the JI's recruiting pool.[30] (In one speech, Maududi put the percentage of professed Muslims who were in fact Muslims "in name only" even higher, at 99.9 percent.[31]) Maududi believed that a vanguard of elite religious intellectuals was necessary to defend Muslims from Hindu domination and to lead the mass of Muslims away from political and cultural obscurity.[32] He recruited heavily from universities and prestigious *madrasahs* in order to develop a small cadre of technocratic, intellectual, and religious elites who could lead the party.[33]

Today, a small number of university-trained *ulema* and conservative intellectuals still lead the JI's rigid hierarchy, and messages are disseminated via a tightly controlled chain of command.[34] Reflecting this zeal for organization and efficiency, one party official described the JI as being run "as if it were a business looking to make a profit. Only our income is not in money, but in souls."[35] As the original JI constitution dictated, sitting at the top of the hierarchy is the *amir*, from whom members must obey any order unless it is sinful.[36] Maududi filled this role for the first thirty years of the organization's existence, and the JI has had only three other leaders since his resignation in 1972. Below the *amir* are his deputy *amirs*, the *shura* (consultative council), the secretary-general, and the secretariat. Trusted political operatives take orders directly from this central ruling body.[37] Because an elite religious status is notoriously difficult to attain in Islamic institutions—and because this standing remains the primary criterion for participation in the JI's leadership apparatus—the party has a very small pool of possible leaders.

This formal structure forms the backbone of an organizational system that is designed to enforce party discipline, to ensure members express sufficient revolutionary ardor, and to maintain a steep hierarchy among the membership. In 1954, the JI created membership categories (which still exist today) that were meant to ensure the fitness of members and assign responsibility for work the party leaders deemed essential. There are three main levels of participation: *arkan* (core members), with singular *rukn* (full voting members); *muttafiq* (affiliated men who carry out party work under the party's supervision but are not voting members); and *hamdard* (sympathizers, or men who support the party's mission but are not officially organized).[38] As of 2011, the JI was believed to have roughly twenty thousand members.[39] The JI officially began to recruit women in the 1950s. They are part of a separate but closely linked organization with a structure that closely mimics that of the men's wing, but both wings are under the same *amir*.[40] Women make up a small (but steadily increasing) percentage of *arkan*.[41]

The JI is very particular about the requirement for membership at each level and carefully controls movement in the organization.[42] *Arkan* are required to attend weekly meetings, and absence without valid cause is grounds for expulsion.[43] In addition, even those well below the leadership level are subject to stringent observation and evaluation of their work and commitment. It can take more than ten years to become a *rukn*. The leadership pays close attention to discipline and dedication; so if a *rukn* misses mandatory meetings without an excuse, he may be demoted to affiliate or even sympathizer. Even the wives and children of members are organized into wings of the party; their participation is mandatory. The strong party allegiances these practices foster mean that the rate of attrition of JI members is far lower than for other confessional parties, like the JUI or PML-N.[44] JI leaders admit that they ask a great deal of their senior members, but they believe that "this is what it takes to reshape a nation."[45]

The JI did not nominate its own candidates immediately after becoming an explicitly political movement in part because there were no elections to contest. It sought instead to influence public policy through outside agitation. One early triumph, achieved in cooperation with the *ulema*, was its participation in passing the Objectives Resolution of 1949, which laid out a set of principles to guide Pakistan's first constitutional convention. The JI also made its voice heard in the debate over the new constitution. Its dislike of the Muslim League and its equal commitment to a strong central state forced it to walk a fine line between opposing the league at every turn and working to ensure that the constitution would create a strong federal government that would unify Pakistan's two wings.[46]

The JI's first direct experience with elections came in Punjab's provincial elections of 1951, but its participation was still hesitant. Instead of running candidates on its own slate, the JI endorsed those candidates from other parties whom it found "pure" and right minded. The fifty-two JI-endorsed candidates were selected by over a thousand village councils across Punjab that sat in judgment of each hopeful's moral caliber.[47] But despite this democratic approach, the JI's candidates were resoundingly unsuccessful, with only one winning office. This failure was owed in part to the Punjab government's clampdown on the JI during the campaign period, but the party had also proved itself too narrowly focused on religious ideology, ignoring its potential constituents' linguistic, ethnic, and economic interests.[48]

The debacle of the 1951 elections convinced some members of the party that the JI could no longer be driven purely by ideological motives. To become politically successful, the party would have to modify its objectives.[49] This early blow spurred dissatisfaction among its members and led to widespread debate about the party's agenda and organization, with one faction advocating for a withdrawal from politics and the other (which included Maududi) for a renewed commitment to achieving political power. At a pivotal conference in Machi Goth in 1957, Maududi made a famous six-hour-long speech in which he argued that political activity was crucial, as politics "was the only way to establish the Islamic way of life (*iqamat-e-din*) and a government based on divine pattern."[50] His arguments persuaded the assembled members, who voted 920–15 to continue their pursuit of political power.

But the JI's early defeat at the polls pointed to a critical weakness, its difficulty mobilizing the masses. Ironically, the party was able to stimulate considerable activity outside the electoral context, as seen in its participation in the anti-Ahmadi riots in 1953. Anti-Ahmadi agitation erupted into violence and resulted in the death of more than two thousand Ahmadis. Although he was not the leader of the uprising and in fact had at first argued against the use of violence, Maududi was convicted of sedition and sentenced to death (the sentence was eventually commuted after he had spent only two years in jail).[51]

Maududi's contribution to the agitation, a virulently anti-Ahmadi book, showed that the party had the ability to engage mass attention, but its dismal electoral performance indicated that the party needed to develop new ways to bring the masses to the polls. One method was to recruit more affiliates; their number grew from 2,900 in 1951 to 25,000 in 1957 and to more than 350,000 in 1992.[52] But Maududi's original conception of the party as a holy community whose members must meet a high standard of purity and righteousness, kept the ranks of full members small and made the JI's leaders somewhat reluctant to engage fully in the dirty business of politics. Despite the decision made at Machi Goth in 1957, the tension between building a holy community and a political party has continued to resurface throughout the JI's history. The imperatives of purity may have led the party to reject the compromises associated with electoral success. As the *amir* for Faisalabad district told journalist Anatol Lieven, "We don't want to rally the masses behind, because they don't help us . . . they are disorganized, illiterate, and can't follow our ideology or stick with our strategy. . . . We don't care if we can't take over the government as long as we keep our characters clean."[53]

Despite the limitations of the vanguard approach when it comes to mass participation (and electoral success), the party remains committed to this vision. Its leaders are confident that "as time goes on the people will realize that we are truly the only party standing up for Islam in all its glory."[54] The JI's website depicts the party's organizational structure as a single vertical line, indicating its vision of leadership as rigidly hierarchical and necessarily exclusionary.[55] While the structure has grown slightly more complex since the party's founding, at its core the JI's hierarchy remains essentially linear. This structure has enabled the JI to greatly increase its actual membership size, establishing more local groups in close proximity to one another, while still retaining tight control over its membership.[56] The JI uses its highly organized members and affiliates to spread the party message at their home mosques, *madrasahs*, and businesses. The party has successfully set up chapters in Pakistan's major urban cities, with its strongest bases in the cities of the Punjab and Sindh.

Unsurprisingly, the JI finds its strongest support among university-educated technocrats and clerics, students and affiliates of academic institutions, and the urban middle- and lower-middle-class faithful. The JI promotes a version of Islam that is modernizing and pragmatic (but not modernist) and largely devoid of "cultural accretions" (i.e., traditional practices, some of which are derived from Hindu conventions), and it appeals to the educated and the upwardly mobile.[57] Unlike other Islamist groups, the JI has a cultural affinity with academics and has deliberately targeted universities and university students in its recruitment efforts. Its student wing, the Islami Jamiate-Talaba (IJT), is one of the most active and visible groups on Pakistan's university campuses.[58] With lower entrance requirements and a focus on mass organization, the IJT has proved a highly effective tool for spreading its parent group's message to the lower-middle-class students who attend public universities and who might not consider attempting the JI's rigorous membership process.[59] Lieven quotes a young IJT member describing his path from curious student to IJT activist: "My family are ANP [Awami National Party], and I am the only one of my brothers and sisters to join the Jamaat. It happened gradually. I went to college and met Jamaat members and was impressed by them and how they work. Once you are affiliated, you learn political awareness and organization skills as well as religious awareness. Then as student members you go to other colleges to organize debates and spread the Jamaat message."[60]

As Nasr points out, the JI's historical focus on written propaganda (which has its roots in Maududi's own vocation as a journalist and pamphleteer) limits its appeal beyond the minority of Pakistanis who are literate. Furthermore, the importance that the JI places on the role of Urdu in Pakistani life makes it less appealing to the many Pakistanis for whom Urdu is a second language or who do not speak it at all.[61] In the urban regions, the JI appeals to the lower-middle-class and middle-class Pakistanis with political leanings who are in many respects excluded from Muslim democratic parties, which strongly favor elite interests. As Lieven writes, in the "depressing social and cultural circumstances [of urban lower-middle-class life] adherence to a radical Islamist network like the Jamaat provides a sense of cultural security, a new community and some degree of social support."[62] Currently, the JI has roughly ten thousand affiliate members in Lahore and fifteen thousand affiliate members in Karachi with a goal of five million affiliates throughout Pakistan.[63]

The JI's lackluster attempts to reach out to the Pakistan's poor may be as much by design as it is an artifact of the party's antecedents. JI leaders' attempts to build mass support for the party's ideology are fruitless because "the poor who are able to vote do so for return favors. This often means the lower classes split their votes among many parties. . . . Their support is not enough to win an election anymore."[64] The JI's most important connection to the lower classes and the rural poor comes through its charitable work. Humeira Iqtidar, who cites the involvement of a JI charity with a peasant uprising in the early 2000s, argues that "no . . . national political party [other than JI] has institutional links, however tenuous, with peasants or small farmers."[65] The party's charitable wing, known as Al-Khidmat Foundation, was widely praised for its relief efforts following the devastating 2010 floods, when it deployed thousands of relief workers across some of the hardest-hit areas of Pakistan. According to JI's leaders, volunteers working under the auspices of Al-Khidmat provided aid to at least half a million flood victims.[66] The JI received similarly good press following the 2005 earthquakes in Pakistan-controlled Kashmir, and Al-Khidmat established several field hospitals and clinics in the affected areas.[67] This activity, a result of the JI's careful organization and highly motivated membership, stood in stark contrast to the perceived ineptness of the government in both crises.

The electoral impact of these activities is as yet undetermined. JI's flood relief work took place primarily in Khyber Pakhtunkhwa, where the group performs best electorally. But it is impossible to say whether the party's comparative success there in the 2013 elections (three National Assembly and seven provincial assembly seats) is the result of the goodwill generated by its charity work or whether it performed the work in areas where it was stronger, both electorally and organizationally. Despite the popular assumption that Islamist parties build mass constituencies through the provision of social services, in-depth studies of this phenomenon question the causal link between social-service provision and electoral success.[68] This case is particularly true for Pakistan and the JI. Pakistani voters are looking less for charity than the sort of large-scale public works projects that only incumbent politicians can offer, while the JI remains deeply ambivalent about using its popularity as a social-services organization to become a mass movement.

While the JI does not have nearly the degree of connection to state networks and government bureaucracy that the Muslim League does, it is not altogether without access. The party's loyal technocrats and university-trained clerics are fairly well incorporated into state networks and have access to governmental resources by virtue of holding academic posts at universities, working in governmental organizations, or receiving government funding for programs. Also, hierarchical Islamists tend to share similar educational backgrounds with the economic elite and have experience with a broader social milieu than the average citizen does.[69] This exposure allows the Islamists some influence and provides access to state goods that may be distributed as patronage.

Equally important, the JI is a major player in Pakistan's educational market. Its influence began during Zia ul-Haq's Islamization campaign of the 1980s and takes two forms—direct, as with JI-controlled *madaris*, and indirect, with JI's influence on public school curricula. Under Zia, state funding for religious education encouraged a boom in *madrasah* foundation during the 1980s. The JI first opened its own *madaris* during that period and is now believed to control (either directly or indirectly) more than two thousand private religious schools.[70] The JI's direct control over the educational market should not be exaggerated, however; the number of JI *madaris* is significant but is dwarfed by the number of *madaris* run by Deobandi *ulema* (an estimated eight thousand in 2005).[71] In addition, the vast majority of students in Pakistan (roughly two-thirds) attend public schools, while *madaris* attract only 1–7 percent of students.[72]

The JI's real importance in the educational arena, therefore, lies in the influence it has had over the curricula of Pakistan's public schools. The content of public education has been a contested field for much of Pakistan's history. During the Zia period public school curricula were seen as a powerful tool for Islamization, as Zia sought to ensure that Pakistani children would "imbibe the lofty ideals and principles of Islam."[73] Zia made Arabic, the language of the Quran, and Islamic religious studies compulsory at all levels. The PML-N perpetuated and even strengthened this trend during the 1990s.[74] The resulting Islamic studies curriculum has been described as "literalistic in its reading of the Qur'an . . . ahistorical . . . homogenizing . . . [and] prescriptive."[75] Further, the general studies curriculum gives a heavily skewed account of Pakistan's history, portrays Pakistan as a country for Muslims alone, and makes "the Ideology of Pakistan [i.e., Islam and the defense of Islam] . . . the cornerstone of education."[76]

Reflecting the JI's ideological influence on Zia's Islamization campaign, the Pakistani public school curriculum and textbooks are heavily influenced by Maududi's belief that in an Islamic society "every subject would become Islamiat [Islamic studies]."[77] The term "the Ideology of Pakistan," itself coined by a JI member, reflects Maududi's pre-partition stance that the subcontinent's Muslims should view themselves as an ideological bloc rather than a national or religious one.[78] Thus, while public school education does not explicitly promote the JI, it does attempt to inculcate in students the values that would lead them to vote for religious parties. The JI's electoral history, however, shows that the sort of social penetration that comes with influence over the curriculum does not necessarily lead to success at the polls, but the JI is not the only party able and willing to capitalize on the religio-nationalistic sentiments inspired by the public school curriculum. As shown by the PML-N's support for Zia's curricular reforms during its time in office, Muslim democratic parties are also able to capitalize on the increasing Islamization of Pakistani society and even uses language and ideas originally developed by the Jamaat to great effect.

Of the three parties examined in this book, the JI has arguably been the most successful at maintaining party discipline. Its narrow hierarchy, strict control over members' behavior, and cellular structure have helped it to maintain a unified message and behavioral adherence, and it is Pakistan's only political party not to be "swallowed up by the patronage system."[79] Only allowing people from certain socioeconomic and educational backgrounds to hold leadership positions also helps the party maintain cohesion and carefully control its messages. These benefits come at a price, however, as the JI's narrow hierarchy and high barriers to membership make it difficult to expand political capacity. Lieven also speculates that while many Pakistanis admire JI members' righteousness, the party's "puritan and intellectual style is rather alien, not just to the mass of the rural population but to the urban proletariat as well."[80]

The JI's core message, furthermore, has not proved an easy sell. The economic elite and its allies in the Muslim League have consistently objected to its insistence on implementing sharia at the national level because it would threaten their financial interests. Maududi argued that anything that poses a threat to Islamic purity, including Western technological advances and the capitalist banking system, should be eliminated from society.[81] (However, the JI conveniently defends Pakistan's "Islamic nuclear bomb.") These positions have been poorly received by the upper classes, which benefit from the current economic order.

Traditional Islamic revival organizations and clerics, meanwhile, have objected to the JI's willingness to participate in politics at all and have widely repudiated Maududi's insistence that sharia should be implemented through political actions and legislation. As Iqtidar makes clear, while the JI is a fundamentalist organization, it is far from a traditional or conservative one. Pakistan's conservative *ulema* reject JI's stance that believers can and should interpret the Quran themselves, without undue reliance on clerical guidance. They also criticize JI's members for beginning a political campaign before they have won the war against their own baser instincts.[82]

Moreover, mass mobilization has been slow. In a nation with 45 percent adult illiteracy (32 percent among men, 60 percent among women), the JI's rigid hierarchy, urban focus, and hyper-intellectualism have made it difficult for the group to form connections with a rural constituency.[83] Furthermore, the JI has entirely rejected the appeals to ethnicity that characterize much of Pakistani politics. Since the founding of the Muttahida Qaumi Movement in the 1980s, the JI has largely lost the support of one of its natural constituencies, the Muhajir (Urdu-speaking immigrant) population of urban Sindh.[84] Thus, the JI has worked to build new alliances across Pakistan (especially Punjab).[85]

While Maududi resigned as *amir* in 1972 and died in 1979, his orientation, philosophy, and approach to the political process still left a strong legacy and continued to bear influence on the party. In particular, Maududi's view that exceptional academic achievement should be a precondition of political service and his use of written manifestos to communicate with followers have made the JI all but inaccessible to the uneducated Muslims of India and Pakistan.[86] As Nasr writes, "Ever since it was formed, the Jama'at has shown an aversion to populism and a disregard for the demands of the poor, preferring instead to trust its political fortunes to a policy that interprets all issues through the prism of religious exegesis and is directed at winning over the elite, suggesting that its objective has been to take over the state from secular leaders rather than give voice to the demands of the masses."[87]

Thus, Jamaat-e-Islami has achieved mixed results in Pakistani elections. Perhaps the high point of its electoral prospects came with the 1958 elections for the Karachi municipal corporation, in which nineteen of the twenty-three JI candidates won their races, forming more than a quarter of the council.[88] The JI had high hopes for the next national elections, but they were canceled with General Ayub Khan's declaration of martial law. In the next thirty years, Pakistanis held only two national elections conducted on a party basis. In subsequent elections, instead of conducting national electoral contests, the JI sought to compete in targeted individual races. As a result, over the years the JI has fared much better at the local and provincial than the national level.

The JI has won 30 percent of the seats in key districts in Punjab and Sindh and more than 15 percent of the seats in six provincial contests. It has won nine prominent mayoral positions and been part of two governing coalitions at the federal level. The JI has developed a close relationship with Pakistan's military, which has allowed it to maintain leadership in local districts and to influence constitutional reform during periods of military rule. In 2002, the JI joined the coalition Muttahida Majlis-e-Amal and had its best national showing, winning 52 out of 272 seats in the National Assembly. In general, however, it rarely wins more than 3–5 percent of seats at the national level. Indeed, the JI had one of its worst showings in the 2013 elections, where it won only 3 seats, all from districts in the KPK.[89]

The JI's failure to break through on the national level can be partly attributed to the high barriers to entry in Pakistani politics. Andrew Wilder, for one, cautions against the assumption that a lack of electoral support points to a lack of popular support, pointing out that Pakistani voters are reluctant to vote for a politician who they believe cannot win. Wilder quotes an unnamed JI candidate in the 1993 national election who complained that even those voters who supported the JI's platform and trusted its candidate voted for the PML-N or the PPP: "Everyone came to me and said, '. . . everything you say is one hundred percent right. We sincerely believe that you are a man that will not tell a lie. . . . You will be true to your call. The only thing is that you will not win."[90] Frustrated JI candidates have come to believe that the deck is stacked against them by the mainstream parties. As one senior leader told me in 2007, "Our current politicians have been 'elected' in a so-called 'democratic' vote. But what is so democratic about rigging elections? What credibility do they have when they are behind political assassinations and corruption at every level of government? This is the 'democracy' they have given us."[91]

Although the Jamaat remains true to Maududi's vision, its struggle to achieve its self-professed goal of "controlling the state apparatus" has led it to make a number of surprising compromises.[92] Iqtidar, whose nuanced anthropological study of the group is an excellent complement to Nasr's now slightly dated work, argues that JI is not monolithic and unchanging but is in fact a constantly adaptive organization. She offers as evidence two major shifts in the JI's ideology and tactics since its founding. First, the JI has adopted the organizing tactics (and occasionally the political platform) of Pakistan's left-wing groups in an effort to recreate their achievements in mass mobilization. Most notably, amid the populist wave that preceded the 1970 elections, the JI's election manifesto offered (somewhat lukewarm) support for land reform, despite Maududi's having adamantly opposed such proposals in the past.[93] This change, and the party's contemporaneous decision to build a presence in Pakistan's labor movement, mark the start of the party's important shift toward populism and attention to socioeconomic issues.[94] As Lieven observes, the JI now puts socioeconomic issues at the center of its appeal to voters.[95] This populist turn both reflects and is the cause of the JI's increasing presence among the lower-middle and even working classes.[96]

More recently, the JI has found itself fighting for supporters with the Jamaat-ud-Dawa, which is officially a charitable organization but is in fact the reincarnation of the now-banned terrorist group Lashkar-e-Taiba.[97] JuD has close historical links to the JI (its founder, Hafiz Saeed, was a former IJT and JI member); yet despite (or perhaps because of) the two groups' closeness on the sharia–secular spectrum, they often compete directly for supporters. The direct competition between the two has increased as the JI has begun to recruit more heavily among the lower classes, which form JuD's base of support, and as JuD has attempted to increase its appeal to the JI's historical constituency of educated, urban middle-class voters.[98] Although JuD does not contest elections, Iqtidar makes clear that JuD members are seen as lost JI voters. The changing face of the average JI supporter has caused the party to begin correcting its original aversion to bread-and-butter issues. In interviews conducted between 2007 and 2013, JI leaders repeatedly asserted that their vision of sharia law would eliminate corruption and injustice. As one said, "Why should a poor farmer pay interest for the loan he needs to grow the crops that feed us all? A society based on sharia law would stop such ruthless practices."[99] Another leader described JI as "the one party that will care for all of the people, including the poor and disadvantaged."[100] A third blamed Pakistan's economic problems, including high food prices and the power crisis, on the corruption and double-dealing of the political elite.[101]

Prominent Pakistani security analyst Ayesha Siddiqa has found that not only is the JI losing support to JuD in urban Punjab but also that local politicians feel obliged to join the JuD-led Difa-e-Pakistan (Defense of Pakistan) Council in an attempt to "buy security" from assassination.[102] Siddiqa and her local interlocutors attribute JuD's recruiting success to its more aggressive stance on jihad, a position that is particularly attractive to Punjabi youths. In its effort to win and retain the support of this constituency, the JI has made startling compromises, such as entering a 2005 alliance with the PPP in the Lahore local government elections.[103] Yet at other times, the JI has found common cause with JuD and other extremist organizations, such as Jaish-e-Mohammad.[104]

As detailed in subsequent chapters, the degree to which the JI holds to its religious fundamentalist and extremist roots largely depends on the political expediency of such a position. While ideology might drive a party's emergence during its initial stages, political relevancy (such as expanding party capacity) forces the JI to make pragmatic political calculations about its stances on a host of policy issues, including developing possible coalitions with secular parties and determining which new groups of voters they try to reach.

Jamiat Ulema-e-Islam: A Network Islamist Party

Jamiat Ulema-e-Islam is a splinter group of Jamiat Ulema-i-Hind (JUH), the organization founded in 1919 by leading Deobandi Islamic scholars in support of the Khilafat Movement.[105] In the 1940s, as independence neared, and with Jinnah and the Muslim League pressing for partition and the creation of a Muslim-majority Pakistan, JUH was forced to take a position on partition. Most JUH leaders decided to join their longtime ally, the Indian National Congress, in opposing the creation of a separate Muslim state. But dissenting clerics in the JUH believed that partition offered the best opportunity for Muslims to reestablish religious and political dominance.[106] The party split over this position in 1945, with each faction following what it considered the most promising path for securing the interests of Indian Muslims.

The pro-partition faction formed the Jamiat Ulema-e-Islam under the leadership of Shabbir Ahmad Usmani, a Deobandi cleric who was also a member of the Muslim League. Usmani and the other founders of the JUI worked together with the Muslim League to achieve partition and the establishment of Pakistan. After partition, he served as a member of Pakistan's Constituent Assembly, the interim national assembly formed to draft a constitution, and he was instrumental in the passage of the Objectives Resolution.[107] The JUI was led largely by *madrasah*-educated rural clerics with close cultural, ethnic, and religious ties to the rural electorate. Despite these connections, some rural peasants initially viewed the JUI with suspicion because of its cooperation and affiliation with the Muslim League over the cause of partition. Although it was understood that the JUI had united with the league only for the purposes of securing the partition of Pakistan, that association raised legitimate questions in the minds of potential JUI supporters who mistrusted the urban, Urdu-speaking, and "irreligious" members of the Muslim League.

The JUI's first foray into the electoral sphere was not a success. In 1946, the party put up candidates for the North-West Frontier's Provincial Assembly, running on a platform of religious integrity and legitimacy. The JUI was effectively shut out of the elections, in which the Muslim League won seventy-five of the eighty-five seats designated for Muslims.[108] From the time of partition through Pakistan's first general election in 1970 (a period during which national elections were not held), the JUI refrained from direct electoral participation and focused instead on becoming a trusted presence in the rural provinces and building a dense network of ethnic and tribal affiliations.[109] To this end, the JUI founded rural *madaris* and *masjids* across Pakistan. (To date, it has established thousands of *madaris* in Pakistan, more than any other religious organization.[110])

Nowhere was this work more important to the JUI's eventual political viability than in the KPK, the mountainous lands also known as the North-West Frontier Province, between Afghanistan and Pakistan. The KPK was quite ethnically, culturally, linguistically, and politically distinct from the rest of colonial India. The majority ethnic group (both then and now) is the Pashtun, a fiercely independent people who have retained their own strict code of honor called Pashtunwali.

In traditional Pashtun culture, a village *mullah* usually wielded political power only to the extent that he "managed to leverage [his] religious credibility." Thus, pre-1980s, some *mullahs* did become political actors in their own right, although their numbers remained small.[111] The connection between religious and political leadership is supported by the fact that tribal groups are largely autonomous, so core political decision making is conducted on a local level. This pattern of local governance mirrors the pattern of the autonomous *masjids* and mosques that are largely free from centralized rule and are guided by local imams and *ulema*. Religious leaders have been able to wield considerable influence with their specific local constituencies. This authority has allowed them to run for local government positions, such as that of *nazim*, a position that oversees all land transactions in a local area.[112]

The connection between religious and political power was only strengthened by the efforts of first the JUH and then the JUI to present the *ulema* as natural wielders of political power. It was most evident in pre–partition attempts to impose sharia in the province, a campaign that attracted a great deal of popular support. The *ulema* had a prime place in the JUH's vision of a sharia government, "keep[ing] watch over matters of shari'a" and guiding legislation.[113] Furthermore, the clout of the *ulema* grew as they became the face of the independence movement. As Sana Haroon writes, their "increasing popularity . . . was as much a function of the expression their politics took as it was an endorsement of their ideological position."[114] After partition, the *ulema* retreated into relative political quiescence, building a power base in their mosques and *madaris* and "assert[ing] a jealous guard over the interpretation of religion, demanding that religious commentators should not only have received a course of religious study, but should have been educated in the particular *dars-i nizami* [course of study] of Deoband."[115]

Organizationally, the JUI took the form of a network Islamist party. Power is not centralized in the hands of a core party leadership but distributed widely among a large network of political adherents in locally based *madrasahs* and mosques. Although the party adheres to the Deobandi school of Islamic thought, by the time of partition Deoband itself had long since ceased to control either the JUH or the JUI ideologically, and many of the so-called Deobandi clerics who founded the JUI had never actually studied at the Dar ul-Ulum itself.[116] Thus, from the start the JUI lacked the strict ideological discipline Maududi had provided the JI. Instead, the JUH was a loose confederation of the relatively autonomous leaders of *masjids* and *madrasahs* who banded together to promote a shared basic ideology and political interests. Each local organization maintains its own leadership and systems of governance.[117]

Network Islamist organizations such as the JUI are led by local *ulema* and clerics who do not work exclusively for the party but continue to lead congregations. Because they have identities and power bases outside the party, they retain a great deal of professional autonomy. These leaders are *of* the people in the sense that they tend to come from the middle to lower class, study at *madaris* rather than at prestigious universities, and operate outside elite social and financial circles. As opposed to the JI, elite intellectual or religious status is not a prerequisite for participation; for the JUI, sheer numbers are everything.[118] The JUI's early leaders set the tone for those who followed. Maulana Abdul Haq, an imam's son from Peshawar, was educated at Deoband and returned to Pakistan before partition and founded his own mosque. Another, Mufti Mahmud, a *pir's* son from the KPK, spent only a year at Deoband and later leveraged his position as a teacher at a prestigious *madrasah* in Multan into his election to the KPK Provincial Assembly.[119] Both men bequeathed their positions in the party to their sons: Sami ul-Haq is the leader of one faction of the JUI, the JUI-Sami, while Mufti Mahmud's son Maulana Fazlur Rehman is the leader of the JUI's most powerful branch, the JUI-Fazlur.

The JUI is commonly described as a party that exists for elections. Because its members come from outside the traditional power structure, winning sufficient support at the polls so they can join electoral coalitions at the provincial or national level is their only way to gain access to patronage goods and to influence policy.[120] As discussed later, this pursuit has often driven the JUI to take surprising stances in an effort to stay in power at any cost.

The success of the network model depends on having a presence in a large number of geographically dispersed grassroots institutions; thus, the location and proximity to religious institutions are crucial considerations for the JUI. In addition to being led primarily by local religious figures, the JUI has tended to build its party offices near religious buildings, such as *masjids*, shrines (tombs of saints), and *madaris*. Proximity to these religious establishments allows the JUI to associate the party with the religious power of the *masjid* or *madrasah* and facilitate the translation of one form of authority to the other.[121] This link is particularly critical in local elections in rural Pakistan, since religious centers equate to population centers and therefore to opportunities for mobilization. Members of the JUI and other network Islamist parties, such as the Jamaat Ulema-e-Pakistan, thus come to view their followers as the religious equivalent of the secular territory-based vote bank, or political *jagir* (fiefdom).[122]

The JUI is a religious movement that turned to politics in order to safeguard its interests—that is, the primacy of the Deobandi *ulema* in the future state of Pakistan. The party's core programmatic commitments thus reflect the Deoband's religious fundamentalism.[123] Similar to the JI, the JUI has pressed from its inception for the imposition of sharia law at a national level and looked to the state to create the conditions in which individual religious faith can flourish. The JUI has made unsuccessful attempts to pass a host of measures based on its members' interpretations of Islamic texts, including laws making the study of Arabic and the Quran mandatory for university admission, requiring that women be veiled in public, prohibiting gambling, and banning dowries.[124]

The party displays a high level of political savvy and a surprising flexibility in pursuit of those goals, however. Between 1971 and 1977, for instance, the JUI was instrumental in winning passage of laws mandating adherence to Islamic rules of inheritance, of the observance of Ramadan, and of abstinence from alcohol, but it did so through parliamentary cooperation with the left-wing PPP under Zulfiqar Bhutto.[125] (Many members of the JUI, scenting political opportunity, in fact defected to the PPP during this time.[126]) During the same period (1972–73), the JUI was able to form a government in the KPK by joining a coalition with the secular Pashtun-nationalist Awami National Party.[127] As a senior JUI leader said in an interview in 2004, "The party has religious concerns, of course, but these do not blind us to practical matters. When we have rubbish piling up that must be hauled away, we don't say 'Allah will provide.' "[128]

While the JUI and the JI largely agree on the issues, they also have significantly disagreed on points that reflect the parties' very different institutional perspectives. For one, the JUI was the first religious organization in South Asia to make protecting Islamic holy sites in Saudi Arabia a political issue. The JUI's strong stance in support of the Saudi state was at least partly motivated by the desire to access Saudi donors, and during the 1970s, the party became a main conduit for the dissemination of Wahhabi Islam (the strain of Islamic thought favored by the Saudi state) in Pakistan.[129] In return, the Saudis provided financial support for rural *madaris*. As Mariam Abou Zahab describes this period in Pakistan's history, "Mosques and *deeni madrasas* (religious schools) with sectarian affiliations were built everywhere, often on State lands, and a new kind of *maulvi* [expert in Islamic law], the 'donor-funded *maulvi*,' appeared, moving around in a Pajero with armed bodyguards."[130] These inflows of money, first from the Gulf States and then supplemented by US support for the Afghan jihad, vastly increased the power of the Deobandi *ulema*, but they also led to intramovement competition for funds and influence. Consequently, the JUI split into eleven factions during the course of the Soviet-Afghan War (late 1979 to early 1989).[131]

Support for the Saudi holy sites was also an emotionally resonant issue for the JUI's rural constituency, many of whom saved their entire lives for the *hajj* (a religiously mandated pilgrimage to Mecca). Thus, being seen as protecting the ancient sites of Mecca and Medina gave the JUI leaders additional religious legitimacy. For the JI, however, Saudi Arabia was not the leader of the pan-Islam movement. While Maududi had good relations with Saudi scholars, he had closer links to scholars and activists in Egypt (Muslim Brotherhood) and Malaysia. Hence, the JI did not see defending the holy sites in Saudi Arabia as a core part of its platform.

Although the two groups collaborated early on, the JUI and the JI have long been bitter rivals. The Deobandi *ulema* took strong issue with Maududi's program (even launching a fatwa campaign against him in 1951), and they were suspicious of his motives, believing that his goal was to control the nature of Pakistan's future Islamist society. Organized by the JI in the run-up to the 1970 elections, the massive popular demonstrations in support of an Islamic government convinced JUI leaders that a platform based on Islam could be politically successful. It left the alliance with the JI, in which it had been a mostly silent partner for over ten years, and put up its own slate of candidates.[132] This split continued through the Zia years, as the JI initially collaborated with the regime while the JUI opposed it. In 1988, the JUI chose to join the Islami Jamhoori Ittehad, the anti-PPP religious coalition.[133]

The JI-JUI split was not entirely the result of political opportunism, however. The two parties had deep ideological differences as well, particularly over the JUI's interpretation of the Quran as demanding social and economic reformation on a broad scale and not simply based on an individual-level observance. Rooted as it was in rural *madaris* and mosques, the JUI's members came into daily contact with the suffering proletariat and were acutely aware of the realities of economic injustice. From its founding, the party has been deeply concerned with the plight of Pakistanis living in poverty and has pressed accordingly for economic reforms such as land redistribution and the provision of interest-free loans. When the ruling ignored these demands, the JUI began to seek alliances with like-minded organizations, and the socialist Pakistan People's Party has been the JUI's closest ally. This element of the JUI's programmatic commitment ran directly counter to the JI's doctrines and the works of its founder Maududi, who argued that socialism in any form is *kufr*, or "un-Islamic," because socialism is intrinsically secular and dismissive of religion.[134] The party's alliance with the PPP proved to be the JUI's most successful political venture, giving it the chance to participate in a ruling coalition and enabling it to implement policy as an incumbent; but in order to obtain these outcomes, the JUI had to moderate its fundamentalist positions.

By 1970, thanks to its success in building schools and institutions that allowed it access to a huge number of rural voters, the JUI had grown to a movement of considerable size. During the 1970s and 1980s, the JUI was able to capitalize on numerous political trends in order to build legitimacy, gain access to the state apparatus, and increase its membership. Some of these changes were short lived, but others dramatically and permanently transformed the party.[135] The late 1960s to the early 1970s saw Zulfiqar Bhutto's rise to power and the consolidation of a long-running leftist trend in Pakistani politics. Forced to confront this new reality, the religious parties responded in sharply different ways. The intensely political JUI embraced Bhutto's populist message and built what would become a long-running, if not always close, relationship with the leftist PPP (now one of Pakistan's largest and most influential political parties). Despite their ideological similarities, however, Mufti Mahmud ran against and defeated Bhutto in an assembly race in the KPK in 1970. This victory underscored the JUI's regional strength, and when Bhutto became prime minister in 1973 (the first following the promulgation of Pakistan's 1973 constitution), he reached out to Mufti as a useful political partner.

A year earlier, in 1972, a similar political bargain between Mufti Mahmud and the head of the left-wing, Pashtun-nationalist National Awami Party (NAP) had made Mufti chief minister of the KPK (even though the JUI had fewer seats than did the NAP in the KPK Assembly). (NAP president Abdul Wali Khan's decision to grant the JUI the chief ministership of KPK in exchange for JUI support at the national level is an interesting example of a historically secular party shifting its position on the sharia–secularism continuum to improve its political prospects.) During his brief time in office (he resigned in 1973), Mufti promoted an aggressive Islamization program. His first address to the people of the province emphasized his intention of bringing its laws closer in line with sharia, and his government banned alcohol, made Ramadan observance mandatory, and revised inheritance laws to better accord with Islamic law.[136]

As noted previously, Mufti also joined with Jamaat-e-Islami to press for federal legislation to declare adherents of the Ahmadiyya sect non-Muslim and limit their ability to freely practice their faith. The Ahmadis had long been subject to persecution for their belief that the founder of their sect, Ghulam Mirza Ahmad, was a messianic figure and prophet. That concept is offensive to traditional Muslims, who view Muhammed as the final prophet of God.[137] The JUI, however, had more pragmatic reasons for attempting to exclude the Ahmadis; the campaign's real goal was to prevent them from being able to serve in plum civil service positions, which the JUI wanted to fill with its own supporters.

While his alliance with the PPP boosted Mufti's personal status, it also undermined the party's credibility as a defender of Islamic virtue. The JUI succeeded in using its newfound clout to pass conservative legislation and signal to its base that it was still a religious party, but it could not escape criticism for entering a marriage of convenience with a secular socialist party.[138] The need to distance itself from the PPP immediately placed a strain on the working relationships between the JUI and the rest of the coalition. At a local level, JUI activists were pushed to distance themselves from the rest of the party leadership and began preaching an even more austere platform of Islamization. Thus the party as a whole moved away from extreme Islamist positions in order to obtain political power and alienated its conservative, religious base, which it then attempted to woo back with extremist policy and rhetoric.[139]

The JUI, which had joined the anti-Bhutto Pakistan National Alliance in 1977, initially welcomed General Zia's military coup, believing that he would rescue Pakistan from Bhutto's secularism and turn the government over to the right-wing parties. But Zia's background and personality made him a better match with the JI, and that party proved the true beneficiary of the early years of his rule. The JUI withdrew from the PNA, which backed Zia, when it became clear that Zia was not going to hold true elections.[140]

The JUI's reach and influence increased significantly, however, as a result of the US-, Saudi-, and Pakistani-backed war against the Soviet forces in Afghanistan. In December 1979, the Soviet Union sent troops to support the Marxist-Leninist government in Kabul, and the Afghans responded by launching a massive insurgency under the banner of jihad. Pashtuns on both sides of the Afghan-Pakistani border highly supported jihad against the Soviet Union, partly because Soviet communism was explicitly antireligious and because the fiercely independent Pashtun people of both countries are unwilling to accept foreign rule. Thus, Afghan Muslims looked to their Pashtun brethren in Pakistan's neighboring KPK for support.

The JUI was perfectly positioned to answer that call, and the proliferation of local Islamic organizations in the KPK and the tribal areas greatly added to the party's network of institutional bases and pool of religious supporters. Deobandi clerics allied with the JUI (including current faction leaders Sami ul-Haq and Fazlur Rehman) built a network of *madaris* in the border areas that provided a steady stream of recruits to the Afghan mujahideen. The Zia government and foreign donors also supported this effort.[141] The Soviets' withdrawal from Afghanistan in 1988 and the resulting drop in donor interest in, and funding for, jihad left a large population of militant *ulema* unemployed.[142] Many of them sought political opportunities with the JUI in the KPK, and the party easily absorbed these would-be entrepreneurs into its vast network. Furthermore, the leaders of what would become the Taliban movement had been educated at JUI-linked Deobandi *madaris* in the KPK.[143] As the Taliban gained control over Afghanistan, the JUI became a crucial go-between for the Pakistani government.[144] Since the end of the Soviet-Afghan War, the party's focus has slowly shifted from leftist-infused Islamism to militancy.

Of the three Islamic party types, network Islamists such as the JUI have the most inherent mass appeal. The JUI's politically active clerics have intimate daily contact with the electorate in small rural *masjids*.[145] Through these networks, the JUI is able to disseminate religious and political messages to a large and receptive audience. As one JUI member told me, somewhat grandiloquently, "Even if we lose a given election, we have such a vast infrastructure within many communities that we are the de facto government in those areas."[146] But its flat organizational structure also means that the JUI has a limited ability to police its members and to develop a uniform message. The JUI's political operatives derive the bulk of their personal power from their status as religious authorities and not as party members. So while they have little incentive to follow the requests or dictates of party leaders, they can still claim to speak on the party's behalf.

The diversity of messages coming out of the JUI has a direct impact on the party's efficacy. Comparative political scientist David Patel, who has studied religious political movements, has found that when a political group communicated a set of divergent messages at several sites within a close geographic range or single neighborhood, Muslim voters responded either by taking no action or by voting at cross purposes. When a single unified message was presented, definitive action resulted. Patel's study of Iraq's Shia and Sunni populations shows that the Shia were able to mobilize a preexisting, well-defined religious hierarchy to "generat[e] common knowledge and shared behavioral beliefs across geographically dispersed Shiite congregations," while the comparatively decentralized Sunni clerics often sent mixed or conflicting messages, preventing Iraq's Sunnis from forming a coherent bloc.[147]

His research may explain why, despite their thinner distribution and less direct contact with voters, hierarchical Islamist parties tend to achieve better electoral results than network Islamists do. It may also help to explain why Pakistan's Islamist parties have failed to capture more than a small percentage of the national vote. Nasr, for example, argues that competition among Islamist parties in the 1970 elections actually decreased their collective share of the vote rather than merely causing it to be divided among the parties.[148]

Historically, the JUI has been disadvantaged in national-level politics by its natural constituency's relative lack of social and political power and by its general lack of incorporation into the state apparatus. The concentration of political and economic power among a small elite class is common to developing democracies and does not favor the success of true mass-based movements. Clientelistic parties tend to be most successful under these conditions because they have the most access to state benefits to offer as patronage and because they can acquire blocks of votes by coercive means through the influence of their elites. Consequently, the JUI has achieved its greatest political power at the national level by joining coalitions, whether with secular parties such as the Pakistan People's Party or with religious parties as in the Muttahida Majlis-e-Amal.[149] Perhaps with this fact in mind, its leaders proclaim their willingness "to join any movement that puts religion in its proper place within government."[150]

Despite these structural disadvantages, the JUI has performed reliably, if never spectacularly, in national elections. Toward the end of the anti-Soviet campaign in Afghanistan the JUI joined Islami Jamhoori Ittehad, a coalition of conservative and religious parties that was formed specifically to contest the dominance of the PPP. Although the PPP took the majority in the 1988 elections with 94 seats and 38 percent of the vote, the coalition presented a strong opposition, winning 56 of the 207 seats and 30 percent of the vote. Campaigning independently in 1990, in the wake of the Soviet withdrawal from Afghanistan, the JUI won only 6 seats and a little less than 3 percent of the vote. By comparison, the ideologically diverse coalition group, led by Nawaz Sharif's faction of the Pakistan Muslim League, decisively won the national assembly with 104 of the 207 seats and 37 percent of the vote. In 1993, the JUI joined and largely led the coalition Islami Jamhoori Mahaz, which then won 4 seats in the National Assembly.[151]

As mentioned previously, the JUI has split into many factions, although few have achieved much, if any, electoral impact. The most important split came in 1991, with factions forming around the two most prominent and charismatic figures—Fazlur Rehman (JUI-F) and Sami ul-Haq (JUI-S).[152] The former is the historical heir to the party's political base, and the JUI-F has historically been far more electorally successful. In the 2013 election, for instance, JUI-F won 10 seats in the National Assembly while JUI-S failed to win any. Rehman's faction also won 13 seats in the KPK Provincial Assembly, where JUI-S was also not represented.[153]

In the 2002 national elections, the Election Commission of Pakistan, under the direction of General Musharraf, increased female and minority representation in the National Assembly by adding 60 reserved seats for women and 10 for minority groups (boosting the total number of seats to 342). Notably, the 70 new seats were not to be filled by direct vote but by party nomination, with each party's share based on its electoral success.[154] With Nawaz Sharif and Benazir Bhutto—the leaders of the two most important parties, the PML-N and the PPP, respectively—disqualified from running, the pro-Musharraf Pakistan Muslim League–Quaid (PML-Q) appeared set to dominate the elections.

In an effort to give voice to the considerable opposition to Musharraf's cooperation with the United States and other Western powers in the war in Afghanistan, the JUI joined six religious parties—including the JUI-F, the JUI-S, and the JI—in a coalition called Muttahida Majlis-e-Amal Pakistan.[155] Although the MMA campaigned as vociferously anti-American, each of its members has long-standing ties to the military, and many non-MMA politicians believed that the military and the intelligence services had in fact midwifed the coalition.[156] (This suspicion was borne out by the MMA's relative moderation on security issues during its time in office.)

The MMA gained 53 seats in the National Assembly (plus an additional 14 of the reserved seats) with a little more than 11 percent of the vote (including 29 of the 35 National Assembly seats from the KPK).[157] It also won enough seats in the KPK Provincial Assembly (48 out of 99) to form a government.[158] The MMA won 6 National Assembly seats in Balochistan, as well, making it an important coalition partner with the PML-Q.[159] As these results indicate, the MMA was strongest in the rural frontier regions of Pakistan that bordered Afghanistan, where anti-Western sentiment was considerably stronger and residents had a direct connection to the Afghan war. Both the PPP and the MMA formed a significant opposition bloc in the National Assembly.

The MMA's share of the vote was the largest of any Islamist party or coalition in Pakistan's history, yet it still received less than half the votes of the PPP or PML-Q.[160] Its relative success was likely owing to the coalition's effectiveness in playing on anti-American sentiment in Pakistan (particularly among the Pashtun population of the northwest), for feelings were running high a year after the American invasion of neighboring Afghanistan.[161] Two factors also helped the MMA: Benazir Bhutto and Nawaz Sharif were in exile and prevented from running, leaving the major parties leaderless, and Musharraf had rigged the election in advance to disqualify a number of popular candidates.[162] Some analysts claim that the military forced certain militants to join a particular party and that many of them chose one or another faction of the JUI as their leaders have long-standing militant ties.[163] While the coalition won National Assembly seats in every province, the high proportion of its parliamentarians elected from the KPK and Balochistan indicate that its roots in Pakistan's population centers (Punjab and urban Sindh) were shallow at best.

The MMA's behavior while in office in the KPK at times vindicated the worst fears of Pakistan's liberal secular elite, but it also displayed surprising moderation in certain areas. One of the government's first moves was to ban such "un-Islamic" features of local life as movie posters, music played on public transportation, and the public display of instruments. Storekeepers who sold pornographic videos "voluntarily" turned them over to the police to be destroyed.[164] The MMA government followed these actions by passing a bill declaring sharia law in the province.[165] Despite this dramatic beginning, after a year in office the MMA still had made few real or substantial changes. Implementation of the Shariat bill passed in June 2003, for instance, required the KPK government to establish a number of committees, none of which had been formed as of October of that year. The government also showed signs of reconsidering controversial legislation in response to opposition from the center.[166] The MMA showed itself truly unwilling to challenge its military patrons. Indeed, JUI-F leader Fazlur Rehman was rumored to be running for the post of prime minister, promising Musharraf his full cooperation should he be selected.[167]

The MMA coalition was fragile from the start, featuring as it did an almost improbable mix of parties, ideologies, and personalities, and the International Crisis Group called it an "unnatural alliance."[168] The coalition brought together multiple factions of the Deobandi JUI (F and S) that had previously opposed each other in elections; the modernizing JI, which has a long and sometimes bitter rivalry with the JUI; the Jamiat Ulema-e-Pakistan, a party of Barelvi *ulema*, whose religious practice is markedly different from that of the Deobandis; the Ahle Hadith, or Wahhabi party Jamiat Ahle Hadith (whose Wahhabi, or Salafi, version of Islam also has significant theological differences with Deobandi Islam); and the Shia party Islami Tehrik Pakistan.[169] Announcing that all of these parties would contest elections together did not put an end to their rivalries, however, and the MMA government in the KPK often found itself trying to accommodate the leaders of minor members of the coalition.[170] Although some of the Sunni parties in the alliance are linked to violent sectarian outfits, such as the Sipah-e-Sahaba, that are primarily focused on killing Shiites, the primary tension in the alliance was not between the Islami Tehrik Pakistan and the Sunni parties but between the JUI factions and the JI. The power struggles between the JUI-F and the JI eventually doomed the alliance, which broke up in 2007.[171]

Despite growing anti-American, anti-Western, and by extension anti-Musharraf sentiment in Pakistan, the 2008 elections were not as readily open to the confessional parties as the 2002 elections had been, mostly because they were held under far freer circumstances than the 2002 Musharraf-controlled contests had been. In the wake of Benazir Bhutto's assassination, the PPP had the greatest momentum going into the election, drawing sympathy from a broad spectrum of the population and being perceived as the greatest threat to Musharraf and the PML-Q. The PML-Q's reputation as a Musharraf puppet worked to the benefit of the PML-N, which by contrast was seen as a legitimate moderate party. Furthermore, the PML-N's charismatic leader, Nawaz Sharif, had been allowed to return from exile. The PPP and PML-N took 168 of the 270 seats in the National Assembly, leaving only 102 seats to be split among the remaining parties.

Although the JI and the JUI-F had previously agreed to boycott the elections to protest Musharraf's continued rule, the JUI-F reneged on this deal at the last minute and won 7 seats and a little more than 2 percent of the vote.[172] Although the JUI-F had partnered with Musharraf's PML-Q in Balochistan during the previous administration and was generally perceived as a pro-Musharraf party, its long-standing ideological and personal ties to the Taliban in Afghanistan made it a natural supporter of the PPP's proposed "political solution" to the conflict in Afghanistan and in Pakistan's tribal areas. Thus, after the elections the JUI-F joined a coalition at the center with the PPP and the Awami National Party (its former rival in the KPK).[173] A JUI leader reminded those who might be surprised by this alliance that "we have much in common with the secularists. There are many policies and principles of governance that we agree on. The media makes it seem like we are always at each other's throat. There is much more cooperation than people know."[174]

The 2013 elections brought the JUI-F modest electoral success: ten National Assembly seats, thirteen seats in the KPK Provincial Assembly, and six in the

Balochistan Provincial Assembly.[175] Despite much discussion, the JI was unwilling to join the reincarnated MMA (or the JUI-F was unwilling to invite it), leaving the JUI-F to run as part of a coalition with a number of smaller Islamist parties.[176] The most important story of the 2013 elections, however, was the Taliban's rampant campaign of violence, which stifled electoral activity in much of the Pashtun belt and even in Pakistan's cities. In December 2012, the Pakistani Taliban had announced that it would target Pakistan's secular parties, and it proved true to its word, attacking campaign rallies and assassinating politicians of the PPP, NAP, and Muttahida Qaumi Movement.[177] The Pakistani Taliban even targeted JUI-F leader Fazlur Rehman for his cooperation with the PPP government.[178] Taliban violence against the NAP, the JUI-F's traditional rival for the Pashtun vote, could not fail to boost the JUI-F's electoral chances. In May 2013, the JUI-F had failed to prevent the Muslim democratic party Pakistan Tehrik-e-Insaf from forming a coalition government in the KPK, and it was negotiating the terms of its cooperation with the PML-N at the center.[179] Some reports suggested that Fazlur Rehman was anxious to position himself as the prime interlocutor in the expected Pakistani government negotiations with the Pakistani Taliban.[180]

As its experiences during the 2013 elections suggest, the JUI has a complex relationship with militancy and with the democratic system that Pakistan's militants have sworn to overthrow. The JUI members have long-standing militant ties. Sami ul-Haq, leader of the JUI-S, is known as the "father" of the Taliban because many of the movement's leaders attended his madrasah at Akora Khattak.[181] Wali Ur Rehman, the Tehrik-e-Taliban Pakistan's deputy chief until his death in May 2013, was a member of the JUI-F before he took up arms.[182] Yet, as noted, the JUI-F was not exempt from terrorist violence during the campaign, and analysts suggested that the Pakistani Taliban turned on Fazlur Rehman not only for his alliance with the secular PPP but also as punishment for his refusal to participate in the pro-militant Difa-e-Pakistan Council.[183]

Interviews with JUI leaders reveal that their own feelings on the issue are somewhat mixed. One senior leader told me that he and his fellow party members were "sworn to peace and will fight our battles on the campaign trail," but they were also "willing to die for [their] beliefs."[184] Another attempted to justify his party's participation in the democratic process by explaining that the JUI was seeking a new form of democracy: "It is true that democracy, prima facie, is at odds with our religion. However, that is just one form of democracy, the one that the West holds to. In fact, there is more than one kind of democracy."[185]

What form, exactly, this new kind of democracy will take is unclear. In interviews, JUI leaders are unable to offer more than vague platitudes regarding their political program. For instance, they promise that the introduction of sharia will automatically end corruption and that the JUI "will provide people with the necessities of life, as well as of the spirit."[186] The JUI's ability to effect radical reform was tested and found wanting during the party's tenure in power in the KPK. Its members remain convinced, however, that their party is "the future of the Muslim nations."[187]

Islamist Parties: Shared Assets and Obstacles

Islamist parties have some strategic advantages over their Muslim democratic counterparts. Islamist parties are closely aligned with educational and religious institutions, so they have a natural means of accessing and connecting with potential supporters. In the case of network Islamists, parties gain physical access to voters through their local mosques and *madaris* (as in the JUI-F's vast network of madaris in Pakistan's Pashtun belt), and in the case of hierarchical Islamists, access occurs through voters' exposure to pervasive cultural, religious, and philosophical ideas (such as the heavily JI-influenced Pakistani public school curriculum). Also, since network Islamist political leaders are almost invariably religious leaders as well, their words are automatically imbued with authority by devout Muslims. A respected cleric delivering a political argument during a sermon can be extremely persuasive simply because of the setting and the listener's receptivity.

Islamist political organizations also hold in their hand a powerful political weapon, the fatwa. The cleric's followers widely regard this religious edict as having the force of scripture. If a Muslim refuses to follow a fatwa, it is believed that he or she will suffer direct spiritual consequences and will have to work harder to be seen as acceptable to God in the afterlife. If a cleric issues a fatwa to Muslim voters to select a certain Islamist party or candidate, as far as that cleric's followers are concerned, voting is no longer a matter of personal choice but one of religious duty. Imam Nazim Ali, Pakistani Deobandi scholar and JUI leader, would preface political fatwas with verses from the Quran that underscored the moral imperative of adherence: "Then it is only a part of the Book that ye believe in, and do ye reject the rest? But what is the reward for those among you who behave like this but disgrace in this life?—And on the Day of Judgment they shall be consigned to the most grievous penalty. For Allah is not unmindful of what ye do" (Quran 2:85).

Pakistani *ulema* have not hesitated to attempt to use fatwas to affect electoral outcomes. For example, renowned Deobandi scholar Maulana Mahmood Ahmed Mirpuri was asked before the 2002 election whether devout Muslims could possibly vote for secular parties whose candidates were "not proper practicing Muslims." Maulana issued a fatwa in response. Using the word *zuroor* (duty) to connote an obligation so great that it is almost a requirement, Maulana essentially argued that true Muslims vote for religiously devout political leaders:

> Pakistan is a Muslim country. It was founded in the name of Islam but, unfortunately, it's [*sic*] aim of being so has not been fulfilled and Islamic Shari'ah has not been implemented.

> It is the duty of all Muslims to work hard and achieve this golden purpose of implementing Islamic Shari'ah in Pakistan. Taking part in elections and voting for suitable candidates is also part of this struggle.
>
> Therefore it is the duty of Pakistani citizens to use their right of vote for candidates who are true Muslims and who want to work for a better society and to implement Islamic law. It is dishonest to use the power of a vote in favour of unsuitable candidates.[188]

Islamist parties, including the JUI and the JI, promoted and defended Maulana's edict during the 2002 campaign.[189]

In the case of *ulema* parties such as the JUI, furthermore, the politicians themselves may issue fatwas regarding their own support. Shortly before the 2013 elections, Fazlur Rehman declared that voting for the Muslim democratic party Pakistan Tehrik-e-Insaf was *haram* (forbidden) under Islamic law.[190] Rehman's fatwa failed to prevent the party from winning a plurality of seats—thirty-five to the JUI-F's thirteen—in the KPK Provincial Assembly.

As the success of the Pakistan Tehrik-e-Insaf on both the national and provincial levels indicates, fatwas are of mixed benefit in Pakistan's electoral campaigns. Because religious institutions are free to issue as many fatwas as they want and fatwas are largely the result of an individual cleric's judgment, any one topic will often be the subject of conflicting fatwas. Fatwas normally carry a time line or a caveat that it applies until conditions change. While religious councils may deem certain fatwas more appropriate than others, few mechanisms exist for preventing fatwa abuse. Fatwas derive their importance from the voices that issue them. While the strength of individual clerics and the platform of key Islamist parties can amplify a fatwa's message, a cleric's words may not carry much weight for those who are not already his followers. In many cases, followers—not leaders—are the ones who monitor the implementation of fatwas, whether they involve catching a politician buying alcohol, seeing women organize freely on college campuses, or finding billboards and television ads that depict women without proper covering. While fatwas have significance to many Muslims in their individual practice, they are difficult to implement on an organization or community level, as the difficulty of forcing state institutions to ban *riba* demonstrates. Although multiple fatwas have ruled against the practice, all of Pakistan's major banks continue to operate on a system of interest and allow customers to obtain interest-bearing savings accounts.

While Islamist parties have limited access to the national-level patronage networks that Muslim democrats rely on, they are able to leverage their local entrenchment in political, religious, and academic institutions to channel material benefits—the most important of which is land—to their constituents. In many rural, postcolonial nations, land is the preeminent measure of wealth and the primary distinguishing characteristic between the rural poor and rural elites. The majority of the rural population still lives and works on land rented from pseudo-feudal landlords. Few tenants have the liquidity to bargain, and fewer still have relationships with banking institutions. Even the smallest parcel of land is of incredible value as a source of collateral for agricultural micro loans and larger credit transactions. It is used as dowries for weddings and passed via inheritance from generation to generation. In this context, the local *patwari*, who is responsible for keeping land records via a complex system of maps, becomes an incredibly important figure. The *patwari* adjudicates all transfers of land, whether by sale, dowry, inheritance, or debt payment. He also resolves all land disputes and has the final say on delineating the boundary lines of local properties. The *patwari* is appointed (or removed) by a single elected official, the *nazim*. Through this mechanism local political strength translates into material advantage in rural areas.

In general, Islamists of both types face significant obstacles to competing effectively on a national stage, even though the country is largely Muslim. Islamist parties enjoy enormous benefits as a result of their close connections to religious institutions, but these affiliations present some political challenges as well. Islamist organizations are, in a very real sense, beholden to their sponsoring religious orders, sects, and mosques. Any political messaging, therefore, must be calibrated to adhere to a specific theological understanding of the Quran. Followers and political leaders alike will scrutinize political statements to ensure their consistency with Islamic text and doctrines. This effort presents difficulties not only because clerics even from the same sect may differ over specific religious questions but also the language Islamist parties use to reach out to prospective supporters is often tedious and lengthy. It is not easy to turn careful theological exegesis into a punchy and memorable sound bite.

Islamist political parties are found to have greater electoral success when the party's economic platform is vague. While it may appear counterintuitive that voters would gravitate toward a party in which the economic specifics go undisclosed, this approach allows the Islamists' most distinguishing factor in gaining voter support, religious ideology, to come to the forefront. Furthermore, a vague platform is easier to communicate informally, and political activists do not need to have a proficient understanding of complex economic conditions and policies. They can capitalize instead on the public's fears about the state's economic status without having to defend any specific solutions.

Islamist organizations have traditionally existed outside ruling political circles both by force and by choice. The dominant political and economic elites at the time of partition recognized that full implementation of sharia would upend the liberal post-feudal economic model on which their power rested. To defend against incursions by overtly religious political parties, the elite secular leaders and Muslim democrats undertook campaigns to repress Islamist groups. The most glaring example of this oppression is found in the repeated incarceration and eventual capital sentencing of Maulana Maududi. Initially imprisoned from 1948 to 1950, he was arrested again after the Lahore riots of 1953. He was eventually convicted of sedition for his writings regarding the Ahmadiyya and was sentenced to death. The court delayed his execution, then commuted and eventually reversed the sentence. The prosecution of Maududi is only one instance of state oppression that Islamist parties see themselves as having experienced. The anti-Ahmadiyya campaign was hugely popular among Islamists, despite (or perhaps because of) the destruction it caused for the Ahmadi community.

The Islamists' outsider status does raise doubts among pragmatic Muslim voters over whether Islamist politicians will have the ability to make good on their campaign promises if they are elected. Given the limitations of purely Islamist ideological positions and policies for political success, it is not surprising that Islamist parties have shifted between moderate and extreme postures across the course of their development. As shown in more detail in subsequent chapters, these moves have been driven by political expediency rather than by ideological imperatives.

CHAPTER 6

ISLAMIC VOTERS IN PAKISTAN

Motives and Behavior

In chapters 4 and 5 I describe the historical catalysts, ideological underpinnings, organizational models, and historical growth of the three main Islamic parties in Pakistan, each of which represents one of the three key party types. Clearly ideology—whether it is religious, as in the case of Islamists, or economic, as in the case of Muslim democrats—drives party emergence and development among Islamic confessional parties. However, ideology alone does not guide voting behavior. In chapter 7 I show how each of these parties and party types become more instrumental and more guided by pragmatic political considerations over time. That is not to say that they adopt more moderate ideologies; rather, they fall sway to instrumentalism. Conventional wisdom holds that participation in electoral politics will push parties to moderate their positions. I argue that in the Pakistani context, participation doesn't necessarily lead to moderation but to instrumentalism, in which such concepts as the enforcement of sharia are less of a goal in themselves but rather a means to an end. Political parties in Pakistan make decisions about where to position themselves on the sharia–secularism continuum based on their electoral level (district, province, nation), their target audience, the political climate, and the relative position of competitor parties. In some instances it makes sense for an Islamic confessional party to become more extreme; in other instances they will moderate. My argument is political parties that shift toward greater extremism do so not strictly out of ideological absolutism or increased fundamentalism but based on internal political calculations about when, where, and from whom to gain votes.

In large part, the underlying pragmatism of Islamic confessional party behavior has been either misinterpreted or missed altogether because scholars have not properly understood the priorities, biases, motivations, and interests of voters in Muslim-majority democracies. In this chapter, through original survey and field research, I try to fill in that missing piece. My conclusions about voter behavior support the argument that Islamic confessional parties are responding directly to targeted electorates when they decide to make more or less extreme programmatic commitments.

One assumption that leads to the misinterpretation concerns the role of religion in Muslim countries. Until recently, social scientists widely asserted that religion would fade from political life as modernization and scientific understanding increased, as it had in many Western countries.[1] Yet faith has not faded to irrelevancy in Muslim societies. Even as the Muslim world modernizes and adopts scientific and technological innovations, religion remains an important part of political life. The aspiration for some expression of religion at the public and political level can be seen in the electoral success of Islamic parties over the past ten years and most clearly in the recent Arab Spring. In Turkey a Muslim democratic party has won two consecutive national elections, in Malaysia, a Muslim democratic party has fared well in recent election cycles, and in Egypt's first post-Mubarak elections, the Islamist Muslim Brotherhood won the presidency (but ultimately was pushed out of office). In Pakistan, through their political participation, Jamaat-e-Islami and Jamiat Ulema-e-Islam have become key players in electoral politics, and the Pakistan Muslim League serves as the main center-right power broker. Even Islamist parties achieved considerable success in 2003, garnering majority control in the KPK province and significant seats in Pakistan's Senate. While their electoral support decreased considerably in 2008, they have remained relevant in the public discourse as influential third parties and with hefty street power. But the starkest example of religio-political parties can be found in Egypt (as noted earlier), where the Muslim Brotherhood and the Salafist Al-Nour (The Light) Party won 60 percent vote in the December 2011 elections. The Muslim world's political experience has shown a different model than the one anticipated by social scientists.

Confronted with these unexpected phenomena, scholars have been pressed to come up with an explanation that goes beyond the purely reductionist and untestable argument that we are seeing the last throes of political religiosity in the struggle between modernity, globalization, and tradition.[2] Yet assumptions continue to determine the debate. After September 11, 2001, the US government tasked a bipartisan committee with detailing the events leading up to the attacks on the United States. In spite of the commission's thoroughness, its final document, *The 9/11 Commission Report*, reiterated common explanations about the cause of Islamist militancy: "Pakistan's endemic poverty, widespread corruption, and often ineffective government create opportunities for Islamist recruitment. Poor education is a particular concern. Millions of families, especially those with little money, send their children to religious schools, or *madrasahs*. Many of these schools are the only opportunity available for an education, but some have been used as incubators for extremism."[3] Essentially, the commission argued that poverty, desperation, religiosity, and viral militancy drive support for extreme Islamist political organizations.

Quantitative research provides more tenable explanations. Jacob Shapiro and C. Christine Fair have classified, summarized, and tested common assumptions about the bases of Islamist militancy in Pakistan in a series of groundbreaking research projects.[4] Although their analysis is descriptive of extremist groups, it appears germane to assumptions about the success of Islamic confessional parties in Pakistan and other Muslim-majority nations. Little distinction has been made in Western analyses of how Islamic political parties differ both among themselves and from Islamist extremist groups. Shapiro and Fair find that five common assumptions hold true to Western policy regarding Pakistan's Islamist extremists, and cognates of these hypotheses are proposed in this book as core popular assumptions about Pakistan's Islamist parties. Common assumptions on militancy hold that (1) there is a "taste for militancy" among Pakistanis who support such groups, meaning that they favor militant actions in general; (2) poverty underlies Islamist extremism or makes violence more accepted; (3) religiosity and personal validation of sharia underlie Islamist extremism; (4) Islamic party support is indicative of the population's Islamist extremism or proclivity for extremism; and (5) support for democracy is synonymous with opposition to Islamist and militant support.[5]

These assumptions about Pakistani Islamist militancy correlate to assumptions about Islamic parties in Pakistan. These assumptions include the following notions: (1) There is a "taste for Islamism" among the supporters of Islamist political parties; (2) support for militant Islamist extremism *causes* Islamist party support and its corollary that (3) Islamist party support causes support for militancy; (4) poverty—and its related condition, illiteracy—generates support for militant organizations and, by extension, for Islamist parties; (5) personal religiosity and belief in sharia generate support for militant organizations and therefore support for Islamist parties; and (6) support for democracy necessarily means opposition to Islamist militancy and therefore opposition to Islamist political parties, and its corollary that (7) antidemocratic beliefs generate support for militant organizations, which in turn lead to support for Islamist parties.[6]

For the purposes of this chapter, I define "militancy" as the use of political violence by organized nonstate groups. Similarly, I define a "militant" organization or group as an organized nonstate (although it may be state-supported) group that uses violence against Pakistani or foreign targets to advance its political agenda. Militant groups in Pakistan are numerous and diverse, with vastly different backgrounds, goals, and aims. Some are in fact supported by the state and target their strikes at India or North Atlantic Treaty Organization and Afghan forces in Afghanistan. Others, especially those formed in the last ten years, have turned against the Pakistani state. They employ a wide variety of tactics, from suicide bombings in crowded civilian areas to commando-style raids on Pakistani military bases and guerrilla warfare against Pakistani troops.[7] One of the few commonalities of such groups, however, is that they almost universally justify their attacks with references to religion. They claim they are freeing "oppressed" Muslims from American or Indian "infidels"; exterminating Pakistan's Shias, whom many militants consider to be non-Muslim; or overthrowing a "godless" state.

I divide the phenomenon of "religiosity" into two types—public and personal. An individual's public religiosity is defined as his or her views on the roles that religion should play in government and that government should take in the management of religion. Perspectives on public religiosity include support for fully instituting sharia in Pakistan, different views of the role that religious scholars and institutions should assume in governance, on how much say the government should have in setting the curriculum for religious schools, and so on. Personal (not necessarily private) religiosity is a measure of personal engagement with religion reflected in the number of times a day a subject prays, the number of times a week he or she attends a mosque or participates in organized religious activity, and the importance of personal religious faith in a subject's worldview. As this chapter discusses, these two types of religiosity are far more loosely correlated than we might assume.

My survey dealt with two distinct levels of attitudes toward democracy. On the one hand, I questioned survey respondents on their beliefs about democratic governance by asking them their opinions of various state institutions, such as local governments and the judiciary, and the provision of services. While not all of these institutions are necessarily democratic in the sense that their members and employees are elected, for most citizens they form the face of Pakistan's current (democratic) constitutional order. Furthermore, Pakistanis expect such institutions to be responsive to their needs in a sort of human-scale microcosm of "democracy." I thus use opinions about these institutions as a proxy for support or distrust of Pakistan's democratic state. I also measure feelings about democracy itself more directly by asking respondents their views on core democratic values.[8]

Survey Hypotheses

All of these assumptions are based on unexamined premises and reveal more about academic and popular bias than about the society they purport to study. Of these egregious biases, the most fundamental one holds that there is no variation between Islamic parties and no meaningful distinction between Islamist parties and Islamist militants. Variations on this theme dominate the current discourse even though the underlying assumptions have received little systematic examination. To address the lack of empirical support for these assertions, I have characterized each of them as theories or explanatory models for Islamic party support. I have developed testable hypotheses based on these theories and conducted original surveys and interviews of Pakistani voters in order to draw some factually based conclusions about voter motivation and support for Islamic confessional parties. I find little support for these common conceptions of Islamic party voter behavior and motivation in the data. Instead, ample evidence reveals that a set of complex, intertwined factors drive voters' motivations.

First, the theory that support for militant Islamic organizations results in support for Islamist parties is favored among Western media and policy analysts because it simplifies Islamic political motivations and actions under a conveniently generalized fanatical umbrella. The theory also assumes that voters who support one militant organization are inclined to support militancy and Islamist movements in general. A Pakistani who supports Islamic militant resistance in Kashmir, for example, is assumed to be more likely to support Islamist militant groups such al-Qaeda, the Taliban, or Hezbollah. In short, the assumption holds that these voters lack political acumen and will simply vote for the Islamist opposition. They are believed not to have distinctive political concerns tethered to the militant or policy actions of a specific organization but simply to have a preference for Islamist organizations in general.[9]

This view underlies the common Western presumption that Pakistan's Islamic parties are somehow tied to al-Qaeda, although evidence of any such linkage has never surfaced. Meanwhile, the premise has strong implications at the level of voter behavior. If those who vote for Islamist parties do so because of a general preference for Islamist organizations, such that the voters make no distinction between their support for militants and their support for political parties, then there is no logical basis for distinguishing among different Islamic parties either. This reasoning leads to a clearly testable hypothesis: $H_0 1$, voters who support any Islamic party, support them all. The alternative hypothesis is that voters who support Islamic parties discriminate among them and lend support only to a specific party or set of parties. Should the alternative hypothesis be supported by the data and voters are found to discriminate between parties, a general preference for Islamism must be ruled out as a viable explanation for Islamic party support.[10]

The second theory derives from the first. If voters have a preference for Islamist organizations as a whole and if no marked boundary exists between Islamist militant groups and Islamic political parties, then support for Islamist militancy leads to support for Islamist political parties. Thus, the more the electorate accepts or even embraces Islamist militant ideologies and activities, the more likely the voters are going to support a political party that falls under the presumed umbrella of an Islamist organization. This commonly held Western view of Islamic parties was touted during the 2008 elections in Pakistan, when Western media assumed that the Taliban's growing influence in the Federally Administered Tribal Areas (FATA) meant that Islamic parties would enjoy success at the polls.[11]

A corollary of the idea that militancy leads to support for confessional politics is that confessional political activism leads to militancy. There is conjecture that voters and parties that are chiefly concerned with implementing sharia have had limited success achieving their goals through electoral politics, so these political actors may be prone to adopting or supporting militant extra-electoral tactics.

Some Islamic parties may even put sharia implementation at the top of their agenda to signal to voters that they are willing to use extra-electoral means to achieve their ends. Support for militancy, it is supposed, extends not only to the conduct of political parties but to organizations outside the political process as well. The argument is that voters who share Islamist militant groups' or terrorist organizations' concerns over the implementation of sharia are less likely to perceive these groups as threats and may be more inclined to see their operations as justifiable. The perceived association between Islamic confessional parties and Islamist militancy, violence, and vigilantism is evidenced by the fact that, prior to Pakistan's 2008 general election, many international observers worried that if Islamic parties prevailed, militants would enjoy a more permissive operational environment.

These fears were briefly realized in the 2002 elections held under General Musharraf when the Muttahida Majlis-e-Amal, a loose coalition of Islamist parties, came in a strong third place.[12] This pro-Taliban coalition also took control of the provincial assembly in the North-West Frontier Province (now Khyber Pakhtunkhwa) and led a coalition in Balochistan that promoted the sustenance of an ideological and religious atmosphere for the Taliban insurgency.[13]

However, the two preceding theories cannot be readily separated, because a causal direction cannot be confirmed at this time. Only the first version—that Islamic militancy causes Islamic political party success—is salient within the context of this study. The theory leads to the following testable hypothesis: $H_0 2$, support for Islamic parties is positively related to support for militant organizations. The alternative hypothesis is that there is no relationship between support for Islamic party ideologies and support for militancy. Although the direction cannot be determined, should the alternative theory be supported by the data, *both* theories must be ruled out.[14]

The fourth theoretical premise is the materialist theory that poverty and illiteracy generate support for Islamist parties. It is based on the argument that voters collectively organize in order to obtain material benefits and that confessional parties maximize the voters' chances of gaining access to jobs, goods, services, and markets.[15] The materialism approach advances the notion that voters are instrumentalist. They emphasize their own religious identity through confessional party membership because it is the best available method to pursue their individual material interests. It assumes that citizens act rationally and make political decisions in relation to costs and benefits. In a state where voters compete for inadequate resources—jobs, food, shelter, water—political power is particularly important because it affords access to material resources. The materialist theory also necessarily assumes that Islamic parties are perceived as the best vehicle for obtaining such material benefits, since it is only if a confessional party wins power that individuals who supported that party are rewarded by having their material needs satisfied. The materialist theory underlies many Western policies toward

Pakistan; the West aids economic development, particularly in the KPK, on the grounds that this effort will decrease political support for both Islamist militants and Islamic parties.[16] This premise again suggests a clearly testable hypothesis: $H_0 3$, lower socioeconomic status is positively correlated to support for Islamic parties. The alternative is that there is no relationship between socioeconomic status and support for Islamic parties.

The argument that religious commitment drives support for Islamic parties rests on sociopsychological theories about voter behavior. Rather than being motivated out of desire for material gains, this set of theories holds that support for political parties is motivated by psychological needs. Individuals join confessional movements to improve the standing of their religious group in order to build self-esteem, perceived social worth, and communal standing in relation to other groups.[17] (Chandra argues that materialist and sociopsychological motivations are not mutually exclusive and that voters may join confessional movements out of desire for both material goods and psychic benefits.) In Pakistan, the linkage between religious identity, psychological need, and Islamic party participation is evidenced in policy debates about educational reform. Much of the West's concern with education in Pakistan has been aimed at curtailing the influence and curricular latitude of *madrasahs*. The common assumption is that such education fosters Islamic fundamentalism, which in turn is assumed to advance Islamism and militancy. In essence, Western policymakers widely perceive *madrasahs* as recruitment centers for Islamist militants and, by extension, for Islamic party supporters.[18] Thus, the debate about educational reform in Pakistan veils the real concern over the proliferation of fundamentalist religious ideology through education; that is, Islamic religiosity leads to or causes Islamist militancy and Islamic party support. This issue suggests a fourth testable hypothesis: $H_0 4$, there is a positive relationship between religiosity and support for Islamic organizations. The alternative hypothesis is that there is no relationship between religiosity and support for Islamic organizations.

Western policymakers and analysts often assume that democracy exists in opposition to Islam. This belief arises in part from the confounding of democracy with secular liberalism, which co-occur so commonly in Western democratic systems and the West's historical experience that they are presumed to be inseparable. More specifically, the secular liberal concept of the separation of church and state is presumed to be a necessary condition for democracy, but it is at odds with those Islamic principles that demand the presence of the divine in all things, including government. Despite this salient point, the perception and presumption is nevertheless that democracy and Islamic political party support are antithetical to each other.

The theory has been tested to some degree with mixed results. Political scientist Kathleen Collins, by studying the conditions under which Islamic political organizations are able to mobilize most effectively, has found evidence for the idea that voters who lack faith in democratic institutions or who disagree with core democratic values are more likely to support Islamic parties. Collins argues that Islamic parties are most successful in states characterized by political and economic uncertainty and where Islamic ideologies compete with failed democratic and nationalist ideologies.[19] Collins's assertion rests on the notion that Islamist parties are better able to coordinate voters' frustration with current governance on vague platforms. When Islamist parties say, "Islam is the solution," they are able to transmit emotive feelings of allegiance on religious identity toward popular political support. While Collins brings up an interesting point about channeling frustrations, she is not able to distinguish between Islamist support at various levels of aggregation. Why are Islamists at the local level able to achieve more electoral success? By contrast, Shapiro and Fair found no clear link between support for democratic processes or principles and support for Islamist and even militant organizations in Pakistan. Their qualitative findings also suggest that Pakistanis do not inherently see democracy and Islamism as incompatible constructs.[20]

Still, the theory remains to be tested and leads to a pair of related hypotheses: $H_0$5a, there is a negative relationship between faith in democratic institutions and support for Islamic parties. The alternative is that there is no relationship between faith in democratic institutions and support for Islamic parties. The second is $H_0$5b, which predicts that there is a negative relationship between endorsement of core democratic values and support for Islamic parties. The alternative is that there is no relationship between agreement with core democratic values and support for Islamic parties.[21]

The relationship between patronage and support for Islamic parties is a less frequent subject of debate (or assumption) in Western discussions about political Islam. I argue in the preceding chapters that regardless of their ideological orientation, the parties' ability to access and distribute state resources is a crucial determinant of power and popular support. Personal access to patronage and its relationship to individual voting patterns and party support is difficult to measure directly, but the survey questions that deal with personal views regarding state institutions do provide some insight into this issue. We would expect that Pakistanis who are shut out of the patronage and favor system, first, would have stronger negative views of those state institutions, such as local government and the police, that are heavily lubricated by patronage and contacts and, second, would be more likely to support the promise of wholesale change held out by the Islamist parties. Thus, to reiterate hypothesis $H_0$5a, we expect that respondents with lower faith in Pakistan's institutions will be more likely to support Islamist movements.

The empirical studies from which these theories have been derived were based largely on the electoral experiences of confessional parties in the West. As detailed in chapter 3, voting theories derived by such examinations are not valid as applied to Islamic parties.[22] Where there have been studies that included Islamic parties, they have usually been conducted in countries with only one Islamic party or they have grouped all parties with any religious orientation into a single category. But, of course, many Muslim-majority countries—such as Indonesia, Pakistan, and Iran—have multiple, viable Islamic parties that differ widely in their interpretations of the Quran and the proper role of Islam in public policy. Theories that fail to differentiate among Islamic parties or to account for the strategic interactions between parties are simply not useful in analyzing the political dynamics in a nation like Pakistan.

To address some of the gaps in our understanding of voter behavior and voting trends regarding Islamic political parties in Muslim-majority nations, I have conducted an original analysis of survey data about voter attitudes and behavior that allows me to draw some inferences about what actually motivates support for Islamic confessional parties. The survey instrument was developed and intricately customized. The questionnaire consisted of ninety-three multiple choice and open-ended items that probed the respondents' views regarding political parties, voting patterns, participation incentives, and religious tendencies. Vignette survey techniques were also used to examine the respondents' views of Islamist groups and militant political movements. Vignette survey techniques embed short messages in stories or anecdotes and allow one to examine how Islamic party slogans—such as "God watches who you vote for" or "Voting is a duty for which you will be held responsible in the afterlife" The techniques "allow one to examine how Islamic party slogans" influence voting behavior and actions toward political organizations.

The survey was administered to a total of 3,532 respondents in two three-month intervals, in 2007 and 2009. The respondents were picked using random stratified sampling and controlling for regional demographics, including gender, religion, and class. I conducted the survey research with a team of research assistants to minimize surveyor bias and nonresponse rates.[23] The respondents were picked using stratified sampling to account for ethnicity, gender, and religious background. While equal participation across provinces was not achieved, weighted samples were used to account for participants in Balochistan.

In analyzing the data, I examined how individuals viewed a series of topics, including their views on the current political system, political parties, and the military. Stepwise hierarchical regression analyses of the survey data were conducted to test the effect of the identified predictor variables on electoral outcomes for Islamist and Muslim democratic parties. The survey analysis surveyed Pakistani voters in general and assessed why they voted for an Islamic party as opposed to other options, including secular parties. The survey examined the assumptions and objectives of Pakistani voters regardless of their affiliation, whether it was for secular, independent, or Islamic parties. If they supported Islamic parties, the survey was able to examine why they voted for a specific Islamic party, such as the JI, JUI, or PML-N. I summarize my findings in the following section; disaggregated data tables may be found in appendix 2.

Although the current analysis did not warrant it, evidence shows that path analysis would be appropriate for subsequent causal studies. Path analysis will be able to examine the logic of Pakistani voters and why they voted for one group over the other. These types of in-depth focus groups provide valuable data and help us examine the logic of political decision making.

Survey Analysis

An analysis of the survey results yields important empirical insights on voting behavior and Muslim confessional parties in Pakistan. The hypothesis (H_01) that voters who support Islamic parties do not differentiate between them and express blanket support for all such organizations is not supported by the survey data (or by raw electoral data, which is examined in greater detail in chapter 7). Both historically and in the present, the JUI, the JI, and the Muslim League have continued to receive very different levels of support, although they are all Islamic parties. Voters make consistent distinctions between Muslim democratic parties and Islamist parties, with the former receiving a relatively higher positive rating than the latter. In 22 percent of the cases, support for the JUI was negatively correlated with support for the JI. Conversely, in 31 percent of cases, support for the JUI was negatively conditionally correlated with support for the JI. Even more dramatically, in 65.5 percent of the cases, support for either Islamist party was negatively conditionally correlated with support for the Muslim League.

This finding signals deep differences in how voters viewed various Islamic parties. In addition, voters for one party were less likely to support another fellow Islamic party. The untested assumption that a unifying interest in Islam and Islamic political rule is strong enough to create overlap and fluidity among the supporters of the three main types of Islamic political parties is false. Not only is there no positive correlation between support for one Islamic party and another, but also there is actually evidence of a negative correlation.

These significant findings bear on political theory regarding Islam and democracy. They suggest that if a voter cannot support the Islamic party of his or her choice, the voter is more likely to support a secular party over another Islamic party. In chapter 7 I discuss specifically how the lack of transference among Islamic parties affects party calculations about pursuing extremist ideologies. Here I examine the significance of this finding in terms of support for the JUI, the JI, and the Muslim democrats on the national and local level and in developing a realistic theory of voter behavior in Muslim-majority democracies.

Known as in-group bias, the phenomenon has been noted, studied, and theorized about in numerous other contexts. The core question scholars have tried to resolve is, given two choices, why would a voter support the candidate or party with whom they have *less* in common? Most models start with the premise that individuals' political behaviors and attitudes are primarily motivated by self-interest. Political scientists James H. Fowler and Cindy D. Kam have recently questioned that premise, arguing that self-interest cannot be the only factor: "Although an individual may derive personal benefits from a certain political outcome, the probability that a single act of participation will significantly affect the outcome is very small in large populations. This gives individuals an incentive to avoid the costs of participation and free ride on the efforts of others, producing the well-known paradox of participation."[24]

Fowler and Kam undertook an empirical study to determine what other determinants influence political participation and voter behavior. They postulated that individuals make political decisions for personal, but nonmaterial, psychic gains such as "satisfying a sense of citizen obligation, affirming their allegiance to the political system, or reinforcing their own sense of efficacy."[25] They also postulated that other-regarding interest is another important motivating factor and should not be presumed to be irrational. Fowler and Kam argue that voters are often mindful of the welfare of others with regard to their political activities. To test these theories, Fowler and Kam conducted a set of field tests to draw out factors other than self-interest that affect the beliefs, actions, and participation of voters in a political system.

The study found that in addition to self-interest, voters tend to use one of two additional methods to guide their political participation—social identification or altruism. Social identifiers have a desire to improve the welfare of certain groups in society (that they either are members of or have psychological attachments to) and possibly at the expense of other groups. A strong distinction exists among these individuals between their in-groups and out-groups. They participate in ways that give them an opportunity to help their preferred groups. An individual may even prioritize in-group interests over narrow self-interest but will not assist an out-group. Altruists are willing to sacrifice narrow self-interest to benefit others in general, regardless of identity or group membership. These individuals will participate when they believe their actions will improve conditions for everyone. Overall, Fowler and Kam concluded that "the benefit from participation may be derived by some combination of self-interest, altruism, and social identity," and these three aspects of political motivation serve as a guide for evaluating the nuances of an individual or group political behavior in a specific political system.[26]

In-group and out-group bias and social identification are particularly salient issues with regard to confessional political parties. It has been empirically demonstrated that religious identity is one of the most inviolable group memberships individuals can adopt.[27] The Muslim faith, as with Catholicism and other hierarchical religions, is particularly prone to creating strong in-group and out-group divisions. What amplifies this development in Muslim-majority countries is the proliferation of religious entrepreneurs and the flattening of the religious hierarchy. While the distinctions between Muslim groups are generally strong and long standing, these divisions can be overcome if the mutual benefit is powerful enough. In other words, Islamic confessional parties may function singularly or collectively depending on whether the political circumstance highlights their broad common adherence to the Muslim faith or their specific differences in the interpretation of Islamic law, material opportunities, psychic goods, or political goals.

These questions are all the more relevant in Pakistan's current political climate, which is marked by uncertainty and upheaval. As the Afghan Taliban's move into the northwest tribal regions and more settled areas of Pakistan has changed the geopolitical landscape, traditional political alliances and affiliations are facing real challenges. Muslim democrats, for example, are threatened by the neo-Taliban expansion because they share little overlap on political issues. In addition, while the Punjabi Taliban are interested in a different set of issues, their geographic proximity with Muslim democrats means they now competing for bases of supporters. Interestingly, as a result of the neo-Taliban expansion, even some Islamist parties now share interests with the state. In Sindh, the Jamaat-e-Islami fears the Taliban incursion because it will reduce its support among the Muhajir Urdu-speaking urban population. The Jamiat Ulema-e-Islam, meanwhile, is reluctant to say anything publicly about the Taliban. The party highly values the perception of being a mediator with the Taliban. If the JUI was seen as leaning too heavily in the other direction, they would fear Taliban excursions into their own power bases in the KPK. The Taliban have been able to carve out a political role given the geographic electoral politics and international issues in Afghanistan. In short, the rise of the Taliban and violent Islamic terrorist groups is resulting in major changes in Pakistan's historical political alliances.

In order to better understand how social identification, altruism, and issues of self-interest may be guiding Pakistani voters' decisions in this complex and unstable political environment, I conducted an original field experiment. Based on the measurement instruments in the "dictator game" used by Fowler and Kam and other political scientists currently working on the issue of voter behavior, I devised a social experiment involving 543 Pakistani college students at Punjab University, Pakistan, in July 2007.

In this version of the dictator game, subjects were asked to identify themselves as supporters of one of three parties: the left-leaning, secular Pakistan People's Party; the right-wing, hierarchical Islamist Jamaat-e-Islami; or the center-right, democratic Muslim League. Each participant was given a hundred rupees and asked to fill out a questionnaire that asked about the respondent's age, gender, strength of party affiliation, time risk, and competitive preferences. After filling out the questionnaire, each participant was then asked to allocate their rupees to themselves (the dictator) and another anonymous respondent (the recipient). The only information revealed to the dictator about the recipient was that individual's political affiliation. The dictator also was told that the recipient would not learn the dictator's identity or party affiliation and that the experimenters would double every rupee that the dictator transferred to the recipient. The structure of the study allows a distinction to be made between a concern for specific groups (social identification) and a concern for others (altruism). The primary benefit of the dictator game relative to other approaches is that it gathers information about respondents' actual behavior rather than their declared preferences.

Previously conducted dictator games have resulted in mean allocations from dictators to out-group recipients of anywhere from 10 to 52 percent.[28] In general, the anonymous nature of the study tends to decrease the amount of money dictators give away. The actions of individuals who give low amounts can be explained easily with the self-interest theory; these individuals are merely accumulating as much money as possible for themselves. But the actions of individuals who give large amounts of money, particularly to out-group recipients, under the condition of anonymity, require further explanation. The simplest explanation is altruism: Individuals give to others either because they want to improve the well-being of others, even if it hinders their personal material gain, or because they are mindful that distributing goods among multiple individuals or groups fulfills a standard of equity.

Two primary results emerged from the dictator game conducted at Punjab University. First, attitudes and behaviors toward out-groups varied greatly among the three parties, and monetary allocations were dependent on the political affiliation of the dictator and the recipient. In the dictators' data results (see tables 6.1 and 6.2), the Muslim democrats showed stronger traits of altruism, while dictators from the JI and JUI showed much higher social identification. The most predictive behavior in the study was whether the dictator and the recipient shared a political affiliation (and was not based solely on the political affiliation of the dictator).

Similarly, party supporters and voters who have stronger social identification vote more strategically because they are conscious of not wasting their vote. Those with less social identification are open to switching parties and voting for the party

Table 6.1. Partisanship and allocations in the Dictator game (%)

Donor	Anonymous recipient	Islamist recipient	Muslim dem. recipient	*N*
All	31.9	29.1	26.3	306
Islamist	29.6	31.5	26.0	173
Muslim dem.	29.2	29.6	32.7	78
Difference	0.4	1.9	−6.7	
p value	0.41	0.23	0.02	

Source = Author's data collected in 2004–2008.

Table 6.2. Muslim Democrats versus Islamists in Dictator game

Donor	Money to Muslim dem. minus amount to Islamist		Money to Muslim dem. minus amount to anonymous		Money to Islamist minus amount to anonymous	
	Mean %	p value	Mean %	p value	Mean %	p value
All	−2.8	.01	−2.2	.09	0.3	.28
Islamist	5.5	.00	−3.6	.03	1.9	.19
Muslim Dem.	2.8	.16	4.1	.10	1.2	.33
PPP	−2.1	.32	−6.2	.19	−6.2	.05

Source = Author's data collected in 2007.

with the best chance to win. Surprisingly, the dictator-recipient shared affiliation provides insights into what calculations voters make locally versus nationally. Voters pay special attention to other party platforms and are very knowledgeable of the electoral landscape.

The second result shows that while students with Islamic party affiliations claimed to have generally higher levels of trust for parties that integrate aspects of Islamism into their party platform, these students demonstrated a higher level of out-group bias toward members of the opposing Islamic party than toward members of the secular party. An individual who identified as a member of the Jamaat-e-Islami party was likely to give more money to a member of the Pakistan People's Party than to a member of the Pakistan Muslim League, even though the Islamic parties have more in common. (Voter biases help explain why, in a democracy that is 97 percent Muslim, secular parties continue to win roughly 50 percent of elections.) This apparent discordance fits with Fowler and Kam's findings that expressed beliefs often do not coincide with revealed actions. Furthermore, it suggests that Pakistani voters are not strictly self-interested but also act on the basis of strong social identification.

The personal views of ordinary Pakistani voters reflect the behavior of their parties. Pakistan's Islamist parties (particularly the JI and JUI) have a long history of direct competition, whether they are in or out of a coalition at the moment. (The short-lived MMA, which collapsed under the weight of internecine squabbling, is a case in point.) This competition is reflected in party leaders' rhetoric regarding the other party; interviews with Islamist politicians show that they are reluctant to speak well of their counterparts in other parties. As one Jamaat-e-Islami leader told me, "We dislike the JUI more than anyone else. They say they uphold Quranic principles but they are the worst at violating them. The vanguard of Islamic parties is the Jamaat-e-Islami. We are the only ones that have Islamic pedigree and credibility."[29] Another JI leader insisted that the "JI does not garner corrupt money or raise false charity funds, like other so-called Islamic parties."[30] As a result, Pakistan's parties are as (or more) likely to partner with those further from them on the sharia–secularism continuum as they are with their ideological compatriots.

Building on this finding that Islamic voters act out of a strong sense of identification with specific organizations rather than out of a generalized pan-Islamic sentiment, the survey found little relationship between support for Islamic parties and Islamic militant organizations (hypothesis $H_0 2$). The survey measured support for Islamic politics in several ways. First, it asked respondents how important they felt it was to live in a country governed by Islamic principles and the extent to which they felt that Pakistan is governed by those principles. Second, it asked about two policy issues that had recently been areas of focus for Islamist political parties—the 2006 Women's Protection Act and requirements that *madrasahs* spend more time on math and science. The Women's Protection Act stirred national debate by contravening portions of the Hudood Ordinance of 1979, which had enforced harsh punishments against women for extramarital sex and made it exceedingly hard for women to prove allegations of rape. The amended law placed rape under the civil code, removed the evidentiary requirement of four male witnesses, and eliminated the threat that women whose rape accusations are dismissed can be countercharged with adultery. Islamist party politicians insisted that these changes would encourage moral laxity, and some even threatened to resign from Parliament. Requirements that *madrasahs* allocate more resources to math and science were also met with vehement Islamist party opposition on the grounds that the state should not dictate the curriculum at religious schools.

Measuring support for militant organizations is sensitive, and several techniques were used to more accurately measure respondents' views. For example, vignettes using slogans of specific militant groups—for one, "We must rid ourselves of deviant Muslims"—was one way to gauge support for militant groups. Interestingly, even strong support for Islamist political parties and policies did not translate into support for militant organizations in any consistent way.[31] The data showed a less than 7 percent crossover between support for militant groups and Islamic parties.

The hypothesis that poverty is positively correlated with support for Islamic confessional parties was partially supported. Consistent with the finding that different kinds of Islamic parties have different bases of support, poverty impacted support for Muslim democrats and Islamists in different ways. On the survey, the variable of socioeconomic position was measured both by assessing the respondents' personal situation and their perceptions of the larger economic picture. It asked respondents who were employed to list how much cash they had earned in the previous year, to rate whether their household's economic situation was better or worse than in the previous year, and to rate whether their community's economic situation was better or worse than in the previous year. It also assessed respondents' perceptions by asking them if the Pakistani economy was on the right track or the wrong track and how Pakistan's economy was doing relative to

India's. I overlaid this information with objective measures of child immunization rates by district, a generally accepted measure of overall economic development.

My survey analysis reveals that poverty is correlated with support for Muslim democratic parties over Islamist parties at the national level of aggregation. According to the materialist approach, voting for mainstream Muslim democrat parties on the national level is rational for poorer voters because Muslim democrats are more likely to win national elections and, if they feel properly beholden to lower-income voters, are more likely to implement policies to help the poor. Moreover, poor voters are more reliant on government largesse for land, jobs, grants, access to markets, and other social services, so they have a greater incentive to curry favor with the Islamic party that is more likely to control those patronage networks. It is true that once in office, Muslim democratic politicians reward regions that lent electoral support.

By contrast, those respondents who felt that the Pakistani economy was doing well compared to India's and who said their personal financial situation was not worsening were more supportive of Islamist parties on a national level. From a materialist perspective, this result may stem from Islamic voters' determining that Pakistan can afford to take a more confrontational stance toward India when Pakistan's economy is strong and that they personally can afford to forgo patronage rewards in order to vote according to social identification and ideology.[32]

At the local level, Islamists were able to gain traction because of the lower information costs. Local politicians are more accessible, especially in public spaces, which are often mosques or local shrines. Islamists have a competitive advantage based on their relationship with religious entrepreneurs, and they are able to connect their possible supporters to the patronage of religious spaces.

The data regarding the link between religiosity and support for Islamic confessional parties (hypothesis $H_0 4$) was also mixed. Public religiosity (preferences about the role of sharia and religion in political life) and personal religiosity (degree of individual adherence, devotion, and daily religious involvement) were weakly correlated with each other and divergently correlated with party preferences.

In terms of public religiosity, there is no consistent correlation between voter preferences and their support for confessional parties. Respondents who favor a greater role for sharia in Pakistan's legal system and those who favor a lesser role for sharia both support the Muslim League more often than do respondents who feel that the role of sharia is just right. Respondents who say that producing "good Muslims" is a crucial goal for schools are not more likely to support Islamic parties. Finally, how highly a voter prioritizes making sharia the law of the land does not predict his or her level of support for Islamic political parties. Part of the reason for this finding is that voters view sharia not as religious law but as synonymous with good governance.

However, the respondents' personal religious identity is relevant to party identity, with a positive relationship between personal religiosity and support for

Islamist parties. Islamist parties spend a great deal of time talking about personal religious devotion and, more important, projecting symbols of religious practice. These symbols evoke personal decisions that "visually tell the narrative." For example, respondents often associated a woman's *hijab* (head covering) with praying five times a day. They also associated a specific color for turbans (green) with more frequent attendance at mosques. This last measure of personal religious devotion (for men) is linked to their level of interaction with Islamist party recruiters. Islamist parties are able to attract new supporters during Friday prayers by passing out leaflets, giving small *bayans* (lectures) with portable microphones, and spending time in chai shops near mosques with congregation attendees.

The relationship between poverty, religiosity, and support for the Muslim League, the JUI, and the JI is summarized in table 6.3. The table includes only religion and poverty measures that explain a variance to a statistically significant degree, using standard nested-model statistics. Only two of four religiosity measures and three of six poverty measures rose to statistically significant levels for at least one political party, further disproving the assumption that a generic link exists between religion and poverty and support for Islamic political parties.

With regard to the hypothesis ($H_0$5a) that there is a negative correlation between faith in democratic institutions and support for Islamic organizations, I found no relationship between trust in governmental institutions and support for Muslim democratic parties, but a significant negative relationship exists between trust in governmental institutions and support for Islamists. I measured trust in democratic institutions through a battery of questions on the rule of law, the judiciary, the local governance, and the delivery of corresponding services. The data shows respondents generally had a high distrust for the civilian government and an exponentially high correlation between these local grievances and support for Islamists. This result fits with my overall theory that support for Islamists is a more local, grassroots phenomenon, whereas support for Muslim democrats is largely on the national level.

Interestingly, the survey revealed no support for hypothesis $H_0$5b, which predicts a negative relationship between a commitment to or support of core democratic values and support for Islamic and especially Islamist parties. This finding runs contrary to popular ideas about Islamic organizations and the compatibility between Islam and democracy in general. Social scientists who specialize in Southeast Asia and Pakistan have noted that Pakistan's Islamist parties commonly phrase their appeals in democratic terms and are at the forefront of a movement toward radical democratization that is uniquely adapted to the regional context. While there may be a disconnect between Western-style liberalism and fundamentalist Islam, Islamist organizations do promote a version of democracy nonetheless. Jamaat-e-Islami, for example, boycotted the 2008 general election on the grounds that the elite influencers were going to rig it. Members of the Islamist political coalition Muttahida Majlis-e-Amal had consistently argued that allowing Pervez

Table 6.3. Regression analyses of survey data

	JUI and JI				Muslim democrats (PML-Q and N)			
	Model 1	Model 2	Model 3	Model 4	Model 1	Model 2	Model 3	Model 4
Constant	−5.23	−5.835	−.347	.415	−2.51	−2.38	−2.41	−2.66
Religion								
More religious people in office	.684	.571	.652	.712	−.381	−.315	−.322	−.345
Regime support								
Democracy support		−.754	−.778	−1.04		−.091	−.078	−.055
Strong leadership		−1.342	−1.45	−1.21		.047	.054	0.67
Institutions, confidence in								
Religious			13.45	12.24			−.871	−.813
State			−.065	−.051			−.031	−.042
Geography								
Walking distance to mosque				−.088				.034
Presence of religious education				−.054				−.051
Economics								
Satisfaction financial situation								
Household				−.075				.068
Employed/unemployed				.035				.084
-2 log likelihood	1159.098	1157.254	1142.341	1127.617	375.41	398.22	365.52	384.24
Improvement (df)								
Correct predictions (%)	84.8	82.6	89.3	85.1	91.3	92.4	91.7	92.5
Pseudo R^2	0.13	0.15	0.12	0.18	0.016	0.024	0.063	0.056
N								

Musharraf to serve simultaneously as the army chief of staff and as the president from 1998 to 2007 was illegal. Leaders of Islamist parties also heavily criticized Musharraf's extralegal dismissal of a Supreme Court justice in March 2007. And Islamic groups currently seeking to win Kashmir's independence from India often use the language of self-determination and *azadi* (freedom).

Overall, data gathered through the survey analysis and the field experiment provides an empirical basis for understanding Islamic voter behavior and motivation. The first and most critical finding is that support for one Islamic organization is not predictive of support for any other Islamic organization. And, more specifically, support for Islamist political parties on a local level is negatively correlated with support for Muslim democratic parties on a national level as a result of demonstrated in-group bias. What this analysis means, essentially, is that Islamist and Muslim democratic parties are not competing for the same voters. Pakistan has two (at least) distinct groups of Islamic voters. Rather than competing with each other for voters directly in any given election, Islamists and Muslim democrats are competing in parallel to mobilize their separate bases of voters.

Election data from Pakistan's seven most recent general elections (1988, 1990, 1993, 1997, 2002, 2008, and 2013) and from four of Pakistan's main provinces—Punjab, Sindh, KPK, and Balochistan—support the conclusion that Muslim democrats do well on a national level and Islamists do well on a local level. Tables 6.4, 6.5, and 6.6 reflect the vote percentages by party at different levels of aggregation for the 2002, 2008, and 2013 elections. (It must be noted that the Pakistan People's Party's participation was severely constrained by the new electoral rules that General Musharraf designed for the 2002 elections. Though the PPP won the largest

Table 6.4. Islamist and Muslim democratic party vote share, 2002

	Islamist parties (JI, JUI, JUP) (%)			Muslim democrats (PML-N) (%)		
Province	District	Province	National	District	Province	National
Punjab	53.5	17.4	12.7	14.4	45.3	78.4
Sindh	48.1	21.4	10.3	12.4	34.4	38.9
KPK	76.4	73.2	54.3	19.2	12.7	29.4
Balochistan	37.3	11.3	8.4	4.5	1.4	8.4

Table 6.5. Islamist and Muslim democratic party vote share, 2008

	Islamist parties (JI, JUI, JUP) (%)			Muslim democrats (PML-N) (%)		
Province	District	Province	National	District	Province	National
Punjab	42.7	15.3	6.7	16.8	34.5	63.6
Sindh	38.1	25.4	7.4	15.4	19.3	33.3
KPK	72.1	61.4	21.8	24.3	31.4	37.3
Balochistan	51.3	9.8	4.4	7.1	13.3	6.2

Table 6.6. Islamist and Muslim democratic party vote share, 2013 (%)

	Islamist parties (JI, JUI, JUP, MDM[a])		Muslim democrats (PML-N)		Muslim democrats (PTI)		Liberal democrats (ANP, MQM, PPP)	
	Province	National	Province	National	Province	National	Province	National
Capital Territory[b]	—	9.76	—	39.74	—	35.65	—	14.84
Punjab	3.81	2.73	52.75	56.23	22.98	21.60	11.69	12.41
Sindh	4.47	5.39	7.46	5.70	7.64	9.43	72.25	71.76
KPK	25.57	28.94	18.56	18.94	22.52	32.70	22.45	16.53
Balochistan	25.70	30.31	15.48	7.82	2.76	5.29	9.77	16.29
FATA[b]	—	28.60	—	12.06	—	16.68	—	7.50

[a] Muttahida Deeni Mahas (MDM), an alliance of five Sunni parties.

[b] Voters in Capital Territory and FATA do not elect provincial assembly members.

number of votes, and a total of eighty-one national seats, it was awarded runner-up status.)

Disaggregation of survey and election data (presented in tables 6.3–6.6), combined with the case histories presented in chapters 4 and 5, paints a fairly clear picture of the core voter for each party type. Muslim democrats tend to win support in national elections from poor voters who have determined that this party is the best mechanism for ensuring personal and community patronage rewards. There is little correlation between public religiosity, personal religiosity, democratic values, or militancy and support for Muslim democratic parties. Muslim democratic voters tend either to abstain or to vote for secular parties on the local level. By contrast, Islamists tend to win support from rural voters whose political decisions are based on advancing or reinforcing their religious and social group ties. Personal religiosity, or intimate involvement with local religious institutions, is correlated with support for Islamists. Furthermore, low confidence in national democratic institutions is also positively correlated with support for Islamist organizations. Islamist voters have determined that their material interests are better served by supporting local nazims with parochial control over land allocations than by supporting far-removed national policymakers. These voters also tend either to abstain or to vote for secular parties on the national level.

One key observation is that Muslim democrats and Islamists are not always competing for the same subset of voters. The assumption that they are vying for the same voters underlies most studies of Islamic electoral politics. This misconstruction has been missed in previous studies and has impeded our academic and policy understanding of the motivations of the various Islamic parties. Chapter 7 explores how these facets of voter behavior inform party conduct, political decisions, and the rise of extremism.

CHAPTER 7

POLITICAL STRATEGY

When Extremism Works

Building on evidence presented in previous chapters about the ideological roots and political histories of Islamic parties in Pakistan, and the calculations and biases of Pakistani voters, this chapter discusses the complex political courtship between parties and voters. I focus particularly on the macro-level strategies Islamist and Muslim democratic parties use to try to maximize vote share. By pairing basic political theory with historical and contemporary qualitative findings, I show how these strategies, above all else, are driven by the parties' analyses of voters' likely responses and may sometimes be at odds with the parties' stated ideological positions. Of particular importance, this study shows that Islamist parties, regardless of their original degree of adherence to the fundamentalist tenets of Islamization, are not solely motivated by ideological principles. In fact, such organizations frequently engage in political strategies that require actions that are counter to their ideological claims, including the use of extra-electoral means (violence) and the formation of coalitions with militant and secular organizations. Similarly, I will show that Muslim democratic parties will sometimes promote a degree of Islamization counter to their own ideological stances in pursuit of a greater share of the vote.

Previous research on Islamic political party formation has tended toward oversimplification by creating a false dichotomy between Islamists and Muslim democrats. Neatly summed up by political scientist Vali Nasr, the stereotype has been that Islamists are ideological and Muslim democrats are pragmatic.[1] Rather than taking that dichotomy as a theoretical possibility, scholars have presumed it to be a matter of fact and used it as the basis of intellectual discourse without ever holding it up to proper scrutiny. As I have demonstrated in this book, there is no motivational homogeneity among Islamic parties of either classification—Muslim democratic or Islamist—and this finding alone upends any notion of a clear dichotomy. Viewing the party types as tied to one motivation simply does not account for the various and complex electoral outcomes in Muslim-majority democracies.

Pakistan is hardly the only nation where intraparty differences in Islamic confessional groups have been important. Kalyvas discussed the case of Algeria and noted the internal disagreements in the Islamic Salvation Front (FIS), a party formed in 1989 that helped spark the Algerian Civil War. From the beginning, ideological and strategic differences existed among the leadership of the FIS concerning the proper role of democracy and the imposition of sharia.[2] The more extreme factions in the FIS used brash, antidemocratic language that provoked a violent government response. It was not a fear of Islamist ideology per se that elicited the state's repressive efforts but the concern that elements of the party would take control and impose an Islamic caliphate, seizing economic power from the secular elites. Had the more moderate voices in FIS won out, the state possibly would have responded less forcefully. This case is simply one empirical example of the fact that no universal Islamist motivational model exists.

One inference that can be drawn from observing intraparty differences within Islamist parties is that the dominant ideological commitments and strategic approaches of such a party can shift over time, depending on which faction gains power and other political circumstances. In Algeria, the government's lack of surety about which FIS camp would prevail is precisely what led it to conclude that it must take definitive action against the group. This example illustrates a core premise of this book: Neither the ideologies nor the political strategies of Islamist parties are rigidly determined. Rather, they are fluid, dynamic, and determined by a number of internal and external factors.

One reason the heterogeneity and fluidity of Islamist party ideology have been missed is that previous scholarship has assumed that political party formation is an inherently state-level activity aimed primarily at shaping national policy. This assumption is so ingrained, Robert Mecham even defines groups that organize and operate below the national level of aggregation as civic organizations rather than as political parties. Of course, the idea that political parties form in order to influence national legislation comes from studies of the formation of secular and confessional parties in Western democracies.[3] As previously demonstrated, however, party formation patterns derived purely from secular Western states are not readily transferrable to developing democracies and are not applicable to Muslim-majority states.

In Pakistan, the geographic level of aggregation is not a proper way to distinguish between party and nonparty organizations. Islamist confessional groups that demonstrate all the requisite characteristics of a political party—running candidates, establishing platforms, and pursuing decades of electoral engagement—are consistently competitive on the local level but virtually nonexistent at the national level. (The reverse pattern is true for Muslim democrats, who have consistently succeeded at the national and have limited support at the local level.) Such patterns not only disprove the notion that national-level success is the raison d'être for any political party, but they also beg the question, Why do Islamists target their party formation and mobilization at lower levels of aggregation while Muslim democrats do so at higher levels? It is unreasonable to view Islamists' consistent and at times overwhelming electoral success at the local level as unintentional or accidental, particularly given the resource disparity between grassroots Islamists and elite-funded Muslim democrats. Rather, it is logical to assert that Islamists deliberately pursue strategies that will ensure electoral gains at the local level, even to the detriment of their ability to compete on a national level. The assertion that some political parties in Pakistan prioritize local-level electoral success is supported by decades of electoral data, but because it runs counter to widely accepted political party formation theory, the case has been largely unexamined in the political science literature. I argue that the narrow-minded focus on national-level data in analyzing political party behavior has obscured important political realities in Pakistan.

As indicated in chapter 5, Islamist parties that are successful on the local level stand to gain material, social, and organizational benefits. For one, control over the local levels of government, including the offices of *nazim* and *patwari*, confers a huge amount of authority over land distribution and ownership, still the central component of class standing in Pakistan's pseudo-feudal economy. Local political power can also drive membership and fundraising for the local religious institutions that sponsor and staff Islamist political parties. Religious authority and political authority are mutually reinforcing in rural districts in Pakistan, so it makes sense for organizations that have religious origins to engage in electoral competition at that level. For rural political entrepreneurs, national elections may be of little relevance, at least compared to the direct benefits of winning local control.

By contrast, in urban areas the *nazim* does not distribute land, nor is land ownership of such huge significance. Local religious institutions are not the sole authority in urban areas, nor are religious leaders even close to the most powerful elites. For the Muslim democratic political entrepreneur in an urban center, local elections simply are not worth the investment. For these actors and organizations, the better payoff is at the national-level elections. As discussed in chapter 4, Muslim democratic parties are the product of ancient aristocracies and efforts by a relatively small number of feudal lords and their families to protect their feudal rule over land, wealth, and power.[4] With the rise of suffrage, that system has morphed into a form of patronage democracy in which the National Assembly has control over the dispersal of desirable material goods, services, and jobs. Traditional elites maintain their political, economic, and social power through their access to the state and consequent ability to distribute or withhold patronage. Electoral success at the national level also gives Muslim democrats a platform to espouse policies that may appeal to targeted voters, but parliamentary inefficacy protects them from having to address the actual implementation or the practical consequences of those policies.

This is not to say that Islamists are wholly uninterested in winning national elections or, conversely, that the Muslim democrats totally eschew political activity on the local level. Quite the contrary, both types of Islamic parties have made and continue to make attempts to attract support on various levels of aggregation. The point, however, is that when trying to understand the behaviors and motivations of these different parties, one must recognize that their core interests are aligned with winning elections on specific levels of aggregation. Moreover, their ongoing political conduct is deeply informed by their local versus national orientations.

In 1957, Anthony Downs proposed a model of political action that, granted, rested upon a number of assumptions and idealized conditions but nevertheless effectively described the primary motivations of party behavior. Downs contended that "political parties in a democracy formulate policy strictly as a means of gaining votes. They do not seek to gain office in order to carry out certain preconceived policies or to serve any particular interest groups; rather they formulate policies and serve interest groups in order to gain office."[5] Such a premise is clearly at odds with the common assumption that Islamic political parties engage in the electoral process in order to establish rule by sharia. But Downs's position that political behavior is collectively self-serving offers important insight into political actions taken in a patronage democracy like Pakistan's. The idea that all political parties and political entrepreneurs, including those perceived as vehemently ideological, are at least partially driven by pragmatic interests in maintaining power is shown here to have a great deal more explanatory power over the behavior of both Islamist and Muslim democratic parties in Pakistan than does the quest for policymaking power alone. The objective of all political activities, according to Downs, is to acquire votes: "Government always acts so as to maximize the number of votes it will receive," and "the actions of government are a function of the way it expects voters to vote."[6] This chapter offers compelling evidence that both Muslim democrats and Islamists adopt ideological postures in the service of what they deem potentially successful political strategies. That is, how they act to acquire votes.

One of the implications of Downs's theory that ideology is a political creation intended to attract voters is that parties are ever changing, reinventing themselves and their ideologies to suit the realities of new electoral cycles. After all, an ideological position favoring certain policies is only advantageous insofar as the electorate desires those policies. When the voters' policy interests shift, a party has to be flexible enough to respond. In multiparty systems, party ideologies tend to be more stable because political territory is divided into smaller portions and that territory is carefully defended to distinguish one party from another.[7] But even in a multiparty system, opposition parties must maintain an ideological position that presents an alternative to whatever the government in power is promulgating. When the realities of governance create incentives for incumbents to make ideological shifts, opposition parties are stimulated to make corresponding adjustments.

As suggested in the introduction to this book, recognizing that Islamic confessional parties in Pakistan are guided as much by practical calculations as by staunch ideology has important implications for our understanding of what drives political extremism. This chapter focuses on presenting detailed historical and current examples of situations in which each of the three main Islamic parties in Pakistan—Muslim League, Jamaat-e-Islami, and Jamiat Ulema-e-Islam—explicitly shifted toward the extreme end of the sharia–secularism continuum in order, they hoped, to capture more votes and solidify their hold on power. In chapter 9, I examine how the United States might build a more efficacious foreign policy and diplomatic approach around this concept of Islamic confessional party instrumentalism.

Pakistan Muslim League: Moving toward Extremism

Over the years, the Pakistan Muslim League has become more incentivized to claim political benefits by moving toward extremist positions. Electoral participation does not necessarily yield moderation; however, it *does* lead to instrumentalism. The PML has signaled its move toward extremism in at least three ways: by affiliating with more extreme groups, by campaigning on a platform that is more extreme than its core positions, and by engaging in violent confrontation with the incumbents and governmental forces.

The Muslim League that led Pakistan to its creation and early development under Jinnah effectively died in 1958 when General Ayub Khan, having led a coup against President Iskander Mirza, outlawed all political parties. The name of the PML, however, endured through many iterations, splinters, reformations, and variations. Ayub Khan utilized the party's name to lend legitimacy to a political party under his own control, the Convention Muslim League, which he created to rubber stamp and support the policies he created as president of Pakistan and under the constitution he produced in 1962. An opposition party arose that called itself the Council Muslim League.

The early 1970s were an important period for the PML because the military rule of Ayub Khan had come to an abrupt end when he handed over power to General Agha Mohammad Yahya Khan in 1969. In 1970, Yahya Khan announced Pakistan's first general elections, and the unicameral National Assembly, when its 1971 term began, reflected East Pakistan's numerical superiority, with 162 seats for members from East Pakistan and 138 for those from West Pakistan. Sheikh Mujibur Rahman's Awami League won an overwhelming majority of votes in East Pakistan and thus a majority of seats in the assembly. The Pakistan People's Party under Zulfiqar Ali Bhutto won the majority of seats in West Pakistan—81 out of 138 seats—but none in the East. The PML's Convention and Council parties were relegated to small minorities in the assembly. Bhutto's PPP and other West Pakistani parties refused to accept East Pakistani political rule. When they pressed Khan, his actions led to a bloody civil war between East and West Pakistan that ended in East Pakistan's victory and its secession, and the creation of Bangladesh. This outcome and the war's heavy casualties provoked a widespread popular movement for Yahya Khan's removal. He installed the PPP and Bhutto as the civilian leadership of the country and stepped down in 1971.

In 1973, the PML Convention and Council parties united only to have another splinter break off in the form of the PML-F (Functional). The PML parties remained in obscurity for much of the decade, which was dominated by the PPP and Bhutto's heavy-handed tactics. This decline in the fortunes of the PML and its progeny presented an important test of its ideological integrity, since these Muslim democratic bodies had historically expressed more moderate policy positions than did the Islamists and had consistently been framed as their ideological rivals. As noted previously, in this climate of languishing political power the PML joined its historical rivals—Jamiat Ulema-e-Islam, Jamaat-e-Islami, Jamiat Ulema-e-Pakistan, and others—to form the nine-party Pakistan National Alliance to oppose Bhutto's PPP.[8] Bhutto sought to limit any opposition by calling a snap election, but fervent campaigning took place nonetheless. Further, as has often been the case, the eventual results were widely disputed.

By joining a coalition party with others so ideologically at odds with its historical positions, the PML's adoption of an extreme position demonstrated the party's political opportunism, consistent with Downs's theory of political economy.[9] Downs asserts that policy positions are not promulgated because of the actual ideological positions of politicians or parties but to signal voters and to retain their political power. However, the formation of the PNA was only the beginning of the PML's politically driven movement toward extremism. In its drive to garner political momentum in the snap election, the alliance, which was dominated by Islamist groups, promulgated a platform that was heavy in religious appeals and explicitly identified the implementation of sharia at the national level as its primary focus.

In short, as a constituent member of the PNA, the Pakistan Muslim League, the long-standing bastion of political moderation and opposition to religiosity in the political arena, ran on a platform of explicit religious extremism. And it worked. As electoral data indicates, the PML's new coalition gained National Assembly seats and significant votes in regional districts.[10] The move to center right began paying off but not without costs. The engagement in such an exercise indicated the flexibility of Muslim democrats regarding their ideological postures, at least temporarily and as a means to attain specific and immediate short-term political ends. In adopting political behavior that is more consistent with extremism than moderation, however, the party's supporters were involved in violence that followed the 1977 elections amid widespread allegations of vote-rigging and intimidation in the PPP's eventual narrow win. By actively affiliating with more extreme groups, campaigning on a platform with more extreme rhetoric than its core positions, and engaging in violent confrontation with the incumbents and governmental forces, the PML signaled its shift toward more extremist positions and actions and its interest in claiming the benefits associated with the strategic move. The PPP had slowly become more unpopular, being viewed as overtly corrupt, elitist, and out of touch with Pakistan's rural masses. Later that year, amid widespread civil disturbance in response to the unpopularity of the PPP and Bhutto, General Zia took power and imposed martial law.

Despite the undemocratic nature of the government that formed under General Zia in 1977, he would later serve to reclaim the Muslim League from obsolescence. In 1985, Zia brought the PML factions together and selected Muhammad Khan Junejo as the prime minister. When Zia was killed in a plane crash in 1988, Pakistan again faced free elections but with grave uncertainty about the PML's capacity to win the popular vote without the sanction and support of the military institution for which it had been serving as a figurehead. Once again the PML faced a formidable PPP opponent, Benazir Bhutto, who assumed her father's leadership role. As it had done in 1977, the PML joined its ideological opponents in a nine-party coalition known as Islami Jamhoori Ittehad.[11] The IJI alliance included its political nemesis Jamaat-e-Islami, and its platform was likewise inconsistent with the PML's moderate postures and positions. Although the theme of sharia was less prominent than it had been in 1977, the platform was nevertheless more religiously conservative and politically extreme than the PML's historical positions and appeals had been. In response to widespread allegations of corruption in the Bhutto camp, the PML under the IJI banner ran on a platform of ethical and moral reform of government. The IJI lost to the PPP, but in the process Nawaz Sharif, who was not officially the PML's leader, emerged as its most prominent figure.

Sharif reaped significant benefits in Punjab, winning 45 seats out of 115, by moving further toward the extreme end of the political spectrum.[12] The PML picked up 20 percent more votes in key electoral districts such as Multan, Khanewal, and Rajanpur.[13] The data shows that electoral success at the national level created a willingness among even the most moderate politicians to harden their positions in order to secure votes. In 1990, the first phase of the transformation was complete. Sharif eventually led a segment of the party to create the PML-N (Nawaz) and to an electoral victory (as part of the IJI) over the PPP in that year's general election. Sharif, formerly a businessman, became prime minister and guided the PML to a resurgence in political power and relevance. The significance of this electoral victory cannot be overstated, because the PML's resurgence came not through waging a campaign based on its traditional political positions and platforms but by gaining legitimization through its association with religiously extreme groups demanding the implementation of sharia.

The political calculation to move center right did come with heavy costs. As with marriages of convenience, the alliance with the Islamists was short lived. When Sharif and the PML-N assumed power in 1990, the Islamist parties had allied with them in opposition to their common problem, the PPP. Once incumbent, however, the semblance of unity rapidly unraveled. Insurgent violence by forces loyal to other Islamist groups was pervasive, and the PML became a target of political opposition.

As the data in chapter 6 indicated, in-group and out-group biases can lead to sharp differences among Islamic parties clustered together. The lack of transference among Islamic parties affects party calculations about pursuing extremist ideologies. Thus, one of Sharif's goals on coming to office was to further differentiate the PML from the Islamists. Sharif announced that his government would undertake a comprehensive national reconstruction plan to speed industrialization, encourage investment, and lift restrictions on new economic development. Sharif needed to craft an economic message that would allow him to break away from the Islamists. If he could gain popularity on economic issues, he would no longer need the ideological assets that the alliance with the Islamists brought.

A key part of this effort was building a base of support in the rural areas that the Islamists had long dominated. Directing the full strength of the national government's patronage machine toward the countryside, Sharif increased funding for rural development programs, established elected village councils, set up PML-N party organizations in rural areas, increased the powers of elected local government, and established village defense forces to complement local security forces at the grassroots level and to create jobs for villagers. He formed coalitions with two ethnic-based parties—the Awami National Party and the Muttahida Quami Movement. He also restricted the powers of local Islamist institutions to apply traditional sharia powers. In this latter policy the PML effectively made a complete about-face from the postures and positions it had adopted in 1977 while a member of the PNA.

Sharif and the PML-N made strategic decisions to try to expand the party's natural constituency by reaching out to peasants, bureaucrats, and Islamist-leaning workers. While Islamists tended to focus on traditional social issues like the Hudood Ordinance, Sharif invited small business owners and provincial technocrats to join his coalition. Then he pursued a state-building and economic-development agenda that he argued would ultimately grow the economy and strengthen Pakistan's global position. Sharif's strategy lives on in the party today; PML-N leaders believe that their success stems from their ability to transcend "contentious, petty issues" and offer the voters "big tents, big ideas, the big picture."[14]

In his effort to vie for the Islamist vote, Sharif decided to break from the Muslim League's historic neglect of (and even antipathy to) sharia law and took up the banner of Islamization. To undercut the Islamist agenda and encourage voters to switch their allegiance, Sharif realized that he would have to send strong signals about his commitment to an Islamic agenda; in fact, he would have to go further than the Islamists themselves to win over the skeptics. This ideological reversal was a clear political gamble. Sharif won passage for the Enforcement of Sharia Act of 1991 (Shariat Bill), which declared the Quran and the Sunnah, the body of Islamic customs and practices, to be the law of the land.

Some would argue that Sharif is in fact religiously conservative; that rather than being a single gambit, the policy provisions of the Sharia Act of 1991 reflect his own convictions; and that his later promulgation of Islamist policy demonstrates a pattern of such behavior. However, evidence in the act itself suggests it was not intended to convert Pakistan to an Islamist state. In article 2 of the act, the language explicitly permits different Islamic sects to interpret the Quran and Sunnah freely as they see fit and to allow jurisprudence to be dictated by their respective interpretations. Apart from the obvious challenge to establishing any meaningful uniformity of law at the national level given such latitude, the clause avoids the exclusionary premises and principles that are central to Islamist extremism.[15] In short, it lays claim to instituting sharia but lacks the rigid language that would permit Islamists to exercise real control over the religious and social expression and behavior of others. Not surprising, Islamist political and religious leaders expressed their discontent with the legislation, contending that it lacked Islamic legitimacy.[16] After the act's passage came significant calls for the Islamization of Pakistan's economic policy.[17] As with previous Islamization policy promulgated by non-Islamists, the act failed to make significant changes to the issues of law and economics that are of greatest concern to more fundamentalist quarters. PML-N members, by contrast, no matter their personal piety, see themselves as hardheaded businessmen who are "practical about our religious positions on Sharia and religious rulings."[18]

Sharif put together a working group to monitor and make recommendations about the enforcement of Islamic laws in the country. The working group adopted a nineteen-point plan that included calls for the implementation of major Islamic legislation, including the creation of sharia courts, transformation of the educational system to impart Islamic teaching, censorship of print and electronic media to suit Islamic morals, mandatory prayer schedules, and the establishment of an Islamic banking system abolishing interest payments. In November 1991, at the behest of the PML-N, Pakistan's supreme religious court declared provisions of twenty federal and provincial laws repugnant to Islam.[19]

Sharif walked a political tightrope by taking such bold steps toward Islamization without utterly alienating his party's traditional core supporters. The biggest problem Sharif faced was over the banning of *riba* (interest payments), which

Islam unequivocally prohibits. Although his government had publicly committed itself to Islamization, its major domestic policy initiative was liberalization and modernization of the economy. If the ban on *riba* was fully implemented, Sharif's new economic policy would likely fail. With no consensus in Pakistan regarding either the content or pace of Islamic reforms, Sharif tried to strike a careful balance and appear as Islamist as possible without actually agreeing to an Islamic economic model. To mobilize Islamist voters, he aggressively pursued liberal fiscal policies and corruption on a national and provincial level. Sharif privatized government banks that were underperforming and, for the first time in Pakistan's history, allowed foreign money exchange to be transacted through private money exchanges. In 1992, Sharif launched Operation Clean-up, an anticorruption campaign against robbers and looters in rural areas of Sindh Province. Having achieved some success with that venture, the campaign continued against murderers, extortionists, and kidnappers in the urban areas of Sindh.

As it turned out, Sharif's efforts to expand the reach of the PML-N to include more fundamentally Islamist voters was partially successful. As noted previously, the electoral data indicates the PML was able to attract them at the national level but was unable to garner their support at the local level.[20] The PML-N's loss of power in 1993 was short lived. The president dismissed Benazir Bhutto and the PPP in 1997, and the PML-N won the subsequent general election and simultaneously took the critical Punjab provincial election.[21] It is critical to note that the PML contested this election without the support of the JUI, the JI, and other Islamist parties; instead, they ran in opposition to the PML. The political platforms on which the PML-N ran were more focused on opposition to corruption than on instituting sharia.

Early in the term and realizing that the party was losing support in the local and regional districts, Sharif turned again to instrumental political considerations. Pragmatism led the PML to embrace sharia implementation. Sharif turned to sharia because of its evocative and emotional appeal to the voters in rural areas, where Islamists and opposition parties had made inroads. While facing opposition from Islamists in the assembly and in provincial regions, Sharif again proposed an Islamization process reminiscent of Zia's efforts. His proposal in 1998 not only included enforcement of prayer and other aspects of religious devotion, but he also alluded to economic reforms consistent with Islam.[22] The measures were met with considerable opposition from the Islamist parties, which argued that Sharif and the PML were unfit to create Islamic governance, given their lack of credibility as good Muslims.[23] The bill passed in the National Assembly but promptly died in the Senate.

Although the Fifteenth Amendment (Constitution) Bill, popularly known as the Shariat Bill, proposed a significant movement toward state implementation of sharia, there was considerable argument in the Parliament about the veracity of the claim that it genuinely expressed the PML's interest in Islamism. Several other explanations provide ample evidence of political gamesmanship in the policy's promulgation at that particular time. Not least of these reports found that the bill's fifth clause pointed to the ulterior motives of the PML and of Sharif in particular. It stipulated that the bill would supersede "anything contained in the constitution, any law or judgment of any court."[24] Members of both secular and religious opposition parties, as well as nonpolitical observers and journalists, uniformly questioned the validity and motivation of the clause. Some openly argued that such broad language offered Sharif unlimited discretionary power and that establishing it was the true intent of the bill, with the Islamist language being a mere Trojan horse.[25]

Despite the debate at the elite level, data shows that Sharif's pragmatic move on the sharia–secularism continuum secured key districts, especially in Punjab Province and the KPK. Electoral analysis shows that the swing vote can be between 5 and 10 percent and can change the outcome for more than fifty to sixty National Assembly seats.[26] It helps explain Sharif's insistence on pushing the Shariat Bill through the lower house of the Parliament in the face of such vociferous opposition; it had tremendous symbolic value in rural areas, where information costs were still high. Sharif took great risks in ultimately modifying the bill to make it more palatable to members of the opposition and religious minorities who had expressed concerns about persecution.[27] The passage of the weakened bill in the lower house served the purpose of signaling solidarity with Islamist-leaning voters, but it posed no real threat to the financial interests of the secular liberal elites, especially as it was well understood that the bill was unlikely to pass in the Senate.

Jamaat-e-Islami: Associating with Violence to Secure Votes

As examined in chapter 5 and in contrast to the PML, the hierarchical Islamist party Jamaat-e-Islami has had a difficult time building mass support since its founding. Its rigidly centralized structure, religious absolutism, romanticization of premodern economic models, and elitist intellectual roots limit its appeal among voters on both ends of the sharia–secularism continuum. One strategy that the JI began to develop in the 1980s and came to rely upon in the 1990s as a means to counteract these disadvantages is establishing an association with other organizations, whether overt or covert. Of particular interest, many of these relationships have involved a connection to and support of extra-electoral groups and activities, including violence.

Political violence is a language of politics in Pakistan. In several instances the absence of a tangible hand in violent action has provided the JI with the political benefits that accrue from the actions without facing legal implications or consequences, and without definitive contradiction of its historical nonviolent posture.

The JI was able to defend these gains through intimidation, street power, and extra-electoral means in many cases. The group's leaders cast their association with violent extremism as part of its defense of the downtrodden: "The Jamaat supports all freedom fighters who are fighting oppression. It is our duty. This is the least we could do. We have always been a political party that represents those less fortunate and those oppressed."[28]

Among the best examples of these practices are the JI's ties with violent action against the Ahmadiyya, and its connection to violent terrorist groups such as Tehrik-e-Nifaz-e-Shariat-e-Muhammadi (TNSM), Hizbul Mujahideen, and the Punjabi Taliban.

The Anti-Ahmadiyya Campaign

Pragmatic political calculations about when, where, and from whom to elicit votes can drive parties to extremist positions. The party views electoral and political influence in broad terms that include legislative, judicial, and constitutional reforms. Jamaat-e-Islami had a role in the development of Pakistan's constitution from the beginning and significantly shaped its most definitive precursor, the Objectives Resolution, which was passed in 1949. Maulana Maududi and the JI significantly influenced the proceedings and the outcome so that it reflected the ideals of a state shaped by Islamic ethics that was tolerant of religious diversity and committed to democracy. Specifically, the document began with the declaration that "sovereignty over the entire universe belongs to Allah Almighty alone," but it also insisted "the principles of democracy, freedom, equality, tolerance and social justice as enunciated by Islam shall be fully observed."[29] The Objectives Resolution was widely seen as a victory for Pakistan's *ulema* in general and for Maududi in particular, as it left a significant mark of Islamist language on the fundamental document of the new nation.[30] Current Jamaat-e-Islami leaders continue to quote the Objectives Resolution and anchor Islamist rhetoric in fulfilling the people's wishes (as demonstrated by the resolution).

Equally important, the Objectives Resolution demonstrated the political influence of Jamaat-e-Islami and the success of its placement on the sharia–secularism continuum. Some viewed the Islamist language of the document as so dominant that the Court of Inquiry into the 1953 riots in Punjab went so far as to argue that Jinnah's proposed secular Muslim state had ended with the passage of the Objectives Resolution.[31] Nevertheless, the document also asserted that "adequate provision shall be made for the minorities to [freely] profess and practice their religions and develop their cultures"; guaranteed "fundamental rights including equality of status, of opportunity and before law, social, economic and political justice, and freedom of thought, expression, belief, faith, worship and association"; and assured that "adequate provisions shall be made to safeguard the legitimate interests of minorities."[32] In 1949, these latter provisions and declarations of tolerance were framed by the *ulema*, and by Maududi in particular, as consistent with the voluntary nature of Islam and the tolerance and diversity inherent in the Islamic faith.[33] A few years and a failed electoral campaign later, however, the Jamaat-e-Islami and Maududi found religious tolerance and the Objectives Resolution that upheld it anathema.

While the sharia–secularism continuum helped guide Jamaat-e-Islami's judicial and legislative agenda, the party's ability to campaign strategically for electoral seats on this continuum remained untested. As the 1951 Punjab elections approached, Maududi and the party entered the fray unsure of how to run an electoral campaign. Part of the JI's constraint is that the members viewed themselves as part of an elite organization, making recruiting and cultivating new members a lengthy and time-intensive matter. Their ambivalence toward electoral action also stemmed from their view that the JI was still functionally a religious organization. Rather than field its own candidates, the JI opted to support candidates who were running and whose piety they assessed to be consistent with religious orthodoxy and the Objectives Resolution.[34] That they considered each candidate's stance on the Objectives Resolution a criterion for their support gives further testimony to the JI's perspective that the resolution represented an ideological victory.

Only one of the fifty candidates that the JI supported won a seat in the provincial assembly, partly because the assessment strategy was not an effective means of predicting electoral success but also because of repression and political patronage from the incumbent provincial powers.[35] Having wasted considerable effort and money for no meaningful return, the JI was reluctant to engage in more electoral competition. When the party faced more opposition and repression in the KPK campaign later in 1951, it withdrew altogether.[36]

In the wake of these defeats the JI and Maududi began to think about how they could successfully mobilize new supporters for their sharia–secularism continuum agenda. After their bitter defeat and the resultant demoralization of core members, the JI needed to find a short-term success. In a clear case of instrumentalism, the JI was gradually drawn toward the exclusionary debate of "who is a Muslim" and the already simmering issue of the Ahmadiyya community in Pakistan. As noted in chapter 5, the Ahmadis' belief that their founder, Ghulam Mirza Ahmad, is a prophet disqualifies them from inclusion in the Muslim *umma* (worldwide community) in the view of orthodox Muslims. Others had been politicizing the poverty in Punjab, agitating against the government as economic oppressors. They also had begun focusing the blame for their economic conditions on the Ahmadis, contending that they were growing wealthy by oppressing poor Muslim people, and in so doing incited a number of protests and riots. It is telling that the JI was neither the instigator of these practices nor the originator of the Ahmadi disputes; in fact, Maududi resisted joining the fray, considering it a nonessential issue. Maududi even sought to shift the discourse from the Ahmadi issue to establishing an

Islamic constitution several times, trying to convince the *ulema* to withdraw from or avoid the Ahmadi conflict without success.[37] However, as the anti-Ahmadi issue erupted into more riots, the government cracked down on the *ulema* and affiliated politicians, pressing the JI to respond.

When confessional parties do position themselves on the extremes, ideological absolutism or increased fundamentalism alone does not sufficiently explain the parties' actions. In this case, the JI changed its ideological stance on the Ahmadiyya issue. The JI had always remained thoroughly disinterested and opposed to the anti-Ahmadiyya agitation, but sensing the need for a pragmatic shift, the JI mobilized Pakistan's first communal riot in 1953. Maududi wrote and published a treatise on the issue (*The Ahmadi Problem*) in order to adopt it as a JI cause and to gather the political momentum carried with it.[38] The JI formed a coalition of religious groups and began a campaign to pressure the Pakistani state into declaring the Ahmadis non-Muslims. The far-ranging campaign asked the state to remove Ahmadis from government and to seize all their property and assets. The demand for extra-electoral means and violence was unprecedented. Hundreds of Ahmadis were killed before the Pakistani state stepped in and imposed martial law. The JI's pragmatic calculation had real—human—costs.

The instrumental move to rally the masses raised the profile of the Jamaat-e-Islami as a genuine power broker. Despite not having electoral votes, the party could intimidate voting bases through street power and extra-electoral means. The government came to view the JI's Maududi as its chief instigator and arrested and charged him with "promoting feelings of hatred between different groups in Pakistan."[39] Maududi was handed the death sentence for sedition, but it was reduced to fourteen years' imprisonment, and he was released within two years. Although the JI had no particular ideological interest in securing the declaration that the Ahmadis were not true Muslims, adopting the issue with its history of violent unrest resulted in Maududi's questionable trial, his imprisonment, his receiving a death sentence that was never executed, and his elevation to the status of hero of the people. The result afforded both Maududi and the party significant political capital.

Street power became one of the key levers for the JI to ensure its political survival. As one JI leader boasted, "Our material is still being read on the street by political party activists. We wrote the book on how to mobilize people quickly. No one does it better than the Jamaat."[40] Again in 1974, the JI widely supported a similar round of rioting and persecution of the Ahmadis in Pakistan. Although the party and its entrepreneurs were not convicted of the actual murders committed by religious extremists, they used extra-electoral means to mobilize their base and intimidate others. Widespread rioting and violence against the Ahmadis were attributed to Islamist religious organizations and to general public action fomented by the JI. Its extra-electoral activity is understood to have been an attempt to garner political support for the party by presenting itself as a protector of Islam, a task that required the identification of a supposed threat to the faith.[41] When the JI condemns opposition parties, it is always on the grounds that those incumbents were not honoring Islamic rule in their establishment and execution of the state's affairs.[42]

Alliance with Extremist Groups

Supporting extra-electoral action against an internal minority group is not the only way in which the JI has sought to identify itself as a legitimate Islamist force. The party's associations with groups engaged in violent action both inside and outside of Pakistan, even while arguing for Islamic democracy inside Pakistan, have significantly signaled its Islamist legitimacy.

Hizbul Mujahideen

A notable example of JI's involvement with extremism is found in the party's identification as a major funder, trainer, and weapons supplier to Hizbul Mujahideen, a group identified as a terrorist organization operating in Kashmir, India, in the late 1980s and 1990s.[43] What is particularly interesting about this action is that one of the JI's primary complaints about the Pakistani government in the 1950s was that it was not waging a legitimate Islamic war or jihad in Kashmir. The party explicitly opposed military action there on the grounds that the Islamic faith was not being advanced or defended by the government's actions, but years later, the JI covertly supported activities that were arguably less consistent with jihad. As with the Ahmadiyya sect, the JI's role was more of a facilitator than of a direct actor in extra-electoral action, including violence, permitting it to signal its solidarity with violent extremists without actually getting blood on its hands. Appealing to voters' sensibilities to achieve Islamic goals allowed the JI to avoid public support for violence, which would not be widely popular.

The Tehrik-e-Nifaz-e-Shariat-e-Muhammadi

Despite having a smaller base of recruits and core supporters to compete with other Islamic parties, the JI claims political benefits through pragmatic negotiations and tacit support of extremist groups. The JI also has affiliations with Pakistani organizations that have been recognized as terrorist groups. The most notable of them is Tehrik-e-Nifaz-e-Shariat-e-Muhammadi, which means "Movement for the Enforcement of Muhammad's Law." In 1990, Sufi Muhammad, a former Jamaat-e-Islami leader, founded the TNSM in the Dir district of the KPK province. Sufi Muhammad's *madrasah* training as an *alim* made him an unconventional JI entrepreneur. He eventually left the party, citing irreparable ideological differences. In particular, he expressed his unwillingness to honor the JI's public position of nonviolence and has been identified as having Wahhabi influences. As with others of this persuasion, Sufi Muhammad's skewed interpretation of Islam justifies violent actions to enforce sharia. At political rallies he would draw on such Quranic scriptures as "So when the sacred months have passed away, then slay the idolaters wherever you find them, and take them captives and besiege them and lie in wait for them in every ambush, then if they repent and keep up prayer and pay the poor-rate, leave their way free to them" (Sura 9:5).

While Sufi Muhammad's stance contrasted to the JI's public stance on nonviolence, their positions mirrored private negotiations of core JI members and former leaders. Qazi Hussein Ahmed, the party's *amir* from 1987 to 2008, described bloodshed in the pursuit of Islamic rule as "inhuman and not Islamic," although he and his staff continued to meet with ex-members of the JI from various extremist organizations.[44] Sufi Muhammad graduated from one of the many small and intellectually disreputable *madrasas* that sprung up on the Afghan border during the anti-Soviet jihad. But while his dubious intellectual pedigree set him apart from the cohort of core JI leaders, his goal—to bring Pakistan under sharia law—certainly fit with their larger objectives.[45]

As is often the case with JI affiliates, the TNSM's violent involvement is driven by conditions bound to particular regional conflicts. Dir is in a mountainous region of what was then called Malakand District (part of what is now Khyber Dakhtunkhwa province) that remained independent after partition and did not accede to Pakistan until 1969. Accession to Pakistan meant, among other things, tax increases on local merchants, who unsurprisingly began to demand a return to the tribal law that had previously governed Dir. Wrangling over the validity of national versus tribal law continued for decades. Muhammad successfully converted this dislike of Pakistani law into support for the imposition of sharia in the region. The TNSM led an armed uprising in Malakand in 1994, demanding the implementation of sharia and ultimately provoking a conflict with Pakistan's military forces. Pakistan's national government gave in to the TNSM's demands, agreeing to impose sharia ordinances in Malakand for several months in May 1994. This accommodation, meant as a temporary concession, became permanent after the TNSM led a violent uprising against the return of secular law. Although the Malakand revolt was ultimately put down, the TNSM's demands were largely met, with the result that Pakistan's national justice system does not currently operate in Malakand. The TNSM ultimately ventured into Afghanistan to assist the Taliban in the war against Western forces and imported neo-Taliban practices in the KPK and Swat regions of Pakistan. As a result of their ideological positions and activities, the group has been alternatively identified as the Pakistani Taliban.[46]

Jamaat-e-Islami has managed its association with the TNSM as it often has with extremist or violent groups—by judicious silence. Even as the Pakistani government has repeatedly arrested the TNSM leaders, the JI has consistently failed to either condemn their violence or even acknowledge the neo-Taliban title assigned to the organization. The JI's practice of avoiding negative statements about or labeling of the TNSM allows the preexisting association between the two groups to serve as a tacit endorsement of the TNSM's actions. Therefore, the JI can imply to extremist-leaning voters it has the capacity to challenge the incumbent Pakistani government, yet still have plausible deniability with more moderate voters.

Jamiat Ulema-e-Islam: Using Religious Spaces as a Party of the Masses

The JUI's move toward the extreme end of the sharia–secularism continuum has been much more gradual and more holistic than the JI's; the network's structure and lack of a central control system means that major shifts occur not by a top-down mandate but by the slow accretion of individual decisions by many local leaders. But similar to its hierarchical counterpart in Khyber Pakhtunkhwa, changes in the JUI's programmatic commitments and tactics have been largely the result of political decisions to bolster the party's status among local populations of voters by affiliating closely with militaristic groups. The JUI has strategically used public places—mostly its large *madrasah* network—to motivate, organize, and recruit a new base of voters and supporters.

As noted in chapter 5, the JUI was born of the Deobandi school of Islamic thought and teaching, which in all its manifestations is concerned with restoring Islamic instruction and culture so that Muslims can recover the geographical and spiritual ground lost in the British colonial rule of India. Initially the Deobandis focused on spiritual revival, supported nonviolent and apolitical educational agendas, and started several schools, originating from the Dar ul-Ulum Deobandi *madrasah* in India. Accordingly, the JUI tradition is based in *madrasahs* in Pakistan. The organization took on a separate political identity from its parent organization Jamiat Ulema-i-Hind in order to support the Muslim League's movement for partition and the formation of Pakistan in 1945. The party gradually acquired a more overt Islamist agenda in the context of partition and the unique regional circumstances of the frontier regions of Pakistan.

The intersection of the frontier regions' fiercely independent Pashtunwali tribal culture, challenging topography, and Islam's pattern of local autonomy fostered the development of relatively isolated religious and political pockets, creating the JUI's loosely affiliated structure. In this environment *madrasahs* thrived, each largely shaped by the interpretations and leanings of their respective *ulema*. The *madrasah* became the *tehsil* (district)–level representative of the JUI's organizational structure. Moreover, it remained the lifeblood and artery of JUI recruitment, as mosque leaders who also happened to be elected party officials of the JUI would give sermons there. The Friday *khutbahs* (sermons) would broaden the party's outreach and goals every week and give the party an avenue to raise money from supporters' almsgiving.

The party had some significant political success in the early 1970s, becoming part of a coalition government with the PPP, whose socialist agenda favored the concerns of the JUI's predominantly rural and poor constituency. To a great degree the JUI had been an obscure group for much of Pakistan's early development, but it came to prominence in the face of growing poverty and the rise of leftist politics among an electorate hungry for promises of economic reform. Here the message of implementing sharia became especially appealing, as Islamic laws regarding *riba* could mean the liberation of a permanently indebted and impoverished underclass that was subject to predatory land rents.

The JUI makes decisions about where to position on the sharia–secularism continuum based on multiple variables, including electoral districts, target audiences, and the relative position of competing parties. Having gained a significant foothold in the political arena on a platform of sharia, JUI leader Mufti Mahmud aggressively pursued Islamization policies that continue to affect the national discourse even now. Ironically, the policies that were successfully passed included a number of stringent and repressive laws concerning personal conduct, but those policies that would have affected the economic issues that were salient to the poor underclass did not become law. Nevertheless, they set the stage for further Islamization and Talibanization in subsequent periods.

Pragmatic Choices and Slow Talibanization

Forced to make pragmatic choices to maintain the party's electoral leverage, the JUI welcomed massive cultural and political shifts that occurred around the Soviet-Afghan War (late 1979 to 1989). With support from the Pakistani state, the United States, and Saudi Arabia, the JUI was able to establish a much denser network of *madrasahs*, and these schools often focused more on training for conflict with Soviet forces in Afghanistan than careful consideration of Islamic texts, law, and teachings. Thus, while Deobandi *ulema* had long been politically potent figures and their *madrasahs* political loci, during the Soviet-Afghan War they also became military loci. During this period *madrasahs* developed at a phenomenal rate, and it is estimated that their numbers more than tripled between the mid-1970s and the mid-1990s.[47] Throughout this time the *ulema* and *alims* in the region declared jihad on the Soviets, advocating direct and violent Pakistani involvement in the Afghan conflict. Afghan mujahideen often lived and trained with Pakistani jihadis, generally in and around the many madrasahs that cropped up in the region. As these fighters returned to Pakistan, having been supported during the Afghan jihad, they sought the income and power that accrued to religious leaders in the region and established more *madrasahs* with decreasing measures of academic grounding.[48] This proliferation of *madrasahs* was well funded by Middle

Eastern Islamist forces, most notably from Saudi Arabia, which had a distinct interest in undercutting the political power of the PPP, whose socialist ideology it found repugnant.[49]

Meanwhile, leadership of the JUI also shifted to Fazlur Rehman, Mufti's son. He fostered further Islamization, and the party itself became increasingly forceful and militant in its rhetoric regarding the enforcement of sharia and the protection of Islam from external forces. Elements in the party shifted from electoral, nonviolent positions to extremist ones and splintered from the party, though they were still widely regarded as JUI affiliates. Among these groups were Harakat-ul-Mujahideen, Jaish-e-Mohammad, Sipah-e-Sahaba Pakistan, and Lashkar-e-Jhangvi, which have been associated with terrorist actions in Pakistan, Kashmir, and Afghanistan and accused of sectarian violence.[50]

The JUI continued to make pragmatic political alliances to ensure these allies' survival and set them up for local electoral power. In the wake of the Afghan war, the Pakistani jihadis were essentially indistinct from the Afghan mujahideen who flooded the KPK province and Federally Administered Tribal Areas, where the JUI had much of its support.[51] While in Afghanistan the mujahideen reorganized to form the Taliban, but in Pakistan they formed a looser network that was interwoven with the JUI, often because individual entrepreneurs held significant sway in their local electoral areas and were under little control of a central party organization. Political entrepreneurship in these instances was more a matter of expediency for consolidating power than an expression of a central organizing ideology. This heterogeneity has created a more complex set of circumstances regarding the JUI's politics. Whereas the JI can be seen as a relatively unitary entity that uses its affiliations to extremist groups for image management and political leverage, the JUI legitimately has certain factions and entrepreneurs whose commitment to electoral processes is questionable.

In a sense, the Taliban's political messaging challenged the JUI. The Taliban had successfully convinced the rural populations of Pakistan and Afghanistan that maintaining their Islamic traditions, sharia, and Pashtunwali codes was only possible by engaging in an anti-Western crusade. The Taliban's approach left the JUI in a bind. In order to maintain its credibility with voters, the JUI had to focus equally on its original demands for the state to implement sharia and on its promotion of pan-Islamic resistance.

The JUI responded to these incentives by instrumentally moving further to the right on the sharia–secularism continuum. Its networked organizational structure demands that the party continue garnering recruits and building symbolic support among a wide voter base. Leading up to the 2002 elections, the JUI saw the opportunity to fill the ideological gap with the war in Afghanistan, the frustration with the Musharraf-US partnership, and the threat to religion under secular authoritarian rule. Moving more to the right, the JUI positioned itself as part of the coalition of religious parties, Muttahida Majlis-e-Amal. Electoral data shows the local, regional, and national success of the JUI in the coalition.[52] Part of its success was in mobilizing its base of voters through the mosque and *madrasah* networks. In addition to its support from the military establishment, the JUI's ability to bring out new voters in several key districts demonstrated the party's street power.[53] Analyzing the data demonstrates that the JUI was able to widen its geographic and overall appeal through a concerted move on the sharia–secularism continuum. And although the JUI had a much poorer showing in the 2008 election (after failing to deliver in the previous administration and facing several corruption charges), the party still managed to gain seven National Assembly seats and fourteen provincial seats and thus a position in the PPP-led coalition.

The JUI's relationship and tacit alliance as mediator with the Pakistani Taliban gives it a strategic edge at the political bargaining table. The Pakistani Taliban's regional focus overlaps with the JUI's primary political strongholds in the frontier regions, and despite the former's lack of engagement in electoral politics, its presence, tactics, and political power require the JUI to be expedient in its response. Whereas the JUI's foray into jihadist rhetoric was predominantly in reaction to an explicit Soviet threat in Afghanistan, the party is historically rooted in religious activism, education, and political activity. By contrast, in recent years the Taliban in Pakistan have been implicated in shootings and bombings of military and government targets in the frontier regions and are among the most prominent suspects in the assassination of Benazir Bhutto.[54] This latter action is clearly not one with which the JUI or any political party in Pakistan can afford to be associated; however, in the face of current anti-Western and anti-moderation sentiment, it is also difficult for political parties to explicitly distance themselves from the Taliban or other extremists. Again, the JUI was forced to make a choice of where it stood on key emotive issues of blasphemy and religious minorities. And in instances involving both issues—for example, the 2009 blasphemy case against Aasiya Bibi and the 2011 assassinations of Salmaan Taseer and Shahbaz Bhatti—the party's movement along the moderate–extreme continuum was driven by political expediency rather than by ideology.

As part of the ruling coalition in the civilian government, the JUI stood silently in November 2010 when Aasiya Bibi, a Christian, became the first woman to be convicted and sentenced to death for blasphemy. Being part of the ruling coalition creates a willingness among even the most ideologically rigid Islamist politicians to soften their positions. While ideologically it made sense for the JUI to publicly support the conviction, doing so would have risked its seat as part of the ruling coalition; hence, the JUI and Fazlur Rehman remained mum and went against his ideological stance. In fact, some prominent JUI members even acknowledged that a change to the blasphemy law might be necessary to prevent any misuse.

When the PPP failed to deliver an additional minister position to the JUI, Rehman decided to quit the ruling coalition in December 2010. And the party's movement along the moderate–extreme continuum was once again driven by political expediency rather than by ideology, when both Taseer and Bhatti were assassinated. The party's move toward extreme political messaging was prominent because both national leaders were assassinated after objecting to existing Islamist blasphemy laws that mete out harsh penalties. Islamist parties, including the JUI, have been deafeningly silent and have not condemned these egregious expressions of the role of violence relative to voting in the Pakistani arena, and arguably it would have been political suicide to do otherwise. Fazlur Rehman was quick to criticize any attempts to amend the blasphemy law, which both Taseer and Bhatti had advocated for because of the law's rampant misuse. While the party's silence can hardly be interpreted as complete agreement with the horrific outcome, the JUI continues to use the Taseer assassination to rally its base in a move that is not unlike the JI's evocative mobilization against the Ahmadiyya sect. Further, the JUI has made a hero of Qadri, Taseer's professed assassin, lauding him as a "Muslim patriot" and continually holding rallies demanding his freedom.

Interviews with party leaders reveal that they see themselves as flexible and pragmatic, to a degree. They often insist that "the Jamiat is open to change their positions based on consultation (*shura*)" and that they are aware that they must be practical and pragmatic to do God's work."[55] In a maneuver that, given the JUI's ties to militant groups, may itself be seen as a sign of strategic positioning, however, they also give open-ended answers to questions about the use of violence. As one JUI leader said, "We do not approve of violence, but our freedom fighters have rights, too. We reserve the right to revisit such issues as long as they are within the Quranic principles."[56] This unwillingness to close off the possibility of using violence appears again in the JUI leaders' (somewhat thuggish) insistence that they control street power in Pakistan: "The JUI knows that in a street fight, we will always win. We own the streets and neighborhoods. The big parties act like bullies, but they know that we rule the day in our areas."[57]

The JUI as Incumbents: Moderation and Extremism

The previously mentioned electoral success of the JUI in the 1970s presents an interesting chapter in the party's history, because it provides a clear example of the rhetorical and ideological flexibility of Islamist parties as they pursue electoral success. As the socialist PPP movement grew in Pakistan leading into 1970, the JUI and the other Islamist parties were forced to choose their positions and rhetoric regarding this new and evidently potent force. Other Islamist groups condemned the PPP and socialism in general as contrary to Islam, since the system is historically rooted in a secular political doctrine. The most adamant voice regarding this issue was that of Maududi's Jamaat-e-Islami, arguing that socialism in any form must be viewed as *kufr* (anti-Islamic).[58]

However, the JUI contended that addressing the needs of the poor and oppressed of Pakistan was central to Islamic conviction; therefore, it favored the PPP's platform of economic reform and redistribution of wealth. On the surface it can be argued that the JUI was not moderating by forming an alliance with an explicitly secular party but was addressing a central concern with another party that shared its fundamental political position. Arguably being born out of the rural *madrasahs* and *masjids*, whose constituents were mostly poor, the JUI had a frame of religious piety that was shaped by its close association with the Pakistani underclass. Frequent close social contact with the people whom the PPP would describe as the proletariat was certainly a factor in the JUI's concerns with economic injustice, and the party pursued such economic reforms as land redistribution and interest-free loans. However, its subsequent actions would call into question the extent to which this platform was driven by a genuine concern for its constituency rather than by the political expediency of identifying an emotionally potent issue for a large block of voters.

The JUI had developed significantly by 1970 in large part because its program of socially visible institution building had endeared it to a large rural constituency. The message of concern for the poor resonated with the populist message of Zulfiqar Ali Bhutto's PPP. Moreover, JUI national leader Mufti Mahmud defeated Bhutto in a provincial assembly election in the KPK province in 1970. Aware of the JUI's strength in the region, Bhutto sought a coalition with the mufti after the former was elected prime minister in 1972 and made the mufti chief minister of a governing coalition in the KPK. As such, the JUI genuinely moderated by forming an alliance with the secular party along shared programmatic and ideological lines and in opposition to extremist groups that maintained their positions but at the expense of electoral failure. Forming such a coalition was a strongly moderating action that received heavy criticism from more extremist quarters, including the JI, and others widely held that the JUI's ascension to power was achieved at the expense of true Islamic values. In a dilemma that is not uncommon in Pakistan, the party took political actions to obtain a place on the national stage that alienated the party's more extreme base. According to Downs, political expediency would therefore demand a policy promulgation that would signal positions consistent with the extremist leanings of the party's voter base.[59]

Not surprising then, once in office the mufti aggressively pursued wide-scale Islamization, resulting in the banning of alcohol, the forced observance of Ramadan, and the revision of inheritance laws according to sharia. In concert with the very organizations that had criticized its allegiance with the PPP, including the JI, the mufti and the JUI sought the policy declaring the Ahmadiyya sect as non-Muslim and curtailing the Ahmadis' religious freedoms. This shift back to vigorous extremism, marked especially by arguments of religious and ideological exclusivity, was necessarily alienating to the JUI's allies in the PPP, and the coalition dissolved in ten months. In essence, gaining national political power demanded moderation and regaining its lost political base demanded extremism. In both instances, political expediency rather than ideology drove the movement along the moderate–extreme continuum.

The JI as Incumbents: Moderation and Extremism

While involved in many extremist activities, including rhetorical and extra-electoral means, Jamaat-e-Islami's electoral and political participation does not necessarily always yield to more extremist positions; however, it does give way to instrumentalism and, in some cases, moderate positions. Evidence shows that electoral success, especially at the national level, creates a willingness among even the most ideologically rigid Islamist politicians to soften their positions in order to secure votes and maintain their power broker status. When functioning as incumbents at the national level, the JI has formed coalitions with secular groups and military leaders and distributed patronage under the guide of Islamization. In softening its position, the JI realizes pragmatic political calculations.

Examples of this tactic include the JI's condemnation of suicide bombings in 2006 and its proclamation against martial law in 2007. In both instances the JI strategically moved along the moderate–extreme continuum, with its calculation driven by political expediency rather than by ideology. In the first instance, the JI risked upsetting its affiliation with extremist groups and prominent former JI members while the second instance risked the JI's being viewed as anti-state (i.e., against the military) after being so closely aligned in earlier periods. It made both of these decisions because the JI held office at the federal level and taking an extreme position would jeopardize its political influence.

Another interesting example of this shift occurred in 2007 during the Lal Masjid (Red Mosque) debate. In March 2007, an assembly of extremists from various groups associated with the JI, including Sipah-e-Sahaba (the militant anti-Shia group) and Jaish-e-Mohammad, occupied the premises of a mosque and seminary school in Islamabad, Pakistan's capital city. The unprecedented occupation happened within a stone's throw of the power centers of Islamabad and under the new, expansive 24/7 media environment in Pakistan. The more than nine hundred occupiers included various extremist leaders, female religious administrators, students, other women, and children. The mosque leaders had established their own sharia court and were demanding that the Islamic law be enforced in Islamabad. Despite the civilian government's repeated attempts to encourage the occupiers to leave the mosque peacefully and to stop their violent activities (which included kidnapping citizens and burning down adjacent buildings), the groups bunkered in the mosque and refused to go peacefully. After a month of negotiations and no progress, General Musharraf ordered a strong military operation to retake the mosque forcefully, during which more than one hundred people were killed.

While the JI recognized the grievances of the mosque's occupiers, the JI had to make a pragmatic political decision on its stance to the operation. As part of the civilian government coalition, the JI faced the issue of challenging an extremist group that wanted to implement sharia in Pakistan, a goal that the two groups shared. Ultimately, the JI sided with the civilian government and stated that citizens cannot challenge the government's writ and take policy into their own hands. While the JI would continue to take paradoxical positions afterward, its political decision reflected both a move from ideological absolutism and the party's acute understanding of maintaining voter support.

JI leaders still insist that the party's positions are guided by the Quran, and, as such, can never be considered extreme. One senior leader said, "We aren't sure why others call us 'extreme'. Our platform is moderate and in line with the Holy Quran. The Prophet noted for us to follow the middle path. The extremists are those who want to rid our country of Islamic principles and want Pakistan to be controlled by external powers."[60]

As demonstrated earlier in this book, no motivational homogeneity exists among Islamic parties of either classification—Muslim democratic or Islamist—and this finding alone upends any notion of a clear dichotomy. Viewing the party types as tied to one motivation simply does not account for the various and complex electoral outcomes in Muslim-majority democracies. Of particular importance, this book shows that Islamist parties, regardless of their original degree of adherence to the fundamentalist tenets of Islamization, are not solely driven by ideological principles. The JI and JUI frequently engage in political strategies that require actions counter to their ideological claims, including the use of extra-electoral means (violence) and the formation of coalitions with militant and secular organizations. Similarly, Muslim democratic parties will sometimes promote a degree of Islamization counter to their own ideological stances in pursuit of a greater vote share. For both Muslim democrats and Islamists, the movement along the moderate–extreme continuum is driven by political expediency rather than by ideology.

The Limits of Strategic Positioning: The Case of the ANP

Not only Pakistan's Islamic or Islamist parties make surprising moves along the sharia–secularism continuum. Secular parties are equally likely to attempt to exploit religious feeling for political advantage. Most frequently, secular parties form political alliances with their religious counterparts when doing so is necessary to solidify their control of a legislature. Maintaining the support of their coalition partners requires that the secular party make at least some effort to pass pro-sharia legislation. Just as Zulfiqar Bhutto oversaw the 1973 constitution, which guarantees Pakistan's status as an Islamic state, so have many secular politicians compromised with religious activists on the local or provincial level. The strategy of making limited concessions to the religious constituency, including the passage of legislation that is important to religious parties but that has little real effect on Pakistan's power structures, has allowed secular and moderate confessional parties to obtain the support of the religious parties and has kept the votes of highly religious Pakistani voters divided among secular, Islamic, and Islamist parties. The violence against secular parties that marked the 2008 and 2013 elections, however, calls the continued validity of this compromise strategy into question, especially for parties operating in Pakistan's western provinces.

Founded as a secular, leftist, Pashtun-nationalist group, the Awami National Party is one example of a secular party that has frequently contracted political marriages of convenience with parties at the other end of the sharia–secularism continuum. Abdul Wali Khan formally established the ANP in 1986.[61] Khan came from a family of Pashtun activists. His father, Abdul Ghaffar Khan, founded and led the left-wing Pashtun group Khudai Khitmatgar (Servants of God), which had partnered with the Indian National Congress to oppose partition.[62] Wali Khan himself had previously led the pro-Moscow faction of the West Pakistan National Awami Party, Pakistan's first leftist party.[63]

Despite its secular credentials, the NAP itself had a long history of engaging with Islamist parties to seek electoral advantage. It partnered with the JUI to form a coalition government in the KPK in 1971–72, ceding the JUI control in the province in exchange for its electoral support at the center. The JUI, under the leadership of Mufti Mahmud, instituted a variety of Islamization measures in the province, banning alcohol, altering the inheritance laws to reflect Islamic precepts, and requiring women to wear the veil in public.[64] When the NAP-PPP modus vivendi fell apart in the mid-1970s, the NAP briefly joined an opposition coalition, the United Democratic Front, that included the JI, but Bhutto banned it in 1975.[65]

Wali Khan returned to formal politics in 1984, and when founding the ANP, he retained the left-wing politics of the NAP but put a greater emphasis on Pashtun nationalism.[66] The group no longer sought to be a national party; instead, the ANP focused its efforts on the Pashtun population of the KPK and Balochistan. Despite its genesis as a coalition of left-wing groups, the ANP saw the PPP as its primary opponent, a not surprising stance given Bhutto's ban on the NAP and the PPP's anti-regionalist policies. Apparently following the principle of "the enemy of my enemy is my friend," after the 1990 elections the ANP agreed to form a coalition government in the KPK with representatives of the Islami Jamhoori Ittehad, the right-wing religious coalition.[67] Wali Khan's wife, Nasim Wali Khan, the party's leader and a political power in her own right, is believed to have engineered this surprising move.

The ANP's alliance with the PML-N (the IJI's main party) throughout the 1990s gave it access to state resources, which it could then redistribute as patronage to its political supporters.[68] The ANP flourished during these years (particularly in those national elections where the PML-N dominated), winning a high of ten National Assembly and thirty-two provincial assembly seats in 1997.[69] The alliance with the PML-N, however, fell apart in 1998 over the issue of renaming the KPK "Pakhtunkhwa," one of the ANP's core demands.[70]

In the 2002 elections (and in the next two elections), the ANP allied itself with the PPP, and the coalition was a more natural fit, given that both parties at least ostensibly share leftist politics. As the PPP's most faithful coalition partner, this alliance brought the ANP into power, both provincially and at the center, from 2008 to 2013 and finally allowed the ANP to achieve its goal of renaming the northwestern province Khyber Pakhtunkhwa.[71] But during the same period the ANP, as the largest secular Pashtun party, became the target of the Pakistani Taliban and allied militant groups, which used terrorism to destroy the party's infrastructure in the KPK. Since the attacks began in roughly 2007, the Taliban have killed more than eight hundred ANP candidates, party workers, and supporters. They targeted party rallies with suicide bombings and ambushed candidates' motorcades. The terrorist threat led one ANP National Assembly member, Wali Khan's son Asfandyar Wali Khan, not to return to his constituency after surviving a 2008 assassination attempt.[72]

Although the Taliban declared it would target all the major secular parties (including the PPP and the MQM) in the 2013 election season, it focused mainly on the ANP, attacking it three times more often than the other secular parties.[73] This disparity may reflect the fact that the Taliban is strongest in the KPK, which is also the ANP's turf, making it easier for militants to stage attacks there; attacking in PPP areas such as Sindh is logistically more difficult. Further, it is also indicative of how gaining the Pashtun people's loyalties has become a major battle in Pakistan's ongoing internal security crisis.[74]

Given the ANP's near-inability to campaign and its longer-standing difficulty operating with its own constituency, it is not surprising that the 2013 elections were a disaster for the party. It was the primary casualty of Imran Khan's "tsunami," with the ANP winning only one seat in the National Assembly (from thirteen) and four in the KPK Provincial Assembly (from forty-eight).[75] Although the ANP's defeat cannot be attributed entirely to terrorism—Imran Khan's popularity in the region and voter dissatisfaction with the ANP's performance were also major factors—the threat of militant violence likely exaggerated the already naturally cyclical nature of Pakistani politics.[76]

For a party that has shown its ability to adapt to a wide variety of coalition partners, the current situation presents unprecedented challenges for the ANP. In the past it has proved its pro-sharia bona fides by partnering with religious parties; however, unless the current security situation improves, any of the confessional parties would risk their special status with the Taliban by working with the ANP. Adapting its policies to meet the Taliban's demands would mean the end of the party as it has existed for twenty-five years. The case of the ANP illustrates the limits of strategic positioning along the sharia–secularism spectrum: Taliban violence threatens to harden what were formerly fluid lines.

CHAPTER 8

LESSONS LEARNED

How Pakistan Informs the Arab Spring and Afghanistan

While much of the discussion in the previous chapters is specific to the Pakistani context, the underlying research could have broader relevance in understanding political behavior in other Muslim-majority nations. Some of the core findings of this study are potentially transferrable to other countries: Islamic confessional groups fit into a three-part typology, certain types of Islamic parties focus on certain levels of electoral aggregation, voters are motivated by social group identification and self-interest, and Islamic parties are fundamentally vote-getting operations rather than vehicles for promoting absolutist ideologies. These concepts would have real salience in Afghanistan, Bangladesh, Egypt, and Morocco, each of which is marked by a predominantly Muslim population, a history of colonial rule, and an emerging democracy that has struggled with military rule. These countries differ in their relative similarity to Pakistan, but the validity of the model proposed in this book is strengthened by the consistency with which the model's patterns appear in these different nations.

As has been found in Pakistan, Muslim democratic parties in such countries as Indonesia and Turkey appear more readily successful than Islamist parties do in electoral contests, drawing much larger vote shares and proportions of the seats in the legislature. Although concerns about Islamism are certainly expressed, explicitly Islamic parties are by far the minority and hold far less electoral power than secular or amorphously religious parties do. Greater religious diversity may in fact buffer against the proliferation and power of Islamic parties and therefore render them even less likely to gain power. What is not clear is whether the relative weakness of Islamic parties in countries such as Afghanistan reduces the threat of Islamist extremism and violence there. It is possible that the greater strength of Islamic parties in Pakistan gives legitimacy to nonviolent conservative Islamic politics and therefore defuses the propensity for violent protest.

I have argued that Islamic party mobilization is best understood in the context of policy choices that target specific constituencies in an electorate. In this chapter

I focus on the lessons learned from Pakistan and how Pakistan's experience with Islamic parties might shed light on political developments in Afghanistan, Egypt, Bangladesh, and Morocco. As the Arab Spring has shown, important preconditions, such as the legitimacy of the political party and party organization, set the stage for implementation, and party mobilization itself is fostered only when credible commitments are made to voter blocs. The literature on political development has long considered the importance of integrating the rural countryside into mainstream (effectively urban) political institutions. The literature's focus, however, has not centered on what types of policies and pledges might be most effective for broadening or solidifying an Islamic party's base. Building on the strategy laid out in chapter 7, this chapter suggests that participation in electoral contests does not necessarily yield moderation; it does, however, lead to instrumentalism. Electoral participation and party mobilization are most effective when policy choices target new constituencies of voters to integrate them into the party's organization. The key to this effort is the party's decision regarding its relative placement along the sharia–secularism continuum.

Signaling Credible Commitments and the Sharia-Secular Model: A Rational Choice Explanation for Islamic Parties

Chapters 6 and 7 have used history and anecdotal evidence to lay the foundation for a sharia-secular model. The experiences of Pakistan's Islamic and Islamist parties highlight the importance of credible commitments to party dynamics, the path dependence of elections, and the decision making of constituencies when given limited information. The cases of Afghanistan, Egypt, Bangladesh, and Morocco provide a rich narrative context in which to test the sharia-secular model and its implications, and augment the larger body of work on the political development of Islamic parties in Muslim-majority nations and in developing countries in general.

Chapters 4 and 5 demonstrate that Islamic parties are complex organizations and may have a wide range of internal characteristics. It is also clear that both Muslim democrats and Islamists took strategic steps to increase mobilization after regime transitions through specific policy choices. Political parties, however, can and often do promise policy provisions in order to court constituencies or to solidify their bases. As such, a political party in the run-up to an election is free to offer policy pledges to all constituencies; however, parties also know that they will potentially be held accountable for delivering on their promised policies and that they cannot reasonably hope to deliver on all promises to all constituencies. As a matter of practical necessity, parties must limit the promises they make. Limitation requires selectivity, which inevitably leads to questions as to why political parties end up supporting certain types of provisions and not others. As noted, Islamic parties make decisions about when, where, and from whom to elicit votes, and these calculations can drive extreme positions.

There is a rich history of work in the political economy literature on the provision of social goods, pork barrel, and patronage to reward or woo specific constituencies. Building on the work of Kaare Strom and Elinor Ostrom, I attempt to sketch the dynamics and strategic choice sets available to Islamic political parties as they decide which constituencies they would like to target with their policy preferences.[1] Islamic parties have an expanded tool kit as they are also able to provide strong social identification through religious symbols and spiritual hierarchies.

This comparative chapter provides a rational choice explanation that helps illustrate whether the arguments made about extremism in Pakistan are relevant in other Muslim-majority nations. The value of the sharia-secular model is that it raises key questions and propositions that can be evaluated over the span of two electoral contests in Afghanistan, Egypt, Bangladesh, and Morocco. Chapter 3 outlines the assumptions of this rational choice explanation in the framework of a game theory model (see appendix 1 for the mathematical resolution). The model does not show how all political parties operate in a democratic context or how political parties contribute to regime durability. The model focuses instead on the limited ways Islamic parties can signal a credible commitment to the population in order to gain support and, together with the consequences of moderate-extreme policy decisions, have an impact on future elections.

The sharia-secular model shows how Islamic parties, regardless of their original degree of adherence to tenets of Islamization, are not driven solely by ideological principles. The basic framework of the model is as follows. Two Islamic parties (party 1 and party 2) in a democratic system are competing for the votes of two blocs (constituency A and constituency B) prior to an election. Constituency A is more numerous than constituency B, so constituency A's votes will be decisive in the upcoming election. Here are a few operating assumptions driving the framework and context of the model:

Assumption 1—The state is fragile under transition and finds it difficult to equally distribute social goods.[2]

Assumption 2—Islamic parties have limited resources in their efforts to support constituencies.

Assumption 3—Islamic parties are interested in maintaining their influence and power.

In stage 1 of the model (which ends with the elections) each Islamic party will attempt to pass legislation through a parliament in which both parties are currently represented. Each party may support one of two pieces of legislation. One is more favorable to constituency A and the other more favorable to constituency

B; furthermore, each constituency dislikes the alternative legislation. Once each party has chosen which piece of legislation to sponsor, its respective representatives will make good faith, visible efforts to enact it prior to the election. The model assumes that whether the party is successful or not, *party support for legislation will be noted by voters*.

Party 1 favors constituency A and intends to support policies favorable to that constituency if elected. The opposite is true of party 2, which supports constituency B and, if elected, intends to support policies that are favorable to that constituency but not favorable to constituency A. The parties' discrete utilities are based on two factors—they increase when the party is elected but decrease if the party supports legislation that contradicts its underlying preferences. Since both parties care most about securing the favor of the larger constituency A for the purposes of being elected, party 2 faces a dilemma when choosing which legislation to support. Because party 1 has a dominant strategy of pursuing a policy favoring constituency A, its policy selection is viable both before and after the election. The crux of the model (see figure A.1) is the decision faced by party 2: Should it support legislation that is opposed to its basic interests in order to win office?[3]

After the elections, the model enters stage 2. In this stage, party 2 will have either stuck to its core constituency and lost the elections, or, by supporting legislation favorable to constituency A and unfavorable to constituency B, managed to win a victory over party 1. If party 1 is in power, it will pass legislation favorable to constituency A; if party 2 is in power, it will attempt to recover from the damage done to its discrete utility by passing as many laws that are favorable to constituency B as it can. But as another round of elections approach, party 2 must perform yet another 180-degree turn in an attempt to woo at least some voters from constituency A or else risk losing its control of the legislature. The main question at this stage is what it will take to convince constituency A to risk voting for a party that has proved itself untrustworthy in the past. Party 2 will have to make huge promises to constituency A's voters for even a fraction of them to consider that voting for party 2 is worthwhile.

Let's illustrate this scenario with the politics of a hypothetical country, the Land of Nod. Nod's citizens are divided into two groups—Sleepyheads and Earlybirds. The majority of Noddians are Sleepyheads who do not get up before noon, and they strongly oppose high prices for mattresses. In the minority are Earlybirds, who own mattress factories. Their own sleeping schedules vary, but they all support keeping mattress prices high. Nod has two main political parties—the Soporifics and the Goodnights. The former support legislation favorable to the Sleepyheads, particularly an enormously popular bill now in the Noddian legislature dictating that normal business hours shall be from 1 p.m. to 9 p.m. The Goodnight Party represents the Earlybirds, who generally oppose the legislation because it prevents them from running their mattress factories more than eight hours a day. The Goodnights recognize, however, that if they vote against the workday bill, they will certainly lose the next national election. The Goodnights thus have a choice: Do they want to oppose the legislation more than they want to win elections?

Let's say the Goodnights choose electoral success over principle. They campaign for the workday legislation, vote for it in overwhelming numbers, and promise even more pro-Sleepyhead legislation if they should come to power in the next election. These tactics are successful, and after the next elections the Goodnights find themselves in control of the legislature (the Earlybirds are willing to stick with a party that has served them well over the years, despite the Goodnights' sudden turn toward pro-Sleepyhead policies). The Goodnights set about passing as much pro-Earlybird legislation as they can, much to the delight of the Earlybirds and the increasing anger of the Sleepyheads, and the prices of mattresses rise dramatically. As the next election approaches, the Goodnights realize they have a problem: While they are pleased that they're passing so much pro–mattress maker legislation, they are bound to lose the next election. Do they accept this fact? Or do they try to win the Sleepyheads back, either by paying lip service to the ideal of sleeping in or by promising to pass a truly blockbuster piece of pro-sleep legislation?

In the next section I assess how Islamic parties operate in Afghanistan, Egypt, Bangladesh, and Morocco according to the basic assumptions of the sharia-secular model, which fits into the rational choice model explained in the preceding paragraphs, highlighting key insights and possible predictive behavior.

Egypt: Islamic Parties Fighting for a Seat at the Table

Similar to Pakistan's long history with Islamic parties, Egypt has a track record of active Islamic political organizations. The best way to understand the evolution of these parties is to examine the 2005 and 2011 elections in Egypt; they illustrate both the recurring trends and the recent changes in the Egyptian political landscape. In Egypt's parliamentary system of government, the parliamentary elections represent key moments in the struggle for party dominance. While it has appeared in various incarnations since its inception in 1866, as of the beginning of 2011 the Egyptian Parliament was a bicameral legislature consisting of the People's Assembly (Majilis Al-Sha'ab), a 454-member lower house, and the Shura Council (Majilis Al-Shura), a 264-member upper house.

The 2011 revolution that ended the Hosni Mubarak regime brought rapid constitutional change. The provisional constitution promulgated by the Supreme Council of the Armed Forces in March of that year limited the People's Assembly to 350 members and the Shura Council to 132, two-thirds of which would be directly elected and a final third appointed by the president.[4] A Constituent Assembly, which was elected by the People's Assembly, wrote a new constitution in 2012 that superseded the provisional constitution. Under the 2012 constitution, the lower house was renamed the House of Representatives but retained 350 members; the Shura Council had 150 members, up to a quarter of which could be appointed by the president.[5]

As with most democratically elected governments in the region, historically there has been a significant dissonance between the official powers of the legislature and its actual powers, largely to the advantage of the executive branch. Egypt has a history of strong dictators, and over time the office of the president came to wield far more power than the constitution had initially envisioned. The army has great influence, which also distorts the balance of power, and it questioned the legitimacy of the Parliament. However, the importance attached to the 2011 parliamentary elections, the first following the revolution, is a sign of the power vested in the Parliament and its potential for transformation and true representation.

The sharia-secular model is based on the premise that Islamist parties are not solely driven by ideological principals and that, given the right incentives, they can moderate their policies. The behavior of Egypt's Muslim Brotherhood in the 2005 elections is a prime example. These elections, to the surprise of no one, saw the National Democratic Party (NDP) (Mubarak's party) continue its dominance of Egyptian politics. After the dust had settled and independent candidates had made the decision to throw in their lot with the NDP, the party won 311 of the 454 seats in the lower house (down from 388 the previous term), giving it a solid two-thirds majority. While the traditional opposition parties fared dismally, the biggest story of the election was the success of the Muslim Brotherhood, which won a record 88 seats for an increase of more than 500 percent from the 2000–2005 term. The number might have been higher without the significant irregularities seen during the vote and voter intimidation by the security forces during the second and third rounds of voting, after it became clear that the Brotherhood was set to do historically well.[6] The Brotherhood's success proved that it could function as a major player in Egyptian politics, despite the fact that the Egyptian political establishment saw it as an adversary.

As Stage 1 of the sharia-secular model predicts, a new set of operating factors began to guide the Brotherhood's decisions during the run-up to the elections. Most important, members' campaign rhetoric began to highlight such concepts as "democracy" and "political participation." As Noha Antar writes, "The experience of elaborating a political program for the legislative elections . . . pushed the movement to publicly clarify its positions on concepts such as party pluralism. . . . Also, the MB [Muslim Brotherhood] declared its acceptance of the republican and parliamentary system. In the MB's interpretation, calling for democracy represents the people's will to be governed by *Shar'a Allah*, divine legislation."[7] Thus, to win votes, the Brotherhood had to signal its policy views to various constituencies, and it had to shape these views so that a significant number of Egyptians voters would support them. As the sharia-secular model predicts, possible supporters must decide the likelihood that a party passing favorable legislation will truly support their interests when in office.

The Muslim Brotherhood had spent more than twenty years laying the groundwork for national electoral success, using a set of tactics that might be found in the playbook of any opposition party, Islamist or secular. It followed a three-pronged approach: gradually building a political support base to elect legitimate representatives to Parliament; gaining control (again through legitimate elections) of Egyptian social and civic groups, such as unions; and making the Muslim Brotherhood into the nation's best social services provider. For many Egyptians, the group appeared "more capable of providing services to the Egyptian population, more reliable in keeping the promises it has made, and even more democratic than the [Mubarak] regime."[8]

The Muslim Brotherhood's time "on the outside" during the 1990s, when it was the subject of a regime crackdown, led it to become a strong defender of democracy, at least for the present. As one senior member said, "The Brotherhood consider constitutional rule closest to Islamic rule. . . . We are the first to call for and apply democracy. We are devoted to it."[9] This tendency continued once the Brotherhood had gained some modicum of power by becoming the only significant opposition party in the Parliament. The Brotherhood's parliamentarians avoided social issues and made common cause with all segments of the opposition, including secular liberals.[10] As one observer wrote of the Brotherhood members in Parliament, "The delegation has not pursued an agenda focused on banning books and legislating the length of skirts. It has pursued an agenda of political reform."[11]

These decisions signal the Brotherhood's credible commitment to possible voters. While some parties may promise and not deliver, the Brotherhood was able to overcome this trust deficit by fulfilling promises on which they had campaigned. The sharia-secular model labels these policy decisions as a costly signal of credible commitment.

This clarity on the question of democracy was necessitated by the deep doubts many Egyptians held about the organization's goals.[12] Furthermore, as with the Jamaat-e-Islami and Jamiat Ulema-e-Islam of Pakistan, the Brotherhood is not simply a political party but a religious organization. In an attempt to maintain the support of conservatives who felt that a multiparty democracy was un-Islamic, the Brotherhood often preserved a certain level of ambiguity regarding how, exactly, it meant to achieve the Islamic state.[13] The Muslim Brotherhood's ambiguity thus stems from the care with which it positions itself on the sharia–secularism continuum. Making a choice relative to competitor parties is paramount. A wrong decision could alienate multiple constituencies of supporters. Consequently, the discontent that fueled the January 2011 revolution was more than palpable in the election results of 2005.

As in Pakistan, the Egyptian electoral process is primarily tactical. While the Muslim Brotherhood continues to be a major political party in the elections, it has capitalized on the demand for change and reform running throughout Egyptian society. Though the Muslim Brotherhood was not a catalyst in the revolution that eventually led to the ousting of Hosni Mubarak, it capitalized on the political unrest, couching its policies in the language of the revolution and using its superior organizational skills to secure strategic gains. As protesters renewed their efforts to ensure fair and transparent elections, the Muslim Brotherhood stood back while the death toll continued to rise in clashes between protesters and security forces. The Muslim Brotherhood's gains came from its passivity. By urging its supporters to refrain from confrontations with authorities, the Brotherhood cultivated its image as a bastion of stability in a country increasingly wracked with insecurity and uncertainty. Even though voters in Egypt have incomplete information, they are able to ascertain that the Brotherhood is not using extra-electoral means of achieving power.

This role of the Islamic parties has led many to posit that the Islamists and the Muslim Brotherhood have always enjoyed immense popularity throughout Egypt, relying mainly on "a platform of social work."[14] Essentializing the role of Islamic organizations might be problematic, but it is proof of the perception they have cultivated for themselves. While the wider policies of the Muslim Brotherhood continue to reference sharia, the group supplements this discourse with allusions to democracy and the need for order. The Brotherhood is able to maintain a balance between two seemingly divergent approaches. This balance is bolstered by a wider compromise between the core principles of the Brotherhood and the need for order fostered by the military establishment. As long as the Islamist parties play by the rules of the establishment—that is, upholding the need for public order and stability in Egypt—the Muslim Brotherhood and other parties can propagate policies that do not directly harm the law and order situation. As predicted by the sharia-secular model, the Brotherhood is making pragmatic political calculations.

Prior to the 2011 overthrow of the Mubarak regime, the indirect nature of the Egyptian presidential elections in Egypt had been subject to increasing criticism. The NDP-controlled People's Assembly nominated and confirmed the presidential candidate, who was then subject to a nationwide "yes or no" referendum. In the past, accusations of manipulation by the incumbent government have dogged these referendums.

A slate of constitutional amendments was introduced prior to the 2005 elections in order to regulate the electoral process. The amendments required any political party participating in the next elections to have been licensed for at least five years and to be able to hold at least 5 percent of the seats in the lower and upper houses of Parliament. The Presidential Electoral Commission, comprising current and former judges and other public figures, was established to assess candidates' eligibility. The elections were plagued by widespread reports of use of force and repressive techniques by NDP officials. It was reported that "security forces and gangs of thugs from the ruling National Democratic Party blockaded access to dozens of polling sites where opposition candidates were strong."[15] Ten deaths were reported to have occurred over the span of the month-long elections, as authorities opened fire on citizens who tried to vote.

With the next slate of elections, the sharia-secular model shows how the two-stage process of supporter-party interaction evolved. Having solidified its role as delivering on credible commitments, the Brotherhood had credibility among key voters. The perception of fraud and discontent spilled over into the 2011 elections, with the newly resurgent civil society wary over the mistakes of the past. Following dissolution of the NDP-dominated People's Assembly and the ousting of Hosni Mubarak earlier in the year, the elections were Egypt's first free and fair contests in decades. The Brotherhood took full advantage of this political opening, announcing in February 2011 that it was forming a political party, the Freedom and Justice Party (FJP), to contest the September parliamentary elections. (As a banned religious organization, the Brotherhood had previously been legally prohibited from forming a party under its own name.)

The sharia-secular model reflects that Islamic organizations frequently engage in political strategies that require actions counter to their ideological claims. The FJP leaders took pains to include Copts and other minorities among the ranks of party members, although party leader (and future president) Mohammed Morsi made clear that he did not think women or non-Muslims were suited for the presidency.[16] The party's platform was designed to appeal to the broadest possible swath of Egyptians, combining support for capitalism with opposition to "manipulation and monopoly," for instance. Announcing its formation shortly after the crowds had departed Tahrir Square, party spokesman Essam Al-Arian argued that "when we look at the revolution's slogans, such as 'freedom,' 'social justice' and 'equality'—all of these can be found in Islamic Law. . . . This revolution is calling for what Islamic Law calls for."[17]

But the Muslim Brotherhood was not the only Islamist party to stake its claim in the electoral landscape. The most significant of the many conservative Islamist parties founded after the revolution was the Al-Nour Party, which has its roots in Alexandria's Salafi (ultraorthodox) population. Al-Nour occupied a position somewhat to the right of the FJP on the sharia–secularism spectrum. While its leaders promised to institute sharia "in a gradual way that suits the nature of society" and reassured voters that they embraced science and modernity, they also made clear that they remained deeply conservative on social issues, such as the interaction between men and women.[18]

The FJP was the primary victor in the 2011 parliamentary elections, winning 152 seats (out of the 322 filled) and 40 percent of the vote in the first round. Al-Nour, however, far outperformed expectations based on its relative youth and lack of experience. Salafi candidates from its bloc received 26 percent of the vote in the first round (more than the major secular parties put together), and the party ended with 78 seats in the legislature, or more than three times as many as the next largest party.[19]

As the sharia-secular model indicates, Al-Nour (Party 2) seeks to define itself against the Muslim Brotherhood, differentiating itself from the more liberal Islamist group in order to peel off more conservative voters. Al-Nour's challenge forces the Brotherhood to make a painful decision of whether it should seek to reassure its conservative supporters that it in fact shares their views on such issues as the role that Islamic law should play in Egypt or, recognizing that reassurance would incur the cost of losing the support of Egypt's more liberal voters, whether it should stick to its middle-of-the-road position.[20]

The key predictive behavior of the sharia-secular model is that electoral participation will push the Al-Nour Party toward instrumentalism. Although Al-Nour's leaders believe that the principles of sharia should be the main source of legislation, the party will be faced with pragmatic choices of institutionalizing policy positions. One example is the question of religious minorities in Egypt. For instance, the Al-Nour Party's platform states that Egypt's Christians can be governed by their own personal and family law.[21]

The sharia-secular model predicts that the legislative battle ahead will largely determine the positions of both parties; each will have to make strategic decisions regarding where to place itself on the sharia–secularism continuum. Much to the dismay of foreign commentators, the Islamist parties have seen the downfall of Hosni Mubarak as an opportunity to incorporate parts of an Islamist agenda into the policy provision of services to key supporters. The parties' pragmatic political decisions on issues ranging from corruption to health care, however, will determine how their constituencies will vote and whether their platforms will moderate or move toward extremism. For both parties, the movement along the moderate–extreme continuum is driven by political expediency rather than by ideology.

Bangladesh: Divergent Islamist Trends from Pakistan

As in Pakistan, Islam has played a dynamic and controversial role in the national identity and national politics of Bangladesh. Bangladesh began life as East Pakistan, and thus religion played a key role in determining its boundaries with the predominantly Hindu Indian state of West Bengal. As in West Pakistan, however, centuries-old divisions along class, sectional, and regional lines gained prominence following partition. The Punjabi elites of West Pakistan looked down on their countrymen of East Pakistan. The stigma in West Pakistan was that Islam, and more generally the culture, in East Pakistan was "tainted" because of its historical intermingling with Hinduism.

Over the years, the list of grievances from East Pakistan against West Pakistan began to grow. As a result, a nationalist movement began to develop in East Pakistan. The Pakistani election of 1970 resulted in the Awami League (AL) of East Pakistan winning by an overwhelming majority, shifting the balance of power from West to East Pakistan. West Pakistan resisted and authorized a brutal suppression of East Pakistan. This clash ultimately culminated in the creation of an independent Bangladesh in 1971.

The formation of Bangladesh went against the notion that all Muslim areas of former British India should unite. Leading the struggle for independence, the AL grew out of the Bangla language movement, which opposed Jinnah's proclamation of Urdu as the national language, and was based on Bengali nationalism, not on Islam.

When civil war broke out in East Pakistan in 1971, members of Jamaat-e-Islami's East Pakistan Wing did not support the independence movement; instead, they supported the Pakistan Army. As a result, following independence, the group was marginalized, and its leaders were even accused of war crimes. Furthermore, Bangladesh's founder and leader of the AL, Sheikh Mujibur Rahman, actively suppressed the group with the intent to create a secular and democratic nation.

Following natural disasters and the AL's corruption and mismanagement, the Bangladesh Army chief of staff Lt. Gen. Ziaur Rahman took power in 1975 (and officially assumed the presidency in 1977).[22] According to the sharia-secular model, as a way to legitimize his rule, the general began to lift the restrictions placed on Islamic parties and the JI in particular. He also removed the constitutional commitment to secularism with a series of amendments that gave primacy to Islamic law. After his assassination in 1981, there was a brief span of civilian rule, which was quickly followed by another military coup in 1982. Under the new military dictator, Lt. Gen. Hussain Mohammed Ershad, the Islamization of Bangladesh continued to expand with the declaration that Islam was the state religion.

Islamic parties thrived under the military dictators. For the first time, these groups were allowed to express their views freely, preach against religious minorities, and endorse particular interpretations of Islamic theology. Furthermore, attacks against Hindus increased with little to no reprimand from the state.

Conventional narratives have portrayed Bangladesh's history as a linear progression from secularism to an Islamic state, with the JI as the main protagonist. While the JI and other Islamic parties did contribute to the growing notion of Bangladesh's being an Islamic state in 1980s and 1990s, it overstates the JI's influence in shaping public discourse. Rather, the sharia-secular model suggests that the dynamics of Bangladesh's principal political parties, the AL and the Bangladesh Nationalist Party (BNP), solidified this trend. The BNP was established under General Ziaur Rahman and from its inception distinguished between Bengali and Bangladeshi nationalism, the latter being explicitly Muslim and separate from the Bengalis of India. The BNP also took an anti-India stance. Meanwhile, the AL had a reputation for having pro-India and pro-Hindu sentiments.

Democracy since the 1990s in Bangladesh has been defined by the intense rivalry between the AL and BNP. During this time, the BNP had to make pragmatic political calculations. Based on the sharia-secular model, the BNP came to rely on the JI's support so that it could wield political influence beyond Parliament. A major part of this support contributed to the party's defense of Islam in the constitution, specifically in the preamble. Under the first term of martial law, a presidential decree replaced the "principle of secularism" with a profession of "absolute trust and faith in the Almighty Allah." The second Parliament of Bangladesh later legitimized the decree.

In January 2010, the Supreme Court ruled that the Parliament did not possess any authority to suspend the constitution and proclaim martial law. Thereby Parliament could not legitimize the actions of martial law regimes. This judgment paved the way for restoring the original language in the preamble of the constitution. Furthermore, the Supreme Court followed with a July 2010 ruling scrapping provisions that had allowed political parties with a manifesto based on faith doctrine to flourish after 1979. The ruling is expected to pave the way for a return to complete secularism in Bangladeshi law.

While the BNP has more actively engaged with Islamic parties, the AL's activities have not been outside the influence of the sharia-secular model. In recent years, despite maintaining "secularism" as its key platform, the party has also played a role in contributing to the burgeoning of Islamic politics in Bangladesh. By 1996, the AL's leadership was no longer willing to stick to its secular agenda and risk being labeled anti-Muslim by the BNP. Shortly before the 1996 elections, AL leader Sheikh Hasina performed a well-publicized hajj. Khaleda Zia, the BNP's leader, responded by accepting a long-standing demand of radical Islamist groups to have the state recognize private *madrasahs*.

Competition for Islamic sentiments between the BNP and AL leaders reflects an overall trend of voter convergence in Bangladesh. Recent electoral analyses show that the distribution of voters has gradually become "distinctly unimodal at the center."[23] This development implies that the ideologically oriented parties to the left and right, such as the Communist Party and Jamaat-e-Islami, would not be in a position to gain enough votes to destabilize the two major parties. Yet, at the same time, the increased convergence of voters in the center increases the competition between the BNP and AL for votes from the left and right, with more emphasis on the right, given the greater electoral influence that right-leaning parties have compared to their left-leaning counterparts. Based on the sharia-secular model, it means more flexibility in terms of policies and ideologies toward the right for the AL and perhaps even increasing cooperation between the AL and BNP. A close alliance between the two parties would lead them to clearly dominate national politics, contributing to political stability in the country and reducing the risk of military intervention.

Afghanistan: Why Islamic Party Origins Matter

As Pakistan demonstrated, ideology drives a party's emergence and is critical to the political development of Islamic confessional parties. Yet while ideology is central during the initial stages, it cannot sustain a party at later stages, particularly when it comes to political relevancy, for which the litmus test is elections. In September 2005, Afghanistan saw its first parliamentary and provincial elections since the allied forces occupied the country after the September 11 attacks on the United States. The elections were held in accordance with the United Nations–sponsored Bonn Agreement after the Taliban were ousted from Kabul. Moreover, the elections were held under the auspices of the 2004 constitution, which was formed by the Hamid Karzai–led interim administration.

The election was contested not on the basis of political parties but by individuals under the single nontransferable vote system. Under this system, candidates stand as individuals and not as members of a party list. The system is used to avoid empowering political parties, which are unpopular in Afghanistan owing to the mujahideen parties' links to foreign governments during the Soviet-Afghan War.

In Afghanistan, the key issue is that political parties are competing with armed guerrilla organizations, and they often work in tandem. Hence, Islamists frequently engage in political strategies that require actions counter to their ideological claims, including the use of extra-electoral means (violence) and the formation of coalitions with militant and secular organizations. The 2005 elections were no different as the elections were held under tight security due to concerns of interference from Taliban militants. Although polling stations were provided special security, the voter turnout was disappointing, as only 57 percent (about 6.8 million voters) cast their votes. The low turnout can be attributed to confusion over the plethora of candidates without a party affiliation and high voter illiteracy in some areas. The presence of American and North Atlantic Treaty Organization troops in the country did not escape the notice of many Afghans, who were hesitant about voting while under virtual occupation.

Therefore, as data on the 2005 elections shows, the electoral contest did not come as a surprise since prominent personalities ruled the roost. The results largely confirmed expectations that many seats would go to leading national and local personalities and to factional groupings. Among the pro-Karzai parliamentarians was his elder brother Qayum of Qandahar Province. About forty parliamentarians were from the Hezb-e-Islami, the Islamic party of anti-US former mujahideen leader Gulbuddin Hekmatyar, but they renounced violence and supported Karzai. Despite the absence of parties, it was widely believed that Karzai supporters formed about 60 percent of the Parliament.[24] In hindsight, the legitimacy of this democratically elected government has been regarded with great suspicion, fueled by its inability to maintain law and order and by Karzai's close relationship with American leaders.

Simplifying the power dynamics in post-Taliban Afghanistan, the 2005 election results ended up bringing to light the complexities of the electoral process and the actors who had a stake in the nation-building process. A motley crew of candidates were elected to the Parliament as a mixture of "Islamists, former mujahideen, drug barons, former Communists, technocrats, academics, independents, women and the Taliban" were accommodated in the form of the fourteen-party, pro–Northern Alliance National Understanding Front. Abdurrab Rasul Sayyaf of Ittehad-e-Islami (renamed Tanzim-e Dawat-e Islami-ye Afghanistan) was a notable mujahideen elected to the Parliament along with the late Burhanuddin Rabbani of Jamiat-e-Islami from Badakhshan.

The key insight of the sharia-secular model that voters have incomplete information about party behavior was evident as optimism around parliamentary elections was at an all-time low during the September 2010 elections. The elections had been delayed from May owing to budgetary and security concerns; however, the delay and the assurances from the Karzai administration did not help matters. Voter turnout was extremely thin, with only 3.6 million casting their votes from the 10 million eligible voters. The Taliban threat loomed large as eleven deaths were reported on the day of the elections. Furthermore, allegations of widespread fraud still remain unchallenged despite Karzai's repeated assertions to the contrary. The Free and Fair Elections Foundation of Afghanistan, the country's biggest electoral monitoring group, reported incidents of ballot stuffing and proxy and underage voting in most provinces.[25]

In the 2010 Afghan elections, the issuance of party lists was still not allowed. Despite changes to electoral laws that allowed parties to field individual candidates, of the 110 political parties that had candidates running for elections, candidates from only 5 parties ran under their respective parties' logos.[26] While it was widely believed that the establishment and thriving of political parties was the key to a fully functioning democracy, the Afghan electoral process remained woefully deprived. The confusion over the change in electoral laws was largely to blame for the dismal representation of political parties. Among the parties fielding candidates, more than half came from the Shia Hezb-e Wahdat-e Islami (Islamic Unity Party), which is led by Second Vice President Karim Khalili. The nascent Hezb-Musharekat-e Melli (National Participation Party) fielded eight candidates, including the party leader Haji Najib Kabuli. Two candidates each were put forward by Hezb-e Muttahed-e Melli (National United Party) of Nur ul-Haq

Ulumi and by Hezb-e Paiwand-e Melli (National Union Party), the party of the Ismaili sect leader Seyed Mansur Naderi.

However, the original 226 party-affiliated candidates presented a much more representative spectrum of Afghanistan's political landscape. There were contenders from all four of the major political currents in Afghanistan: Islamist (or former mujahideen) parties such as Jamiat-e-Islami, Hezb-e Islami, Sayyaf's Da'wat-e Islami, and Mahaz-e Milli-ye Islami-ye Afghanistan, or Harakat; former leftists such as the Democratic Party and the Peace and National Welfare Society; new, pro-democratic parties such as the Labour and Development Party and the Hezb-Azadikhwa Afghanistan; and ethno-nationalists like the Afghan Mellat (Afghan Nation) and the National Congress Party.

The individuals who were able to secure votes in the elections capitalized on their names as major players in Afghanistan. Further, political party backing came into its own as electoral laws were relaxed. However, by and large, without party politics and a democratic culture that was conducive to electing democratic leaders, it was inevitable that already powerful and well-known individuals, as opposed to nascent politicians, would make substantial gains in the polls.

The sharia-secular model recognizes that Islamist organizations are tethered to practical political considerations. Some individuals found themselves at the receiving end of patronage from the US government, which still has a military presence in the country. President Karzai is one such example, as he was willing to defer to Western wishes in return for support for his regime. A mutual web of interests was drawn between foreign powers and the local elite, especially in the wake of the war on terror, with Afghanistan occupying a central place in international politics. The strategic gains made by the local politicians thus have to be viewed not only on a national basis but also in terms of external influences.

The choice of strategic behavior for most political actors in Afghanistan has been to strike a balance between appealing to the electorate and allaying the fears of the American authorities. In many ways, international actors subsume the place of Afghan citizenry in the sharia-secular model. The fractured nature of a country still reeling from a long, drawn-out war paves the way for more opportunist politicians to take advantage of certain situations in order to gain small victories that might result in their elections.

Owing to the unpopular, ongoing war in the country, some politicians have sought to appeal to the frustrated masses. This tactic has led to a rise in the popularity of some politicians, such as those belonging to the left-wing Democratic Party and the National Peace Activists Party or those of the democratic Labour and Development Party and the Azadikhwahan. A multitude of political parties are cropping up, in hopes of bridging the leadership chasm that currently defines Afghani politics. However, because there seems to be a widespread distrust of political parties, it has been a difficult journey. Most strong candidates wish to run as independents with a party's implicit backing.

Candidates seem to adopt this sort of moderate behavior because they do not wish to upset the various stakeholders in Afghan politics. As the sharia-secular model indicates, electoral participation does not necessarily yield moderation. To avoid confrontation, individuals aspire to seamlessly slip into government positions without troubling the status quo too much. For example, Anwar al-Haq Ahadi served as the minister of finance in President Karzai's administration while retaining his position as the head of a powerful Pashtun nationalist party called the Afghan Mellat party.[27] This duality for retaining public office is a necessary corollary to the middle or more moderate stance that politicians take officially, since the promise of going into government leads to a tamping down of the stance that the party would otherwise like to take.

Furthermore, this disjunction between individuals and political parties means that parties can take seemingly extreme stances yet not affect the chances of their sympathizers in politics. In the sharia-secular model, this disconnect reflects the networked nature of political parties in Afghanistan and is most similar to the JUI's experience in Pakistan. Moreover, the threat of assassination in a highly volatile country discourages some politicians from taking more reconciliatory stances in public forums. The September 2011 suicide bombing death of Burhanuddin Rabbani, head of the High Peace Council, which is the commission that negotiates with the Taliban, is yet another reminder of the high stakes involved in taking conciliatory stances.

However, in order to reassure the Americans of their commitments to peace, politicians constantly go back and forth and assume multiple stances as they sympathize with the militants' grievances and, at the same time, do not condone the violence they wreck across the country. The model would predict that those political parties not directly fielding candidates in official positions would take more extremist stances as they are bound neither by patronage of the US-led coalition nor by the larger interests of the country. Thus, these regional parties adopt stances that appeal to their constituencies directly, and they might, at times, involve supporting the militancy. As shown in Pakistan, many wrongly assume that these parties are primarily interested in winning *national* elections; however, Islamic party instrumentalism becomes clear only by taking seriously parties' interests in winning *local* elections as well.

Afghanistan Analysts Network senior analyst Thomas Ruttig tries to explain why the 2010 elections yet again pit myriad numbers of independents against each other: "A questionable law, technical problems in implementing it, an astonishing lack of awareness about legal developments on the part of some parties and, it seems, the lack of courage on the part of others to run under their party name has led to a situation in which only five political parties are fielding candidates in the September 18 poll. In all, just 31 candidates will sport a party logo. That is out of a total number of around 2500 candidates. Let's call these the 'officially party-affiliated candidates.'"[28]

The ability to switch between adhering to the party's brand and making individual decisions gives Islamists more flexibility in Afghanistan. Dominant Islamist parties, such as the Jamiat-e Islami, Hezb-e Islami, and Afghan Mellat, already have people in top government positions and do not want to jeopardize their favorable standing by emphasizing their organizational brand. It is no secret that President Karzai is weary of political parties. These parties, therefore, had no qualms about dropping their official party logo as they banked on the individual prominence of their candidates to win seats in the 2010 election. The tribal leader who initiates and builds a party relies on the networks he has prior to entering electoral politics. His original network, the legitimacy it imparts upon him over time, forms the customs, code, communal law that forms the basis of the leader's party strategy. Thus, the right elder, the right cleric is the one perfectly poised with pre-existing networks at the time he enters politics. Critically, institutions are so fragile and newly formed that a leader's pre-existing networks are crucial to the ability to form a party in the first place. In other words, a would-be party leader can't join the JI in Pakistan or the GOP in the United States because in Afghanistan there is no JI or GOP to join.

Morocco: Where Incumbency Leads to Moderation

As reflected in the Pakistani experience, the relaxation of ideological positions signals a shift in approach for confessional parties that is best described as instrumentalist. Buoyed by the winds of change blowing from the optimism generated by the Arab Spring, the Justice and Development Party (PJD) won the November 2011 elections by a landslide.

The results of the 2007 parliamentary elections had surprised many observers. While the Istiqlal (Independence) Party finished the race in a leading position, with fifty-two seats (16 percent of the popular vote), the PJD had followed with forty-six seats (14 percent of the popular vote). Expectations prior to the election were high regarding the Islamists' potential gains, especially against the background of Western and domestic polls predicting the unstoppable rise of the PJD. During the final phase of the election campaign, the party leadership expressed high optimism, stating publicly that seventy to eighty seats were within reach and that the party would be the strongest bloc in the Parliament. Initial statements from prominent party figures were characterized by an angry tone and harsh accusations of vote buying by other parties. Local and international monitoring groups confirmed that the elections were conducted in a fair and transparent manner. Remarkably, voter turnout plunged to a historical low of 37 percent, down from 51 percent in the 2002 elections and 58 percent in 1997.

The success of the Islamist PJD, headed by Abdelilah Benkirane, marks a major shift in the politics of Morocco. As had voters in Egypt, the voters in

Morocco turned to a centrist Islamist party (in this case the PJD) as an alternative in the quest to satiate their thirst for real change. The PJD's success can be attributed, by and large, to a "combination of good organization, an outsider status and not being too much of a threat to Morocco's all-powerful king."[29] The turnout for the elections was disappointing, however, as only 45 percent of registered voters, or 13 million out of 21 million eligible voters, cast their votes.[30] It has been posited that the low turnout is part of a wider disillusionment with the political process and the system that sustains it. "This [low turnout] sends a strong signal to authorities that Moroccans are not buying the proposed reforms," Najib Chawki, an activist with the movement, told Reuters.[31]

As the sharia-secular model suggests, the Islamists' relaxation of their ideological positions signals an incrementalist shift in their approach. Based on this observation, it would be erroneous to describe the PJD as ideologically absolutist. The PJD uses Islam as a reference, or more of an indicator of the moral values prevailing in the region, and has strategically chosen key positions on the sharia–secularism continuum. The party's focus seems to be oriented toward more secular issues, such as eliminating corruption and restructuring a flagging economy. It has avoided issues that create consternation for most Islamist parties, such as mandating the wearing of the *hijab* and banning the sale of alcohol.

The PJD has made economic and legal issues the foundation of its platform, eschewing the more controversial social questions that are at the heart of some Islamist party platforms.[32] The PJD gained support in recent years by tapping people's disillusionment with their government, which was seen as removed from voters' needs, and by focusing on the poor and jobless youths.

The sharia-secular model focuses on sending costly signals of credible commitment. The PJD sent several such costly signals and helps explain how far the party has come since the last elections in 2007, the first year in which the PJD fielded candidates in all constituencies. In these elections, the Socialist Union of Popular Forces lost nearly a quarter of its erstwhile seats to the conservative monarchist Istiqlal Party, whose leader Abbas El Fassi was elected as prime minister following the vote. However, this victory came amid allegations from the JDP regarding the "use of money" by the other parties to win the elections. Saad-Eddine Othmani, then leader of the PJD, even asserted that the PJD was "the [real] winner of the elections."[33]

The PJD's failure in the 2007 elections follows another unsuccessful run to capture a majority in Parliament in the 2002 elections. However, it must be noted that "since 2002 the party has become less preoccupied with debates on ideological and religious issues" and has greatly benefited from being on the opposition benches as mistrust against the incumbent governments mounted.[34] The only obstacle in the party's path was the fear that the leadership might not be able to translate the party's ideological opposition into substantial reform and change. While these concerns have remained, 2011 is a different world, with Morocco feeling the pinch of the economic downturn more than ever. The desire for change manifested in the Arab Spring, and the PJD eventually prevailed.

The PJD's success has followed a trajectory similar to that of many other parties emerging from the fringe. At a fundamental level the party's appeal to Islam sets it apart from other parties, probably leading to its initial alienation, but the PJD's ability to transcend the label of "Islamism" has been the main reason for its mainstream success. Islamic parties make decisions about where to position themselves on the sharia–secularism continuum, and the PJD's strategic behavior of avoiding hot-button issues (*hijab* and alcohol) has been consistent throughout. However, in the context of Morocco, these moderate stances were necessary for the party's political survival if it was to gain the king's patronage since he retains the final say in matters pertaining to defense, security, and religion.

Since the PJD always saw itself as a nationalist party, it took decisions that would not pander to regional and parochial interests. However, since the Islamist vote was its most valuable and core vote bank, the party continues to assert such policies as "Islamic financing" that would pander to the Islamic constituents but at the same time would appease the more secular elite and establishment.

The PJD seems to strike an ideal balance between staying true to its core values while being willing to cooperate with other parties to reach a viable compromise and middle ground on some issues. However, one must not read too much into its choice of coalition partner, the nationalist Istiqlal Party, which came in second with sixty seats in 2011.[35] The PJD's choice proves that there is not much compromise there, as it is a conservative party backed by the establishment. Thus, cooperation with the establishment is a major theme running through the policies adopted by the PJD. The PJD's main victory, therefore, has been the fine line it has trod in relation to the populist stance for reform that it has assumed and the expectations that the establishment has from it—that is, the hope that the PJD will stem the revolutionary tendencies and "defuse protests prompted by the Arab Spring."[36]

In the sharia-secular model, the PJD's stance comes closest to that of the Pakistani Muslim democrats. The PJD is seen as a midway compromise between such populist demands as eradicating corruption and appeasing the same system that begat that very corruption. This seemingly contradictory notion cuts across boundaries and is a problem facing both most regimes of the region and those wishing to institute change from within the system.

Initially it was the PJD's different, if not radical, stance that allowed it to make small footholds in previous elections and the public's imagination. However, to become a truly national party, it was important for the party to make certain strategic decisions. This mixture of the old and the new, and the Arab Spring and stability, makes the PJD an atypical candidate for politics at a time of great uncertainty and reemphasis on democratic processes. The PJD continues to "play by the rules" of the machinery of Moroccan politics. Because the PJD has been part of the political ecosystem, it inevitably shies away from delicate issues, reactionary politics, high-risk political endeavors, or the like. The PJD is becoming synonymous with the entrenched bureaucracy that, like a large ship, it is impossible to turn quickly.

Conclusion: Why Pakistan Matters

This sharia-secular model parallels major aspects of Islamic party electoral experiences in Afghanistan, Egypt, Bangladesh, and Morocco. This chapter has focused primarily on how strategic policy choices made party mobilization possible and has demonstrated that the shared struggle for Islamist votes led political parties to take different paths. In particular, Islamists in stage 1 (the period up to and including the first set of elections) were able to signal their commitment through Islamization policies, whereas in stage 2 (the period up to and including the second set of elections), Islamists or Muslim democrats signaled their commitment through patronage to multiple segments of society. However, that the model fails to account for or address the common downfall of both groups—namely, military intervention—is noteworthy.

Examining the sharia-secular model illustrates the strengths and weaknesses of its insights. The strengths of the model center on the importance of credible commitments to party dynamics, the path dependence of early elections, and the decision parameters of constituencies with limited information. The model is a simplified version and does not incorporate additional factors that have shaped various cases, such as the roles of military (including international) and paramilitary forces. Moreover, it is virtually impossible to reduce the entire population of a nation into two main constituencies, because there exist other more nuanced coalitions that may not be adequately represented by either constituency A or constituency B.

As noted, core findings of the sharia-secular model are potentially transferrable to other countries: Islamic confessional groups fit into a three-part typology, certain types of Islamic parties focus on certain levels of electoral aggregation, voters are motivated by social group identification and self-interest, and Islamic parties are fundamentally vote-getting operations rather than vehicles for absolutist ideologies.

CHAPTER 9

FOREIGN POLICY IMPLICATIONS AND NEW TRENDS

Awareness of the broader context, history, and motivations underlying the behavior of Islamic confessional parties in Pakistan could vastly improve the ability of foreign policymakers to successfully navigate the ever-changing and often bewildering political terrain there. Oversimplified and uninformed depictions of party politics, and in particular misperceptions of Islamist parties, in Pakistan have affected international policy in negative ways, resulting in clumsy mismanagement or total neglect of potentially vital relationships. Understanding that both pragmatic political and religious considerations motivate Islamic political parties will impact how the US government deals with Islamic political actors, both allies and antagonists. More specifically, understanding that extreme Islamist politics is not driven solely by ideological absolutism should open new opportunities for Western diplomacy.

US policy toward Pakistan in the post-9/11 world has focused overwhelmingly on security concerns, particularly in the porous border region between Afghanistan and Pakistan. This mountainous 1,600-square-mile area on both sides of the border is now the hub of a global militant Islamist insurgency. International stakeholders have become increasingly concerned about the influence of Islamic extremism as these territories have become host to training camps and *madrasahs* for extremist groups, including the Taliban and al-Qaeda. This region is incredibly difficult to effectively police in part because the political boundaries are purely artificial creations of former colonial powers. In many ways, while they do have socioeconomic differences, the Pashtun peoples of Pakistan share several meaningful features with the Pashtuns in bordering Afghan territories. Movement back and forth between the two areas has long been a normal part of life in the region, reflecting ancient tribal and kinship bonds that remain regardless of the imposition of an arbitrary border. Given these historical realities, while US military action starting in 2001 was originally targeted at Afghanistan, many high-profile targets have migrated into the border regions of Pakistan. Even tacit Pakistani military cooperation with international stakeholders is frowned upon by much of the frontier electorate, in no small part because the Taliban and al-Qaeda are able to bring patronage resources to the region and perceived legitimate religious authorities support the insurgents.

A much smaller proportion of international aid to Pakistan comes in the form of development support to impoverished regions. The distribution pattern of these funds belies the claim that they are intended to blunt the endemic poverty that is assumed to spur extreme Islamist politics. In reality, funds are given not to the poorest areas but to those of primary security significance, where it is believed that development will lead to security and stability. Development aid in these regions includes funding for health initiatives to improve child and maternal health outcomes and for educational improvements and school-building projects. Money for these efforts has been limited, resulting in modest deliverables and low support from the Pakistani government. Security issues have hampered efforts to provide developmental support, resulting in personnel turnover, project delays, and cessation of projects.

Beyond simply sending money, a major role for the foreign policy apparatus is interacting with counterparts in Pakistan to coordinate efforts and promote advantageous policy approaches. In this realm, the actions of Western officials are of particular interest and concern. During President Musharraf's military rule, the United States largely ignored the country's civilian opposition, both Islamic and secular, even when they held crucial blocks of power in the National Assembly. This single-minded focus was perhaps inevitable when Pakistan was ruled by martial law and when the United States, above all else, required military support and cooperation during Operation Enduring Freedom in Afghanistan. Since Musharraf's fall and the rise of civilian parties such as the Pakistan People's Party and the Pakistan Muslim League–Nawaz, however, Western officials' interest of powerful National Assembly concerns is both justified and riskier.

The lack of engagement with important groups outside the executive branch is most pronounced in terms of Western dealings with Islamic parties, especially regionally important Islamists. From 2001 to 2007, the Islamist coalition party of the Muttahida Majlis-e-Amal was a potent political force in Pakistan, but some Western officials not only limited but also avoided contact with its members. The same approach was adopted toward other network and hierarchical Islamist groups with sway in the National Assembly or strategically important districts. Beyond simply refusing to engage these parties, much of the West's policy directed toward Islamic political parties in Pakistan has been designed to suppress, disable, or circumvent them. Founded on the demonstrably faulty conventional wisdom that political Islamism is driven by economic disenfranchisement and militaristic zeal, Western officials have undertaken to limit or weaken confessional Islamic parties by limiting its engagement and providing few avenues for capacity building.

The data on voting behavior presented in chapters 6 and 7 and the historical findings laid out in chapters 4 and 5 call into serious doubt the motivational assumptions underlying these policies and suggest that such efforts might well be counterproductive. Islamic parties are neither a recent development in Pakistan nor an outgrowth of militant Islam; rather, they are foundational to the nation itself and its democratic political process. It can be reasonably concluded that such parties will remain an integral fixture of the political landscape regardless of third-party efforts to eradicate them or limit their growth. These parties can (and should) be differentiated from violent Islamist militias, though in some instances they do have loose ties to such groups. While the Islamic parties have complex attitudes toward violence, they are invested in the political process and would not stand to gain from a transition to autocratic religious rule. As such, despite their rhetoric, these parties are important potential allies for Western powers.

The historical conduct and core interests of Pakistan's Islamic political parties suggest that they could actually be useful allies in the effort to allay and limit the spread of violent Islamism if properly incentivized. While Islamist parties have recently deemed it an electoral advantage to affiliate to varying degrees with militaristic organizations, these affiliates (such as the Taliban) are actively working to destabilize the political system that Islamist parties depend on for their own survival. Rather than pushing Islamic parties further into the arms of extremists through policies of suppression, Western powers would be wise to exploit the tensions between these groups and look for points of shared interest with Islamic parties that may serve as the basis of dialogue and cooperation.

This new approach will require a major realignment of perspective as the West must interact with political parties that are considered moderate in the Pakistani context rather than with those that would be seen as moderate by American norms. To be sure, this shift poses domestic political challenges for Western allies. There is a risk of being seen as cooperating with polarizing groups that employ anti-Western rhetoric and have connections to the Taliban and other extremists. However, Western policymakers would do well to look beyond the rhetoric of Islamic parties, to determine their underlying motivations, and to create innovative ways to provide support to groups that espouse antiviolence measures.

In the area of public diplomacy, and particularly on the education front, we should be directly challenging the myth that the West is opposed to Islam. We should send the message that expanding quality education is a priority across Pakistan and that religious schools play an important role in that task (as some would argue that in the West). We should also stress that violent radicalism is the main issue both for Pakistan and the West. The West should make clear that its problem is not with *madrasahs* but with murderers. Political officers in Pakistan should be visiting religious scholars, *madrasah* principals, political activists (including hard-line leaders from the Jamiat Ulema-e-Islam and the Jamaat-e-Islami), and student leaders. The task is not to endorse or agree with these people but to keep channels of dialogue open and in particular to challenge the wilder inaccuracies about Western policy. Senior Western diplomats should consider visiting a *madrasah* or a group of student Islamists and giving a short talk. They should take an opportunity to stress core messages on how we respect religiosity in Pakistan and on how we view terrorism, not Islam, as posing a problem. They could also briefly mention the depth of religious practice in the West and observe how school choice is encouraging better-quality education.

Muslim democratic parties have shown more consistent support for key Western values, democratic political processes, and economic initiatives while also distancing themselves from Islamic militancy. Thus, the West has a cultural foundation from which it can reach out to these groups. Muslim democratic parties tend to be a reliable presence in the National Assembly, have access to state resources and infrastructure, and hold significant influence in Pakistan's urban regions and among influential ruling elites. All of these factors make them potentially important partners in an effort to shift Western aid from purely military objectives to more development-directed projects. This move cannot be achieved, in fact, without the support of the Muslim democrats. Unlike Islamists, Muslim democrats are well positioned to establish relatively stable governments that are capable of maintaining social and economic order. They are better able to do so in part because of their greater degree of incorporation into the establishment and because of their social ties to those elites whose interests invariably shape policy. At the same time, Muslim democrats are also able to meet the demand for the presence of religion in government, given their ability to use Islamic rhetoric and even promulgate Islamist-leaning policy with greater credibility than explicitly secular parties can. The latter are prone to conflict periodically with the wider population's religious mores, which can be exploited and easily linked to strong anti-Western sentiment.

Muslim democratic parties are more viable vehicles for implementing Western policies than either Islamist or secular parties, being harder to associate with Western agendas in Pakistan, and yet offer little risk of establishing inadvertent connections to extremist or terrorist groups in the international community. In essence, political parties in Pakistan face three public relations challenges: They must appear sufficiently Muslim and anti-Western for the electorate, sufficiently cosmopolitan for the ruling elites, and sufficiently pro-Western for the United States and other Western powers. Secular parties achieve the second and third goals competently while Islamists achieve the first quite convincingly. Muslim democrats, on the other hand, are poised to achieve all three, albeit never perfectly.

Islamic Activism in the Twenty-First Century

As the Arab Spring revolts of 2010–12 showed, the old guard in many Muslim countries is being challenged and even unceremoniously pushed aside. Much of this upheaval stems from the highly effective tactics of Islamist activists who are uniquely skilled at bold offensives carried out through social media networks such as Facebook, Twitter, and YouTube. These activists have repeatedly demonstrated how dangerous they can be, crippling ruling parties by shaping first public perception and then voting patterns. Whether in Turkey, Pakistan, Tunisia, or elsewhere, this new kind of "combat" has forever shaken the already weak foundations of local and national politics in Muslim-majority nations. Islamists who are determined to unseat the opposition are using the social media matrix as its newest weapon. They are changing the way many millions of people live and will live, as well as how they choose their leaders.

Everywhere Islamists operate they are more adept at using social media than the established governments are. In Arab countries the Islamists have long been the most organized opposition force, and some movements have lasted several decades. They have had the time and experience needed to hone their skills and tradecraft, from producing hard-hitting propaganda to organizing hard-nosed street protests. As soon as the technology became available in the early twenty-first century, younger Islamists took to social media sites well ahead of the other politically active groups, especially incumbent bureaucrats.

Despite official control of the internet in Muslim nations, blocking access to all opposition sites for long periods is not easy. When one goes down, another pops up. In today's internet-driven information whirlwind we detect clear echoes of celebrated media-guru Marshall McLuhan's postprint global village prognostications of the 1960s. Indeed, his most famous dictum describes well the asymmetrical nature of politicking social media style: "The medium is the message."

Another valuable skill social media gave these early adopters was the ability to recruit new members for the Islamic cause and to recruit them en masse. The various governments they were opposing, whether civilian or military, either did not have the capacity or did not perceive the need to campaign on the internet. Over time, this public relations tardiness proved damaging, and the Muslim world's regimes have had trouble catching up.

Furthermore, unlike secular parties, the Islamists can draw upon religious iconography and traditions to entice members into the fold. In the early years of social media, Islamists began sending out clips of sermons and lectures, reaching a wider audience than they had previously dreamed possible. This early practice eventually gave birth to thousands of blogs and forums, drawing ever more engaged and greater numbers of supporters. Those in power offered nothing comparable, not exactly a desirable outcome from the government's perspective.

The power of Islamist social media networking was uniquely demonstrated when riots broke out all over the Muslim world in 2012 in reaction to a crude YouTube video that denigrated the Prophet Muhammad. This global upheaval did not rely on word of mouth but was in fact generated and coordinated through Islamist social media outlets. The same was true earlier when deadly riots broke out in Pakistan and Afghanistan after a confrontational Christian pastor in Florida infamously conducted a public burning of the Quran. When a Danish newspaper published cartoons critical of the Prophet Muhammad as a buffoon, Islamist groups across the Muslim world also used social media to whip crowds into a frenzy.

In each case social media was used to stir up the hornet's nest, to spread the word, and to organize action on the ground. Traditional TV and radio broadcasters were quick to pick up on each story and follow it. But without social media stoking the anger of millions, it is doubtful any of these events would have caught the attention of a global audience.

Since most Islamist organizations already had many followers years before the advent of social media, the new technology simply became a new way of boosting their profiles and "products," which in turn brought the groups still more foot soldiers. Egypt's Muslim Brotherhood has kept its social media campaigns tightly linked to recruitment channels that had been operating since the 1980s. This tool greatly expanded the group's base of supporters and volunteers and ultimately helped them (briefly) achieve power in Egypt before Brotherhood leader and Egyptian president Mohammed Morsi was ousted by the military. In Pakistan, Pakistan Tehrik-e-Insaf made heavy use of social media during the 2013 election campaign, posting more press releases and announcements on Twitter than all of the other political parties combined. This effort significantly helped the party's ground game in the national elections.

As with both of President Barack Obama's presidential campaigns (which also depended heavily, some say decisively, on social media), the Islamists have always used door-to-door, street-by-street canvassing. Very often they have firsthand knowledge of which neighborhoods are going to vote for them and which are on the fence. They mine their detailed knowledge of the political terrain to help decide which districts to invest in; this consideration is especially important in a winner-take-all electoral contest where a 5–7 percent swing in the vote can be decisive. Thus, much of social media is aimed at the critical middle-class voter, the only bloc capable of delivering those extra percentage points in a close election. Coupling the expansive social media networks with a traditional ground force has proven to be an invaluable strategy for the Islamists.

Naturally, the long-range goal of these media-wise Islamists is to compete and win in the mainstream political arena. They have achieved this objective in some countries, where they have campaigned toe-to-toe and come out ahead against well-established, even well-entrenched political machines. Their preferred candidates are winning more races than they are losing. The fact is, the Islamists are out-hustling, out-working, and out-mobilizing their opponents.

Though Islamists use social media throughout the Muslim world to oppose and resist the powers that be, this technology continues to be useful when they themselves become the powers that be. For example, the Islamist Adalet ve Kalkinma Party currently governing Turkey has proved itself skillful at controlling public opinion with persuasively slanted communiqués issued on social media sites. This ability is especially important as the regime combats serious unrest and agitation by young liberals and groups of secular protesters.

Of course, the protesters are themselves using social media to build pressure and push their demands. Both sides are waging social media warfare to shape and control the narrative. The AKP's official Web presence is designed to appeal to its younger base, with many videos and visuals. Continuing the egalitarian style of its successful preelection social media campaigns, the AKP site allows anyone to post a comment or create a blog or forum. Discussion is encouraged (up to a point).

Of course, Islamists are not all of one mind, and thus their social media activity is frequently aimed at each other. Though they share the same basic religious beliefs, infighting and factionalism is common between groups. At times they try to outdo each other while playing the religious card. One Islamist party will post the latest sermon by a prominent member, and in reaction a rival party will post a clip of a sermon with greater intensity. These parties not only openly compete to attract the most "likes," but they also work hard at maintaining a holier-than-thou image.

Social networking inspires copycats. When Egypt's Muslim Brotherhood introduced a new social media gimmick to attract volunteers, Pakistan's Jamaat-e-Islami party was quick to adopt the same method. When AKP runs a popular contest via social media platforms to draw in Turkish voters, Pakistan's PTI party launches a similar contest.

The various Islamist groups also use social media as a watchdog for Islamic traditions. One party, for instance, might obtain a camera phone clip of an adversary drinking at a private party. The video will be immediately uploaded to various social networks, along with expressions of outrage and shock. In response, the maligned party will post a clip of their rivals at a party where they were fraternizing with women (perhaps an older clip that was being held back for just such retaliation). This exposure is equivalent to the negative ads that appear during campaign season in the West.

But social media cannot achieve all goals. For instance, it cannot produce viable political candidates out of thin air. A candidate's viability is a matter of human presence and depends on the contender's personality, public speaking style, level of charisma, and ability to draw voters. Social media can certainly amplify and exploit these traits, but it cannot create them. Further, candidates still need to appear before large crowds and talk about matters of substance, such as pressing issues and the party's position. This outreach is basic to building esprit de corps and mobilizing voters and must be carried out in person, not only on the internet.

Another major limitation of social media is that it cannot carry out the hands-on ground game. All of the Islamic parties still depend heavily on volunteers to do the old-fashioned but crucial legwork and canvassing. The Islamists can hype the party's platform on social networks, but this effort can only boost and disseminate the message. The core campaign must still involve a traditional ground force.

Yet another drawback of social media for Islamists is its weaker penetration in rural areas, which make up an important part of most Muslim-majority nations. Rural residents tend to be less sophisticated users of internet services, and many may not be able to afford the cost of access. In Pakistan and other countries, not all of the outlying regions have internet connectivity, and the connection is not always reliable even when a link can be established. Social media is still largely an urban phenomenon. Mobile short message service (SMS) and text messaging, however, are rapidly changing the picture.

Social media has largely failed the Islamists in the crucial area of fund-raising. The internet is still a limited platform for raising money in Muslim nations. Financial systems in most of these countries are not as simple and secure as in the West, where such services as PayPal and others are available. In the Middle East and surrounding regions, campaign financing is still a matter of cash and carry, hand to pocket. Social media cannot manage such transactions effectively, at least not yet, in the region.

When the Islamists' social media activity escalates beyond mere harassment and becomes a serious threat to a sitting government, the conflict can turn violent. A range of "hard power"—everything from covert surveillance and moles planted inside the group to police intimidation, assassination, and even military action—has been brought to bear against various religious parties, factions, and individuals. As the Western media has reported for years, many Islamic parties do indeed have links to terrorist organizations like al-Qaeda, Lashkar-e-Taiba, Sipah-e-Sahaba, and so on. In short, if force is used against the parties, the Islamists are quite capable of not only defending themselves but also mounting offensive operations of their own.

But during a time of crisis, the leading Islamist parties are equally able to outfox the authorities via so-called "smart power." By collecting real-time reports from their network of on-location "spotters" they can quickly assess the tactical situation in areas where riot police and crowd control units are operating. This hot-spot mapping allows the Islamists to efficiently deploy ground forces and countermeasures where they are most needed either to confront the threat or simply to outmaneuver it. Using Twitter, Facebook, and other tools, the Islamists can rapidly organize and launch street protests of nearly any size, as well as synchronize flash mobs and other guerrilla actions. In addition, Islamists use their social media output to attract traditional TV, radio, and print coverage, creating a powerful multilevel platform.

The Islamists know how to play hardball. Their Web strategies include widely disseminating a mix of facts and propaganda regarding government and military corruption, exposing the ruling party's inability to deliver basic goods and services and neglect of certain ethnic regions and minorities, and even gossiping about individual politicians and elites. Sometimes Islamic insurgents will go for the throat and hack into secure computer networks maintained by government, military, and corporate entities.

Social media is inherently democratic. Facebook and Twitter, among other services, make citizen reporting easy. Anyone can be an investigative journalist today. While in the past it might take years and major funding to organize and mobilize enough bodies to threaten a sitting government, now it takes only a few hours and an internet connection to kick off a revolution. Social media insurgents operate around the clock, spreading their messages far and wide, reaching millions, winning friends and influencing voters, telling truths or lies as the need arises, helping to reshape the social and political landscape from North Africa to the Black Sea. Their actions will ultimately lead to a reconfiguring of many global political alignments.

The Future Is Now

Even though direct engagement with Islamist parties will represent an incredible political gamble on the part of the West and the parties themselves—and without any guarantees that mutually agreeable programmatic commitments are achievable—the political system in Pakistan is currently undergoing a structural upheaval that makes engagement with Islamists essentially unavoidable. In April 2010, the National Assembly approved passage of the Eighteenth Amendment to Pakistan's constitution that devolves huge amounts of power from the president to provincial and local authorities. Among the several areas of devolution, a few have potentially far-reaching consequences for religious, economic, health, and human rights issues. Chief among them is the administration of educational and minority affairs. Education, already a highly politicized issue because of the implications of giving curricular control to Islamization, will become a provincially determined issue. The necessary implication is that struggles over the inclusion of "Western" academic curricular items and the teaching of girls will become more drawn out and rancorous. The capacity of the United States and other Western nations to modernize through education may be significantly reduced in specific areas.

Shifting minority affairs to regional and local government will also have significant implications for religious minorities, especially in rural areas. Given the challenges to the Ahmadiyya and Sikh communities in the past and the recent assassinations of political figures who challenged the enforcement of sharia, human rights challenges may increase significantly in Islamist-dominated areas. Because Islamist political parties are so much more successful at lower levels of electoral aggregation, these changes mean that Islamist political figures will have more power over policy considerations than at any time in Pakistan's history. If Western aid is going to take on more of a development focus, foreign governments will have to reach agreements with those Islamists who hold regional and local authority.

Building workable relationships with Islamist parties, particularly network Islamists such as the JUI, is necessary to ensure that new development aid is effectively directed toward health care and education initiatives. Both of these policy areas have been a rhetorical focus for the West but have seen limited results. The difficulties that have plagued development projects in the frontier regions are a direct result of the Western powers' having tried to impose solutions without the cooperation and support of local Islamists. Not only have these efforts been underfunded and poorly managed, but also they have received little institutional state support. Moreover, evidence shows that local Islamist politicians and religious authorities have actually impeded their implementation. Wary of outside influence and resources that could undermine their own patronage structures and thereby usurp local authority, Islamist parties and militant groups have continued reaching out to a new segment of voters and supporters. In some cases, these groups take credit for new schools, roads, or clinics built by the West. In others, security challenges have halted projects and have caused high personnel turnover.

These problems cannot be solved by providing money alone or formulating policy that attempts to circumvent local interests. Local government officials and religious leaders must be given incentives to cooperate. Again, this strategy is less a matter of ideology and more a matter of pure political calculus. Health and education are highly valued commodities in Pakistan; local leaders perceived as making significant improvements on behalf of their communities in these areas stand to gain an enormous amount of prestige and political capital. Network Islamists, despite their rhetorical stance, are politicians in pursuit of votes and political security, and an *imam* or *ulema* who is seen as bringing improved health care and education to his constituents will have greater assurance of achieving both. Therefore, the successful implementation of development initiatives in the frontier region means giving full ownership and credit to local political authorities. If they are seen as the architects and providers of services, local officials have clear incentives to protect and support their implementation. Furthermore, these officials must have the leeway to craft public outreach and marketing strategies, which may include publicly denouncing the very Western aid organizations with whom they work in order to avoid the stigma of being controlled by outside interests. Western agencies must accept that these conditions are necessary for effective developmental policy in the region.

Of course, direct or even indirect cooperation with some Islamist political actors will remain impossible. Although I strongly argue that it is counterproductive for the West to view all Islamists as either ideologically intransigent or wholly opposed to Western interests, some individuals or local offshoots are indeed so closely linked to militant Islamism that there is no longer light between them. In these cases, targeted efforts to disempower these political actors may be required. Since Islamist politicians derive much of their power from their mutually reinforcing control over local religious institutions and the mechanisms of land distribution, Muslim democratic proposals for land reform may be one of the most promising strategies for undermining militant Islamist authority.

Were Muslim democrats to propose selective land reform policies, they could significantly reshape the local election patterns that have prevailed in the frontier and other rural regions of Pakistan. Specifically, the selective purchase and distribution of land to peasants, freeing them from land rents and providing them generational wealth and bargaining power, would provide a means of building a coalition between urban and rural interests and diluting the power of Islamist messages that focus on endemic poverty.[1] These changes would drastically undercut the power of local *nazims* and their *patwaris* in the rural areas. At the moment, it would be nearly impossible for the National Assembly to agree to such widespread land reform; however, it may be feasible to achieve narrow, regionally focused land reform in key rural areas to reduce the power of specific Islamist political entrepreneurs who are most closely associated with militant groups. Such a strategy is possible, given that these associations are not the predominant pattern and it is publicly known who maintains such associations. In short, targeted land redistribution could serve as a method to reduce the power of Islamist militants and to extend the reach of more moderate Muslim democrats in selected rural areas.

While many of these policy prescriptions are specific to the Pakistani context, the underlying research could have much broader relevance to understanding political behavior in other Muslim-majority nations. Some of the core findings of this study are potentially transferrable to other countries. Islamic confessional groups fit into a three-part typology, certain types of Islamic parties focus on certain levels of electoral aggregation, voters are motivated by social group identification and self-interest, and Islamic parties are fundamentally vote-getting operations rather than vehicles for absolutist ideologies. Some of the countries where these concepts would likely have salience are Bangladesh, Egypt, and Indonesia. These countries are predominantly Muslim but not Arab, have a history of European colonial rule, and are emerging democracies that have struggled with military rule. They differ in their relative similarity to Pakistan, but the validity of the model proposed in this book is strengthened by the consistency with which the pattern is found across these different nations.

As has been found in Pakistan, Muslim democratic parties in such countries as Indonesia and Turkey appear more readily successful than Islamists are in electoral contests, drawing much larger vote shares and proportions of the seats in the legislature. Although concerns about Islamism are certainly expressed, explicitly Islamic parties are by far the minority and hold far less electoral power than secular or amorphously religious parties do. Greater religious diversity may in fact buffer against the proliferation and power of Islamic parties and therefore render them even less likely to gain power. What is not clear is whether the relative weakness of Islamic parties in countries such as Bangladesh reduces the threat of Islamist extremism and violence there. The greater strength of Islamic parties in Pakistan possibly gives legitimacy to nonviolent conservative Islamic politics and therefore defuses the propensity for violent protest.

The similarities of social circumstances in the Muslim world—histories of colonialism, regionalism, feudalism, and factionalism—make predominantly Muslim nations likely to share dynamics that foster religio-political entrepreneurship. Among the critical similarities of Islamic political parties across regions is that they offer entrepreneurs options that are not available solely through religious or political entrepreneurship. In each of these nations, leadership has historically been attached to religious entrepreneurs, granting them the kind of access to power and resources that typically accrue to political entrepreneurs in Western political systems. However, this power has long been in tension with secular feudal political power, which is now expressed by proxy through democratic electoral politics. In religious political parties, both types of power can be combined but with specific limits. Those who strongly favor the religious identity are restricted in their access to electoral means and vice versa.

The drive toward engagement in electoral politics in Pakistan has been shown to be strategic rather than ideological. At the individual level entrepreneurs often have more incentives to participate electorally than extra-electorally. Whereas religious entrepreneurship offers power and access to some material goods, political entrepreneurship derived from the religious faction offers greater access to power, wealth, status, and influence locally, regionally, and possibly nationally. These patterns favor the development of Islamist parties of both types; however, such parties are systematically excluded from the electoral majority by the ruling elites and never dominate the national parliaments of Muslim countries. Nonetheless, they may have much more significant electoral power at the regional, provincial, or local levels because of both entrepreneur and voter strategies. As such, they cannot be ignored or excluded if policies are to be implemented at that level. As a matter of broad policy importance, they are also susceptible to persuasion that is not ideological, regardless of their public anti-Western postures.

The common history of feudal patterns of wealth distribution in predominantly Muslim nations favors the development of Muslim democratic parties. Although the preceding comparison is limited in scale and depth, it bears out the argument that Islamist parties have relatively little success in national electoral contests across multiple nations but that Muslim democrats are more likely to win elections. The Islamists in each country are marginal political groups at the national level, while Muslim democrats are more inclined to be incorporated electorally and to wield some influence in the Parliament, if not actually dominate it. In each case the commitment to religious ideological rhetoric is marginal among Muslim democrats, and their propensity for supporting secular liberal policy and practice is high. However, they are sensitive to the local political climate and may avoid overt secular or Western-friendly activity or rhetoric in order to secure their voter base. Effectively, they are prone to Islamization when it is politically expedient and insofar as it does not disrupt the financial affairs of the feudal elites.

In addition to the dynamics that drive different types of political actors, voters in predominantly Muslim countries are likely to practice voting behavior that must be accounted for in shaping international policy. The autonomy of Islamic groups; the sharp differences of sect, ethnicity, and region; and the uneven distribution of material resources in all these countries also set the stage for strategic voting practices among Islamic voters. The strategies they employ tend to be specific to different levels of aggregation. At the national level they are more likely to vote for Muslim democrats (or even secular parties) who are more incorporated into state networks and therefore more likely to provide material benefits. At the local level they may be more inclined to elect Islamists who offer both psychic and material benefits. The nature of such benefits can vary widely.

Despite these broad similarities, the sheer diversity of political party types and dynamics found in the Pakistani political arena must serve as a clear indication to Western policymakers and researchers that careful scrutiny is required. Precisely because so many different factors can and do shape the development, ideology, and practice of political parties in predominantly Islamic nations, each party must be examined carefully and considered in its own historical, social, and economic context.

Few areas of study could be considered more relevant to assisting US foreign policy. The aftermath of September 11 led to an outpouring of books, articles, and commissioned reports on how we should communicate with the Muslim world. Conferences on strategic communications and messaging were all the rage. Foreign affairs journals covered the topic. The 2008 elections led to a flurry of public diplomacy proposals for the incoming administration. Overall, the recommendations generally called for public diplomacy input during policy creation, for new public diplomacy offices inside and outside government in cooperation with the private sector, and for increased public diplomacy budgets. Diverse internal recommendations, such as improving language skills among our Foreign Service officers, were also proposed. The 2003 report "Changing Minds, Winning Peace," chaired by Edward Djerejian, is probably the most comprehensive of these efforts and still reads well today.[2] Nonetheless, in spite of this outpouring and the implementation of some recommendations, we are still wrestling with questions about the effectiveness of public diplomacy in Muslim countries.

The American government is not alone. One American senior advertising executive said, "You think our government has difficulty communicating with non-Western audiences—so do we."[3] Previous studies include little examination of and comparison with the experiences of the private sector.

Understanding the operating environment is the beginning of any business plan or military operation, and this is why public diplomacy is so critical. Previous studies have downplayed or ignored what Muslim populations actually think or do. The focus was instead on what the West can do unilaterally, not what the West can do vis-à-vis the attitudes and practices found on the ground. Essential to understanding the public environment in Muslim countries is examining the political organizations that represent them. Too much is at stake to ignore them.

APPENDIX 1

The sharia-secular model is an adaptation of a classic two-player signaling game. Parties 1 and 2 are both preparing for an upcoming election. The voters know that each party prefers either constituency A or constituency B, but they do not know where the parties' real preferences lie. The probability that a party actually prefers constituency B is r, meaning that a party actually prefers constituency A with probability $1 - r$. Values for r are not provided here, but it might be reasonable to assume that r is equivalent to the proportion of voters favoring constituency B.

Party 1, as mentioned previously, will always attempt to pass legislation favoring constituency A; therefore, the upper left path, in which party 1 courts constituency A by working to pass favorable legislation, is a strictly dominant strategy both before and after the election. Party 2, however, will have to choose between espousing a policy that favors the majority constituency (including working in the run-up to the vote to pass legislation to prove its commitment) (selected with probability p) and one that favors its true constituency (selected with probability $1 - p$).

Constituency A voters, therefore, face a dilemma when $p > 0$ (when $p = 0$, there is a separating equilibrium). Given that both parties are sending the same signals, they must decide how likely it is that either party will truly support their interests when in office. A party may be lying (probability q) or telling the truth (probability $1 - q$).

Figure A.1 represents the first stage of the game: the first elections. The terminal nodes are labeled with payoffs for parties (top) and constituency A (bottom). The payoff variables are defined as follows, with Y > F and S > N > R.

There are three equilibrium in stage 1: partially separating, pooling, and separating. We solve first for the partially separating equilibrium, where party 2 mixes strategies (that is, neither lies all the time nor tells the truth all the time).

$$(0.1)\quad q = \frac{pr}{pr + 1(1 - r)}$$

Figure A.1. Sharia-secular model 1

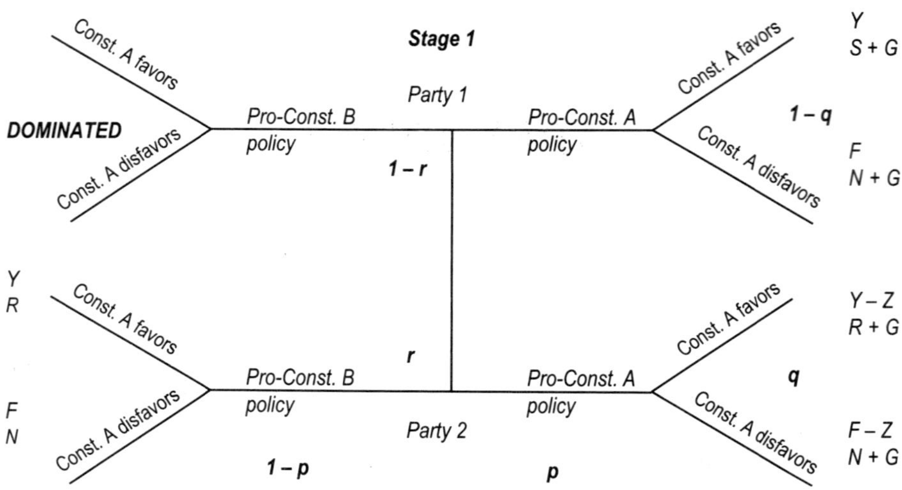

Table A.1. Payoff variable definitions

Y—payoff to winning party	G—benefit to constituency A if policy passed in its favor prior to election
F—payoff to losing party	R—payoff to constituency A if it elects party 1
Z—cost to party 2 of supporting constituency A	S—payoff to constituency A if it elects party 2
	N—payoff to constituency A if it abstains

Rearranging, we get:

$$(0.2)\ p=\frac{1-r}{r}\left(\frac{q}{1-q}\right)$$

Now, set the payoffs to constituency A for supporting a party favoring its policy equal to the payoffs for denying support to such a party.

$$(0.3)\ q(R+G)+(1-q)(S+G)=q(N+G)+(1-q)(N+G)$$

This equation reduces to:

$$(0.4)\ q^{*}=\frac{S-N}{S-R}$$

Plugging (0.4) into (0.2), we get the optimal mixing probability of party 2, the optimal percentage of the time that party 2 will try to attract constituency A's support:

$$(0.5)\ p^* = \frac{1-r}{r}\left(\frac{S-N}{N-R}\right)$$

Next, we look at the pooling equilibrium, where both parties always support policies favoring constituency A. In this case, $p^* = 1$, so $q^* = r^*$. We are left with:

$$(0.6)\ r^* = \frac{S-N}{S-R}$$

If $r = r^*$, constituency A is indifferent between supporting and not supporting a party that signals favorable policies before the election.

If $r > r^*$, constituency A will decide not to support either party. This decision will lead party 2 to defect and signal a strategy favoring constituency B.

If $r < r^*$, constituency A will always support a party that signals a favorable policy. Thus, party 2 will only defect when the payoff to losing (with no constituency A support) exceeds the payoff to supporting constituency A and winning. In mathematical terms:

$$(0.7)\ F > Y - Z \text{ or } Z > Y - F$$

For a separating equilibrium, the voters have full information. In other words, $r = 0$, which must be below r^* by construction. This is identical to the previous situation, and party 2 will defect when the condition in (0.7) holds.

Two-Stage Game

Introducing a second election complicates the analysis slightly (see fig. A.2). There are two scenarios. In the first, party 1 won the election and presumably carried out policies favorable to constituency A. In the second, party 2 chose to support constituency A's policies before the election but then betrayed constituency A while in power. In both cases, party 2 is now at a disadvantage (presuming that the populations of the two constituencies remain unchanged).

Party 1, if elected, is a known supporter of constituency A (it has probability 0 of favoring constituency B). Party 2, in order to be elected, must send an even stronger signal to constituency A that it will introduce favorable policies. This stronger signal will be costlier.

Party 2, if elected, is known to favor constituency B. Party 1 is still an unknown, but it does not have to go very far to be perceived as better than party 2. Once again, party 2 must send a strong signal to constituency A that it will change its ways. This signal will be costlier.

Here, ZZ represents the cost of the stronger signal party 2 must send, and GG represents the larger gain that constituency A receives from the stronger signal.

Since one party's type is known in this second stage, the character of the game changes significantly. We will deal with the two scenarios in turn.

Scenario 1: Party 1 elected in the first term

Constituency A voters will not choose to abstain here. They are choosing between party 1, which is a known quantity they know they will be happy with, and an unknown in party 2. In order to choose party 2, they must get a higher payoff to take the risk of being disappointed. Assuming constituency A is risk neutral, they choose party 2 when:

(0.8) $r(R+GG)+(1-r)(S+GG) \geq 1(S+G)$

Rearranging we get:

(0.9) $GG \geq G+r(S-R)$

Therefore, party 2 must offer an additional policy benefit upfront to constituency A that exceeds the benefit offered by party 1. Party 2 will offer this benefit when its cost does not exceed the utility difference between winning and losing the election.

Figure A.2. Sharia-secular model 2

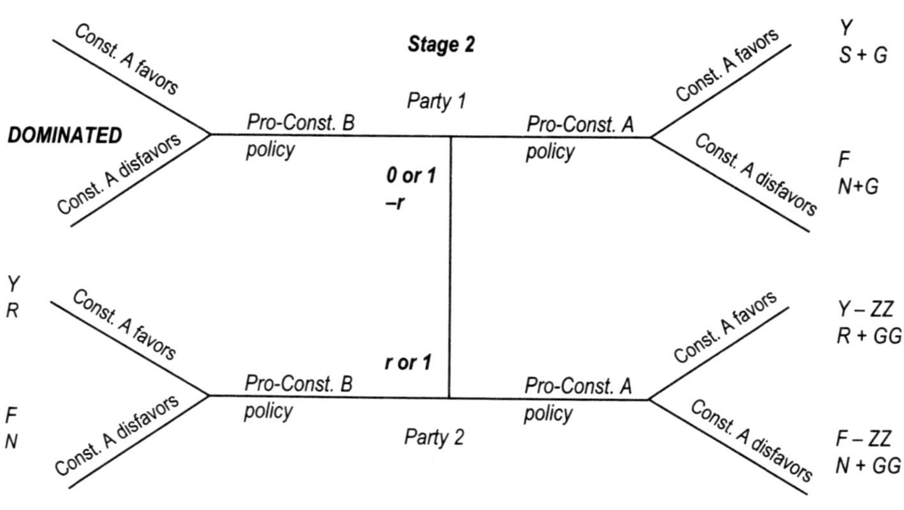

(0.10) $Y - ZZ > F$

The key, therefore, is what cost ZZ accompanies the policy GG in (0.9). This will determine which policy party 2 chooses. The minimum utility for party 2 in this scenario is F, and the maximum utility is $Y - ZZ$, where ZZ is determined by GG in (0.9).

Note that, just as in stage 1, the condition $r > r^*$ must hold for party 2 to be elected.

(0.11) $r(R + GG) + (1 - r)(S + GG) > N + GG$

Reduces to:

(0.12) $r > \dfrac{S - N}{S - R}$

Scenario 2: Party 2 elected in first term

Constituency A voters may choose to abstain here. Party 2 is known to be traitorous, and party 1's type is still unknown. At first glance, it appears that constituency A could still vote for party 2 if party 2 sends a strong enough signal before election. Constituency A could support party 2 over party 1 if:

(0.13) $R + GG > (1 - r)(S + G) + r(R + G)$

This reduces to:

(0.14) $GG > G + (1 - r)(S - R)$

However, since party 2 is known to be traitorous, constituency A will always favor abstaining over voting for party 2, since $R + GG < N + GG$. Whether party 1 is then elected is irrelevant to party 2's utility. Party 2, recognizing this, will always choose to favor constituency B and receive utility F.

Combining the Two Stages:

Will party 2 act differently in stage 1, given the possible results in stage 2? As shown above, party 2 is guaranteed a utility of F in stage 2 when it wins in stage 1. When party 2 loses in stage 1, it receives a minimum utility of F in stage 2 and may receive higher utility, depending upon the parameters r, S, and R, as well as the relationship between ZZ and GG.

So should party 2 be more likely to cede the election in stage 1? While it depends on the precise numbers, it seems unlikely in most cases. Party 2 will apply a discounting factor to the utility in stage 2. This discounting factor will reduce any utility difference between the two scenarios.

Stage 2 is most likely to matter in cases where $F \approx Y - Z$ (see equation (0.7)). In these cases, where party 2 is on the fence about choosing one policy or another, it may lean toward its underlying preference in hopes of getting a higher utility from stage 2.

In Pakistan's case, the major constituency (constituency A) was the large agrarian voter base with Islamist leanings, including middle-class farmers, small land owners, and the landless. The JI (party 1) knew that it wanted to gear its policies towards mobilizing constituency A, and offered specific targets through the Islamization program and Hudood Ordinance and other noted civil service redistribution measures, such as the removal of the Ahmadis. The smaller constituency (constituency B) consisted of the pro-business/merchant class that wanted Pakistan to liberalize its trade policy and open its markets to attract investment by foreign capital and were favored by party 2, or the Muslim democrats. In the 1971 election, the opposition was very small, winning less than 18 percent of the Pakistan Parliament. The Muslim democrat opposition (party 2) decided to not publicly oppose the JI legislation for fear of reprisals from constituency A.

Figure A.1 illustrates the importance of the first stage, that is the first election, and its possible path dependence. The voters do not know party type, but they do know that each party favors either constituency A or constituency B. The probability that a party favors constituency B is represented here by r (with party 2 as the example), meaning that a party favors constituency A with probability $1 - r$ (with party 1 as the example). Values for r are not provided here, but it might be reasonable to assume that r is equivalent to the proportion of voters favoring constituency B.

Party 1, as mentioned, will always attempt to pass legislation favoring constituency A; therefore, the upper left path is a strictly dominated strategy. This is akin to the JI pushing for pro-Islamist policies during the early part of its parliamentary control. Party 2 will choose between a policy that favors either the majority constituency (selected with probability p) and one that favors its true constituency (selected with probability $1 - p$). In this case, the smaller opposition in Pakistan chose the former.

In the face of the unanimous selection of policies in their favor, constituency A voters face a dilemma when $p > 0$ (when $p = 0$, there is a separating equilibrium). In other words, they must decide the likelihood that a party passing favorable policies will truly support their interests when in office. The party may be lying (probability q) or it may be telling the truth (probability $1 - q$). This raises the issue of how voters decide whether or not to trust a political party to enact those policies promised during the election cycle, such as the 1977 build-up to elections in Pakistan. Voters have incomplete information, so in order to foster voter trust, political parties must counter the legitimate concern that they may be making false promises. One way they are able to do so is to issue a costly signal of credible commitment. For example, in the JI and Islamists' cases, the government gave up a tremendous tax base when it forgave past land dues to signal a credible commitment. They also made a public demonstration of redistributing civil service jobs to Islamist supporters.

As noted, the model is designed to explore the consequences of certain policy decisions and how these affect the learning curve of the electorate. Depending upon the result of the first stage (first election), the voters will have different preferences for the two parties in the second election, and this shift will result in different utility-maximizing behavior by party 2 in stage 2. This dynamic illustrates the principal insights needed to examine Pakistan Period 2.

In solving the model (working out its various scenarios), there are three equilibriums: a separating, partially separating, and pooling equilibrium. One of the pooling equilibriums occurs in stage 2 (second election). First, the electorate learns whether party 1 and party 2 followed through on the promises made in the first election. Second, party 2 must now make a choice regarding its position and whether it should favor constituency A or constituency B. Even though its latent preference would be for constituency B, the only way party 2 can increase its overall support is to support constituency A, and in fact to go further (beyond party 1) in providing policy provisions that support constituency A. If it simply matches the policy provisions of party 1, voters will still be inclined to go with party 1, since they have little incentive to switch their allegiance.

The other observable implication, or separating equilibrium, of the model is that some constant proportion of the population will tend to vote consistently with one party. This association seems to be the result of incomplete information and the strength of the initial identity and the momentum of allegiance to the original party. This partially separating equilibrium suggests path dependence and first-mover's advantage to the first election.

To summarize the sharia-secular model in the context of Pakistan, the following propositions are made:

Proposition 1: Party 2 (Muslim democrats) faces a strategic decision in the second election, since voters will be trying to understand what its underlying preferences are.

Proposition 2: Party 1 (JI and Islamists) can retain core support regardless of whether it supports policies for constituency A (pro-peasant) or constituency B (pro-business).

Proposition 3: The key learning aspect for voters (who have incomplete information) is whether they can trust party 1 or party 2 to follow through on the promises they made regarding policies for their party's respective constituency.

APPENDIX 2

Table A.2.1. National Assembly Election Results, 2013

	PTI	PML-N	PPP	MQM	ANP	JI	JUI-F	JUP	MDM	Other Parties	Inde-pendent	Polled Votes	Registered Voters	Polled Votes %	Remarks
NA-1	90,500	4,232	7,121	117	24,468	7,051	4,738	100	4,827			143,154	320,578	46.18	
NA-2	79,125	5,159	10,666		12,137	8,020	18,787		3,477			137,371	336,122	43.45	
NA-3	66,528	22,370	22,045	475	5,902	11,954	27,987					157,261	384,086	46.30	
NA-4	55,134	20,412	12,031	261	15,795	16,493	12,519	1,166	1,519			135,330	352,416	40.34	
NA-5	70,053	11,648	10,171		21,435	19,869	14,131					147,307	320,675	49.89	
NA-6	54,266	34,537	5,121		20,316				11,110			125,350	299,273	47.08	
NA-7	40,254	3,527	6,856		38,264	22,664	53,610		1,032			166,207	376,144	46.22	
NA-8	30,089	2,678	3,848	387	15,953	11,034	33,836			37,044		134,869	327,423	43.63	
NA-9	42,068	32,090	7,002	293	44,769	4,578	14,427					145,227	336,177	45.12	
NA-10	46,531	11,491	15,345	170	19,436	19,107	39,269	3,426				154,775	321,660	51.00	
NA-11	38,233	12,659	26,928		11,506	15,536	26,623	220				131,705	329,285	42.00	
NA-12	19,661	7,227	4,949		37,437	2,166	21,651		329	56,680		150,100	351,675	44.12	
NA-13	48,576	21,416	6,824		14,201	4,886	28,672		252			124,827	362,779	43.90	
NA-14	68,129	13,789	10,041	130	7,211	3,558	32,041		9,209			144,108	409,775	42.68	
NA-15	51,481	29,815	2,263	327	7,559	5,105	13,226	93	29,224			139,093	314,969	51.64	
NA-16	24,067	5,411	4,700		4,479	1,777	21,137					61,571	214,703	30.81	
NA-17	96,549	69,721	1,107	526		4,408	3,504					175,815	338,273	56.48	
NA-18	41,391	69,839		253		6,805	1,390		9,309			128,987	336,924	55.57	
NA-19	116,979	114,807	16,474	699		5,117	19,860					273,936	531,865	55.55	
NA-20	75,197	106,467				3,321	29,001					213,986	415,191	54.60	
NA-21	25,615	91,013		510		3,219	43,342					163,699	392,364	45.13	
NA-22	2,370	12,214	105	27		679	18,572		344			34,311	204,979	35.78	
NA-23		11,865					12,337		530		17,498	42,230	127,028	40.24	
NA-24	21,394	8,501	67,769	697		392	92,395		749			191,897	390,996	56.14	
NA-25	47,543	2,871	46,262				77,595	1,044				175,315	366,793	53.26	
NA-26	25,392		2,320			12,831	78,294		112			118,949	444,059	39.00	
NA-27	18,405	56,824			2,909		85,051	45				163,234	330,921	53.00	
NA-28	23,336	11,917	530		21,151	29,170	21,290	306				107,700	360,019	35.07	
NA-29	88,513	24,212	7,919	742	14,690	11,240	21,026	1,068				169,410	521,072	35.37	
NA-30	49,976	33,027	16,373		15,595	11,367	16,704	189	618			143,849	460,748	35.88	
NA-31	6,120	30,916	11,061		21,682	4,579	8,407					82,765	296,723	31.67	
NA-32	24,182	2,463	19,877		6,728	20,520	15,928			29,772		119,470	208,810	63.66	
NA-33	15,397	17,343	26,803		4,262	42,582	6,567					112,954	368,035	32.14	
NA-34	45,066	5,818	6,275		8,959	49,475	22,552		77			138,222	504,694	30.15	

Table A.2.1. National Assembly Election Results, 2013 (Continued)

	PTI	PML-N	PPP	MQM	ANP	JI	JUI-F	JUP	MDM	Other Parties	Inde-pendent	Polled Votes	Registered Voters	Polled Votes %	Remarks
NA-35	51,312	18,207	19,081		8,709	16,397	22,329					136,035	311,172	45.95	
NA-36	1,795	4,028	753	24		5,652	4,631				9,005	25,888	179,304	29.92	
NA-37	294	26		191	229	182	47		5,062		30,524	36,555	162,660	58.09	
NA-38															Postponed
NA-39	3,805	857	7,726		2,723	1,017	4,175				7,922	28,225	125,687	38.05	
NA-40	8,239	2,469	1			284	12,233		2		18,055	41,283	160,666	48.52	
NA-41	667	8,022	62		198		3,045		347			12,341	92,719	0.00	
NA-42	2,454	429	11			271	3,468					6,633	108,056	11.57	
NA-43	6,948	1,690	697			10,023	3,613				13,929	36,900	168,514	26.14	
NA-44	7,069	15,114	4,127		1,378	11,972	6,249					45,909	185,040	32.43	
NA-45	9,198	530	262		2,113	4,124	1,180				29,697	47,104	175,036	39.92	
NA-46															Repoll at some polling stations
NA-47	11,328	4,310			2,805	727	10,240		350			29,760	121,265	39.76	
NA-48	73,878	52,205	9,178	172	42	25,048	733					161,256	292,142	59.55	
NA-49	57,383	94,106	44,984	171	79	9,968	200					206,891	334,241	64.36	
NA-50	47,210	134,439	45,203	232		7,465	7,356					241,905	442,458	57.10	
NA-51	39,842	121,067	67,146	338	371	3,121	412	995				233,292	452,466	54.22	
NA-52	69,769	133,143		275		2,736	558		2,107			208,588	455,186	57.04	
NA-53	110,593	102,430	14,870	152		3,338	1,966	1,782	657			235,788	382,115	61.90	
NA-54	68,687	76,336	13,185	100		2,970	197	468				161,943	300,816	55.36	
NA-55		75,306	6,216	101	135	2,034	1,031	91		88,627		173,541	324,022	55.47	
NA-56	80,577	67,221	4,091	86		6,463	272					158,710	288,423	56.04	
NA-57	56,007	59,920	1,807			2,915	5,637	1,449				127,735	353,751	52.61	
NA-58	74,526	85,244		689								160,459	359,058	83.09	
NA-59	33,721	59,819	31,726				1,966	375	643		60,284	188,534	309,334	64.00	
NA-60	48,076	130,821	11,101				335					190,333	486,070	63.00	
NA-61	45,892	114,282		75			581					160,830	443,677	61.00	
NA-62	62,880	102,230	8,186	350		2,183						175,829	389,451	55.69	
NA-63	42,805	116,013	5,103	196		2,895	242					167,254	386,957	53.87	
NA-64	11,813	151,690	67,212	402				455	336			231,908	415,491	60.48	
NA-65	8,885	102,871		234		6,767						118,757	323,341	62.30	
NA-66	36,296	133,085	29,624			9,492			84			20,8581	384,131	56.83	
NA-67	7,011	109,132										116,143	365,609	63.02	
NA-68	45,584	140,828	21,418	208					6,591			214,629	373,233	59.96	
NA-69	80,331	119,193										199,524	336,551	61.72	

Table A.2.1. (Continued)

	PTI	PML-N	PPP	MQM	ANP	JI	JUI-F	JUP	MDM	Other Parties	Inde-pendent	Polled Votes	Registered Voters	Polled Votes %	Remarks
NA-70	38,099	94,594	2,939	588			7,954					144,174	343,920	62.64	
NA-71	133,224	73,373	924	143								207,664	386,930	57.61	
NA-72	126,088	66,372	1,102	213								193,775	371,374	63.69	
NA-73		97,688	3,223	464		1,593			577			103,545	336,765	68.31	
NA-74	6,199		13,489	228		1,396					118,196	139,508	375,159	68.16	
NA-75	49,131	130,300	9,916	191		1,499						191,037	321,768	61.54	
NA-76	17,758	101,797	35,750	296		3,220			189			159,010	329,266	58.21	
NA-77	10,444	98,057		1,179		961						110,641	294,667	61.48	
NA-78	11,297	88,162	23,274	379								123,112	301,973	62.57	
NA-79	22,420	118,516	21,716	898		1,438						164,988	335,868	56.85	
NA-80	25,015	96,039				1,302						122,356	343,277	59.92	
NA-81	28,578	122,041	40,163			5,774						196,556	344,031	61.74	
NA-82	36,373	126,349		81		2,153	278	38				165,272	343,634	59.12	
NA-83															Terminated
NA-84	42,336	103,176	21,343	50		2,252	1,251					170,408	308,900	59.84	
NA-85	55,215	124,591	11,174	90		2,131						193,201	331,974	60.35	
NA-86	24,998	77,512	46,258			826			127			149,721	289,317	63.58	
NA-87		93,651	17,220	279		11,123						122,273	367,617	58.61	
NA-88		87,002	6,784	189		3,576			909			98,460	277,976	64.54	
NA-89	8,236	74,324	3,431	103		1,144			71,598			158,836	290,555	59.00	
NA-90	1,890	41,620	423	279		388			37,794		52,106	134,500	238,856	66.67	
NA-91		87,048	768	1,339							91,301	180,456	279,042	67.82	
NA-92	12,248	91,903	6,544	167		2,200						113,062	354,476	60.70	
NA-93	95,490	117,534	1,623	241				190				215,078	352,845	64.40	
NA-94		103,581	66,372	86		452						170,491	385,561	63.80	
NA-95	27,838	108,457	15,937	853		2,919	542		151			156,697	318,739	53.06	
NA-96	30,097	105,182	13,667	36		3,536	461		102			153,081	303,568	52.00	
NA-97	31,436	104,638		109		2,324	166		1,059			139,732	328,632	52.18	
NA-98	20,778	118,832	37,372	497		12,795						190,274	363,205	56.88	
NA-99	20,212	97,143	36,897	489					2,042			156,783	318,029	56.25	
NA-100	6,490	89,826	6,833	195		2,129						105,473	288,271	64.14	
NA-101	11,592	99,924		237		6,667	375					118,795	352,057	57.85	
NA-102	5,653	93,691	3,566	400		1,045						104,355	284,417	62.21	
NA-103	4,454	75,877	659	620							76,199	157,809	259,256	63.69	
NA-104	19,318	85,113				3,330						107,761	374,975	54.99	
NA-105	40,094	64,796	10,826	123		3,721				78,171		197,731	394,060	51.73	
NA-106	31,422	83,024	34,775	75				244				149,540	413,565	53.91	

Table A.2.1. National Assembly Election Results, 2013 (Continued)

	PTI	PML-N	PPP	MQM	ANP	JI	JUI-F	JUP	MDM	Other Parties	Inde-pendent	Polled Votes	Registered Voters	Polled Votes %	Remarks
NA-107	61,083	94,196										155,279	400,622	53.00	
NA-108	25,406	73,789	29,883	105		18,270					85,009	232,462	430,517	57.60	
NA-109	13,813	135,501	44,528			1,443						195,285	384,637	55.36	
NA-110	71,573	92,848	2,203			6,365						172,989	342,125	52.46	
NA-111	31,153	137,474	51,046	426				266				220,365	399,981	56.89	
NA-112	37,061	129,571	23,450	1,035		7,560						198,677	363,004	57.34	
NA-113	52,694	118,192				223		796				171,905	353,741	56.50	
NA-114	18,535	131,607		101		2,698						152,941	381,496	57.05	
NA-115	13,369	71,493	1,335	242		663						87,102	247,582	57.50	
NA-116	9,108	91,409	40,291			876						141,684	271,905	55.74	
NA-117	51,359	95,481	3,118	193		783						150,934	272,892	57.73	
NA-118	43,616	103,346	14,054	45			1,534	88				162,683	334,256	50.60	
NA-119	40,821	107,735	3,930	18			454	113				15,3071	305,570	50.93	
NA-120	52,354	91,683	2,605	35		953	1,152		22			148,804	295,826	51.85	
NA-121	68,307	114,474	5,882			2,996	1,723					193,382	388,441	51.75	
NA-122	84,517	93,389	2,833	49					165			180,953	326,028	58.48	
NA-123	40,617	126,878	3,770	55			593	571				172,484	347,941	50.53	
NA-124	42,561	119,312	6,990	41	119			101				169,124	322,562	53.56	
NA-125	84,495	123,416	6,152	154				369	258			214,844	429,485	51.90	
NA-126	97,785	90,332	2,770	142		3,226						194,255	359,492	55.00	
NA-127	45,787	102,080	6,233	167			497					154,764	330,154	49.00	
NA-128	78,369	124,107	3,408	87		9,483			323			215,777	418,384	64.00	
NA-129	35,781	94,007	11,633	50			1,203					142,674	273,648	54.08	
NA-130	22,066	88,842	32,569	24		8,780						152,281	290,930	54.76	
NA-131	21,637	73,742		254		1,130	365					97,128	273,993	55.56	
NA-132	16,467	93,140	33,439	52		3,573	123					146,794	291,232	56.85	
NA-133	25,874	68,909	4,796			4,623						104,202	291,283	55.31	
NA-134	14,131	44,397		117		1,087						59,732	250,183	60.75	
NA-135	40,628	82,150	9,786	154		4,652			256			137,626	285,289	59.09	
NA-136	33,408	73,775		373								107,556	285,503	61.22	
NA-137	8,896	61,329	12,007	344								82,576	287,484	61.08	
NA-138	13,127	75,694	20,526				1,654	4,937				115,938	282,555	66.50	
NA-139	21,725	102,565	28,594	209		5,399			849			159,341	301,506	62.00	
NA-140	30,431	69,212		467		1,878						101,988	291,601	63.74	
NA-141	11,989	96,737	4,536	418		1,105	259					115,044	309,577	62.78	
NA-142	18,325	85,243				1,923						105,491	278,336	64.48	

Table A.2.1. (Continued)

	PTI	PML-N	PPP	MQM	ANP	JI	JUI-F	JUP	MDM	Other Parties	Inde-pendent	Polled Votes	Registered Voters	Polled Votes %	Remarks
NA-143		90,652	14,351	141		14,924						120,068	272,742	62.78	
NA-144	18,648	105,162	36,723	87		1,773			653			163,046	293,394	58.00	
NA-145	12,319	89,025	26,601	73								128,018	293,394	58.00	
NA-146	11,999	109,998	27,401			1,123						150,521	278,408	60.84	
NA-147	8,195	87,266	58,234			138						153,833	264,607	61.86	
NA-148	64,763	81,830	49,918	205		633						197,349	350,801	58.51	
NA-149	83,640	73,898	20,719	128		3,802		1,815				184,002	338,005	56.11	
NA-150	92,761	79,680	12,208	128				76	1,808			186,661	373,331	51.67	
NA-151	38,647	95,714	56,858	188				216				191,623	362,313	56.00	
NA-152	64,611	81,015	32,514	302		2,582						181,024	332,921	58.29	
NA-153	18,155	94,413	90,179	741								203,488	349,714	60.00	
NA-154	75,955	45,634	11,173	285			1,593				86,177	220,817	370,150	67.40	
NA-155	42,398	60,524	22,480	662							85,452	211,516	356,995	63.69	
NA-156	20,837	69,397		239			1,193		13,598		79,675	184,939	314,492	62.32	
NA-157	27,842	96,162		591		2,037	1,908		3,117			131,657	334,495	60.80	
NA-158	72,126	94,050	28,237	441			421					195,275	323,568	61.77	
NA-159	68,114	116,903	4,132	1,576		1,975	493	185				193,378	320,985	63.20	
NA-160	38,023	99,553	13,877	85		3,889	147	51				155,625	306,875	60.73	
NA-161	43,646	94,012	10,894	304		3,201						152,057	304,942	60.71	
NA-162	88,974		9,609	1,633		353						100,569	306,359	59.65	
NA-163	16,311	89,126				117						105,554	276,191	64.33	
NA-164	27,958	67,984		429								96,371	260,811	64.93	
NA-165	55,279	71,804		446				434				127,963	270,634	63.03	
NA-166	49,270	87,209		129					3,379			139,987	292,076	67.07	
NA-167	35,416	99,907	4,379	524		650	110		5,057			146,043	331,598	62.17	
NA-168	54,334	69,049	42,292	510	826			538				167,549	312,836	61.91	
NA-169	27,226	72,956				171	756		219		89,673	191,001	321,145	63.46	
NA-170	81,131	83,895	19,554	451		1,596			1,675			188,302	319,983	63.47	
NA-171	17,514	62,849	57,276			2,629	37,961		56			178,285	347,789	52.00	
NA-172	38,643	49,230	336	247			290					88,746	345,974	47.30	
NA-173	24,858		60,258	376		2,517	1,803				82,521	172,333	358,766	52.68	
NA-174	6,964	101,705	25,363	414		6,193		80	221			140,940	369,102	59.52	
NA-175	13,805	110,573	6,581	491		1,365	1,284					134,099	355,184	64.00	
NA-176	10,840	88,322	17,183	502	206		1,600		140			118,793	338,237	62.00	
NA-177	13,757	22,719	49,822	324	269		746		8,948		103,327	199,912	357,013	64.02	
NA-178	33,212	63,228	26,048	353	77		1,765		233		79,417	204,333	349,646	61.70	

Table A.2.1. National Assembly Election Results, 2013 (Continued)

	PTI	PML-N	PPP	MQM	ANP	JI	JUI-F	JUP	MDM	Other Parties	Inde-pendent	Polled Votes	Registered Voters	Polled Votes %	Remarks
NA-179	9,476	110,197	73,199	290	209		7,601					200,972	341,765	61.91	
NA-180	2,555	57,158	41,548	357		634			4,185		72,044	178,481	296,167	61.17	
NA-181	20,699	119,403	81,393	1,916								223,411	348,176	68.11	
NA-182	32,212	85,292	75,127	541		43,242						236,414	388,333	67.58	
NA-183	197	61,891	24,613	282			1,642		800			89,425	296,231	58.00	
NA-184		94,429	64,175	313		987	293		4,270			164,467	291,600	60.51	
NA-185		88,379	6,105	467			3,274					98,225	334,038	52.13	
NA-186	52,958	74,491		479		906	589		221			129,644	310,421	63.69	
NA-187	360	88,872		156		419				92,972		182,779	282,844	67.26	
NA-188	1,897	89,262		228							90,537	181,924	303,678	67.99	
NA-189	46,686	95,060	15,031	760					467			158,004	309,222	59.88	
NA-190	40,225	83,353	8,683	639		641		953	1170			135,664	324,085	61.27	
NA-191	6,653	55,037	18,377	325		1,240			3,572	79,306		164,510	326,972	84.77	
NA-192	16,426	79,208	80,499	281			3,679					180,093	339,364	58.18	
NA-193	17,158	86,232	46,190	330		664	820					151,394	288,381	56.84	
NA-194	15,837	19,444	49,762	189		946	1,542		677		64,272	152,669	298,013	57.18	
NA-195	18,347	1,015	97,778	685		1,556						119,381	307,811	56.05	
NA-196	27,865	106,595	56,342	344								191,146	342,027	58.72	
NA-197	31,648	80,944	67,728	863		2,003	184					183,370	328,977	59.41	
NA-198	8,584		52,684	28,569		1,191	16,712		1673			109,413	254,082	52.00	
NA-199	1,272		85,120	1,915			2,060		1,923			92,290	273,483	57.35	
NA-200		210	86,579	1,219	79	806	118		840			89,851	291,682	60.37	
NA-201		683	124,472	1,345		169						126,669	276,383	58.44	
NA-202	2,210	1,355	53,165	597			26,628			54,890		138,845	260,355	56.05	
NA-203			41,919	379			8,861			77,065		128,224	228,663	59.24	
NA-204	2,187		50,128	651								52,966	299,653	47.51	
NA-205			65,720	661				366				66,747	252,714	51.19	
NA-206			87,789	493		233			2,657			91,172	258,115	47.31	
NA-207	1,290		83,918	1,343		56	20,478		3,575			110,660	282,819	54.24	
NA-208	7,589	45,801	51,025	632								105,047	257,664	43.14	
NA-209			54,881	490		2,669						58,040	238,513	46.62	
NA-210	561		55,808	122								56,491	251,995	0.00	
NA-211			67,338	5,340						83,960		156,638	287,886	59.09	
NA-212	1,064	25,978	93,884	3,248								124,174	312,206	62.82	
NA-213	2,520		113,199	33,874					2,381			151,974	374,425	0.00	
NA-214		25,687	135,502	781			5,732	26				167,728	293,868	61.72	

Table A.2.1. (Continued)

	PTI	PML-N	PPP	MQM	ANP	JI	JUI-F	JUP	MDM	Other Parties	Inde-pendent	Polled Votes	Registered Voters	Polled Votes %	Remarks
NA-215	1,506	66,481	91,809	696					4,973			165,465	285,128	60.92	
NA-216	904		76,941	2,569		376			633	86,982		168,405	276,049	64.26	
NA-217			71,916	352					2,924	75,862		151,054	277,325	61.00	
NA-218			95,724	1,607			73		1,284			98,688	288,653	62.85	
NA-219			1,4701	141,035	2,646	13,498						171,880	302,211	58.81	
NA-220			10,522	135,886				10,990	4,410			161,808	274,281	60.03	
NA-221	14,544		59,821	13026					997			88,388	269,066	52.02	
NA-222	1,499		100,095	2,358		1,838						105,790	260,060	59.08	
NA-223	1,486	68,118	91,956	8,700		124		215	3428			174,027	300,955	63.45	
NA-224	4,534		128,723	1,185				27				134,469	365,308	56.10	
NA-225	340		110,738	1,114								112,192	320,072	60.12	
NA-226			82,017	34,687		364	222		7,842			125,132	329,640	58.26	
NA-227		3,515	113,218	3,556		204	198					120,691	299,736	59.75	
NA-228	86,134		99,700	4,920			2,778					193,532	295,065	68.84	
NA-229															Repoll at some polling stations
NA-230															Repoll at some polling stations
NA-231			129,500	6,378					1,823			137,701	369,425	56.21	
NA-232		56,838	76,876	444								134,158	299,644	54.36	
NA-233		65,181	110,292	323					135			175,931	310,078	67.50	
NA-234			65,916	3,010					2,518	90,787		162,231	281,956	59.58	
NA-235	370		62,231	1,617						74,062		138,280	226,448	62.52	
NA-236	1,395		100,906	10,034				41				112,376	331,648	51.30	
NA-237	1,080	23,598	86,746	2,985								114,409	362,768	58.10	
NA-238			79,181	1,135			2,635				88,954	171,905	305,732	60.56	
NA-239	34,408		27,814	39,251	6,394	6,939	20,954		6,689			142,449	373,762	41.12	
NA-240	21,096		19,360	87,805	1,246	4,222	6,024		10,784			150,537	287,170	56.80	
NA-241	27,827		3,361	95,584	7,190	11,438	11,697					157,097	312,861	52.87	
NA-242	10,889	9,462	2,277	166,836		5,155						194,619	307,684	65.54	
NA-243	29,875		5,831	192,638		8,578						236,922	424,198	57.86	
NA-244	26,495		1,390	133,885		9,230			7,045			178,045	318,697	61.00	
NA-245	54,937		2,432	115,776		22,452						195,597	382,932	54.28	
NA-246	31,875		1,716	137,874		10,321						181,786	357,781	51.63	
NA-247	35,349		3,326	126,263				3,311				168,249	303,774	57.24	
NA-248	26,348		84,530	6,489			9,054					126,421	295,536	46.04	
NA-249			64,974	109,952				7,647				182,573	304,528	60.90	

Table A.2.1. National Assembly Election Results, 2013 (Continued)

	PTI	PML-N	PPP	MQM	ANP	JI	JUI-F	JUP	MDM	Other Parties	Inde-pendent	Polled Votes	Registered Voters	Polled Votes %	Remarks
NA-250	76,305		4,556	28,374	701	11,149	747					121,832	365,531	35.48	
NA-251	40,388	13,223	6,637	81,603		2,7166			462			169,479	342,155	49.53	
NA-252	49,622		3,301	91,339		16,342			2,580			163,184	321,191	53.43	
NA-253	61,913		10,127	101,386	285	12,651			8,242			194,604	519,854	39.33	
NA-254															Terminated
NA-255	19,033		3,378	136,982	1,213	9,338						169,944	347,277	0.00	
NA-256	69,072		4,347	151,788	856			18,732				244,795	459,185	54.23	
NA-257		9,060	13,459	125,405	149	10,410						158,483	371,013	52.90	
NA-258	17,697	52,751	36,329	17,854	466							125,097	393,793	44.58	
NA-259	16,007		4,737	281	889	483	7,622		13,512	38,552		82,083	264,293	41.58	
NA-260	7,653	8,692	15,857	174	547		26,019		7,183	30,338		96,463	429,794	41.01	
NA-261	2,920	999	440	98	4,274		48,712					57,443	248,179	54.17	
NA-262	382	798	3,435		3,111		25,254			37,814		70,794	184,824	49.35	
NA-263	3,227	23,374	22,147		1,095	367	31,031					81,241	214,322	51.06	
NA-264	1,884	1,470			3,143		30,870					37,367	215,250	45.04	
NA-265	6,037	6,668	1,942	154	1,441	218	7,402				22,874	46,736	211,471	42.47	
NA-266			17,404	377		778	7,852	1,026			41,604	69,041	409,664	39.35	
NA-267	95	2,272	124	146			1,012				42,240	45,889	147,595	61.28	
NA-268	575	6,724	374	29			10,717	252		19,873		38,544	183,932	34.78	
NA-269															Withheld
NA-270	1,320		35,142				2,838				56,658	95,958	238,664	43.78	
NA-271		7,388	6,170				2,655					16,213	158,164	19.06	
NA-272		942				1,108	2,973			15,835		20,858	267,667	29.56	
Grand Total	7,679,954	14,874,104	6,911,218	2,456,153	453,057	963,909	1,461,371	67,966	360,297	1,148,592	1,695,150	38,071,771	84,552,238	45.03	
%	20.17230562	39.06858969	18.15312978	6.451375745	1.190007683	2.531820755	3.838463412	0.178520721	0.946362595	3.016912452	4.452511547				

Source: Data compiled by the author from several sources including Pakistan Election Commission, 2013.

PTI Pakistan Tehrik-e-Insaf
PML-N Pakistan Muslim League (N)
PPP Pakistan Peoples Party Parliamentarians
MQM Muttahidda Qaumi Movement
ANP Awami National Party
JI Jamaat-e-Islami Pakistan
JUI-F Jamiat Ulema-e-Islam (F)
JUP Jamiat Ulema-e-Pakistan
MDM Mutahida Deeni Mahaz

Table A.2.2 Punjab Assembly

	PTI	PML-N	PPP	MQM	ANP	JI	JUI-F	JUP	MDM	Other Parties	Inde-pendent	Polled Votes	Registered Voters	Polled Votes %	Remarks
PP-1	21,435	50,982	0	125		6,201		516	13,579			92,838	232,524	58.73	
PP-2	13,233	43,335	15,868			1,760	1,047					75,243	215,116	55.06	
PP-3	29,784	58,916	22,700	755			131	928				113,214	239,695	50.83	
PP-4	36,886	60,159	23,440	178		1,164	92	742				122,661	212,632	61.71	
PP-5	15,139	65,445	3,030	905		1,521	297					86,337	221,451	59.79	
PP-6	49,398		14,590	94		2,443	694				51,826	119,045	233,735	53.42	
PP-7	48,440	47,666	14,529	65		1,620	1,490		212			114,022	178,947	65.20	
PP-8	49,876	40,442	7,250			4,717	1,333	126	254			103,998	203,168	59.14	
PP-9	29,797	29,524	2,849	130		1,342	325					63,967	125,581	55.28	
PP-10	36,521	42,539		50	152	2,841			830			82,933	175,230	55.44	
PP-11	44,430	43,267	4,455	511	77	1,565	1,303					95,608	178,065	55.32	
PP-12	35,836	34,034	7,355	89		2,411						79,725	145,956	55.74	
PP-13	33,595	30,346	5,913	148		2,535						72,537	140,497	55.06	
PP-14	32,684	36,852	6,943	147		4,614	179					81,419	147,837	57.07	
PP-15	28,437	24,055	2,734	648	160	4,506		566				61,106	198,413	56.34	
PP-16	18,549	38,791	990			1,768	5,392	203				65,693	189,894	50.27	
PP-17	22,747	40,897	24,282	69		4,688	1,251	146	917			94,997	218,325	64.00	
PP-18	46,133	59,126	5,461	292				161				111,173	221,636	66.42	
PP-19	26,240	37,745		714		8,006	4,707	1,737				79,149	193,865	60.67	
PP-20	32,827	62,088	8,082	77		1,266	89					104,429	250,385	62.48	
PP-21	24,472	75,003	5,302	140								104,917	235,685	61.40	
PP-22	17,728	57,235			73			40				75,076	214,102	63.00	
PP-23	23,578	54,949				4,445			1,524			84,496	229,575	59.20	
PP-24	27,951	38,604		367		996						67,918	174,407	59.63	
PP-25	28,146	48,594	5,788	143		1,473						84,144	215,044	54.83	
PP-26	28,653	44,150	2,094	59		953						75,909	175,082	50.10	
PP-27	8,465	49,069	2,737	882		5,621						66,774	211,475	57.08	
PP-28	32,657	58,531	6,749	148		2,888						100,973	170,693	60.71	
PP-29	10,547	47,559	17,983	139		9,936						86,164	187,077	55.39	
PP-30	3,762	37,624	5,138	102				314				46,940	151,703	58.56	
PP-31	12,235	29,841				1,232						43,308	131,745	63.71	
PP-32	5,098	43,221		295		7,295				55,358		111,267	184,576	62.76	
PP-33	19,637	58,714	10,345	235			5,939					94,870	179,071	56.00	
PP-34	23,676	33,853	3,345	25		3,262	2,599					66,760	141,130	54.00	
PP-35	8,637	31,740	12,319	51		5,107					41,853	99,707	186,445	61.64	
PP-36	4,250	37,509	2,152	22		484	1,045					45,462	167,491	62.78	
PP-37	31,608	56,347	2,779	41					616			91,391	173,964	61.00	
PP-38	15,952	27,034	8,497	195		7,074					39,240	97,992	187,920	57.00	
PP-39	38,173	42,348	1,408									81,929	177,331	60.22	

Table A.2.2. Punjab Assembly (Continued)

	PTI	PML-N	PPP	MQM	ANP	JI	JUI-F	JUP	MDM	Other Parties	Inde-pendent	Polled Votes	Registered Voters	Polled Votes %	Remarks
PP-40	3,392	45,854	613	60		207						50,126	159,230	63.39	
PP-41	6,597	39,818	4,068	116	519	1,900						53,018	183,289	55.76	
PP-42	7,797	50,616	229	83			538					59,263	160,631	69.94	
PP-43	31,122	37,100		90		2,311						70,623	193,648	56.17	
PP-44	56,247	40,861	352			3,234		131				100,825	193,385	56.15	
PP-45	59,746	29,228	660	106								89,740	189,434	62.58	
PP-46	53,110	42,810	1,059	134		1,288						98,401	181,940	64.83	
PP-47	5,021	39,213	1,147	291		1,381	170		379		48,243	95,845	149,764	66.48	
PP-48			10,308	151		170			72		33,473	44,174	152,166	68.32	
PP-49	1,818	0	6,582	159		1,762					64,197	74,518	193,175	71.31	
PP-50	5,119	464	18,646	232		634	3,304		7,711		42,087	78,197	216,819	66.01	
PP-51													0	0.00	Terminated
PP-52	14,603	54,814	5,911			2,124						77,452	154,283	61.15	
PP-53	14,996	44,754	12,639	461		3,474			516			76,840	165,955	58.23	
PP-54	21,989	50,641	10,018	92		2,306	19		34			85,099	163,311	58.10	
PP-55	4,491	52,861		348		177						57,877	144,745	62.02	
PP-56	3,838	2,535		134		1,219	1,067				24,906	33,699	149,922	60.57	
PP-57	4,820	37,762	7,700	84		2,988						53,354	145,808	62.28	
PP-58	7,026	27,686	6,145								29,068	69,925	156,165	52.77	
PP-59	12,100	47,116	12,305	328		1,525						73,374	162,151	56.00	
PP-60	7,066	43,970	2,625			309						53,970	173,717	58.00	
PP-61	9,141	8,661		152		1,105			559		25,882	45,500	149,427	59.56	
PP-62	13,450	53,406	8,496	620		597						76,569	193,850	59.99	
PP-63	8,663	60,309	25,025			1,458						95,455	162,936	60.71	
PP-64	5,858	23,723	18,488								55,789	103,858	181,095	62.37	
PP-65	14,654	64,645	17,571	37			84					96,991	177,078	58.53	
PP-66	29,670	53,906	5,750	32		937		12				90,307	166,556	59.75	
PP-67	34,189	60,964	4,354	20		2,763			160			102,450	180,495	59.16	
PP-68	28,168	40,235	4,035	18		1,146	132	938	165			74,837	187,876	58.98	
PP-69	15,670	33,198	10,987	26		5,051	1,498	423				66,853	153,393	57.46	
PP-70	24,607	56,694	8,062	42		1,361			404			91,170	155,507	62.39	
PP-71	18,205	56,007	3,680	22					843			78,757	19,0615	59.64	
PP-72	22,003	53,899	5,130	53		2,850			255			84,190	141,369	61.06	
PP-73	18,746	47,300	18,451			10		386				84,893	166,805	62.87	
PP-74	6,742	38,230	32,659	30		1,147			80			78,888	140,379	63.78	
PP-75	4,085	54,764										58,849	182,439	52.56	
PP-76	13,432	28,396		301		1,431			175			43,735	156,162	64.99	
PP-77	4,588	36,284	3,834	64							38,607	83,377	149,486	63.60	
PP-78	10,217	42,870		39		158	11	202	40,938			94,435	199,428	51.93	

Table A.2.2. (Continued)

	PTI	PML-N	PPP	MQM	ANP	JI	JUI-F	JUP	MDM	Other Parties	Inde-pendent	Polled Votes	Registered Voters	Polled Votes %	Remarks
PP-79	10,007	29,052		38			545					39,642	151,961	66.62	
PP-80	1,963	27,639		249								29,851	133,483	65.79	
PP-81	820	41,700	2,907			2,499						47,926	186,178	64.43	
PP-82		37,356										37,356	135,409	67.48	
PP-83	5,766	32,126	299	160							40,928	79,279	143,633	68.31	
PP-84	8,072	20,288	12,213			589				26,501		67,663	148,649	63.66	
PP-85	9,099	39,170	6,175	191		2,906	629	471				58,641	169,178	60.22	
PP-86	19,308	40,655	3,990	38		11,151	650					75,792	156,477	66.37	
PP-87	36,316	53,582		146		525	2,295		430			93,294	155,799	64.52	
PP-88	2,766	37,216	17,642	42		299			102			58,067	148,122	64.05	
PP-89	12,161	55,046	26,641	91								93,939	156,241	64.62	
PP-90	42,719	46,679	5,714	165								95,277	158,416	64.04	
PP-91	9,949	34,075	8,430	88		16		145	55			52,758	149,711	53.25	
PP-92	12,553	55,559	8,937	36		6,593	433	224	151			84,486	169,028	51.78	
PP-93	10,254	47,033	8,676	28		4,854		248	76			71,169	140,570	53.00	
PP-94	16,951	47,744		23		2,889	282					67,889	162,998	51.00	
PP-95	14,704	47,126	7,127			2,839	119		1,331			73,246	191,699	52.10	
PP-96	13,878	38,430	6,033	9		1,341	43					59,734	136,933	50.85	
PP-97	8,011	29,756		409								38,176	179,310	56.77	
PP-98	16,659	55,769	16,061	671								89,160	183,895	56.52	
PP-99	3,820	33,469		210		1,864			1,602			40,965	153,347	52.18	
PP-100	14,618	54,118	9,033	168	284		40		639			78,900	164,682	59.77	
PP-101	3,931	24,430	2,487			1,573						32,421	147,473	63.47	
PP-102	1,449	30,452	2,644			459						35,004	140,798	64.81	
PP-103	4,063	41,453		371		829						46,716	168,531	60.12	
PP-104	7,455	42,814	3,867	58		15,544	164					69,902	183,526	56.00	
PP-105	3,800	55,021	6,261	252		1,452		36				66,822	198,218	59.16	
PP-106	4,211	51,543				1,676						57,430	171,795	66.17	
PP-107	3,283	48,674	516	151							52,269	104,893	173,660	63.87	
PP-108	5,662	32,310		12		1,216						39,200	184,487	54.07	
PP-109	14,753	39,860		27		1,998						56,638	190,488	54.10	
PP-110	16,322	27,863	5,410	188		1,896				51,361		103,040	194,905	55.53	
PP-111	31,215	35,515	3,739	43		2,413						72,925	199,155	47.95	
PP-112	13,254	39,428	18,399	111		17,579						88,771	203,718	53.31	
PP-113	16,018	51,586				3,461		430				71,495	209,847	54.16	
PP-114	32,795	40,428		14		1,574						74,811	219,254	54.30	
PP-115	20,893	42,562		32		4,363						67,850	181,368	54.20	
PP-116	7,622	52,826	12,412									72,860	177,687	54.23	
PP-117	20,533	30,537	18,875	171		4,872	139					75,127	180,389	60.00	
PP-118	12,703	16,348				491	119			39,353		69,014	132,724	56.20	

Table A.2.2. Punjab Assembly (Continued)

	PTI	PML-N	PPP	MQM	ANP	JI	JUI-F	JUP	MDM	Other Parties	Inde-pendent	Polled Votes	Registered Voters	Polled Votes %	Remarks
PP-119	5,042	28,441	19,734	44		1,132	237					54,630	161,684	55.91	
PP-120	8,676	19,529	10,101	102		871	1,069					40,348	162,670	48.45	
PP-121	19,922	65,642	24,910	954		1,129		15				112,572	207,346	57.92	
PP-122	38,283	43,167	2,549	73			140	132				84,344	163,182	53.02	
PP-123	32,066	49,455						132				81,653	168,181	51.76	
PP-124	23,348	55,565	7,600	178		6,991		483				94,165	179,902	54.76	
PP-125	10,037	59,706	20,030	253		877		205				91,108	162,636	59.48	
PP-126	9,740	50,455	11,380			1,576	56					73,207	150,792	56.54	
PP-127	20,962	51,125	3,549	546		1,644						77,826	175,187	55.88	
PP-128	3,517	36,529				42		169				40,257	130,148	56.62	
PP-129	13,806	63,257	4,633	455								82,151	161,362	54.86	
PP-130	24,481	56,740	3,780			613		699				86,313	175,239	56.13	
PP-131	6,890	39,820		40		2,116		41				48,907	167,372	57.75	
PP-132	5,221	45,505		398		1,951						53,075	152,140	60.00	
PP-133	8,012	45,473										53,485	157,190	55.00	
PP-134	5,548	33,984		75		221						39,828	148,712	55.59	
PP-135	30,260	59,999	3,914			746						94,919	174,838	56.42	
PP-136	6,369	47,475	3,384			395						57,623	159,173	60.20	
PP-137	20,621	50,936		350		4,432	584					76,923	172,144	50.69	
PP-138	17,806	47,051	6,983	33		1,753	810		345			74,781	162,112	50.18	
PP-139	25,802	44,670	2,251	33		539	3,159					76,454	162,347	50.86	
PP-140	28,243	37,615	1,184			1,025	742					68,809	133,479	52.91	
PP-141	23,188	58,857	2,218	32		748	275					85,318	169,792	51.00	
PP-142	20,305	44,130	2,886	84								67,405	135,778	50.81	
PP-143	16,424	57,919	1,514	7		1,990	338	276				78,468	168,723	48.71	
PP-144	22,827	64,113	3,918	28			407	309				91,602	179,150	51.96	
PP-145	17,945	59,521	4,347	19		676		264				82,772	164,342	52.47	
PP-146	23,841	55,850	2,367	25		563	68		537			83,251	158,220	53.77	
PP-147	30,174	36,781	1,873			1,890						70,718	131,002	56.68	
PP-148	54,893	49,784	1,038	47		1,005	635		70			107,472	195,026	56.30	
PP-149	30,913	47,933	3,680	88		2,482	851		60			86,007	194,015	52.24	
PP-150	34,219	57,232	3,805	195			1,018		78			96,547	194,426	51.24	
PP-151	58,183	54,374	1,224	46		1,890						115,717	218,510	54.00	
PP-152	36,977	34,667	1,739	41		1,002	237					74,663	140,832	55.00	
PP-153	20,031	51,590	5,541	172			288	23				77,645	187,492	46.00	
PP-154	21,007	37,472	1,718	85		7,905	132					68,319	142,662	57.00	
PP-155	42,942	62,838	4,590	15		207		74				110,666	246,334	48.80	
PP-156	38,582	47,477	2,641			682		8,558	483			98,423	182,781	55.57	
PP-157	20,721	45,947	13,237	17		4,683						84,605	174,402	51.00	

Table A.2.2. (Continued)

	PTI	PML-N	PPP	MQM	ANP	JI	JUI-F	JUP	MDM	Other Parties	Inde-pendent	Polled Votes	Registered Voters	Polled Votes %	Remarks
PP-158	8,953	35,130	18,182	17		3,195	2,119					67,596	143,839	57.66	
PP-159	19,350	60,603	6,108	21			1,899	148				88,129	187,298	51.83	
PP-160	59,486	71,677	4,332	61		10,714			57			146,327	292,435	52.30	
PP-161	18,181	60,311	1,826	24								80,342	185,547	56.16	
PP-162	8,171	28,019	6,206	117		523	701					43,737	127,842	60.13	
PP-163	8,167	40,772		174		616						49,729	137,298	54.50	
PP-164	12,913	45,425		173		5,710	60					64,281	162,919	54.87	
PP-165	7,310	33,073	10,528			407	36				37,741	89,095	157,919	57.31	
PP-166	9,063	22,709	6,285	498		1,082		62				39,699	141,368	57.60	
PP-167	19,621	41,573	5,716	256		1,642		23	3,298			72,129	194,921	53.61	
PP-168	6,589	22,001		34		1,384					24,813	54,821	154,586	60.15	
PP-169	7,228	26,000	4,981	46		163						38,418	139,298	59.51	
PP-170	5,359		7,624			840					36,444	50,267	157,578	58.20	
PP-171	28,302	37,342	5,658	232		3,363						74,897	165,494	60.46	
PP-172	6,801	29,032	3,449	68								39,350	149,601	60.85	
PP-173	6,958	30,819	22,404	526		429						61,136	138,635	60.95	
PP-174	3,489	27,390	3,244	103								34,226	137,506	61.21	
PP-175	27,881	33,758		28		1,673	636	795				64,771	149,494	66.40	
PP-176	7,628	23,899	4,971	62		454	225	5,861				43,100	133,061	66.21	
PP-177	11,468	61,520	10,429	73			2,806					86,296	155,042	61.00	
PP-178	10,560	34,335	2,946	171		8,381		7,120				63,513	146,464	62.00	
PP-179	12,242	45,012	17,677	169		884						75,984	145,996	64.00	
PP-180	17,102	26,766		422		962				31,840		77,092	145,605	64.61	
PP-181	11,230	47,067	6,635	195		207						65,334	146,150	62.68	
PP-182	6,814	32,553	7,467				76					46,910	163,427	61.75	
PP-183	3,979	34,349				2,354		1,391		35,160		77,233	133,427	65.90	
PP-184	25,198	41,772				1,252						68,222	144,909	52.68	
PP-185	8,819	26,886	11,006	259								46,970	156,085	61.48	
PP-186	7,699	38,178	16,069	48			1,076					63,070	177,214	62.23	
PP-187	4,916	60,717	17,757									83,390	151,054	58.77	
PP-188	2,713	47,222	25,107	83								75,125	137,862	62.66	
PP-189	38,787	37,421	3,984									80,192	157,415	60.22	
PP-190	16,362	63,366	17,701	42		1,127			877			99,475	187,674	56.00	
PP-191	3,188	45,739	34,103	83		474						83,587	137,101	61.00	
PP-192	18,893	42,073	9,364			1,506						71,836	154,852	58.77	
PP-193	5,019	30,137	23,479	77								58,712	131,790	60.94	
PP-194	37,174	29,866	12,611	72			633	115				80,471	166,255	53.13	
PP-195	40,877	31,940	6,783	83		3,126		183				82,992	157,967	56.67	
PP-196	28,826	33,030	10,000	61								71,917	175,778	50.45	

Table A.2.2. Punjab Assembly (Continued)

	PTI	PML-N	PPP	MQM	ANP	JI	JUI-F	JUP	MDM	Other Parties	Inde-pendent	Polled Votes	Registered Voters	Polled Votes %	Remarks
PP-197	26,352	28,129	9,751	29			388	260				64,909	130,547	58.08	
PP-198	29,728	32,112	12,204	52		1,131						75,227	155,174	52.00	
PP-199	26,593	35,817	25,518	511		2,137	332					90,908	183,261	52.00	
PP-200	16,575	42,992	26,220	186								85,973	184,989	56.94	
PP-201	24,367	35,233	25,118	160		1,034						85,912	152,663	60.95	
PP-202	27,845	34,647	24,520	176		365						87,553	163,983	57.66	
PP-203	22,073	30,396	14,718	77								67,264	157,741	58.54	
PP-204	9,072	26,930	19,729	137		7,410	458					63,736	156,298	59.20	
PP-205	9,592	39,760	33,127	231			2,168					84,878	156,398	64.00	
PP-206	10,681	43,228	31,509	154								85,572	164,242	60.00	
PP-207	16,553	29,108	12,291	110		319					30,237	88,618	156,819	63.48	
PP-208	17,052	19,994	6,707	107							28,710	72,570	142,746	64.28	
PP-209	11,880	21,678	11,239	1,062							30,282	76,141	135,670	62.99	
PP-210	16,431	19,220	6,501			514					32,733	75,399	146,490	56.61	
PP-211	23,426	22,236	6,001	417			2,526				32,717	87,323	146,020	63.16	
PP-212	12,230	31,286		137			18		4,858		38,820	87,349	155,360	63.80	
PP-213	7,856	33,452	5,027	118		168			4,691		36,329	87,641	159,132	59.01	
PP-214	16,021	34,465		437			362		997			52,282	179,755	59.14	
PP-215	5,213	45,039		106		421						50,779	154,740	62.52	
PP-216	21,577	34,208	10,855	1,842								68,482	139,616	62.11	
PP-217													0	0.00	Terminated
PP-218	26,151	33,033	931	168		2,141	220				34,738	97,382	162,989	64.11	
PP-219	34,333	46,986	3,068	2,996		712	204					88,299	158,016	60.45	
PP-220	8,742	44,011		153								52,906	178,625	61.50	
PP-221	27,830	55,462	9,848	90		13,616		26				106,872	190,599	58.72	
PP-222	18,860	37,169		70								56,099	179,865	62.09	
PP-223	16,785	42,563		1,513		717						61,578	140,048	59.91	
PP-224	42,676	35,049	16,535									94,260	179,075	59.96	
PP-225	36,017	45,689	2,591	16		77						84,390	168,938	62.08	
PP-226	6,004	49,542	2,238			62						57,846	157,217	64.94	
PP-227		48,153		252				275				48,680	157,166	64.30	
PP-228	11,621	37,134	6,539	82				437				55,813	161,262	61.37	
PP-229	8,459	37,721	3,244	652		3,067	1,523			44,937		99,603	160,397	65.03	
PP-230	50,734	66,906	2,435	168		351			2,855			123,449	190,984	66.73	
PP-231	22,537	39,388	6,830	160		4,948						73,863	155,915	65.68	
PP-232	2,284	43,665		67		1,035					50,260	97,311	169,010	66.38	
PP-233	22,913	40,091	7,326	63		56	118					70,567	162,588	57.68	
PP-234	13,956	23,937	15,701	229								53,823	147,470	58.00	
PP-235	20,661	26,324	15,845	64		9,134						72,028	165,366	60.90	
PP-236	19,481	44,694		190					277			64,642	169,445	63.21	

Table A.2.2. (Continued)

	PTI	PML-N	PPP	MQM	ANP	JI	JUI-F	JUP	MDM	Other Parties	Inde-pendent	Polled Votes	Registered Voters	Polled Votes %	Remarks
PP-237	9,379	34,049		652		720	194				45,436	90,430	151,700	63.92	
PP-238	29,223	46,474	1,033	77		3,264			447			80,518	158,206	64.82	
PP-239	37,020	31,354	14,625	307			520		777			84,603	161,777	61.96	
PP-240													0	0.00	Withheld
PP-241	7,704	22,590	27,511	50					48			57,903	153,107	55.29	
PP-242	6,383	27,289	5,512	31		567			559		28,173	68,514	146,044	48.80	
PP-243	14,952	26,983	2,069	126			258		1,005			45,393	149,880	48.50	
PP-244	21,478	18,196	4,012	71		4,474	282		910		22,213	71,636	161,312	47.43	
PP-245	5,127	13,968		116					3,413		17,908	40,532	147,784	48.90	
PP-246	8,674	2,057	20,889	307		1,293	1,405		394		32,105	67,124	14,4793	55.05	
PP-247	4,070	56,197	9,535	216		2,110		45	50			72,223	188,927	56.01	
PP-248	1,794	48,090	19,616	127		1,496	233		68			71,424	180,175	63.26	
PP-249	4,415	27,054	3,433			685			136		40,136	75,859	177,165	63.90	
PP-250	5,309	54,876	1,521	135		419	726		876			63,862	178,079	63.10	
PP-251	30,835	32,905	4,462	165		600	15,782					84,749	160,772	63.00	
PP-252	4,632	11,095	17,475	60	247	591	2,847				20,408	57,355	176,446	62.18	
PP-253	4,283	24,536	17,707	275		1,070			381		35,269	83,521	148,286	69.00	
PP-254													0	0.00	Terminated
PP-255	7,307	22,364	6,046	121	115		108		2,880		47,266	86,207	160,010	67.88	
PP-256	25,109	30,061	730	477					105			56,482	71,895	64.06	
PP-257	2,701	33,080	7,617	226		1,775	22,230					67,629	144,518	60.92	
PP-258	3,651	46,189	24,947	199			7,137					82,123	145,042	59.81	
PP-259	3,624	46,027	40,785	34	149		4,584		90			95,293	155,216	54.05	
PP-260	3,487	20,139	22,945	325		319		70	3,676		29,713	80,674	137,186	59.81	
PP-261	1,415	26,804	9,704	192		517			2,415		41,925	82,972	132,206	62.94	
PP-262	35,684	25,144		199		1,659						62,686	155,838	66.61	
PP-263	8,201	21,670	32,572	142								62,585	145,616	67.11	
PP-264	5,419	30,003		174								35,596	140,126	69.15	
PP-265	8,734	34,049	29,042	360			3,676					75,861	139,250	72.34	
PP-266	13,469	0	23,051	186							31,499	68,205	155,679	64.50	
PP-267	1,443	23,655	13,247	248		4,222	8,895		194	31,926		83,830	152,164	58.00	
PP-268	3,601	36,873	3,224	232		76	18		433			44,457	143,541	54.00	
PP-269		37,047	20,237	168		632			15,699			73,783	140,599	58.22	
PP-270		52,848	23,508	845		174	200					77,575	151,023	62.20	
PP-271	21,178		4,271	378		30,070	2,272					58,169	166,603	48.30	
PP-272	25,238	40,468	4,663	307			1,089					71,765	167,435	55.98	
PP-273	18,282	40,135		358		600						59,375	150,450	64.65	
PP-274	21,160	36,570		171		430						58,331	159,971	62.75	
PP-275		51,792		19		635	356					52,802	151,061	68.00	

Table A.2.2. Punjab Assembly (Continued)

	PTI	PML-N	PPP	MQM	ANP	JI	JUI-F	JUP	MDM	Other Parties	Inde-pendent	Polled Votes	Registered Voters	Polled Votes %	Remarks
PP-276		31,751		36		111				44,568		76,466	130,682	68.00	
PP-277	394	47,357		651		906						49,308	158,022	70.59	
PP-278	2,647	38,673	4,426	44				4,207				49,997	145,656	65.11	
PP-279	20,434	44,516	7,390	161		1,823	1,612		330			76,266	157,699	59.30	
PP-280	17,558	16,173	7,499	100			1,956		414			43,700	152,413	59.65	
PP-281	20,222	36,704	6,341	271		262	773		224			64,797	163,392	60.70	
PP-282	21,240	36,993	4,279	652		930		779				64,873	160,693	65.31	
PP-283	4,039	34,989	11,525	68					4,753	43,337		98,711	170,744	64.83	
PP-284	3,847	21,094	25,903	147		828				26,665		78,484	156,228	64.54	
PP-285		32,648	25,948	141		1,839	398					60,974	134,291	56.00	
PP-286	11,081	22,898	32,246	55			1,229					67,509	140,892	55.70	
PP-287	4,547	30,258	19,334	59		231	110	157				54,696	138,704	60.29	
PP-288	4,517	10,992	19,248	379		550	353				19,940	55,979	127,931	63.55	
PP-289	4,590	5,873	15,520			357	3,371				20,289	50,000	133,420	39.35	
PP-290	11,592	42,881	19,409	179		620	272	140				75,093	146,512	0.00	
PP-291	7,461	12,294	20,036	49		507	559				21,759	62,665	135,025	67.35	
PP-292	7,540	14,685	36,068	291		709	129					59,422	146,005	57.63	
PP-293	18,403	29,650	12,513			9,267		2,411				72,244	176,271	55.84	
PP-294	12,504	33,409	19,123	139								65,175	157,032	61.43	
PP-295	11,564		52,318	581		738						65,201	161,650	54.49	
PP-296	24,722	46,375	24,165	683		1,660						97,605	167,406	59.00	
PP-297	24,478		43,292	559		1,859						70,188	139,435	0.00	
Grand Total	4,951,216	11,365,363	2,464,812	51,374	1,776	489,772	153,398	45,010	134,369	431,006	1,456,231	21,544,327			
%	22.98%	52.75%	11.44%	0.24%	0.01%	2.27%	0.71%	0.21%	0.62%	2%	7.76%			78.01	

Source: Data compiled by the author from several sources including Pakistan Election Commission, 2013.

PTI Pakistan Tehrik-e-Insaf
PML-N Pakistan Muslim League (N)
PPP Pakistan Peoples Party Parliamentarians
MQM Muttahidda Qaumi Movement
ANP Awami National Party
JI Jamaat-e-Islami Pakistan
JUI-F Jamiat Ulema-e-Islam (F)
JUP Jamiat Ulema-e-Pakistan
MDM Mutahida Deeni Mahaz

NOTES

In notes that cite an interview, all interviewees wish to remain anonymous.

1. Introduction

1. "JI Welcomes Opposition Alliance for LB Polls," *The Nation* (Pakistan), July 19, 2005; and "Opposition Vows to Resist Government Candidates," *The Nation* (Pakistan), September 23, 2005.

2. Seyyed Vali Reza Nasr, *The Vanguard of the Islamic Revolution: The Jama'at-I Islami of Pakistan* (Berkeley: University of California Press, 1994), 172.

3. Humeira Iqtidar, *Secularizing Islamists?: Jama'at-e-Islami and Jama'at-ud-Da'wa in Urban Pakistan* (Chicago: University of Chicago Press, 2011).

4. Muhammad Waseem and Mariam Mufti, *Religion, Politics and Governance in Pakistan*, Religions and Development Research Programme, Working Paper 27 (Birmingham, UK: University of Birmingham, 2009), 42.

5. Owais Tohid, "Interview: Maulana Fazlur Rehman," *Newsline*, July 15, 2003.

6. For some examples of such competition in the 2013 elections, see Gandhara, "Once Allied, Religious Parties Compete against Each Other in Northwest Pakistan," *Radio Free Europe/Radio Liberty*, May 10, 2013, www.rferl.org/content/gandhara-pakistan-religious-parties/2498256 5.html.

7. See Jillian Schwedler, "Can Islamists Become Moderates? Rethinking the Inclusion/Moderation Hypothesis," *World Politics* 63, no. 2 (2011), for a comprehensive review of recent scholarship on this point.

2. Islam and Democracy in Pakistan

1. Kalyvas, *Rise of Christian Democracy.*

2. Some surveys put this number as high as 73 percent, with the percentage of Muslims supporting a traditional theocracy as low as 18. See Moataz A. Fattah, *Democratic Values in the Muslim World* (Boulder, CO: Lynne Reiner, 2008). Similarly, Ronald Inglehart's analysis of data from the 1999–2000 World Values Survey (the most recent for which data are available) found that 68 percent of Pakistanis—the second-lowest percentage in the survey—expressed support for democracy. (The country expressing the least support for democracy was Russia, at 62

percent, and the next lowest country before Pakistan was the Philippines, where 82 percent of respondents favored democracy.) See Ronald Inglehart, "How Solid Is Mass Support for Democracy—and How Can We Measure It?," *Political Science and Politics* 36, no. 1 (2003): 51–57. Inglehart's data are swiftly becoming out of date, however; Pakistan was actually polled in 1996, a political lifetime ago.

3. Zakaria, "Rise of Illiberal Democracy."

4. Rajeev Bhargava, "The Distinctiveness of Indian Secularism," in *The Future of Secularism*, ed. T. N. Srinivasan (New Delhi: Oxford University Press, 2006), 20–53; and Talal Asad, *Formations of the Secular: Christianity, Islam, Modernity* (Stanford, CA: Stanford University Press, 2003).

5. Esposito and Voll, *Makers of Contemporary Islam*.

6. Iqtidar, *Secularizing Islamists?*, 7.

7. Ibid.

8. As Dennis Galvan makes clear, this does not meant that political parties in Senegal are completely distinct from organized religious groups. Senegal's political parties extend the reach of liberal democratic parties (which find their strongest support among the elites and in the urban coastal areas) by distributing patronage to Senegal's mass populations through the "familist" networks created by Sufi brotherhoods. The brotherhoods are an ideal vehicle for this purpose because they are trans-ethnic and allow the Senegalese to envision a large, diverse group of members as part of their own "kin" network. What's more, they "represent the most legitimate and popular social organizations in the country." See Dennis Galvan, "Democracy without Ethnic Conflict: Embedded Parties, Transcendent Social Capital and Non-violent Pluralism in Senegal and Indonesia," paper presented at the 97th annual meeting of the American Political Science Association, San Francisco, CA, September 2001, 8. While the leaders of the brotherhoods may issue fatwas commanding their followers to vote for a certain candidate, their decision to do so is not based on the candidate's successful appeal to Islamic values but rather on the result of a purely economic negotiation.

9. My conception of the sharia-secular continuum bears some resemblance to Ishtiaq Ahmed's typology of four ideological orientations among the Pakistani public, which range from "a sacred state excluding human will" to "a secular state excluding divine will." Ishtiaq Ahmed, *The Concept of an Islamic State: An Analysis of the Ideological Controversy in Pakistan* (Stockholm: Edsbruck, University of Stockholm, 1985). As cited in Waseem and Mufti, *Religion, Politics and Governance in Pakistan*, 12.

10. To be clear, the distinction between Islamists and Muslim democrats concerns the various organizations' public positions on state enforcement of religious mores and not party members' personal adherence to sharia law or practices. Mecham, "From the Sacred to the State."

11. J. M. Otto, *Sharia and National Law in Muslim Countries* (Amsterdam: Amsterdam University Press, 2008), 10.

12. "The Objectives Resolution," *Islamic Studies* 48, no. 1 (2009), 90.

13. Ibid., 93.

14. G. W. Choudhury, "Constitution-Making Dilemmas in Pakistan," *The Western Political Quarterly* 8, no. 4 (1955): 589–600.

15. Wintrobe, *Rational Extremism*.

16. Vali Nasr, "The Rise of 'Muslim Democracy,'" *Journal of Democracy* 16, no. 2 (April 2005): 13–14.

17. Ibid., 13.

18. Kalyvas, *Rise of Christian Democracy*, chapter 1.

19. Nasr, "Rise of 'Muslim Democracy,'" 16.

20. Robert LaPorte, Jr., "Pakistan in 1995: The Continuing Crises," *Asian Survey* 36, no. 2 (1996): 180.

21. Charles Kurzman and Ijlal Naqvi, "Do Muslims Vote Islamic?," *Journal of Democracy* 21, no. 2 (2010): 51.

22. In the elections of 1977, for instance, only the second it ever contested, the PPP was opposed by the Pakistan National Alliance (PNA) on primarily religious grounds. Despite the PNA's heterogeneity (it was a diverse coalition of Islamist, moderate, and even secular parties), its platform promised to "enforce Islamic law throughout Pakistan . . . and to ban the sale of wine and liquor, gambling of every kind, the payment of interest, and the use of 'obscenity.'" The popularity of this approach forced PPP leader Zulfiqar Ali Bhutto to "Islamize" his own platform, replacing references to socialism with "the more appealing term of *Musawat-i-Muhammadi* (Islamic egalitarianism)." Syed Mujawar Hussain Shah, *Religion and Politics in Pakistan (1972–88)* (Islamabad: Quaid-i-Azam University, 2005), 211.

23. Owen Bennett Jones, *Pakistan: The Eye of the Storm* (New Haven, CT: Yale University Press, 2003), 248. Bhutto famously (if perhaps apocryphally) once responded to the clerics' criticism of his drinking by declaring that he did drink, but "unlike you [the mullahs], I don't drink the blood of the people." See Tariq Ali, "Imperial Delusions," *Macalester International Review* 16 (2005): 41.

24. Bennett Jones, *Pakistan*, 229.

25. John Bray, "Pakistan at 50: A State in Decline?," *International Affairs* 73, no. 2 (1997): 321.

26. Vali Nasr, "Military Rule, Islamism and Democracy in Pakistan," *Middle East Journal* 58, no. 2 (1994): 195–209.

27. Bennett Jones, *Pakistan*, 231.

28. The Pakistan Army (when it is not ruling Pakistan directly) has often interfered in electoral politics in an attempt to prevent any one party from fully consolidating power. At times the army has supported the PML-N (as seen in the formation of the IJI) and at other times the PPP (as in the 2007 National Reconciliation Order, negotiated during General Musharraf's presidency, which granted amnesty to PPP politicians facing corruption charges but not to those from the PML-N).

29. Jamal Malik, "Muslim Culture and Reform in 18th Century South Asia," *Journal of the Royal Asiatic Society*, 3rd series, 13, no. 2 (2003): 227–43.

30. Michael R. Anderson, "Islamic Law and the Colonial Encounter in British India," Women Living Under Muslim Laws, Occasional Paper no. 7 (1996), www.wluml.org/node/5627.

31. With the doubtful exception of General Musharraf, who resigned his post as army chief of staff in November 2007 and ruled as a civilian president until he stepped down in August 2008.

32. Malik, *Politics and Islam*, 160.

33. Ibid., 162–63.

34. Mohammad Waseem, "Functioning of Democracy in Pakistan," in Zoya Hasan, ed., *Democracy in Muslim Societies: The Asian Experience* (Los Angeles: Sage Publications, 2007), 182.

35. R. E. Looney, "Excessive Defense Expenditures and Economic Stabilization: The Case of Pakistan," *Journal of Policy Modeling* 19, no. 4 (1997): 381–406.

36. Ayesha Siddiqa, *Military Inc.: Inside Pakistan's Military Economy* (London: Plato Press, 2007).

37. Chandra, "Elite Incorporation," 56.
38. Stephen M. Lyon, "Power and Patronage in Pakistan" (Ph.D. diss., University of Durham, 2002), 57.
39. Ibid., 187.
40. Matthew Nelson, *In the Shadow of Shar'iah: Islam, Islamic Law, and Democracy in Pakistan* (New York: Columbia University Press, 2011).
41. Lyon, "Power and Patronage in Pakistan," 201.
42. Andrew Wilder, *The Pakistani Voter: Electoral Politics and Voting Behavior in the Punjab* (Oxford: Oxford University Press, 1999).
43. Kalyvas "Commitment Problems," 379.
44. Malik, *Politics and Islam*, 154.
45. Ibid., 155.
46. For a contemporary (East Pakistani) account of the 1956 constitution and the debate surrounding its promulgation, see G. W. Choudhury, "The Constitution of Pakistan," *Pacific Affairs* 29, no. 3 (1956): 243–52.
47. Talbot, *Pakistan: A Modern History*, 240–43.
48. Seyyed Vali Reza Nasr, *Islamic Leviathan: Islam and the Making of State Power* (Oxford: Oxford University Press, 2001), 135.
49. Riaz Hassan, "Islamization: An Analysis of Religious, Political and Social Change in Pakistan," *Middle Eastern Studies* 21, no. 3 (1985): 263–84.
50. William L. Richter, "The Political Dynamics of Islamic Resurgence in Pakistan," *Asian Survey* 19, no. 6 (1979): 551–52.
51. Hussain Shah, *Religion and Politics in Pakistan*, 241.
52. Richter, "Political Dynamics," 551.
53. Nasr, *Islamic Leviathan*, 131.
54. Mumtaz Ahmad, "The Crescent and the Sword: Islam, the Military, and Political Legitimacy in Pakistan, 1977–1985," *Middle East Journal* 50, no. 3 (1996): 384.
55. Hassan, "Islamization," 264.
56. Talbot, *Pakistan: A Modern History*, 273.
57. Hassan, "Islamization," 269.
58. Nasr, *Islamic Leviathan*, 139.
59. Hassan, "Islamization," 268–69.
60. Talbot, *Pakistan: A Modern History*, 273.
61. Hassan, "Islamization," 269.
62. Nasr, *Islamic Leviathan*, 140.
63. Hussain Haqqani, *Pakistan: Between Mosque and Military* (Washington, DC: Carnegie Endowment for International Peace, 2005), 149.
64. Hussain Shah, *Religion and Politics in Pakistan*, 267–70.
65. Talbot, *Pakistan: A Modern History*, 279.
66. Hassan, "Islamization," 264.
67. Ahmad, "Crescent and the Sword," 378.
68. Nasr, *Islamic Leviathan*, 137.
69. Ibid., 147.
70. Ibid., 138.
71. Ahmad, "Crescent and the Sword," 376.
72. Nasr, *Islamic Leviathan*, 138.
73. Richard Kurin, "Islamization in Pakistan: A View from the Countryside," *Asian Survey*, 25, no. 8 (1985): 852–62.

74. Ahmad, "Crescent and the Sword," 383.

75. Talbot, *Pakistan: A Modern History*, 251–53.

76. Ibid., 285.

77. C. Christine Fair, "The Militant Challenge in Pakistan," *Asia Policy* 11 (2011): 105–37.

78. Nasr, "Rise of Sunni Militancy," 139–80.

79. See, e.g., Sayyid A. S. Pirzada, "The Role of the Deobandi Ulama in Pakistan's Politics," in *Political System in Pakistan,* vol. 4. *The Islamic State of Pakistan*, ed. Verinder Grover and Ranjana Arora (New Delhi: Deep & Deep, 1995), 627–41.

80. Nasr, "Rise of Sunni Militancy," 149.

81. Ibid., 147–48.

82. Alix Philippon, "Sunnis against Sunnis: The Politicization of Doctrinal Fractures in Pakistan," *The Muslim World* 101 (April 2011): 347–68.

83. Ibid., 349.

84. Joshua White, "Beyond Moderation: Dynamics of Political Islam in Pakistan," *Contemporary South Asia* 20, no. 2 (2012): 184.

85. William Ziring, "From Islamic Republic to Islamic State," *Asian Survey* 24, no. 9 (1984): 932.

86. Steven Kull, "Muslim Public Opinion on US Policy, Attacks on Civilians and al Qaeda," World Public Opionion.org, April 24, 2007, www.worldpublicopinion.org/pipa/pdf/apr07/START_Apr07_rpt.pdf.

87. Pew Forum on Religion and Public Life, "The World's Muslims: Religion, Politics and Society," Pew Research Center, April 30, 2013, www.pewforum.org/Muslim/the-worlds-muslims-religion-politics-society-beliefs-about-sharia.aspx#views.

88. C. Christine Fair, Neil Malhotra, and Jacob N. Shapiro, "Islam, Militancy, and Politics in Pakistan: Insights from a National Sample," *Terrorism and Political Violence* 22, no. 4 (2010): 495–521.

89. Ibid., 514.

90. British Council Pakistan, *Pakistan: The Next Generation* (Lahore: British Council, 2009).

91. British Council Pakistan, *Pakistan: The Next Generation Goes to the Ballot Box* (Lahore: British Council, 2013). www.nextgeneration.com.pk/pdf/next-generation-goes-to-the-ballot-box.pdf.

92. Ibid., 45.

93. British Council, *Pakistan* (2009).

3. Islamic Parties in Pakistan

1. Masoud, *Why Islam Wins*, 60–61.

2. Lipset and Rokkan, *Party Systems and Voter Alignments*, 63.

3. Cox and McCubbins, *Legislative Leviathan*; and Aldrich, *Why Parties?*

4. Stathis N. Kalyvas, "From Pulpit to Party: Party Formation and the Christian Democratic Phenomenon," *Comparative Politics* 30, no. 3 (April 1998): 293–312; and Cox and McCubbins, *Legislative Leviathan*.

5. Aldrich, *Why Parties?*

6. Ibid., 91.

7. Masoud, *Why Islam Wins*.

8. Lipset and Rokkan, *Party Systems and Voter Alignments*.

9. Kalyvas, "Commitment Problems," 296–97.

10. Kalyvas, "From Pulpit to Party."
11. Ibid., 302.
12. Kalyvas, "Commitment Problems."
13. Spiess, "Epilogue," 331.
14. Ibid., 337.
15. Kalyvas, "Commitment Problems," 379.
16. Chandra, *Why Ethnic Parties Succeed*, 121–22.
17. Gunther and Diamond, "Species of Political Parties," 175–76.
18. Lewis, *The Crisis of Islam*.
19. Chandra, *Why Ethnic Parties Succeed*, 56.
20. Gunther and Diamond, "Species of Political Parties," 176.
21. Downs, *Economic Theory of Democracy*, 144.
22. Mecham, "From the Sacred to the State," 9.
23. Ibid., 9.
24. Kesgin, "Evolution of Political Islam in Turkey," 13, 17.
25. Ibid., 14.
26. Schwedler, "Can Islamists Become Moderates?," 347–76.
27. Carrie Rosefsky Wickham, "The Path to Moderation: Strategy and Learning in the Formation of Egypt's Wasat Party," *Comparative Politics* 36, no. 2 (2004): 205–28.
28. Schwedler, "Can Islamists Become Moderates?," 352.
29. Janine A. Clark, "The Conditions of Islamist Moderation: Unpacking Cross-Ideological Cooperation in Jordan," *International Journal of Middle East Studies* 38, no. 4 (2006): 539–60.
30. Schwedler, "Can Islamists Become Moderates?," 348.
31. Janine A. Clark and Jillian Schwedler, "Who Opened the Window? Women's Activism in Islamist Parties," *Comparative Politics* 35, no. 3 (2003): 293–312.
32. Schwedler, "Can Islamists Become Moderates?," 355.
33. Mona El-Ghobashy, "The Metamorphosis of the Egyptian Muslim Brothers," *International Journal of Middle East Studies* 37, no. 3 (2005): 374.
34. Jillian Schwedler, *Faith in Moderation* (Cambridge, MA: Cambridge University Press, 2006).
35. Joshua T. White, "Beyond Moderation: Dynamics of Political Islam in Pakistan," *Contemporary South Asia* 20, no. 2 (2012): 179–94.
36. Robert Quinn Mecham, "From Islamist Movement to Islamist Party: Why Islamist Leaders Form Political Parties," paper presented at the Second Global International Studies Conference, Ljubljana, Slovenia, July 24, 2007, 4–5.
37. Kaare Strom, "A Behavioral Theory of Competitive Political Parties," *American Journal of Political Science* 34, no. 2 (1990): 574.
38. Vickie Langohr, "Of Islamists and Ballot Boxes: Rethinking the Relationship between Islamisms and Electoral Politics," *International Journal of Middle East Politics* 33, no. 4 (2001): 591–610.
39. Lyon, "Power and Patronage in Pakistan," 209–10.
40. Ibid., 213.
41. Iqtidar, *Secularizing Islamists?*, 103.
42. Schwedler, *Faith in Moderation*, 197–98.
43. Iqtidar, *Secularizing Islamists?*, 203.
44. Sultan Tepe, "Moderation of Religious Parties: Electoral Constraints, Ideological Commitments, and the Democratic Capacities of Religious Parties in Israel and Turkey," *Political Research Quarterly* 65, no. 3 (2012): 468.

45. Downs, *Economic Theory of Democracy*.

46. This discrepancy was first noticed in Morris Fiorina, *Representatives, Roll Calls, and Constituencies* (Lexington, MA: DC Heath, 1974).

47. Girish J. Galuti, "Revisiting the Link between Electoral Competition and Policy Extremism in the U.S. Congress," *American Politics Research* 32, no. 5 (2004): 495–520.

48. For an excellent summary of this debate, see Morris Fiorina, "Whatever Happened to the Median Voter?," paper presented to the MIT Conference on Parties and Congress, Cambridge, Massachusetts, October 2, 1999. http://www.stanford.edu/~mfiorina/Fiorina%20Web%20Files/MedianVoterPaper.pdf. Fiorina presents eight different categories of explanation for the polarization of American politics—ranging from actual ideological polarization among the electorate to structural conditions, such as nationalization of elections—but without endorsing any one explanation.

49. Edward L. Glaeser, Giacomo A. M. Ponzetto, and Jesse M. Shapiro, "Strategic Extremism: Why Republicans and Democrats Divide on Religious Values," *Quarterly Journal of Economics* 120, no. 4 (2005): 1283–1330.

50. Ibid., 1287.

51. Gunther and Diamond, "Species of Political Parties," 176.

52. Ibid., 171.

53. Ibid., 173.

54. Ibid., 175.

55. Ibid., 173.

56. Ibid., 171.

57. Ibid., 173.

58. Ibid., 175.

59. Chandra, "Why Ethnic Parties Succeed," 23–25.

60. According to the 2008–9 Pakistan Social and Living Standards Measurement Survey. see http://finance.gov.pk/survey/chapter_10/10_Education.pdf; and Pakistan Bureau of Statistics, "Chapter 2. Education," in *Pakistan Social and Living Standards Measurement Survey (PSLM) 2010–11*, //www.pbs.gov.pk/sites/default/files/pslm/publications/pslm…prov2010–11/education.pdf.

61. We revisit these points in chapters 6 and 7 with detailed data.

4. Muslim Democratic Parties

1. Craig Baxter, Yogendra K. Malik, Charles H. Kennedy, and Robert C. Oberst, *Government and Politics in South Asia, 5th ed.* (Boulder, CO: Westview, 2002), 6.

2. Peter Hardy, *The Muslims of British India* (London: Cambridge University Press, 1972), 43.

3. Ian St. John, *The Making of the Raj* (Santa Barbara, CA: Praeger, 2012), 143.

4. Bhupen Qanungo, "A Study of British Relations with the Native States of India, 1858–62," *The Journal of Asian Studies* 26, no. 2 (1967): 251–65.

5. Henry Smith Williams, ed., *The Historians' History of the World: A Comprehensive Narrative of the Rise and Development of Nations as Recorded by over Two Thousand of the Great Writers of All Ages* (New York: Outlook Company, 1904), 166–67.

6. Baxter et al., *Government and Politics*, 7–8.

7. John Emory Godbey and Allen Howard Godbey, *Light in Darkness, or Missions and Missionary Heroes: An Illustrated History of the Missionary Work Taking up Principally the Work in India* (New York: General Books, 2010), 180.

8. John W. Cell, *Hailey: A Study in British Imperialism, 1872–1969* (New York: Cambridge University, 1992), 39.

9. Iftikhar Malik, *The History of Pakistan* (Westport, CT: Greenwood Press, 2008), 103.

10. Ibid., 104.

11. H. Rashid, *Inside Bengal Politics* (Dhaka: The University Press Limited, 2003).

12. Baxter et al., *Government and Politics*, 7–8.

13. Norman Van Cott, *India's Parties* (New Delhi: Trow Books, 1999), 15.

14. Gunther and Diamond, "Species of Political Parties," 172.

15. Stephen P. Cohen, *The Idea of Pakistan* (Lahore: Vanguard Books, 2005), 56.

16. Nelson, *In the Shadow of Shar'iah*.

17. Ian Talbot, *Pakistan: A Modern History* (New York: St. Martin's Press, 1998).

18. Seyyed Vali Reza Nasr, *Mawdudi and the Making of Islamic Revivalism* (New York: Oxford University Press, 1996), 18.

19. Malik, *History of Pakistan*, 113–14.

20. Nasr, *Mawdudi*, 18.

21. Ibid.

22. Malik, *History of Pakistan*, 119.

23. Talbot, *Pakistan: A Modern History*, 28.

24. L. Carl Brown, *Religion and State: The Muslim Approach to Politics* (New York: Columbia University Press, 2000), 150.

25. Ibid., 149–50.

26. Baxter et al., *Government and Politics*, 195.

27. Malik, *History of Pakistan*, 121.

28. Choudhary, Rahmat Ali, "Now or Never: Are We to Live or Perish Forever?" (1933), in G. Allana's *Pakistan Movement Historical Documents* (Karachi: Department of International Relations, 1969), www.columbia.edu/itc/mealac/pritchett/00islamlinks/txt_rahmatali_1933.html.

29. Malik, *History of Pakistan*, 121.

30. Baxter et al., *Government and Politics*, 14.

31. Ibid., 204.

32. Akbar S. Ahmed, *Jinnah, Pakistan and Islamic Identity: The Search for Saladin* (London: Routledge, 1997), 74.

33. Ayesha Jalal, *The Sole Spokesman: Jinnah, the Muslim League, and the Demand for Pakistan* (Cambridge: Cambridge University Press, 1994), 33, 35.

34. Ibid., 35–36.

35. Rashid, *Inside Bengal Politics*.

36. Ahmed, *Jinnah*, 68.

37. Jalal, *Sole Spokesman*, 42.

38. Ibid., 43.

39. Deepak Pandey, "Congress-Muslim League Relations, 1937–39: 'The Parting of the Ways,'" *Modern Asian Studies* 12, no. 4 (1978): 636.

40. Jalal, *Sole Spokesman*, 147.

41. Talbot, *Pakistan: A Modern History*, 73.

42. Ibid., 70.

43. Rashid, *Inside Bengal Politics*.

44. S. M. Ikram, *Indian Muslims and Partition of India* (New Delhi: Atlantic, 1992), 387; and Ian A. Talbot, "The 1946 Punjab Elections," *Modern Asian Studies* 14, no. 1 (1980): 65–66.

45. Rashid, *Inside Bengal Politics*.

46. Ahmed, *Jinnah*, 192.

47. Ibid., 195.

48. Baxter et al., *Government and Politics*, 184. The assembly had actually formulated a constitution in 1954, after seven years of work; but in what was, in hindsight, an early sign of Pakistan's troubles with presidential authoritarianism, Governor-General Ghulam Muhammad dismissed it, claiming it had lost the confidence of the people. G. W. Choudhury, "Constitution-Making Dilemmas in Pakistan," *World Affairs* 8, no. 4. (1955): 589–600.

49. Choudhury, "Constitution-Making Dilemmas in Pakistan," 592.

50. Khalid bin Sayeed, "Collapse of Parliamentary Democracy in Pakistan," *Middle East Journal* 13, no. 4 (1959): 394.

51. Baxter et al., *Government and Politics*, 195.

52. bin Sayeed, "Collapse," 389.

53. Baxter et al., *Government and Politics*, 184, 197.

54. Marvin G. Weinbaum, "Civic Culture and Democracy in Pakistan," *Asian Survey* 36, no. 7 (1996): 641.

55. Gunther and Diamond, "Species of Political Parties," 176.

56. Baxter et al., *Government and Politics*, 195; and Gunther and Diamond, "Species of Political Parties," 176.

57. Baxter et al., *Government and Politics*, 198.

58. Afzal, *Political Parties in Pakistan*, 66a, 67a.

59. Safdar Mahmood, *Pakistan: Political Roots and Development, 1947–1999* (Oxford: Oxford University Press, 2000), 126–27.

60. Rasul B. Rais, "Pakistan in 1988: From Command to Civilian Politics," *Asian Survey* 29, no. 2 (1989): 199–206.

61. Talbot, *Pakistan: A Modern History*, 284.

62. Mahmood, *Pakistan*, 127.

63. Seyyed Vali Reza Nasr, "Democracy and the Crisis of Governability in Pakistan," *Asian Survey* 32, no. 6 (1992), 523.

64. Ibid.

65. Ibid.

66. Ibid., 524.

67. Mahmood, *Pakistan*, 129.

68. Talbot, *Pakistan: A Modern History*, 110–11.

69. S. N. Jamal, "Nawaz Sharif Outlines His Islamic Agenda," in *Political System in Pakistan*, vol. 4, *The Islamic State of Pakistan*, ed. Verinder Grover and Ranjana Arora (New Delhi: Deep & Deep, 1995), 680.

70. Charles Kennedy, "Repugnancy to Islam–Who Decides? Islam and Legal Reform in Pakistan," *Journal of Comparative and International Law* 41 (1992): 779.

71. Ibid., 779–80.

72. Rais Ahmed Khan, "Pakistan in 1992: Waiting for Change," *Asian Survey* 33, no. 2 (1993): 130.

73. Hasan-Askari Rizvi, "Pakistani in 1998: The Polity under Pressure," *Asian Survey* 39, no. 2 (1999): 180.

74. In early 1990, for instance, an anti-PPP rally featured a portrait of Zia, which was unveiled to cheers from the crowd of thousands. See Lawrence Ziring, "Pakistan in 1990: The Fall of Benazir Bhutto," *Asian Survey* 31, no. 2 (1991): 113–24.

75. Ibid., 116.

76. Ibid., 122.

77. Rais A. Khan, "Pakistan in 1991: Light and Shadows," *Asian Survey* 32, no. 2 (1992): 197–206.

78. Mohammed Hanif, "Pakistan Elections: How Nawaz Sharif Beat Imran Khan and What Happens Next," *The Guardian*, May 13, 2013, www.guardian.co.uk/world/2013/may/13/pakistan-elections-nawaz-sharif-imran-khan.

79. "Provincial Agenda," *The Friday Times*, March 22, 2013.

80. M. Ilyas Khan, "Pakistan Election: Taliban Threats Hamper Secular Campaign," *BBC News*, April 4, 2013, www.bbc.co.uk/news/world-asia-22022951.

81. Declan Walsh, "Taliban Attacks in Northwest Pakistan Are Reshaping Ballot," *New York Times*, April 21, 2013.

82. Syed Hassan Ali, "Parties Modify Election Campaign in View of Terror Threat," *The Dawn*, April 15, 2013, dawn.com/2013/04/15/parties-modify-election-campaign-in-view-of-terror-threat/.

83. Lyse Doucet, "Elections in a Time of Taliban," *International Herald Tribune*, May 11, 2013.

84. Amir Mir, "LeJ Terror Suspect Contesting on PML-N Ticket," *The News* (Pakistan), May 6, 2013.

85. Kashif Hussain, "PML-N Banks on a Sectarian Leader?," *The Daily Times* (Pakistan), April 22, 2013.

86. Election Commission of Pakistan, "Party Position (National Assembly)," June 3, 2013, www.ecp.gov.pk/overallpartyposition030620131600.pdf.

87. Election Commission of Pakistan, "Party Position (Provincial Assemblies)," June 5, 2013, www.ecp.gov.pk/overallpartypositionPA.pdf.

88. Davis was a contractor for the Central Intelligence Agency who shot and killed two men in downtown Lahore in January 2011. (He later claimed that the men had been following him and were attempting to kill him.) A third Pakistani citizen was struck and killed by a consulate emergency response vehicle on its way to the scene. The United States insisted that Davis had diplomatic immunity, and he was eventually allowed to leave Pakistan after reparations had been paid to the families of his victims. The incident caused a temporary chill in US-Pakistani relations, but its most important impact was on public opinion. For ordinary Pakistanis, Davis's case for some merely underlined Pakistan's weakness in the face of American power, as well as America's disregard for Pakistani life. See Mark Mazzetti, "How a Single Spy Helped Turn Pakistan against the United States," *New York Times Magazine*, April 9, 2013, www.nytimes.com/2013/04/14/magazine/raymond-davis-pakistan.html?pagewanted=all.

89. Savita Pande, "Pakistan after Abbotabad," *Indian Foreign Affairs Journal* 6, no. 2 (2011): 165–86.

90. Ibid., 171.

91. Shantanu Guha Ray, "'I Am Not Close to the Pakistani Army': A Recent Opinion Poll Says 68 Per Cent of Pakistanis Want Imran Khan to Lead the Country," *India Today*, July 11, 2011.

92. Qaswar Abbas, "Short Road to Power," *India Today*, November 14, 2011.

93. Pankaj Mishra, "Imran Khan Must Be Doing Something Right," *New York Times Magazine*, August 16, 2012.

94. Anas Malik, "Pakistan in 2012: An Assertive Judiciary in a Pre-Election Year," *Asian Survey* 53, no. 1 (2013): 41.

95. "Does PTI Matter?," *Friday Times*, June 10, 2011.

96. Fahd Husain, "The Great Leap Forward: Imran Khan's Soaring Popularity," *Newsline*, November 30, 2011.

97. Mishra, "Imran Khan," 2012.

98. "Fielding Candidates," *Friday Times*, March 15, 2013.

99. Mohammed Hanif, "Pakistan Elections," *The Guardian*, May 13, 2013, www.guardian.co.uk/world/2013/may/13/pakistan-elections-nawaz-sharif-imran-khan.

100. Mishra, "Imran Khan," 2012.

101. "Viral Video Forces Imran Khan to Clarify Stance on Ahmadis," *Regional Times*, May 6, 2013.

102. Amir Zia, "Tsunami or Passing Storm?," *Newsline*, April 28, 2013.

103. Ibid.

104. "The Khan Bowls too Wide," *Tehelka*, May 7, 2012.

105. "National Conference to Remember Qazi Hussain, Professor Ghafoor," *Business Recorder*, January 29, 2013.

106. Arif Rafiq, "The Emergence of the Difa-e-Pakistan Islamist Coalition," *CTC Sentinel* 5, no. 3 (March 22, 2012), www.ctc.usma.edu/posts/the-emergence-of-the-difa-e-pakistan-islamist-coalition.

107. Election Commission of Pakistan, "Party Position (National Assembly)," June 3, 2013, www.ecp.gov.pk/overallpartyposition030620131600.pdf.

108. Hanif, "Pakistan Elections."

109. "New KP Chief Minister Says: We'll Prove Ourselves in Two Months," *The Dawn*, June 4, 2013.

110. Wilder, *Pakistani Voter*, 1999.

111. Anthony Downs, "An Economic Theory of Political Action in a Democracy," *Journal of Political Economy* 65, no. 2 (1957): 135–50.

112. Haqqani, *Pakistan*, 207.

113. Peter Blood, ed., "The Government: Islami Jamhoori Ittehad," in *Pakistan: A Country Study* (Washington: US Library of Congress, 1994), http://countrystudies.us/pakistan/67.htm.

114. Hans Anwar and James Rupert, "Pakistan Minister Assassinated after Blasphemy Law Challenge," *Bloomberg Businessweek*, March3, 2011, www.businessweek.com/news/2011–03–03/pakistan-minister-assassinated-after-blasphemy-law-challenge.html.

115. Charles H. Kennedy, "Pakistan in 2004: Running Very Fast to Stay in the Same Place," *Asian Survey* 45, no. 1 (2005): 105–11.

116. See, e.g., Amir Mir, "Punjab Govt May Not Act against LeJ, PML-N Has Seat Adjustments with Defunct SSP," *The News* (Pakistan), February 22, 2013, www.thenews.com.pk/Todays-News-13–21114-Punjab-govt-may-not-act-against-LeJ-PML-N-has-seat-adjustments-with-defunct-SSP.

5. Islamist Parties

1. Gunes M. Tezcür, *Muslim Reformers in Iran and Turkey*, 49.

2. Downs, *Economic Theory of Democracy*.

3. Jamiat-Ulema-i-Hind, "About Us," 2009, http://jamiatulama.org/about_us.html.

4. Malik, Iftikhar Haider. *State and Civil Society in Pakistan: Politics of Authority, Ideology, and Ethnicity*. Basingstoke, UK: Macmillan, 1997.

5. Interview with senior JI member, 2007, Lahore, Pakistan.

6. Barbara D. Metcalf, *Islamic Revival in British India: Deoband, 1860–1900* (Princeton, NJ: Princeton University Press, 1982).

7. M. Naeem Qureshi, *Pan-Islam in British Indian Politic: A Study of the Khilafat Movement, 1918–1924* (Leiden, the Netherlands: Brill, 1999).

8. Jamiat-Ulema-i-Hind, "About Us."

9. Nasr, "Rise of Sunni Militancy," 169–73.

10. Ibid., 172.

11. Nasr, *Mawdudi*.

12. Khalid bin Sayeed, "The Jama'at-i-Islami Movement in Pakistan," *Public Affairs* 30, no. 1 (1957): 61.

13. Iqtidar, *Secularizing Humanists?*, 123.

14. Interview with senior JI member, 2007, Lahore, Pakistan.

15. Sayeed, "Jama'at-i-Islami Movement," 67–68.

16. Interview with senior JI member, 2007, Lahore, Pakistan.

17. Ibid.

18. Sayeed, "Jama'at-i-Islami Movement," 64.

19. Abdul Rashid Moten, "Mawdūdī and the Transformation of Jamā ʔat-e-Islāmī in Pakistan," *The Muslim World* 93, no. 3/4 (2003): 392.

20. Sayeed, "Jama'at-i-Islami Movement," 61.

21. Interview with senior JI member, 2007, Islamabad, Pakistan.

22. Ibid.

23. Nasr, *Mawdudi*, 28–29.

24. Ibid., 4–5.

25. Interview with senior JI member, 2008, Karachi, Pakistan.

26. Nasr, *Mawdudi*, 42.

27. Nasr, *Vanguard of the Islamic Revolution*, 123–24.

28. Interview with senior JI member, 2008, Karachi, Pakistan.

29. Interview with senior JI member, April 2007, Karachi, Pakistan.

30. Moten, "Mawdūdī and the Transformation," 396.

31. Hussain Shah, *Religion and Politics in Pakistan*, 271.

32. Nasr, *Mawdudi*, 5.

33. Nasr, *Vanguard of the Islamic Revolution*, 64.

34. Interview with senior JI member, 2008, Lahore, Pakistan.

35. Interview with senior JI member, May 2008, Lahore, Pakistan.

36. Sayeed, "Jama'at-i-Islami Movement," 65.

37. Interview with senior JI member, 2009, Lahore, Pakistan.

38. Nasr, *Vanguard of the Islamic Revolution*, 48.

39. Iqtidar, *Secularizing Islamists?*, 95.

40. Nasr, *Vanguard of the Islamic Revolution*, 58.

41. Ibid., 96. In 1983 the JI had 4,776 members, of whom 160 (3.3 percent) were women; in 1989 it had 5,723 members, of whom 321 (5.6 percent) were women. A 2010 paper puts the number of female *rukn* at around 3,000, which would make them about 15 percent of the current total. In addition, JI's women's wing has 900,000 female affiliate members and supporters. See Niloufer Siddiqui, "Gender Ideology and the Jamaat-e-Islami," *Current Trends in Islamist Ideology* 10 (August 17, 2010), www.currenttrends.org/research/detail/gender-ideology-and-the-jam aat-e-islami.

42. Interview with senior JI member, 2007, Lahore, Pakistan.

43. Bahadur, *Democracy in Pakistan,* 148.
44. Interview with senior JI member, 2007, Lahore, Pakistan.
45. Interview with senior JI member, May 2013, Islamabad, Pakistan.
46. Nasr, *Vanguard of the Islamic Revolution*, chapter 6.
47. Moten, "Mawdūdī and the Transformation," 395.
48. Nasr, *Vanguard of the Islamic Revolution*, 128.
49. Interview with senior JI member, 2007.
50. Moten, "Mawdūdī and the Transformation," 396.
51. Nasr, *Vanguard of the Islamic Revolution*, 139.
52. Ibid., 96.
53. Anatol Lieven, *Pakistan: A Hard Country* (New York: PublicAffairs, 2011), 152.
54. Interview with senior JI leader, June 2007, Lahore, Pakistan.
55. Jamaat-e-Islami Pakistan, "Organizational Structure," http://jamaat.org/site/page/6 .
56. Interview with senior JI member, 2007, Lahore, Pakistan.
57. Iqtidar, *Secularizing Islamists?*, 114.
58. Seyyed Vali Reza Nasr, "Students, Islam, and Politics: Islami Jami'at-I Tulaba in Pakistan," *Middle East Journal* 46, no. 1 (1992): 59–76.
59. Iqtidar, *Secularizing Islamists?*, 78.
60. Lieven, *Pakistan*, 151.
61. Nasr, *Vanguard of the Islamic Revolution*, 85. Iqtidar, conducting fieldwork twenty years after Nasr, also found that most conversations with JI members were conducted in Urdu and that the majority of the group's literature was published in that language. See Iqtidar, *Secularizing Islamists?*
62. Lieven, *Pakistan*, 138.
63. Interview with senior JI member, 2007, Lahore, Pakistan; and Iqtidar, *Secularizing Islamists?*, 95.
64. Interview with senior JI leader, April 2013, Islamabad, Pakistan.
65. Iqtidar, *Secularizing Islamists?*, 79.
66. Yousaf Ali, "Islamic Charities Most Effective in Relief Activities," *The News (Pakistan)* August 26, 2010.
67. Intikhab Amir, "Battagram: Religious Groups Play Key Role in Relief Operation," *The Dawn (Pakistan)*, October 25, 2005.
68. See, e.g., Jenny B. White, "Islamist Social Networks and Social Welfare Services in Turkey," in *Islamist Politics in the Middle East: Movements and Change*, ed. Samer S. Shehata (Milton Park, UK: Routledge, 2012); and Janine Astrid Clark, "Patronage, Prestige, and Power: The Islamic Center Charity Society's Political Role within the Muslim Brotherhood," in Sehata, *Islamist Politics*.
69. Interview with senior JI member, 2007, Islamabad, Pakistan.
70. C. Christine Fair, *The Madrassah Challenge: Militancy and Religious Education in Pakistan* (Washington, DC: USIP, 2008), 21.
71. "Pakistan Forms Body to Register Seminaries by 30 September," *The Dawn*, July 30, 2005.
72. Rebecca Winthrop and Corinne Graff, *Beyond Madrasas: Assessing the Links between Education and Militancy in Pakistan* (Washington, DC: Brookings, 2010), 13.
73. Quoted in A. H. Nayyar and Ahmed Salim, *The Subtle Subversion: The State of Curricula and Textbooks in Pakistan* (Islamabad: Sustainable Development Policy Institute, 2002), 3.
74. Ibid., 4.

75. Shiraz Thobani, *Islam in the School Curriculum: Symbolic Pedagogy and Cultural Claims* (London: Continuum, 2010), 33–34.

76. Ibid., 34.

77. Nayyar and Salim, *Subtle Subversion*, 10.

78. Ibid., 16.

79. Lieven, *Pakistan*, 27.

80. Ibid., 152.

81. Interview with senior JI member, 2007, Islamabad, Pakistan.

82. Iqtidar, *Secularizing Islamists?*, 111–16.

83. "Pakistan," *CIA World Factbook 2013*, https://www.cia.gov/library/publications/the-world-factbook/geos/pk.html.

84. Nasr, *Vanguard of the Islamic Revolution*, 87.

85. Interview with senior JI member, 2007.

86. Nasr, *Mawdudi*, 14.

87. Nasr, *Vanguard of the Islamic Revolution*, 81.

88. Moten, "Mawdūdī and the Transformation," 397.

89. At the time of this writing, it is possible that the JI will win more seats, since numerous contests were postponed due to violence preceding the elections and by-elections will be held to fill seats won by politicians returned from more than one constituency; but the 3 seats that the JI won represent only 1 percent of the 261 seats available. Elections results at Election Commission of Pakistan, "General Elections 2013," May 2013, www.ecp.gov.pk/electionresult/AllResults.aspx?assemblyid=NA.

90. Wilder, *Pakistani Voter*, 171.

91. Interview with senior JI member, 2007, Lahore, Pakistan.

92. Iqtidar, *Secularizing Islamists?*, 100.

93. Ibid., 86.

94. Ibid., 87, 93–97.

95. Lieven, *Pakistan*, 150.

96. Iqtidar, *Secularizing Islamists?*, 120.

97. Stephen Tankel, *Lashkar-e-Taiba: From 9/11 to Mumbai* (London: International Centre for the Study of Radicalisation and Political Violence, 2009), 5–6, www.ps.au.dk/fileadmin/site_files/filer_statskundskab/subsites/cir/pdf-filer/Tankel_01.pdf.

98. Iqtidar, *Secularizing Islamists?*, 120–25.

99. Interview with senior JI member, May 2007.

100. Interview with senior JI member, October 2008.

101. Interview with senior JI leader, February 2009.

102. Ayesha Siddiqa, *The New Frontiers: Militancy and Radicalism in Punjab*, SISA Report No. 2 (Haslum, Norway: Centre for International and Strategic Analysis, 2013), 14, http://cdn.criticalppp.com/wp-content/uploads/2013/02/2013–02–04...SISA2_The_New_Frontiers_-_Ayesha_Siddiqa.pdf.

103. Iqtidar, *Secularizing Islamists?*, 120. Iqtidar quotes a JuD leader criticizing the JI for having gone the electoral route, since the JI now has to "run after the *vote bank* . . . and modify their stances constantly" (125, emphasis original). Ironically, this quote directly follows a section in which Iqtidar discusses how JuD, in an attempt to broaden its appeal, has publicly moderated its official position on killing Shia and the followers of Sunni traditions other than Ahl-e-Hadith. Iqtidar thus offers proof that even groups that seek power through extra-constitutional means are not immune to the dictates of public opinion.

104. Interview with senior JI member, 2007, Islamabad, Pakistan.

105. White, *Pakistan's Islamist Frontier*, 25.

106. Ibid., 26.

107. Ibid.

108. Talbot, "1946 Punjab Elections," 65–66.

109. Jalal, *Self and Sovereignty*, 450.

110. Interview with leading JUI member, 2008, Islamabad, Pakistan.

111. White, *Pakistan's Islamist Frontier*, 31.

112. Interview with senior JUI member, 2007, Islamabad, Pakistan.

113. Sana Haroon, "The Rise of Deobandi Islam in the NorthWest Frontier Province and Its Implications in Colonial India and Pakistan, 1914–1996," *Journal of the Royal Asiatic Society of Great Britain & Ireland* 18, no. 1 (2008): 52: "Establishment of the Deobandi-dominated JUS [Jamiyatul Ulema Sarhad, the NWFP branch of the JUH] was the beginning of the process by which Deobandi *ulama* of the NWFP began to rationalise and regularise their authority as a natural political leadership in the province, urging that Muslim religious life and public participation could not be separated."

114. Ibid., 53.

115. Ibid., 59.

116. Ibid., 58.

117. Interview with senior JUI member, 2007, Islamabad, Pakistan.

118. Ibid., Lahore, Pakistan.

119. Haroon, "Rise of Deobandi Islam," 60–62.

120. International Crisis Group, "Islamic Parties in Pakistan," *Asia Report* 216 (2011): 10.

121. Interview with senior JUI member, 2007, Lahore, Pakistan.

122. Nasr, "Rise of Sunni Militancy," 153.

123. Interview with senior JUI member, 2008, Lahore, Pakistan.

124. Ibid.

125. Ashok K. Behuria, "Sects within Sect: The Case of Deobandi–Barelvi Encounter in Pakistan," *Strategic Analysis*, 32, no. 1 (2008): 69.

126. Anwar H. Syed, "Pakistan in 1976: Business as Usual," *Asian Survey* 17, no. 2 (1977): 181.

127. Saeed Shafqat, "From Official Islam to Islamism: The Rise of Dawat-ul-Irshad and Lashkar-e-Taiba," in *Pakistan: Nationalism without a Nation*, ed. Christophe Jaffrelot (London: Zed Books, 2002), 135.

128. Interview with senior JUI leader, June 2004.

129. Despite Saudi support for the Deobandi groups, there are significant, if subtle, theological differences between Deobandi and Wahhabi thought. Deobandi clerics follow the Hanafi *fiqh* (school of interpretation of the Quran), as do most South Asian Muslims. Wahhabis, however, follow the Hanbali fiqh, more common in the Gulf States. Wahhabism, furthermore, is often described as more severe and austere than the Deobandi trend. (See Husain Haqqani, "The Ideologies of South Asian Jihad Groups," *Current Trends in Islamist Ideology* 1 (2005): 12–26.) Few Pakistanis call themselves Wahhabi, however; most who belong to this tradition describe themselves as Ahle Hadith. While there is an Ahle Hadith political party, it is quite weak, and Jamaat-ud-Dawa is in fact the most important organization espousing Ahle Hadith views (see Iqtidar, *Secularizing Islamists?*).

130. Mariam Abou Zahab, "The Regional Dimension of Sectarian Conflicts in Pakistan," in *Pakistan: Nationalism without a Nation*, ed. Christophe Jaffrelot (London: Zed Books, 2002), 115.

131. Shafqat, "From Official Islam," 138.

132. Nasr, *Vanguard of the Islamic Revolution*, 117–18, 165.

133. Rasul B. Rais, "Pakistan in 1988: From Command to Conciliation Politics," *Asian Survey* 29, no. 2 (1989): 202.

134. Nasr, "Rise of Sunni Militancy."

135. Interview with senior JUI member, 2008.

136. Haroon, "Rise of Deobandi Islam," 64.

137. Sadia Saeed, "Pakistani Nationalism and the State Marginalisation of the Ahmadiyya Community in Pakistan," *Studies in Ethnicity and Nationalism* 7, no. 3 (2007): 132–52.

138. Interview with senior JUI member, 2007, Lahore, Pakistan.

139. Ibid.

140. Behuria, "Sects within Sect," 70.

141. Ibid., 70–71.

142. White, *Pakistan's Islamist Frontier*, 32.

143. Sumita Kumar, "The Role of Islamist Parties in Pakistani Politics," *Strategic Analysis* 25, no. 2 (2001): 277.

144. Iftikhar H. Malik, "Pakistan in 2001: The Afghanistan Crisis and the Rediscovery of the Frontline State," *Asian Survey* 42, no. 2 (2002): 206.

145. Interview with senior JUI member, 2007, Lahore, Pakistan.

146. Interview with JUI senior leader, July 2008, Lahore, Pakistan.

147. David S. Patel, "Islam, Information, and Social Order: The Strategic Role of Religion in Muslim Societies" (Ph.D. diss., Stanford University, 2007), 52.

148. S. V. R. Nasr, "Democracy and Islamic Revivalism," *Political Science Quarterly* 110, no. 2 (1995): 280.

149. Interview with senior JUI member, 2009, Islamabad, Pakistan.

150. Interview with senior JUI member, April 2008, Islamabad, Pakistan.

151. D. Nohlen, F. Grotz, and C. Hartmann, *Elections in Asia: A Data Handbook*, vol. 1 (New York: Book Affairs, 2001), 678.

152. "Pakistan," in *The Columbia World Dictionary of Islamism*, ed. Antoine Sfeir (New York: Columbia University Press, 2007), 272.

153. Election Commission of Pakistan, "General Election Result—2013: National Assembly Result," 2013, www.ecp.gov.pk/electionresult/AllResults.aspx?assemblyid = NA; and Election Commission of Pakistan, "General Election Result—2013: KPK Assembly Result," 2013, www.ecp.gov.pk/electionresult/AllResults.aspx?assemblyid = PK.

154. Ian Talbot, "Pakistan in 2002: Democracy, Terrorism, and Brinkmanship," *Asian Survey* 43, no. 1 (2003): 205.

155. Ibid., 204.

156. International Crisis Group, "Pakistan: The Mullahs and the Military," *Asia Report* 49 (March 2003): 14–15.

157. Counting the number of MMA delegates to the National Assembly is surprisingly difficult, as different sources often give different tallies. This variation is in part because elections in the Federally Administered Tribal Areas (FATA) are legally required not to have parties, so that all candidates from that region are listed as independents. The MMA was known to have backed seven successful candidates out of the twelve returned from FATA, and most analysts count those seven in the total, bringing the MMA total up to fifty-three. (See Rahimullah Yusufzai, "The Real Test," *Newsline*, November 12, 2002.) Furthermore, each party that received above a certain threshold of the vote was allowed to appoint its proportional share of

the 70 seats reserved for women and minorities. The proportion of these seats that each party is able to claim is based on its share of the directly elected representatives, not of the total vote. Thus the MMA, with a little less than 20 percent of the 272 directly elected seats, was allowed to appoint fourteen candidates to the reserved seats. (See Zahid Hussain, "Test of Faith," *Newsline*, October 13, 2003.)

158. Yusufzai, "The Real Test."

159. Shahzada Zulfiqar, "Reversal of Fortune," *Newsline*, November 12, 2012.

160. Yusufzai, "The Real Test."

161. Zulfiqar, "Reversal of Fortune."

162. Yusufzai, "The Real Test"; and Ashutosh Misra, "Rise of Religious Parties in Pakistan: Causes and Prospects," *Strategic Analysis* 27, no. 2 (2003): 190.

163. Misra, "Rise of Religious Parties," 190.

164. Amir Mohammed Khan, "The Day the Music Died," *Newsline*, February 10, 2003.

165. Rahimullah Yusufzai, "No Gain, No Pain," *Newsline*, October 13, 2003.

166. Yusufzai, "The Real Test."

167. Hussain, "Test of Faith."

168. International Crisis Group, "Pakistan," 5.

169. C. Christine Fair, "Militant Recruitment in Pakistan: Implications for Al Qaeda and Other Organizations," *Studies in Conflict & Terrorism* 27 (2004): 489–504.

170. Yusufzai, "The Real Test."

171. "Not So Holy Alliance," *Friday Times*, November 30, 2012.

172. Matthew J. Nelson, "Pakistan in 2008: Moving beyond Musharraf," *Asian Survey* 49, no. 1 (2009): 16–27.

173. Ibid., 22.

174. Interview with JUI senior leader, June 2011.

175. Geo TV, "Election Results 2013," http://election2013.geo.tv/. Results are as of May 25, 2013, with seven National Assembly constituencies still undecided.

176. "Not So Holy Alliance."

177. "Terrorising Pakistan's Secular Parties," *The Dawn*, April 27, 2013, http://dawn.com/2013/04/27/terrorising-pakistans-secular-parties/.

178. Aman Azhar, "The Return of the Holy Warriors," *Newsline*, January 25, 2012.

179. "The Maulana and His Fatwa," *Friday Times*, May 24, 2013; and "No Decision yet on JUI-F, PML-N Coalition," *The Dawn,* May 18, 2013, http://dawn.com/2013/05/18/no-decision-yet-on-jui-f-pml-n-coaliti on/.

180. Ali Hussain and Zulfiqar Ahmad, "Engaging with Taliban: Fazl Vying to Become Part of PML-N Government at All Cost," *Business Recorder*, May 23, 2013, www.brecorder.com/general-news/172/1188418/.

181. Imtiaz Ali, "The Father of the Taliban: An Interview with Maulana Sami ul-Haq," *Jamestown Foundation Spotlight on Terror* 4, no. 2 (2007), www.jamestown.org/single/?no_cache=1&tx_ttnews%5Btt_news%5D=4180#.Uce2jvmsim4.

182. Mushtaq Yusufzai, "TTP Withdraws Talks Offer to Govt," *The News (Pakistan)*, May 31, 2013.

183. Zia Ur Rehman, "Militants Turn against Pakistan's JUI-F Islamist Party," *CTC Sentinel* 5, no. 4 (2012): 15–17.

184. Author interview with senior JUI leader, May 2008, Lahore, Pakistan.

185. Author interview with senior JUI leader, August 2008, Lahore, Pakistan.

186. Author interview with senior JUI leader, April 2008, Lahore, Pakistan.

187. Interview with JUI senior leader, May 2008, Lahore, Pakistan.

188. Maulana Mahmood Ahmed Mirpuri, "Fatwa on Voting for Secular Groups," INFAO Fatwa Management System, 2009, www.e-infad.my/FMS_en/index.php?option=com_fatwa&task=vie wlink&link_id=1802&Itemid=59.

189. Interview with senior JUI member, 2009, Lahore, Pakistan.

190. "Political 'Fatwa': Voting for PTI Is Haram, Says Maulana Fazl," *The Express Tribune* (Pakistan), May 5, 2013, http://tribune.com.pk/story/544667/political-fatwa-voting-for-pti-is-haram-says-maulana-fazl/.

6. Islamic Voters in Pakistan

1. Gill, "Religion and Comparative Politics," 117.

2. Ernest Gellner, *Muslim Society* (Cambridge: Cambridge University Press, 1981); and Dwight B. Billings and Shauna L. Scott, "Religion and Political Legitimation," *Annual Review of Sociology* 20 (1994): 186.

3. National Commission on Terrorist Attacks upon the United States, *The 9/11 Commission Report: Final Report of the National Commission on Terrorist Attack upon the United States* (New York: Norton, 2004), 367.

4. Shapiro and Fair, "Why Support Islamist Militancy?"

5. Ibid., 80–81.

6. Shapiro and Fair, "Why Support Islamist Militancy?"

7. See Fair, "Militant Challenge in Pakistan," 105–37.

8. Shapiro and Fair, "Why Support Islamist Militancy?"

9. Ibid.

10. Ibid.

11. Fair, "Militant Challenge in Pakistan," 105–37.

12. K. Alan Kronstadt, *Pakistan's Domestic Political Developments: Issues for Congress*, CRS Report for Congress (Washington, DC: Library of Congress, 2003), 3. http://fpc.state.gov/documents/organization/29970.pdf.

13. Magnus Norell, "The Taliban and the Muttahida Majlis-e-Amal (MMA)," *China and Eurasia Forum Quarterly* 5, no. 3 (August 2007): 63.

14. Shapiro and Fair, "Why Support Islamist Militancy?"

15. Chandra, "Why Ethnic Parties Succeed," 10–11.

16. Shapiro and Fair, "Why Support Islamist Militancy?," 90.

17. Another approach is the party identification school. The central position of this model focuses on the mediating role of long-term psychological predispositions in guiding voter behavior. It assumes that partisanship is motivated more by sociological factors than material factors. If two separate groups or parties are on better terms with one another in comparison to another party or parties, they may work together on the grounds of mutual goals and mutual disdain for another group. The party identification approach is especially applicable to ethnic groups and confessional parties as in many instances they represent minorities in a nation-state.

18. White, *Pakistan's Islamist Frontier*, 4.

19. Kathleen Collins, "Ideas, Networks, and Islamist Movements," *World Politics*, 60, no. 1: 71, 73, 74.

20. Shapiro and Fair, "Why Support Islamist Militancy?"

21. Ibid.

22. Carlos Garcia-Rivero and Hennie Kotzé, "Electoral Support for Islamic Parties in the Middle East and North Africa," *Party Politics* 13, no. 5 (2007).

23. Target respondents were fourteen to sixty-four years of age. The geographical coverage was limited to the four provinces of Pakistan, and the Federally Administered Tribal Areas region was not included. The poll was conducted with a 95 percent confidence interval, with a 2.65 percent margin of error.

24. J. H. Fowler and C. D. Kam, "Beyond the Self: Social Identity, Altruism, and Political Participation," *Journal of Politics* 69, no. 3 (2007): 813.

25. Ibid., 815.

26. Ibid., 816.

27. Roy, *Globalized Islam*; Pickering, "Durkheim's Contribution"; Yamagishi, Jin, and Kiyonari, "Bounded Generalized Reciprocity," 161–97; Yamagishi and Mifune, "Does Shared Group Membership Promote Altruism?", 5–30; and Whitt and Wilson, "The Dictator Game," 655–68.

28. Fowler and Kam, "Beyond the Self," 816.

29. Author interview with JI senior leader, May 2013.

30. Author interview with JI senior leader, January 2009.

31. See table 6.3, which also shows that contrary to $H_0$4, support for militant organizations is not positively correlated with support for Talibanization, as discussed earlier in chapter 5.

32. Respondents from communities that saw their economic conditions improving also were more supportive of Islamist parties.

7. Political Strategy

1. Nasr, "Rise of 'Muslim Democracy,'" 13.

2. Kalyvas, "Commitment Problems," 382.

3. Cox and McCubbins, *Legislative Leviathan*; Aldrich, *Why Parties?*; and Kalyvas, *Rise of Christian Democracy.*

4. Badruddin Umar, *The Emergence of Bangladesh: Class Struggles in East Pakistan (1947–1958)* (New York: Oxford University Press, 2004).

5. Downs, *Economic Theory*, 137.

6. Ibid.

7. Ibid., 143–44.

8. Haqqani, *Pakistan*, 207.

9. Downs, *Economic Theory.*

10. T. Mehdi, *Elections in Pakistan, 1970–2008* (Lahore: Sanjh Publications, 2010).

11. Blood, "The Government: Islami Jamhoori Ittehad."

12. Mehdi, *Elections in Pakistan*, 34.

13. Ibid., 38.

14. Interview with senior JI member, 2008.

15. "Shariat Act: Text and Commentary from Pakistan," *South Asia Bulletin* 10, no. 2 (1990).

16. Talbot, *Pakistan: A Modern History*, 318.

17. Ibid., 317.

18. Interview with senior JI member, 2008.

19. Blood, *Pakistan: A Country Study*, 252–53.

20. Mehdi, *Elections in Pakistan*, 21.

21. Craig Baxter, *Bangladesh: From a Nation to a State* (Boulder, CO: Westview Press, 1997), 90–100.

22. "Pakistan Premier Proposes an Islamic Society Based on Koran," *New York Times*, August 28, 1998.

23. Kamal Siddiqi, "Nawaz to Go Ahead with Islamization Bill," *Indian Express*, September 9, 1998.

24. Kamal Siddiqi, "Sharif Goes Ahead with Shariat; 2 More Generals Quit," *Indian Express*, October 9, 1998.

25. Siddiqi, "Nawaz to Go Ahead."

26. Mehdi, *Elections in Pakistan*, 45.

27. Siddiqi, "Nawaz to Go Ahead."

28. Author interview with senior JI district leader, October 2012.

29. "The Constitution of Pakistan: Annex [Article 2(A)]: The Objectives Resolution," Pakistani.org., www.pakistani.org/pakistan/constitution/annex_objres.html.

30. Zaidi, *The Emergence of Ulema*, 95–98.

31. Punjab Disturbance Court of Inquiry, "Report of the Court of Inquiry Constituted under Punjab Act II of 1954 to Enquire into the Punjab Disturbances of 1953," 1954, 203.

32. "Objectives Resolution."

33. Oh, *The Rights of God*, 97.

34. Nasr, *Vanguard of the Islamic Revolution*, 127–28.

35. Mehdi, *Elections in Pakistan*, 45; and Nasr, *Vanguard of the Islamic Revolution*, 128–29.

36. Nasr, *Vanguard of the Islamic Revolution*, 129.

37. Ibid., 131, 132–33, 134–35.

38. Ibid., 136.

39. Ibid., 137.

40. Author interview with senior JI leader, June 2008.

41. Khan, "Persecution of the Ahmadiyya Community," 224–25.

42. Nasr, *Vanguard of the Islamic Revolution*, 134–35.

43. Task Force on Terrorism and Unconventional Warfare, House Republican Research Committee, "The New Islamist International," *1993 Congressional Reports: Intelligence and Security*, February 13, 1993, www.fas.org/irp/congress/1993_rpt/house_repub_report.html.

44. Quoted by Omar S. Bashir, "Explaining Islamist Pressures on State Behavior: The Jamaat-i Islami and Pakistani Foreign Policy" (Ph.D. diss., University of Oxford, 2009), 2.

45. White, *Pakistan's Islamist Frontier*, 35.

46. Jacob Shapiro and Christine Fair, "Understanding Support for Islamic Militancy in Pakistan," *International Security,* 34, no. 3 (Winter 2009/2010): 86.

47. Tahir Kamran, "Evolution and Impact of 'Deobandi' Islam in the Punjab," *The Historian* 4, no. 1 (January–December 2006): 39, 40.

48. White, *Pakistan's Islamist Frontier*, 31.

49. Kamran, "Evolution and Impact," 40.

50. Ibid., 29.

51. White, *Pakistan's Islamist Frontier*, 32.

52. Mehdi, *Elections in Pakistan*, 101.

53. Ibid., 65.

54. Shapiro and Fair, "Understanding Support," 87.

55. Interview with senior JI leader, 2008.

56. Interview with senior JI leader, 2009.

57. Interview with senior JI leader, 2008.

58. Nasr, "Rise of Sunni Militancy."

59. Downs, *Economic Theory*, 137.

60. Author interview with senior JI leader, July 2012.

61. Eliza Van Hollen, "Pakistan in 1986: Trials of Transition," *Asian Survey* 27, no. 2 (1987): 148.

62. James W. Spain, "The Pathan Borderlands," *Middle East Journal* 15, no. 2 (1961): 165–77.

63. M. Rashiduzzaman, "The National Awami Party of Pakistan: Leftist Politics in Crisis," *Public Affairs* 43, no. 3 (1970): 394–409.

64. Azhar, "Return of the Holy Warriors."

65. Lawrence Ziring, "Pakistan: A Political Perspective," *Asian Survey* 15, no. 7 (1975): 636–37.

66. Nasreen Ghufran, "Pushtun Ethnonationalism and the Taliban Insurgency in the North West Frontier Province of Pakistan," *Asian Survey* 49, no. 6 (2009): 1099.

67. Ziring, "Pakistan in 1990," 121.

68. Zalan, "The Twilight of the Frontier's Iron Lady," *Newsline*, February 26, 2012.

69. Muhammad Shakeel Ahmad, "Electoral Politics in NWFP: 1988–99" (Ph.D. diss., Quaid-i-Azam University, Islamabad, Pakistan, 2010), 233.

70. Ameen Jan, "Pakistan on a Precipice," *Asian Survey* 39, no. 5 (1999): 700–701.

71. Muhammad Mushtaq, Ayaz Muhammad, and Syed Khawja Alqama, "Politics of Power Sharing in Post-1971 Pakistan," *Journal of Politics and Law* 4, no. 1 (2011): 249–60.

72. Tauseef-ur-Rahman, "The Rise and Fall of ANP," *The News (Pakistan)*, May 29, 2013.

73. "PIPS Report: Awami National Party Bore the Brunt of Pre-election Violence," *Pakistan Express Tribune*, May 25, 2013.

74. Ijaz Khan, *Pashtuns in the Crossfire: Pashtun Politics in the Shadow of "War against Terrorism"* (Bradford, UK: Pakistan Security Research Unit, 2007).

75. Election Commission of Pakistan, "General Elections 2013: National Assembly," www.ecp.gov.pk/electionresult/AllResults.aspx?assemblyidqNA; and Election Commission of Pakistan, "Party Position (Provincial Assemblies)," June 7, 2013, www.ecp.gov.pk/overallpartypositionPA07–06–2013.pdf; and Associated Press of Pakistan, "Election 2008 Results," www.app.com.pk/election/.

76. Mureeb Mohmand, "Moving Aside: ANP Suffers Unprecedented Whitewash in Stronghold," *The Express Tribune*, May 13, 2013.

8. Lessons Learned

1. See Strom, "A Behavioral Approach,"; Ostrom, "A Behavioral Approach," 1–22

2. Social goods are public and club goods provided to citizens and include education, tax relief, transportation, welfare services, law and order, and other social services.

3. The voters' utility functions are specified as discrete payoffs for each possible scenario (e.g., party 2 wins the election but passes unfavorable legislation). The voters will try to maximize payoffs given incomplete information regarding what "type" each party represents (it is presumed that the voters have no prior information about party type). As discussed below, three possible equilibriums may result from this model: separating, partially separating, and pooling.

4. Egypt's Government Services, *Constitutional Declaration 2011*, www.egypt.gov.eg/english/laws/constitution/.

5. Nariman Youssef, "Egypt's Draft Constitution Translated," *Egypt Independent*, December 2, 2012, www.egyptindependent.com/news/egypt-s-draft-constitution-translated.

6. Yoram Meital, "The Struggle over Political Order in Egypt: The 2005 Elections," *Middle East Journal* 60, no. 2 (Spring 2006): 275.

7. Noha Antar, *The Muslim Brotherhood's Success in the Legislative Elections in Egypt 2005: Reasons and Implications*, EuroMeSCo Democratization and Human Rights Project, October 2006, 34, www.ikhwanweb.com/uploads/lib/55X3HT7GA6EFHS2.pdf.

8. John Walsh, "Egypt's Muslim Brotherhood," *Harvard International Review* (Winter 2003), 32.

9. Ibid., 35.

10. James Traub, "Islamic Democrats," *New York Times*, April 29, 2007.

11. Samer Shehata and Joshua Stacher, "The Brotherhood Goes to Parliament," *Middle East Report* 240 (Fall 2006): 33.

12. Traub, "Islamic Democrats."

13. Antar, *Muslim Brotherhood's Success*, 4.

14. Amro Hassan, "Egypt Islamist Parties the Big Winners in Second Round of Voting," *Los Angeles Times*, December 25, 2011, http://articles.latimes.com/2011/dec/25/world/la-fg-egypt-elections-20111225.

15. "Editorial: Egypt's Ugly Election," *Washington Post*, December 10, 2005.

16. Nathan Lean, "Egypt Elections: After Court Ruling, the Real Concern Is Not the Muslim Brotherhood," *Christian Science Monitor*, June 15, 2012.

17. "Al-Arian: Brotherhood's Freedom and Justice Party to Be Based on Islamic Law," *Egypt Independent*, February 23, 2011, www.egyptindependent.com/news/al-arian-brotherhoods-freedom-and-justice-party-be-based-islamic-law.

18. Ariel Zirulnick, "Who's Who in Egypt's Elections," *Christian Science Monitor*, November 29, 2011.

19. Hesham Sallam, "Egyptian Elections: Full Results after Round 2," *Ahram Online*, January 5, 2012, http://english.ahram.org.eg/NewsContent/33/100/30973/Elections-/News/Egypt-Elections-Full-results-after-round-.aspx.

20. David D. Kirkpatrick, "Egyptian Vote Forces Islamists to Confront Their Divide over Rule by Religion," *New York Times*, December 4, 2011.

21. Said Shehata, "Profiles of Egypt's Political Parties: Al-Nour," *BBC News*, November 25, 2011, www.bbc.co.uk/news/world-middle-east-15899539.

22. M. Rashiduzzaman, "Bangladesh in 1977: Dilemmas of the Military Rulers," *Asian Survey* 18, no. 2 (1978): 126–34.

23. Akhtar Hossein, "Anatomy of Hartal Politics in Bangladesh," *Asian Survey* 40, no. 3 (May–June 2000): 521.

24. Kenneth Katzman, *Afghanistan: Elections, Constitution, and Government*, CRS Report for Congress (Washington, DC: Library of Congress, May 25, 2006), http://fpc.state.gov/documents/organization/67158.pdf.

25. Jon Boone, "Afghanistan Election: Fraud Could Delay Result for Months, Observers Warn," *Guardian*, September 19, 2010, www.guardian.co.uk/world/2010/sep/19/afghanistan-election-fraud-delay-result.

26. Thomas Ruttig, "Afghanistan's Elections: Political Parties at the Fringes Again," *Foreign Policy*, September 13, 2010, http://afpak.foreignpolicy.com/posts/2010/09/13/afghanistans_elections_political_parties_at_the_fringes_again.

27. "Government & Politics: Political Parties/Groups and Leaders in Afghanistan," Afghanistan Online, last updated May 17, 2012, www.afghan-web.com/politics/parties.html.

28. Ruttig, "Afghanistan's Elections."

29. "Morocco's Arab Spring Election Won by Islamists," *USA Today*, November 27, 2011, www.usatoday.com/news/world/story/2011–11–27/morocco-elections-islamist-victory/51421964/1.

30. "Morocco's Election: Yet Another Islamist Victory," *The Economist*, December 3, 2011, www.economist.com/node/21541058.

31. "Islamist PJD Party Wins Morocco Poll," BBC News Africa, November 27, 2011, www.bbc.co.uk/news/world-africa-15902703.

32. Amr Hamzawy, *Party for Justice and Development in Morocco: Participation and Its Discontents* (Washington, DC: Carnegie Endowment for International Peace, 2008).

33. "Moroccan Nationalists in Poll Win," Al Jazeera, September 9, 2007, www.aljazeera.com/focus/moroccoelections2007/2007/09/2008525122526993418.html.

34. Amr Hamzawy, "The 2007 Moroccan Parliamentary Elections Results and Implications," *Web Commentary*, September 11, 2007, http://carnegieendowment.org/files/moroccan_parliamentary_elections_final.pdf.

35. "Islamist PJD Party Wins," BBC News, November 2011.

36. Ibid.

9. Foreign Policy Implications and New Trends

1. Myron Weiner, *Party Building in a New Nation: The Indian National Congress* (Chicago: University of Chicago Press, 1967), 490.

2. Edward P. Djerejian, "Changing Minds, Winning Peace: A New Strategic Direction for U.S. Public Diplomacy in the Arab and Muslim World" (Washington, DC: Advisory Group on Public Diplomacy for the Arab and Muslim World, 2003).

3. Ibid.

SELECTED BIBLIOGRAPHY

Afzal, Rafique. *Political Parties in Pakistan.* National Institute of Historical and Cultural Research. Islamabad: QAU, 2000.

Aldrich, J. H. *Why Parties? The Origin and Transformation of Political Parties in America.* Chicago: University of Chicago Press, 1995.

Axelrod, R. *The Evolution of Cooperation.* New York: Basic Books, 1984.

Axelrod, R., and R. Hammond. "The Evolution of Ethnocentric Behavior." Paper prepared at the Midwest Political Science Convention, Chicago, April 3–6, 2003.

Bahadur, K. *Democracy in Pakistan: Crises and Conflicts.* New Delhi: Har-Anand Publications, 1997.

Bates, R. "Capital, Kinship, and Conflict: The Structuring Influence of Capital in Kinship Societies." *Canadian Journal of African Studies* 24, no. 2 (1990a): 151–64.

———. "Macropolitical Economy in the Field of Development." In *Perspectives on Positive Political Economy,* edited by J. Alt and K. Shepsle, 31–54. Cambridge, UK: Cambridge University Press, 1990b.

Baxter, C., Y. K. Malik, C. H. Kennedy, and R. C. Oberst. *Government and Politics in South Asia.* 5th ed. Boulder, CO: Westview Press, 2002.

Brown, Jonathan A. C. "Did the Prophet Say It or Not? The Literal, Historical, and Effective Truth of Hadīths in Early Sunnism." *Journal of the American Oriental Society* 129, no. 2 (2009): 259–85.

Cell, J. W. *Hailey: A Study in British Imperialism, 1872–1969.* New York: Cambridge University Press, 1992.

Chandra, K. "Elite Incorporation in Multi-Ethnic Societies." *Asian Survey* 4, no. 5 (2000): 26–61.

———. "Why Ethnic Parties Succeed: A Comparative Study of the Bahujan Samaj Party across Indian States." Ph.D. diss., Harvard University, 2000.

Coase, R. "The Nature of the Firm." *Econometrica,* New Series 4, no. 16 (1937): 386–405.

———. "The Problem of Social Cost." *Journal of Law and Economics* 3, no. 1 (1960): 1–44.

Cohen, M., R. Riolo, and R. Axelrod. "The Role of Social Structure in the Maintenance of Cooperative Regimes." *Rationality and Society* 13, no. 1 (2001): 5–32.

Cohen, S. *The Idea of Pakistan*. Lahore: Vanguard Books, 2005.

Coleman, J. *Foundations of Social Theory*. Cambridge, MA: Belknap Press of Harvard University Press, 1990.

———. *The Mathematics of Collective Action*. Chicago: Aldine, 1973.

Cox, G. W., and M. D. McCubbins. *Legislative Leviathan: Party Government in the House*. Berkeley: University of California Press, 1993.

Deutsch, K. "Social Mobilization and Political Development." *American Political Science Review* 55, no. 3 (1961): 493–514.

Downs, A. *An Economic Theory of Democracy*. New York: Harper, 1957.

Dresch, P., and B. Haykel. "Stereotypes and Political Styles: Islamists and Tribesfolk in Yemen." *International Journal of Middle East Studies* 27, no. 4 (1995): 405–31.

Esposito, J. L., and J. O. Voll. *Makers of Contemporary Islam*. New York: Oxford University Press, 2001.

Fearon, J., and D. Laitin. "Explaining Interethnic Cooperation," *American Political Science Review* 90, no. 4 (1996): 715–35.

Garcia-Rivero, C., and H. Kotzé. "Electoral Support for Islamic Parties in the Middle East and North Africa." *Party Politics* 13, no. 5 (2007).

Gill, A. "Religion and Comparative Politics." *Annual Reviews in Political Science* 4 (2001): 117–38.

———. *Rendering unto Caesar*. Chicago: University of Chicago Press, 1998.

Godbey, J. E., and A. H. Godbey. *Light in Darkness, or Missions and Missionary Heroes: An Illustrated History of the Missionary Work Taking up Principally the Work in India*. New York: General Books, 2010.

Granovetter, M. "The Strength of Weak Ties." *American Journal of Sociology* 78, no. 6 (1973): 1360–80.

Greif, A. "Cultural Beliefs and the Organization of Society: A Historical and Theoretical Reflection on Collectivist and Individualist Societies." *Journal of Political Economy* 102, no. 5 (1994): 912–50.

Gunther, R., and L. Diamond. "Species of Political Parties: A New Typology." *Party Politics* 9, no. 2 (2003): 176–77.

Haqqani, H. *Pakistan: Between Mosque and Military*. Washington, DC: Carnegie Endowment for International Peace, 2005.

Hardin, R. *Collective Action*. Baltimore: Johns Hopkins University Press, 1982.

Hardy, P. *The Muslims of British India*. London: Cambridge University Press, 1972.

Huntington, S. *Political Order in Changing Societies*. New Haven, CT: Yale University Press, 1968.

Iannaccone, L. "Introduction to the Economics of Religion." *Journal of Economic Literature* 36, no. 3 (1998): 1465–95.

Ikram, S. M. *Indian Muslims and Partition of India*. New Delhi: Atlantic, 1992.

Inglehart, R. *Modernization and Postmodernization: Cultural, Economic, and Political Change in 43 Societies*. Princeton, NJ: Princeton University Press, 1997.

Jalal, A. *Self and Sovereignty: Individual and Community in South Asian Islam since 1850*. London: Routledge, 2000.

Kalyvas, S. "Commitment Problems in Emerging Democracies: The Case of Religious Parties." *Comparative Politics* 32, no. 4 (2000): 296–97.

———. *The Rise of Christian Democracy in Europe*. New York: Cambridge University Press, 1996.

Kamali, Mohammed. *Shariah Law: An Introduction*. Oxford: Oneworld Publishers, 2008.

Keddie, N. "The New Religious Politics: Where, When, and Why Do 'Fundamentalisms' Appear?" *Comparative Studies in Society and History* 40, no. 4 (1998): 696–723.

Kesgin, S. P. "The Evolution of Political Islam in Turkey: Comparing Party Programs of 'Islamic' Parties in Government." Master's thesis, University of Kansas, 2004.

Khan, A. "Persecution of the Ahmadiyya Community in Pakistan: An Analysis under International Law and International Relations." *Harvard Human Rights Journal* 16 (2003): 224–25.

Kitschelt, H. *The Logics of Party Formation: Ecological Politics in Belgium and West Germany*. Ithaca, NY: Cornell University Press, 1989.

Kitschelt, H., and A. McGann. *The Radical Right in Western Europe*. Ann Arbor, MI: University of Michigan Press, 1995.

Lerner, D. *The Passing of Traditional Society: Modernizing the Middle East*. New York: Free Press, 1958.

Levine, D. *Popular Voices in Latin American Catholicism*. Princeton, NJ: Princeton University Press, 1992.

Lewis, Bernard. *The Crisis of Islam: Holy War and Unholy Terror*. Random House Digital, Inc., 2004.

Lipset, S. *Political Man: The Social Bases of Politics*. Garden City, NY: Doubleday, 1960.

Lipset, S. M., and S. Rokkan. *Party Systems and Voter Alignments: Cross-National Perspectives*. New York: Free Press, 1967.

Lustick, I. "Agent-Based Modeling of Collective Identity: Testing Constructivist Theory." *Journal of Artificial Societies and Social Simulation* 3, no. 1 (2000).

Malik, M. *Politics and Islam*. Lahore: Jalal Press, 2009.

Marwell, G., and P. Oliver. *The Critical Mass in Collective Action*. New York: Cambridge University Press, 1993.

Masoud, Tarek. "Islamist Parties: Are They Democrats? Does it Matter?" *Journal of Democracy*, 19, no. 3 (July) 2008.

———. "Why Islam Wins: Electoral Ecologies and Economies of Political Islam in Contemporary Egypt." Ph.D. diss., Yale University, 2008.

McAdam, D., S. Tarrow, and C. Tilly, eds. *Dynamics of Contention.* New York: Cambridge University Press, 2001.

Mecham, R. Q. "From the Sacred to the State: Institutional Origins of Islamist Political Mobilization." Ph.D. diss., Stanford University, 2006.

Metcalf, B. *Islamic Revival in British India: Deoband, 1860–1900.* Princeton, NJ: Princeton University Press, 1982.

Nagel, J. "Constructing Ethnicity: Creating and Recreating Ethnic Identity and Culture," *Social Problems* 41, no. 1 (1994): 152–76.

Nasr, S. V. R. *Mawdudi and the Making of Islamic Revivalism.* New York: Oxford University Press, 1996.

———. "The Rise of Sunni Militancy in Pakistan: The Changing Role of Islamism and the Ulama in Society and Politics." *Modern Asian Studies* 34, no. 1 (2000).

Nohlen, F., C. Grotz, and C. Harmann. *Elections in Asia: A Data Handbook.* New York: Book Affairs, 2001.

North, D. *Institutions, Institutional Change and Economic Performance.* Cambridge, UK: Cambridge University Press, 1990.

———. *Structure and Change in Economic History.* New York: W. W. Norton, 1981.

Oh, I. *The Rights of God: Islam, Human Rights, and Comparative Ethics.* Washington, DC: Georgetown University Press, 2007.

Olson, M. *The Logic of Collective Action: Public Goods and the Theory of Groups.* Cambridge: Harvard University Press, 1965.

———. *The Rise and Decline of Nations.* New Haven, CT: Yale University Press, 1982.

Ostrom, E. "A Behavioral Approach to the Rational Choice Theory of Collective Action." *American Political Science Review* 92, no. 1 (1998): 1–22.

Pickering, W. "Durkheim's Contribution to the Debate on Church and State," *Durkheim Studies* 12: 2006.

Przeworski, A., and J. D. Sprague. *Paper Stones: A History of Electoral Socialism.* Chicago: University of Chicago Press, 1986.

Rabb, Intisar A. "Doubt's Benefit: Legal Maxims in Islamic Law, 7th–16th Centuries." Ph.D. diss., Princeton University, 2009.

Roy, Oliver. *Globalized Islam, The Search for a New Ummah.* New York: Columbia University Press, 2004.

Sartori, G. *Parties and Party Systems: A Framework for Analysis.* New York: Cambridge University Press, 1976.

Schelling, T. *Micromotives and Macrobehavior.* New York: W. W. Norton, 1978.

Schumpeter, J. *Capitalism, Socialism and Democracy.* New York: Harper & Row, 1975.

Shapiro, J., and C. Fair. "Why Support Islamist Militancy? Evidence from Pakistan." *International Security* 34, no. 3 (2009).

Spiess, C. "Epilogue: Rethinking Party Theory in the Light of South Asian Experience." In *Political Parties in South Asia,* edited by Subatra K. Mitra, Mike Enskat, and Clemens Spiess. Westport, CT: Praeger Books, 2004.

Strom, Kaare. "A Behavioral Theory of Competitive Political Parties." *American Journal of Political Science* (1990): 565–98.

Talbot, I. A. *Pakistan: A Modern History.* New York: St. Martin's Press, 1998.

———. "The 1946 Punjab Elections." *Modern Asian Studies* 14, no. 2 (1980): 65–66.

Tarrow, S. *Power in Movement: Social Movements, Collective Action, and Politics.* New York: Cambridge University Press, 1994.

Tezcür, G. *Muslim Reformers in Iran and Turkey: The Paradox of Moderation*. Austin: University of Texas Press, 2010.

Umar, Badruddin. *The Emergence of Bangladesh: Class Struggles in East Pakistan (1947–1958).* New York: Oxford University Press, 2004.

White, J. T. *Pakistan's Islamist Frontier: Islamic Politics and U.S. Policy in Pakistan's North-West Frontier*. Religion and Security Monograph Series no. 1. Arlington, VA: Center on Faith and International Affairs, 2008.

Whitt, S. and Wilson, R. K. "The Dictator Game: Fairness and Ethnicity in Postwar Bosnia." *American Journal of Political Science* 51, no. 3 (2007): 655–68.

Wickham, Carrie. *The Muslim Brotherhood: Evolution of an Islamist Movement.* Princeton, NJ: Princeton University Press, 2013.

Wilder, Andrew. "The Pakistani Voter," in *Electoral Politics and Voting Behavior in the Punjab.* Oxford: Oxford University Press, 1999.

Williams, H. S., ed. *The Historians' History of the World: A Comprehensive Narrative of the Rise and Development of Nations as Recorded by over Two Thousand of the Great Writers of All Ages.* New York: Outlook Company, 1904.

Wintrobe, R. *Rational Extremism: The Political Economy of Radicalism*. New York: Cambridge University Press, 2006.

Yamagishi T., Jin, N., and Kiyonari, T. "Bounded Generalized Reciprocity: Ingroup Boasting and Ingroup Favoritism." *Advances in Group Processes* 16 (1999): 161–97.

Yamagishi, T., and Mifune, N. "Does Shared Group Membership Promote Altruism? Fear, Greed, and Reputation." *Rationality and Society* 20, no. 1 (2008): 5–30.

Zaidi, Syed M. Z. *The Emergence of Ulema in the Politics of India and Pakistan, 1918–1949: A Historical Perspective*. Lincoln, NE: Writers Club Press, 2003.

Zakaria, F. "The Rise of Illiberal Democracy." *Foreign Affairs* 4, no. 10 (1997).

INDEX